Android Epistemology

Android Epistemology

Edited by

Kenneth M. Ford,
Clark Glymour, & Patrick J. Hayes

Menlo Park / Cambridge / London
AAAI Press / The MIT Press

Copublished and distributed by The MIT Press, Massachusetts Institute of Technology, Cambridge, Massachusetts and London, England.

ISBN 978-0-262-51904-5 (pb.:alk.paper)

Library of Congress Cataloging-in-Publication Data

Android epistemology / edited by Kenneth M. Ford, Clark Glymour &
    Patrick J. Hayes.
        p.   cm.
    Includes bibliographical references and index.

    1. Androids. 2. Robotics. 3. Artificial intelligence. I. Ford, Kenneth M.
II. Glymour, Clark N. III. Hayes, Patrick J.
TJ211.A54 1995   95-30527
629.8'92--dc20   CIP

The MIT Press is pleased to keep this title available in print by manufacturing
single copies, on demand, via digital printing technology.

Contents

Acknowledgments

We wish to thank the many people who contributed their time and talents to the success of this book. We must especially thank the program committee of the workshop from which it sprang and our indefatigable referees for their invaluable service. The most essential contribution was, of course, from the authors of the papers themselves. We would also like to thank Jeff Yerkes and Kathy Howell without whom the volume would never have seen the light of day. Mike Hamilton (AAAI Press) and Bob Prior (MIT Press) collaborated to make the publication process a pleasure.

We would also like to acknowledge the workshop's primary benefactors: The National Science Foundation, American Association for Artificial Intelligence, Florida High Technology and Industry Council, and The Institute for the Interdisciplinary Study of Human and Machine Cognition at the University of West Florida.

Preface

Most of the chapters in this book have evolved from talks originally presented at The Second International Workshop on Human & Machine Cognition held at the Eden Condominiums on Perdido Key Florida during May 9-11, 1991. The International Workshop on Human & Machine Cognition convenes every other year to address a central interdisciplinary topic bearing on artificial intelligence and cognitive science. The special topic for the 1991 meeting was the Android Epistemology. Other workshops in this series have focussed on The Frame Problem (1989), Expertise in Context (1993), and Smart Machines in Education (1995). This workshop series has become known for its operating scheme: first, find an exciting interdisciplinary topic; next, select a small group (about forty) of the most interesting participants; and finally, plop them down in a spectacular location conducive to the free exchange of ideas (and sometimes argument) that often continues informally late into the night. Thus far this recipe has worked well.

It should be noted that although the workshop took place in 1991, the papers that appear here are actually of much more recent vintage. They were completed some time after the workshop (in some cases *far* after) and have benefited both from the spontaneous exchanges that happened in that halcyon setting and an extensive review process.

Ken Ford, Clark Glymour, & Pat Hayes, Editors

Introduction

Kenneth Ford, Clark Glymour, & Patrick Hayes

Until very recently, systematic thought about knowledge, beliefs, attitudes, desires, preferences and obligations has been concerned with only two kinds of agents: humans and gods. Until this century, the best mechanical analog for thought was clockwork (recognizably inferior to biology), and the fantasy of creating something with knowledge could be achieved only by giving the mysterious quality of life to some dead or inert mass, risking the gods' wrath or vengeance. Frankenstein's monster was the most vivid imaginable thinking creation of human science. Times have changed. The invention of the computer in the first half of this century produced the first machine which would do what you told it to do, giving new life to the project of thinking about the structure of knowledge, reason, belief, and desire in machines. We now have very powerful theoretical characterizations of what machines can and cannot do, a few general ways of structuring computation—or in other words, general designs for machines—and a good bit of practical knowledge about what works and what doesn't in machine design, some of it inspired by the biological machines we find in nature. But the human community has only begun to probe the space of possibilities for machines that can be said to know or think or believe or want. The theory of computation itself, while providing the boundaries, also indicates this vast unexplored space which they enclose.

Android epistemology, as the editors understand the term, is the business of exploring the space of possible machines and their capacities for knowledge, beliefs, attitudes, desires, and action in accordance with their mental states. Parts of the enterprise naturally concern the functions of machine components and processes; parts of it concern characterizations of machine behavior; parts of it, the proofs of boundaries on what is possible behavior for machines sharing some feature; and parts of android epistemology inevitably involve trying to decide what to say and what not to say about machine parts, states and processes using the psychological terms we use for one another, and similarly, what engineering vocabulary is useful in psychological descriptions of biological machines. Wherever psychologists propose that human thought or belief or desire are generated by some machine process, psychology is android epistemology. Humans are just a special case; only gods are left out of android epistemology.

Android epistemology is not a methodology or a discipline. The very idea of a disciplinary methodology—that there is one proper, professional way to do things—is by nature exclusionary. Academic disciplines tend to adopt methods and ideas as their own, becoming defined by them and eventually restricted by them, no matter how productive they have been. We have chosen a new name to emphasize the way that a single theme unifies various strands of contemporary science. Artificial intelligence is the discipline most obviously and self-consciously engaged in android epistemology, but the subject naturally includes robotics, neural networks, work on "artificial life," much of linguistics, and cognitive psychology. New areas will wish to define themselves as new ideas are explored. For example, something that might be called computational ecology seems now to be emerging, and who can know what will be next? Android epistemology is the insight that epistemology is about the processes in the machine, not the stuff it is made of. The force of this idea can be seen in the way in which it violates all kinds of traditional disciplinary boundaries in science, bringing together engineering and the life sciences, placing mathematical linguistics in the heart of electrical engineering and requiring moral philosophers to understand computation theory. University deans, forced to work within the old hierarchies, weep with frustration, and the work often has to be done in new 'interdisciplinary'—and often undisciplined—research centers and institutes which escape the old categories. We live in interesting times.

With the exception of the editors' essay and the contributions by Marvin Minsky and Herbert Simon, the essays in this volume arose from a workshop held at Pensacola, Florida which brought together a wide variety of opinions and disciplines. Some of them propose contributions to android epistemology; the majority of the contributions, however, offer arguments for or against the very idea. We have selected the papers partly to display the variety of these views and of their disciplinary backgrounds. While the essays are not conscious attempts at objective surveys, many of them might also serve to introduce a reader to an area of research, and we indicate some of the relevant areas. Without pretense of neutrality, in what follows we introduce the reader to the views and their champions.

The very idea of android epistemology incenses many philosophers. Android epistemology suggests to them a final abandonment of all that is specially human and humane. The first essay in this collection, written by the editors, argues to the contrary that various parts of the idea of android epistemology have had a role throughout the history of western philosophy and that contemporary android epistemology is not a rejection but a fruition of a grand tradition in philosophical theories of knowledge and of mind. Were they reborn into a modern university, we claim, Plato and Aristotle and Leibniz would most suitably take up appointments in the department of computer science.

In the second essay, Herbert Simon, one of the pioneers of artificial intelligence, offers a clear statement of a central approach to android epistemology, often called the representationalist hypothesis or, less respectfully, 'good old-fashioned artificial intelligence' or GOFAI. He considers features of human cognitive processes and argues that they can be programmed and realized in machines. Simon's morals for android epistemology include (1) the mind is a nearly decomposable system whose aggregate behavior can be described without much concern for lower level implementation; (2) human intelligence uses selective heuristic search, indexed memory, serial processing for problems that cannot be solved by recognition, and a variety of representations. Simon's essay offers examples from a number of AI programs as well as insightful comments on issues of affect and motivation.

Anatol Rapoport places the opposition to the very idea of android epistemology within a long tradition of resistance to scientific demolition of supposed special, admirable, and unique features of human beings and their place in the universe. The opposition to android epistemology, he argues, is the vitalists' last stand, the very last line that can be drawn if there is to be something special and historically conditioned about humans. One sort of argument that android epistemology cannot include humans is that there is something, some X, that people can do but machines cannot. Rapoport considers one of the vitalists' best cases to be rapid recognition of what might be called physically vague features of situations—faces, chess positions, and so on. His essay is an invitation to the reader to consider what the future may hold for computer vision and pattern recognition, as well as our capacity to understand the basis of "higher order" recognition in human perception.

Margaret Boden's contribution to this book discusses another proposed value for the X that machines can't do: they can't do anything creative. She emphasizes that "creativity" is itself a physically vague predicate we are helpless to define behaviorally but whose instances we think we can often recognize. Boden proposes that the occurrence of an idea is creative for an agent, P-creative, if that agent could not have had that idea before, and historically creative, H-creative, if no agent could have had that idea before. She denies that there can be any systematic explanation of the latter, but she claims robots can be P-creative. P-creativity, Boden suggests, is a relation between an idea and a set of generative rules or procedures—a "conceptual space": the generation of an idea is creative with respect to a conceptual space when it occurs outside of that space, by some other means, perhaps using other rules or procedures. It follows that the notion of creative [full stop] is a grammatical mistake, like the notion of higher [full stop], and that knowing an agent's thought is creative with respect to some conceptual space requires knowing how it came to have that particular thought.

Antoni Gomila's interesting essay on persons and cognitive systems argues that reflexive mental characteristics—the agent's sense of self and self-control—are generated from the agent's social setting and cannot be understood fully in terms of individual information-processing mechanisms. Nonetheless, Gomila claims, it is the agent's information-processing mechanisms that enable the social environment to have such a formative role, and emergence of internal mechanisms for using natural language—an emergence which he maintains is entirely maturational—is the crucial step in the process by which the social setting forms the person. The essay is nicely informed by work in developmental psychology. We editors have lots to argue about with Gomila, but his essay is clear and lively and can serve here as a pointer to the growing interest of social scientists in android epistemology and the new perspectives they bring.

One of those little known well-known facts of computation theory is that no computationally bounded agent can, even in the limit, reliably discriminate androids from nonandroids. Turing proposed an "imitation game" to be the test of success for artificial intelligence. What does computation theory have to say about its reliability? Selmer Bringsjord argues that the Turing Test for conscious intelligence in an artifact or android is not reliable against perhaps improbable but nonetheless possible combinations of performance by a simple machine—a very dumb finite automaton—and judgment by testers. He considers and rejects a number of replacements for the Turing Test, arguing that some do not restore reliability while another test, which requires the equivalence of programs between human and android, may not itself be computable. Bringsjord prefers a proposal due to Kugel which holds that people are not bounded by Turing computability, but instead compute a larger class of functions, the limiting recursive functions. Limiting recursion is a model for learning in which the agent eventually gets the correct answer (whatever it may be) and sticks with the correct answer, but the agent cannot say when the correct answer has been obtained. While the equivalence of programs is not computable, it is learnable in the limit. A Kugel test for conscious intelligence is a test for the enhanced learning capacity of limiting recursion. Bringsjord eventually rejects this test for the same reasons he rejected Turing's. While we do not always endorse its arguments, we recommend the chapter to the reader for its sprightly use of computation theory in philosophical questions.

We have included Kalyan Basu's essay in this collection for its forceful and compact statement of objections to android epistemology drawn from recent and contemporary English and German philosophy. We dispute virtually every unpoetic claim Basu makes for the singularity of human beings, but space and editorial politeness make us refrain from giving arguments here. We believe that anyone reasonably informed about computer science and cognitive psychology will be able to provide some of them. Although none are directed explicitly to Basu's essay, the elements of many replies are contained in other chapters in this collection.

Ronald Chrisley's chapter bravely attempts to unite android epistemology with a philosophical movement generated over the last 30 years by a number of philosophers associated with Oxford University. That movement combines pieces of logic, phenomenology, and aspects of philosophical essentialism in an attempt to characterize features of "content." Marked by a decided preference for a priori claims and a distaste for genuinely formal work, the Oxford movement has been isolated from and hostile to developments in computer science, cognitive psychology, and artificial intelligence. Chrisley claims, however, that parallel distributed processing requires distinctions about content and characterizations of "non-conceptual" content, and vice-versa. Chrisley's chapter may introduce the reader to a style of philosophical writing and reasoning that is becoming increasingly prevalent in the best philosophical circles in England and North America.

Lynn Stein's essay is a brief, clear, and lively discussion of the robotic use of memory and imagination in planning goal-directed motion. In the Meta-Toto system, a history of robotic movements is used to form an internal map of surroundings which the robot then uses to imagine the results of various sequences of motions and thus to plan motion towards a goal. Stein's description invites the reader to think about how imagination might be used in combination with programmed or acquired causal knowledge for other sorts of robotic planning. One of the editors is already heading for his basement with a floppy in one hand and a soldering iron in the other. Look out for a robot that imagines itself into the bottom of a well. Glymour would claim he had reproduced Thales. Stein is the representative here of a large body of work in what artificial intelligence calls "planning," that is, thought about action. There is a growing controversy about the extent to which intelligent actions are planned, as opposed to being quick reactions to immediate problems arising in the android's current situation. The truth, as always, probably includes aspects of both positions, but the debate fits thoroughly under the banner of android epistemology.

Most of what is known has to be learned, so mechanisms of learning are a central topic in android epistemology. The essay by Stary and Peschl discusses machine learning from the perspective of the programmer, the philosopher, and the psychologist. They discuss a number of computational learning architectures, and suggest that evaluating success in learning is a matter of evaluating how well a system adapts to an environment. We hope readers will take this chapter as an invitation to the literature on computational learning theory, where traditional philosophical questions have received a sharper formulation and surprising answers and where important problems the philosophical tradition overlooked have been raised and solved. (See, for example,

K. Kelly, *The Logic of Reliable Inquiry,* Oxford University Press, 1995; D. Osherso, M. Stob, and S. Weinstein, *Systems That Learn,* MIT Press, 1985).

Cary deBessonet's essay gives an individual perspective on what AI workers call "knowledge representation." DeBessonet describes a form of "semantic net" that treats relations of instantiation and causation and that distinguishes between associations that are "typical" of a term—what philosophers might call almost analytic—and associations that are "penumbral" or more contingent. His concern is a version of a familiar problem in machine reasoning, namely that of designing systems that allow rapid inference that is neither deductive nor probabilistic. We are able, for example, to almost instantly recognize the tension between the claim that "A flock of birds ate all the figs" and the claim that "A bird ate all the figs" even though it is hard to specify any simple way in which they might be logically contradictory. That this problem is familiar does not make it any simpler, however: android epistemology is replete with familiar, difficult problems. DeBessonet's chapter is an accessible discussion of one way of addressing some of these problems computationally and may serve to introduce some readers to the surprising complexities of apparently "ordinary" reasoning.

James Gips' deceptively simple and direct essay raises a whole range of questions about how a robot could be ethical; if we are computationally bounded systems, the questions have important implications for us as well. Gips briefly and clearly reviews the basic approaches to ethical theory common in philosophy and asks the salient question "how could ethical systems of various sorts be made computable?" Gips's question parallels more familiar questions about epistemic norms: how could an android be rational, deductively consistent, probabilistically coherent? The most rudimentary computation theory reveals a tension between the ideals of logic and probability, on the one hand, and the demand of computability on the other. Much of the richness of artificial intelligence consists in finding ways to compromise the ideals to abide by the computational constraint. The same form of tension applies to various sorts of ethical theories—to utilitarian and deontological theories, for example—but the parallel inquiry has not even begun. Gips' essay is an invitation.

The chapter by A. F. Umar Khan accepts the invitation. His paper discusses strategies a robot can use to keep on the straight and narrow. One of the insights of this essay is that a robot can have internalized, rule-based (whether utilitarian or otherwise) self-control only if it can learn at least the immediate consequences of its actions, for only then can the system intelligently (and thus responsibly) adapt its rules to circumstances. Machine ethics, he argues directly and convincingly, is inseparable from machine learning.

Henry Kyburg's chapter outlines a theory of rational, probabilistic inference that Kyburg claims is a norm for any agent, human or otherwise, that has to work with incomplete knowledge of its surroundings. According to Kyburg, a body of evidence of database necessitates, for any specified interval (between 0 and 1), whether or not the probability of an event lies in that interval. Kyburg's theory, which he has developed in more detail elsewhere, is presented in its most succinct form in this essay. Again, this essay hints at a growing volume of research and controversy about ways that androids can, and perhaps must, use probabilistic machinery to cope with an uncertain world.

Paul Churchland's contribution to this book is a real piece of android epistemology, a proposal for a mechanism to produce features of stereoscopic vision rapidly by using a feedforward neural network. Churchland presents experimental demonstrations of the behavior of the architecture and, treating it as a model of human stereoscopic vision, derives predictions about human anatomical connections in the optical cortex. Churchland is well known for his use of neural models rather than more traditional computational architectures and serves here as our representative of this very active and successful 'connectionist' school.

Finally, Marvin Minsky imagines a future dialog about the sad limitations of these little androids who call themselves "human." We don't want to have dinner with anyone who reads it without laughing. We urge you to buy this book: Minsky's essay is worth the money, all by itself.

Android Epistemology

1 The Prehistory of Android Epistemology

Clark Glymour, Kenneth M. Ford, & Patrick J. Hayes

Contemporary artificial intelligence (AI) can be viewed as essays in the epistemology of androids, an exploration of the principles underlying the cognitive behavior of any possible kind of mechanical agents. Occasional hyperbole and flimflam aside, artificial intelligence is a wonderful subject, full of new ideas and possibilities, unfettered by tradition or concern (other than inspirational) for the accidents of human constitution, but disciplined by the limits of mechanical computation. More than other new sciences, AI and philosophy have things to say to one another: any attempt to create and understand minds must be of philosophical interest. In fact, AI is philosophy, conducted by novel means. That AI emerges from ideas of computer science is, of course, a familiar observation. The central insights of Babbage, Turing, von Neumann and other pioneers on how a machine might actually be built that could manipulate and be influenced by symbols are widely recognized. But for all the novelty, many of the central ideas that animate artificial intelligence, and even particular techniques and themes prominent in contemporary practice, have a long philosophical ancestry. In fact, the sources of key assumptions and insights underlying much of AI—such as that the mind is computational, that computational devices can be a simulacrum of the mind, the fundamental idea that machines can "calculate" with symbols for things other than numbers, and that there is a plethora of possible artificial minds yet to be invented—are deeply embedded in the history of philosophy. This background includes the history of logic, the emergence of combinatorics, the merging and separating of theories of deduction and computation from psychological theories, the formation of the first program for a possible cognitive agent, characteristic designs of programs for machine learning, characterizations of conditions for causal inference, and no doubt a good deal more. In addition to any list of ideas, there is what might best be characterized as an attitude towards machinery. AI has an engineer's respect for things that work and a pragmatic willingness to try anything that will produce the results needed. In the spirit of medieval astronomy, it wants only to save the phenomena, not to hypothesize psychological truth. While important parts of modern science have emerged from trying to understand machines—thermodynamics and steam engines, for example—the direct intellectual merging of philosophy and engineering seems strange, even rather outrageous, in our modern academic culture. But many earlier philosophers seem to have had a similar kind of affection and respect for machinery. This essay attempts briefly to survey some of the philosophical sources of contemporary ideas about artificial intelligence. More extended treatments can be found in Glymour (1992) and in Haugeland (1985).

Back to the Greeks: Plato and Aristotle

According to both Plato and Aristotle, the objects of knowledge have a special *formal structure*. The sort of thing a person may know is that one thing or kind of property is a *finite combination* of other things or kinds of properties. *Man* is a combination of *rational* and *animal*. *Triangle* is a combination of *closed, rectilinear, figure,* and *three-sided*. Plato and Aristotle differed about the metaphysics, of course. For Plato these combinations are ideal objects or forms; for Aristotle they are essential attributes of concrete objects. For both philosophers, however, all knowledge consists of knowing such combinations of forms or essential attributes of a thing or kind. For example, according to Plato, knowledge of virtue is knowledge of which simple forms are combined into the form of virtue. Any AI knowledge engineer will recognize the idea and be attracted by its computational virtues. The anticipations are, however, more detailed. In the *Meno*, Socrates and Meno search for an answer to the question "What is virtue?" Socratic method is to collect positive and negative examples and to search for hypotheses that cover the positive and exclude the negative. In the course of the dialogue, Meno points out through a question the first theorem of computational learning theory: how will they know when they have found the correct answer? Meno's point, of course, is that they cannot, solely on the basis of a finite sample, decide the truth of a contingent, universal claim by any rule that will yield the truth in all logically possible circumstances consistent with the sample. Socrates' response to Meno is that the process of discovery is what is now called in artificial intelligence *explanation-based reasoning*. Everyone, according to Plato, already knows implicitly at birth all of the laws of forms. The process we think of as empirical discovery is simply a matter of realizing which formal truth, or consequence of laws of forms, applies to a particular set of cases and adding that truth to one's explicit knowledge.

The conjunctive view of the objects of knowledge suggests questions about combinations of properties. Ultimately, on either the Platonic or Aristotelian view, any kind of property that can be the object of scientific knowledge can be analyzed into a combination of simple properties that cannot be further analyzed. The number of distinct kinds that can be the objects of knowledge then consists of the number of distinct combinations of these simple properties, whatever they are. What is the number of pairs of distinct properties if there are n properties altogether? What is the number of triples of distinct properties if there are n properties altogether? What is the number of distinct combinations of any particular number m of properties drawn from n properties? How can these distinct combinations be enumerated and surveyed? If one has the Platonic-Aristotelian conception of the form of knowledge, these are fundamental questions.

In Europe, it was just such questions that gave rise to the mathematical subject of combinatorics, the study of the numbers of possible combinations satisfying given conditions. The first mathematical results of this kind in the West seem to occur in a commentary on Aristotle by Porphyry, written in the 3rd century A.D. Porphyry wished to comment on all of the similarities and differences among five Aristotelian "voices," and so he posed the problem of enumerating all the distinct pairs of things that can be obtained from a collection of five things. He observed that one might think that this number is 20, because one can choose the first thing of a pair in any of five ways, and the remaining member of the pair in four distinct ways. But Porphyry correctly argued that the number of pairings is not 20:

> Such is not the case; for though the first of the five can be paired with the remaining four, when we come to the second, one of the pairs will already have been counted; with the third, two; with the fourth, three and with the fifth, four; thus there are in all only ten differences: 4+3+2+1. (cited in Edwards, 1987, p. 20)

Roughly 250 years later, Boethius wrote commentaries on Porphyry's commentary on Aristotle, and in them he provided a more general, alternative proof. But Porphyry's combinatoric result seems not to have been significantly extended until the Renaissance. Even without technical advances, however, combinatoric ideas remained important.

In the Middle Ages, the conception of the objects of knowledge as combinations of simple attributes that make up a kind or a complex property led to a conception of the method for acquiring knowledge. The method, insofar as it deserves the name, consisted of trying to "analyze" a thing into its simple properties (analysis) and then trying to put it back together by combining those properties (synthesis). Sometimes—in Renaissance chemistry, for example—"analysis" meant physically decomposing a substance into "simpler" substances, and "synthesis" meant physically reconstituting a substance of that kind, but for the most part the analysis and synthesis were purely mental.

Ramón Lull and the Infidels

After the reintroduction of classical learning into Christian Europe, one would expect that Christian intellectuals would have applied the methods they had learned from Aristotle and Plato to the study of God, and they did. God, too, had fundamental properties, and one could consider the combinations of His attributes. In the 13th century, the questions of how to enumerate, organize, and display God's attributes led to a fundamental insight, one that we nowadays take for granted. It concerns the odd life of the great Spanish philosopher, Ramón Lull, a 13th century Franciscan monk.

The notion of mechanical aids in carrying out an algorithm and the notion of an algorithm itself are ancient, perhaps prehistoric. But one of the central insights of modern computational thinking, the idea that machines can aid nonnumerical and nongeometrical reasoning through manipulating discrete symbols, first appeared in the West, as far as we know, in the writings of Ramón Lull. The source of Lull's idea lay in a traditional metaphysical view and in the slowly emerging mathematics of combinatorics. Lull's motives, however, were entirely religious.

Lull's life illustrates that a philosopher can also be a man (or woman) of action, if only bizzare action. Lull grew up in a wealthy family and passed his early adulthood in the court of James II of Spain. He spent his time with games and pleasantries and is reputed to have made great efforts to seduce the wives of other courtiers. Accounts have it that after considerable effort to seduce a particular lady, she finally let him into her chambers and revealed a withered breast. Taking this sight as a sign from God, Lull gave up the life of a courtier and joined the Franciscan order, determined that he would dedicate his life to converting Moslem civilization to Christianity, and in a curious way, philosophy gained from that dedication.

Lull moved to Majorca and spent several years mastering the Arabic language, studying and writing tracts (of which he eventually authored hundreds) against Islam and for Christianity. About 1274, Lull had a vision of the means by which Moslems could be converted to Christianity. Stimulated by the idea, he wrote another book, his *Ars Magna.* While Lull's fundamental style of thought is mystical and obscure, it contains one logical gem.

In effect, Lull's idea was that Moslems (and others) may fail to convert to Christianity because of a cognitive defect. They simply were unable to appreciate the vast array of the combinations of God's or Christ's virtues. But thanks to this vision, Lull believed that infidels could be converted if they could be brought to see the *combinations* of God's attributes. Further, he thought that a *representation* of those combinations could be effectively presented by means of appropriate machines, and that supposition was the key to his new method. Lull designed and built a series of machines to be used to present the combinations of God's virtues.

A typical Lullian machine consisted of two or more disks having a common spindle. Each disk could be rotated independently of the others. The rim of each disk was divided into sections or *camerae*, and each section bore a letter. According to the application for which the machine was intended, the letters would each have a special significance. They might denote, for example, an attribute of God. One Lullian machine, for example, has the letters "B" through "R" around the rims of an inner disk, and around the outer disk Latin words signifying attributes of God: Bonitas (B), Magnitudo (C), Eternitas (D) and so on. A Lullian machine was operated by rotating the two disks independently, much as we would a star finder or (some years ago) a circular slide rule. At any setting of the disks, *pairs* of God's attributes would be juxtaposed on the rims of the inner and outer disks. Rotating the disks would create different pairings. One would thus discover that God is Good *and* Great, Good *and* Eternal, Great *and* Eternal, and so forth. The heretic and the infidel were supposed to be brought to the True Faith by these revelations.

Lull lectured on several occasions at the University of Paris. He traveled throughout Europe attempting to raise money for missions to North Africa to convert Moslems to Christianity. He himself is reported to have made three such trips to Africa. Tradition has it that on his third trip, at the age of 83, he was stoned to death, but some biographers are so lacking in romantic sentiment that they dispute this account.

This story may seem a bizarre and slightly amusing tale of no particular philosophical significance. But buried within Lull's mysticism and his machines is the seed of a collection of powerful ideas that only began to bear fruit 350 years later, in the 17th century. One of the great ideas implicit in Lull's work is that nonmathematical reasoning can be done, or at least assisted, by a mechanical process; the other is that reasoning does not proceed by syllogism, but by combinatorics. Reasoning is the decomposition and recombination of representations. The decomposition and recombination of attributes can be represented by the decomposition and recombination of *symbols*, and that, as Lull's devices illustrate, is a process that can be made mechanical.

Computation and Discovery in the 17th Century:
Pascal, Leibniz and Bacon

Lull's work was known even in the 17th century, when a version of his ideas was taken up by Leibniz. Interestingly, the 17th century has a hidden history that strived, but failed, to articulate a theory of reasoning that combines logic, algebra, and combinatorics.

In 1642, Blaise Pascal, the French philosopher, mathematician, and inventor, perfected what until recently had been generally thought of as the first automatic calculating machine.[1] Like Lullian machines, Pascal's machine used rotating wheels, but unlike Lull's, it actually did something—addition and subtraction—including carries or borrows. This machine, called Pascaline, seems very simple now but was a contemporary public sensation raising both excitement and fear—not unlike today's AI research program; and, skeptics might add, Pascal's machine had a defect that AI may share: it cost more to produce than people were willing to pay for it. Although the Pascaline's functionality was limited, it showed that tasks that previously might have been expected to require human attention or thought could be made fully, automatically mechanical. The process of building the calculating device seems to have had a substantial impact on Pascal's philosophical thinking. With a prescience for enduring controversy, in his *Pensées*, Pascal (1670/1932) remarked that "The arithmetical machine produces effects which approach nearer to thought than all the actions of animals." What animals have that the calculator lacked, Pascal wrote, is will.

Pascal's *Treatise of the Arithmetical Triangle*, in which the Binomial Theorem is first established, helped to make it evident that the analysis of combinations arising from the Aristotelian and Platonic traditions was an aspect of algebraic relations among numbers. Descartes' mathematical work had shown that geometry, the traditional mathematical language of the sciences, also had an algebraic side and that important geometrical properties could be characterized algebraically. By the middle and latter parts of the 17th century, algebraic relations, usually presented as geometrical statements of ratios, had become the form in which natural science expressed the laws of nature. Kepler's third law was essentially such a relation, and so was the Boyle-Mariotte law of gases, and the inverse square law of gravitation. It was only natural to suppose that the actions of the mind—thought—must also have laws that can be described by such relations, and that the combinatorics of analysis and synthesis are a hint of them. Gottfried Leibniz came to that very conclusion.

Pascal's *Treatise* was published in 1654. The next year Leibniz, then 19 years of age, published his first work, a Latin treatise on logic and combinatorics, *De Arte Combinatoria*. He did not yet know of Pascal's work, but he learned of it subsequently, and in later years when he journeyed to Paris, he tried unsuccessfully to meet with Pascal, who had retreated to religious quarters at Port Royal. Pascal had shown that the same combinatorial numbers or binomial coefficients also arise in relations between the terms of certain infinite series, and reflection on the properties of series eventually helped lead Leibniz to the discovery of the differential and integral calculus.

Leibniz's first work was really a combinatorial study of logic in the Aristotelian tradition. It is the only work on logic that Leibniz ever published. Over the course of the rest of his life, Leibniz wrote a long series of unpublished and incomplete papers on logic. They show the formation of some of the key modern ideas about deductive inference and proof, and they also show how very difficult the issues were for one of the greatest philosophers and mathematicians of the century. Leibniz's logical theory is not consistent and thorough (Leibniz had a difficult time completing anything), but it contains many ideas that were successfully elaborated in later centuries, and it also shows clearly the limitations of the Aristotelian framework.

Following tradition, Leibniz assumed that every proposition consists of a predicate applied to a subject and that in this regard the structure of language reflects the structure of the world. In the world, substances *have* attributes. But Leibniz gave this notion a twist. Substances don't, in his view, *have* attributes in the sense that one and the same substance could have an attribute or not have it. A substance *just is* a combination of attributes. You, for example, are nothing but the combination of all of the properties that you have. So there is no property that you in fact have that *you* could not have—an entity that didn't have some property you have wouldn't be you. So, finally, every property you have, you have *necessarily*. The same holds for any other substance in the world. Whatever properties a substance has, it has necessarily.

In Leibniz's theory, every concept *just is* a list or combination of primitive concepts. All true propositions are true because the list of primitive concepts of the subject term is appropriately related to the list of primitive concepts of the predicate term. Leibniz says that every true proposition is true because it is an instance of the identity A = A. He meant that if a proposition is true, the subject and predicate lists will be such that by eliminating irrelevant parts of one or the other, the same combination of concepts or attributes is found in the subject as is found in the predicate. So every true proposition can be given a proof. The proof of a proposition consists of the following:

1. Producing the combinations of simple concepts that are, respectively, the concept denoted by the predicate of the proposition and the concept denoted by the subject of the proposition.

2. Showing that the concept of the predicate is included in the concept of the subject, or vice-versa, according to what the proposition asserts.

Leibniz wrote extensively about these two steps. He never succeeded in making clear just how the analysis of concepts was to be obtained—of course, neither had Aristotle or the Scholastic tradition of analysis and synthesis. Leibniz envisioned the creation of an enormous dictionary or encyclopedia; his vision was ridiculed by Swift in the latter's account of Laputan scholarship and has not had a good reputation since the 18th century. In the 1950s, Bar-Hillel noted that a successful mechanical translator, in order to properly distinguish ambiguities such as "pen" in "the ink is in the pen" and "the sheep are in the pen," would have to have access to a huge database of all of human knowledge. Bar-Hillel's observation was considered a *reductio ad absurdum* argument for the impossibility of machine translation. But something like Leibnizian "dictionaries" are indeed being constructed in AI and used in machine translation, albeit with a rather more complex theory of the structure of knowledge, but still based on the idea—now with the backing of 20th century logical theory—that in a computational sense a concept simply is a combination of all that is known about it, so that a suitably rich enumeration and organization of all this knowledge is sufficient to capture the concept.

If a universal dictionary could be assembled that expressed each concept in terms of the simplest concepts, Leibniz was convinced that the production of scientific knowledge would become *automatic*. He thought an *algorithm* or mechanical procedure could be found to carry out the second part of the procedure for giving proofs. The way to formulate such a procedure is to treat the problem as though it is part of *algebra*. Each simple term and each complex term should be given a letter or other symbol (Leibniz sometimes suggested using numbers as symbols for concepts), and then one would use algebraic methods to search for algebraic identities. On other occasions, he suggested representing concepts by geometrical figures, such as lines, and trying to carry out the second step of the aforementioned two-step process by geometrical procedures. The essential thing is that there is a *mathematics of reason* (in fact, that is the title of one of the logical papers Leibniz completed), and this mathematics can be carried out automatically.

Again, much current AI research, given more adequate flesh by developments in logic, is based on a modification of Leibniz's vision. One entire subfield of AI is concerned with "computational logic," a phrase that Leibniz would have understood immediately. Pascal and Leibniz would perhaps also have understood one aspect of the computational difficulties of this field. The reasoning process is indeed governed by combinatorics, quite aside from problems of undecidability. Combinatorial analysis shows that the search spaces of reasoning expand too rapidly to submit to straightforward enumeration, so the mathematics of reasoning seems to require "dictionaries" of heuristics, which are the subject of active research.

Pascal's success with calculating machines inspired Leibniz to devise his own machine, which he called the Stepped Reckoner. Although conceptually much more sophisticated than either the Calculating Clock or the Pascaline, Leibniz's Stepped Reckoner appears never to have operated properly; its manufacture was beyond machining techniques of the day. Leibniz's efforts to build a better machine led him to realize that a binary notation would permit a much simpler mechanism than required for his and Pascal's decimal-based devices. He envisioned a binary calculator that would use moving balls to represent binary digits (Leibniz, 1679).[2] As noted by Augarten (1985), the notion of binary representation had more than practical import for Leibniz. He regarded the remarkable expressiveness of binary enumeration as a sort of natural proof of the existence of God, asserting that it demonstrated that God, the omniscient *one* (1), had created everything out of *nothing* (0). Thus as did Lull and Pascal before him, Leibniz attached deep religious significance to his efforts at mechanization.

Pascaline's wheels carried numerals, and it performed arithmetic, but Leibniz saw that these machines were manipulating symbols in ways that were best understood in combinatoric terms and that there was nothing about the idea which restricted it solely to arithmetic. During the first half of this the 20th century, when the idea of mechanical arithmetic had become commonplace, this insight was still rare. An early British government report on the significance of computing machines declared that they were not worth the investment of much research effort, on the grounds that there was not a great need for more gun-aiming tables.

In 1620, Francis Bacon's *Novum Organum* sought to provide the inductive method for the new science. Bacon describes a nearly algorithmic procedure, often ridiculed by 20th century philosophers of science for whom the very idea of discovery by algorithm was anathema. Bacon's discovery procedure assumes the investigator is in search of the "form" of a phenomenon, which for Bacon, as for Aristotle and Plato, meant at least a conjunction of features essential, necessary, and sufficient for the phenomenon. The investigator should then collect positive instances of the phenomenon, forming them in a table. Again, negative instances, otherwise as like positive instances as possible, should be collected in a table. Third, a table should be formed of instances exhibiting the phenomenon in varying degrees, if the phenomenon admits of such variation. Now the investigator should find—Bacon doesn't say how—whatever combination of features is common to all positive instances, absent from all negative instances, and concommitant in degree with the degree of the phenomenon in the table of degrees.

Bacon's problem setting, and his method, were revived around the middle of this century in the study in cognitive psychology of "concept learning." Procedures proposed by Bruner, and later by Hunt, and still later by statistical concept learners, have their logical and historical roots in Bacon's new method.

The Cartesian Way

René Descartes' mathematical innovations created linkages that proved essential to the very idea of a mechanics of mind. Descartes' algebraic geometry transformed aspects of the traditional geometrical formalism for the mathematical description of nature into systems of algebraic equations. With that transformation, an algebraic expression became possible for Kepler's laws, Boyle's law, and so on. The binomial theorem in turn established connections between algebra and combinatorics, the mathematics of mind.

Yet, philosophically, Descartes was unconnected with the invisible thread that bound Hobbes, Leibniz and Pascal. The Cartesian conception of mind was not, like Hobbes', of a material device that represents by physical symbols and reasons by computation. Descartes' mind, it is almost too banal to note, was of an entirely different substance than matter; Descartes' mind could exist were nothing material to exist; Descartes' mind could be influenced by material conditions, but it was not bound by and characterized by the principles that constrain matter.

This idea is tantalizingly close to the modern conception of software. Software is also immaterial and remarkably unconstrained by physical principles, yet when provided with a suitable material substrate (not a pineal gland), it can have startling material effects. The Cartesian error was only to think of it as a *substance* rather than something like a pattern or a specification. But perhaps Descartes can be forgiven—philosophers and lawyers are still not quite clear about exactly how to describe software. Fortunately, however, programmers are able to create and use it with some confidence.

For the purposes of our topic, Descartes' principal contemporary influence is on the opponents of artificial intelligence, through two ideas. First, Descartes thought of procedures, algorithms, methods, and rules as inextricable from meaning and intention. Descartes' rules for inquiry are not even approximately mechanical as are Hobbes'; instead, Descartes formulated his rules in terms for which there are only inner criteria: examine whether ideas are *clear*; examine whether ideas are *distinct* from others. It was this very subjective twist on method that irritated Descartes' materialist critics, such as Pierre Gassendi. In our century, the Cartesian view of method seems to have prompted (no doubt through more proximate sources, such as phenomenalism) Wittgenstein's argument that a purely subjective language is impossible, because extra-linguistic criteria are required to constitute correct or incorrect usage, and a language without standards of use is not a language at all. Wittgenstein's private language argument has been recast by Saul Kripke as an argument about the irreducibility of rules or algorithms to material or physical relations. Briefly, Kripke argues that rules—for example, the rule for addition—require *meanings* that somehow determine how the rules apply to a potential infinity of as yet unexamined cases. But meanings are *normative;* meanings have to do with how language ought to be used. And, to conclude the argument, norms are not part of the physical world.

The second Cartesian influence on contemporary discussions occurs through a strategy of argument that is ubiquitous in contemporary philosophical opposition to artificial intelligence. Descartes' criterion for possibility is imagination: If p is (or can be) imagined, then p is possible. Hence, if the denial of p can be imagined, then p is not necessary. In combination with some other ideas about possibility and necessity—for example, the idea that fundamental scientific identifications of properties ("water is H_2O") entail that the identity claims are necessary—the Cartesian fallacy sows considerable confusion. A well-known recent example of this confusion is Searle's Chinese room argument. Searle wants to refute the thesis that *any* physically possible system that implements a program for understanding Chinese with sufficient speed therefore understands Chinese. Searle imagines that he is placed in a room containing baskets full of Chinese symbols and a rule book (in English) for matching Chinese symbols with other Chinese symbols. People outside the room (who understand Chinese) slide questions written in Chinese under the door. In response he manipulates the symbols according to the rules in the book and answers by sliding strings of Chinese symbols back out under the door. The rule book is supposed to be analogous to the computer program, and Searle to the computer. These answers are indistinguishable from those of a native Chinese speaker, although, according to Searle, neither he nor the room nor the two of them together understand Chinese. Even if one were to (mistakenly) grant his second conclusion (that the whole system didn't understand Chinese), Searle's fantasy is only a counterexample to anything of interest to artificial intelligence if one supposes that because Searle can imagine himself running the program, that this *is* actually possible. But before he could generate a single output Searle-in-the-box would become bored and his Chinese friends would have long since found better things to do.

Minds and Procedures: Hobbes to Kant

Thomas Hobbes, the 17th century autodidact and mathematical eccentric best known for his writings on political philosophy, also formulated a rather clear anticipation of Newell and Simon's notion of intelligence as a physical system that manipulates symbols:

> By ratiocination, I mean computation. Now to compute is either to collect the sum of many things that are added together, or to know what remains when one thing is taken out of another. Ratiocination, therefore, is the same with addition and subtraction; and if any man add multiplication and division, I will not be against it, seeing multiplication is nothing but addition of equals one to another, and division nothing but a subtraction of equals one from another, as often as is possible. So that all ratiocination is comprehended in these two operations of the mind, addition and subtraction.
>
> But how by the *ratiocination* of our mind, we add and subtract in our silent thoughts, without the use of words, it will be necessary for me to make intelligible by an example or two. If therefore a man sees something afar off and obscurely, although no appellation had yet been given to anything, he will, notwithstanding, have the same idea of that thing for which now, by imposing a name on it, we call it *body*. Again, when by coming nearer, he sees the same thing thus and thus, now in one place and now in another, he will have a new idea thereof, namely, that for which we now call such a thing *animated*. Thirdly, when standing nearer, he perceives the figure, hears the voice, and sees other things which are signs of a rational mind, he has a third idea, though it have yet no appellation, namely, that for which we now call anything *rational*. Lastly, when, by looking fully and distinctly upon it,

he conceives all that he has seen as one thing, the idea he has now is compounded of his former ideas, which are put together in the mind in the same order in which these three single names, *body, animated, rational,* are in speech compounded into this one name, *body-animated-rational,* or *man.* In like manner, of the several conceptions of *four sides, equality of sides,* and *right angles,* is compounded the conception of a *square.* For the mind may conceive a figure of four sides without any conception of their equality, and of that equality without conceiving a right angle; and may join together all these single conceptions into one conception or one idea of a square. And thus we see how the conceptions of the mind are compounded. Again, whosoever sees a man standing near him, conceives the whole idea of that man; and if, as he goes away, he follows him with his eyes only, he will lose the idea of those things which were signs of his being rational, whilst, nevertheless, the idea of a body-animated remains still before his eyes, so that the idea of rational is subtracted from the whole idea of man, that is to say, of body-animated-rational, and there remains that of body-animated; and a while after, at a greater distance, the idea of animated will be lost, and that of body only will remain; so that at last, when nothing at all can be seen, the whole idea will vanish out of sight. By which examples, I think, it is manifest enough what is the internal ratiocination of mind without words.

We must not therefore, think that computation, that is, ratiocination, has place only in numbers, as if man were distinguished from other living creatures (which is said to have been the opinion of Pythagoras) by nothing but the faculty of numbering; for *magnitude, body, motion, time, degrees of quality, action, conception proportion, speech* and *names* (in which all the kinds of philosophy consist) are capable of addition and subtraction. (Hobbes, 1962, pp. 25-26)

There are several important thoughts in this passage. One is that reasoning is a psychological process, so that a theory of logical inference should be a theory of the operations of the mind. Another is that representations can have an encoding by, or be analogous to, numbers. A third is that the theory of reasoning is a theory of appropriate combinations; just what the objects are that are combined is obscure in this passage, but other passages suggest that Hobbes thought of the mind as composed of particles, and some of these particles, or collections of them, serve as symbols (or, as Hobbes would say, names) for things, and it is these physical symbols that are combined or decomposed in reasoning.

Later English writers of philosophical psychology, Locke, Hume, Mill, and Maudsley, for example, thought of the content of a theory of mind as, at least in part, a theory of mental procedures, specifically procedures in which mental objects—"ideas"—are linked or "associated." Associationist psychology typically avoided Hobbes' mechanical formulations, and his connection of procedures with algorithms and numerical encodings had no influence. Instead, mental procedures were explained in terms of "similarity" and "vivacity" and temporal proximity of occurrence of ideas.

The procedural viewpoint was given a very different turn in the closing decades of the 18th century in Kant's *Critique of Pure Reason* and his related works. As with the associationist writers who influenced him, Kant gives no hint that mental processes are computational, but he offers an original view of those processes themselves, quite unlike anything before. Kant is the modern father of the notion of top-down processing.

Kant recognized that the logical theory which he had inherited from Aristotle, and which he assumed to be sound and complete, could not account for mathematical inference. Euclid's geometrical proofs, which prove by construction the existence of objects with specified properties, cannot be turned into valid syllogistic arguments, nor can Euclid's proofs of theorems in number theory be obtained by syllogism. Yet Kant was convinced that classical mathematics and much else (including that all events are governed by causal regularities and features of Newtonian physics) is known *a priori* and not derived from inductions founded on experience. Kant's solution to the conundrum is that the content of experience is literally a *function* (in the mathematical sense) of the procedures of mind and of unknowable features of things in themselves. The difference between what is needed to obtain Euclid's proofs and what Aristotle's logic can do is built into the mind itself, not as axioms but as procedures that automatically construct the content of experience from the deliverances of sense. Things in themselves deliver, in unknowable ways, sensation, or what Kant sometimes calls the matter of experience; the "faculty of intuition" then contributes spatial and temporal features; and the "schematism of the understanding" contributes object identity, causal regularity, and the synthesis of the individual pieces into a unified experience. The faculty of intuition automatically constructs images, for example, that satisfy the requirements of Euclidean axioms, and the schematism ensures that nothing random happens in experience. Kant repeatedly remarks that the process of synthesis and the operation of the schematism are unconscious, and he observes that how the schematism works will likely remain unknown (immediately thereafter he plunges into lengthy remarks about how the schematism works).

The 19th Century: Boole, Frege and Freud

George Boole's work can be seen as a continuation of Leibniz's vision. Boole provided an algebra of logic and considered the algebra important because it provided a method for correct reasoning. Boole, too, viewed the mathematical theory of reasoning as a description of psychological laws of nature, but he also realized the contradiction between this analysis and the obvious fact that humans make errors of reasoning.

> The truth that the ultimate laws of thought are mathematical in their form, viewed in connection with the fact of the possibility of error, establishes a ground

for some remarkable conclusions. If we directed our attention to the scientific truth alone, we might be led to infer an almost exact parallelism between the intellectual operations and the movements of external nature. Suppose any one conversant with physical science, but unaccustomed to reflect upon the nature of his own faculties, to have been informed, that it had been proved, that the laws of those faculties were mathematical; it is probable that after the first feelings of incredulity had subsided, the impression would arise, that the order of thought must, *therefore*, be as necessary as that of the material universe. We know that in the realm of natural science, the absolute connection between the initial and final elements of a problem, exhibited in the mathematical form, fitly symbolizes that physical necessity which binds together effect and cause. The necessary sequence of states and conditions in the inorganic world, and the necessary connection of premises and conclusion in the processes of exact demonstration thereto applied, seem to be coordinate.

Were, then, the laws of valid reasoning uniformly obeyed, a very close parallelism would exist between the operations of the intellect and those of external Nature. Subjection to laws mathematical in their form and expression, even the subjection of an absolute obedience, would stamp upon the two series one common character. The reign of necessity over the intellectual and the physical world would be alike complete and universal.

But while the observation of external Nature testifies with ever-strengthening evidence to the fact, that uniformity of operation and unvarying obedience to appointed laws prevail throughout her entire domain, the slightest attention to the processes of the intellectual world reveals to us another state of things. The mathematical laws of reasoning are, properly speaking, the laws of *right* reasoning only, and their actual transgression is a perpetually recurring phenomenon. Error, which has no place in the material system, occupies a large one here. We must accept this as one of those ultimate facts, the origin of which it lies beyond the province of science to determine. We must admit that there exist laws which even the rigor of their mathematical forms does not preserve from violation. We must ascribe to them an authority the essence of which does not consist in power, a supremacy which the analogy of the inviolable order of the natural world in no way assists us to comprehend. (Boole, 1951, pp. 407-408)

Caught by the image of logic as the laws of reasoning akin to the law of gravitation, Boole did not try to resolve this difficulty by supposing that his was the theory of some ideal agent; he did not think that he was describing other minds than ours, imaginary minds still somehow recognizably similar to our own.

About thirty years later, Frege gave the first adequate formulation of the logic of propositions—Boole had in effect described something closer to mod 2 arithmetic—and formalized a system of logic that included both first-order logic and the quantification over properties, although the latter part of his system was, as Russell showed, not consistent. Frege insisted on separating logic from psychology, and so he did not suffer Boole's embarrassment over human error. Frege's achievement, and the logical developments of the next fifty years that extended it, at last put in place one of the principal tools for the study, among many other things, of android epistemology. Another conceptual tool arose at nearly the same time from physiology.

While the 18th and early 19th centuries witnessed thinkers such as Pascal, Leibniz, and Boole struggling to find a mechanical basis for reasoning, the end of the 19th and the beginning of the 20th century saw two remarkably different ways of reconciling psychology with the notion that reasoning is computation. Each of these lines of work leads to a branch of contemporary AI research. The "symbolic" approach to AI emphasizes structures of reasoning, while "connectionist" artificial intelligence focuses on brain-like architectures.

Prefaces to modern connectionist works usually trace the ideas back as far as Hebb's (1949) *The Organization of Behavior;* occasionally writers will note passages of William James near the turn of the century that have a connectionist flavor. But the basics of connectionist models of computation and of mind were fully developed by the late 19th century in the private views, and some of the public views, of neuropsychologists. We know of no better statement from this time than Sigmund Freud's private writings, where a great many details, including what is now called "Hebbian learning" and the "Hebbian synapse" are described. Freud was trained as a neuroanatomist by Ernst Brucke, one of Europe's leading physiologists and an uncompromising materialist. Early in the 1890s physiologists learned of synaptic junctions, and in Vienna that revelation immediately led to connectionist speculations by the senior research assistants in Brucke's laboratory, including Freud. While others published similar views, Freud developed his ideas in his unpublished *Project for a Scientific Psychology,* written in 1895. Freud's theory of dreams began in that essay, and the last chapter of Freud's first book on dreams is clearly derived from it. (For a more detailed account of Freud's connection with connectionism, see Glymour, 1991.)

We return now to the symbolic tradition. Kant held that the objects of experience are constructed or "synthesized," but he was not at all clear about what they are constructed from or how the details of such a construction could work. After Frege's work, a few philosophers began to have novel ideas about what a "construction" or "synthesis" might be. The three most important philosophers first influenced by Frege were Bertrand Russell, Ludwig Wittgenstein, and Rudolf Carnap. Russell had an important correspondence with Frege, and Carnap went to Jena to study with him. Frege's anti-psychologism may have had a curious and healthy effect, for Carnap especially had no hesitation in developing a mathematics of cognition that, while motivated by psychological ideas, did not pretend to describe how people actually reason. This attitude was crucial to the pragmatic approach of early work in AI.

Russell and Carnap each proposed (at about the same time) that extensions of Frege's logical theory, or Frege's logic in combination with set theory, could be used to describe the construction of physical objects from the data of sensation. Russell and Whitehead had developed techniques to carry on

Frege's logicist program to reduce mathematics to logic; Russell and Carnap, independently, thought that the same techniques could be used to give an account of the possibility of knowledge of the external world.

Russell's idea was that starting with variables ranging over basic entities (the sense data) and with predicates denoting properties of sense data (such as *red*), one could then *define* terms that would denote *sets* of sense data. Physical objects would literally be sets of sense data, or sets of sets of sense data or sets of sets of sets of sense data, and so on. Similarly, higher order properties of physical objects (such as the property of being a tree) would also be appropriate sets of sense data (or sets of sets of sense data, etc.). Russell sketched these ideas in a popular book, *Our Knowledge of the External World*, but he made no attempt to describe any logical details. Meanwhile, Carnap actually produced an outline of such a system.

Carnap's book, *The Logical Structure of the World*, was published in 1928. Carnap assumed that the fundamental entities over which the variables of his system range are what he called *elementary experiences*—an elementary experience is all that appears to someone at a particular moment. In addition, he assumed one relation between elementary experiences is given in experience, namely, the relation that obtains when one recollects that two experiences are similar in some respect or other. (For example, they might both be experiences that contain a red patch somewhere.) The construction of the world begins with a finite list of pairs of elementary experiences; for each pair in the list, the person whose experiences they are recollects that the first element in the pair is in some respect similar to the second element in the pair. Qualities such as color and tone are then defined as certain sets (or sets of sets or sets of sets of sets, etc.) formed from this list. Objects are to be constructed in the same way.

One of the most remarkable things about Carnap's logical construction of the world is that it is not presented only as a collection of logical formulas that are to be applied to terms denoting elementary experiences and the relation of recollection. Carnap also described the construction as a *computational procedure*. That is, along with each logical construction he gave what he called a "fictitious procedure" that shows how to calculate a representation of the object constructed from any list of pairs of elementary experiences. The procedures are perfectly explicit, and they could be represented in any modern computer language. Carnap was the first philosopher (indeed the first person) to present a theory of the mind as a computational program. The use of logical representations immediately suggested (to Carnap anyway) that computation can be done not just on numbers, but on symbols that represent nonnumerical objects. This was really Ramón Lull's idea, and Hobbes' idea after that, but in Carnap's work it begins to look as though it might really work.

William Aspray (1981) has given a persuasive account of the origins of the theory of computation, as it emerged in this century, from philosophical issues in the foundations of mathematics rooted in the 19th century. We think it is fair to say, however, that while the development of the essentials of recursion computation theory was motivated by philosophical issues, the profession of philosophy contributed nothing to them. Gödel gave an account of his incompleteness results to the Vienna Circle, but the audience seems to have missed their import. Alonzo Church was at the center of things, but in the 30s and 40s he was in the mathematics department at Princeton, and there is no evidence that anyone in the philosophy department at the time had an inkling of the revolution going on around them.

Late in the 1920s or thereabouts, Frank Ramsey developed the idea of subjective utility theory and the theory of measurement of subjective utilities. Belatedly, Carnap approached Ramsey's conception of probability, and by the middle of the century, Carnap proposed that we think of inductive norms as the design principles for an android that would begin life with some probability distribution and carry on by conditioning on the evidence it acquired throughout life. When, early in the 1960s, electronic digital computers began to be available for research, the first expert systems for medical diagnosis used Bayesian methods much as Carnap had imagined. Whether there was any direct influence from the philosophical tradition, we do not know. Russell, too, came late in life to think of epistemology as principles of android design. His last serious work, *Human Knowledge, Its Scope and Limits*, abandons the idea of building up the world from sense data and considers especially the general knowledge of kinds and causes that systems must innately have in order to convert sensation into knowledge of the world.

Carnap had two students, Walter Pitts and Herbert Simon, who contributed directly to the formation of the subject of artificial intelligence in the middle of this century, and Simon, of course, contributed many of the leading ideas in the subject. And Carnap had another student, Carl Hempel, who contributed indirectly to the first commercial computer programs for automated scientific discovery. For all of their influence, neither Carnap nor Hempel seems to have had a glimmer of the possibilities in android epistemology, and both flatly denied—Hempel repeatedly and vehemently—the possibility of machine discovery.

Hempel's influence came through his students. One of his doctoral students at Princeton, Gerald Massey, had a doctoral student at Michigan State, Bruce Buchanan, who went to work at Stanford in what was then a very odd job: helping to design and implement programs for chemical identification with mass spectroscopy. Joshua Lederberg and others had developed algorithms for identifying the hydrocarbon compounds consistent with chemical law and a given formula, and the task was to use these algorithms as part of an inference engine. In the Dendral and Meta-Dendral programs, Hempel's theory of explanation and his instance-based approach to hypothesis confirmation were adapted and applied.

Conclusion

The history of modern computing has as a central theme the development of methods for representing information in a physical form which is both stable enough to be reliable as a memory and plastic enough to be changed mechanically. The algorithms of Pascal's and Leibniz's calculating machines were physically represented in their mechanical structure. It was not until Babbage's (1792-1871) Analytical Engine that a machine was designed that did not directly physically embody the algorithms that it could execute. Significantly, it used a punched-card technique for encoding information and algorithms which was originally developed for use in mechanical looms of the late 19th century. The engineers were beginning, quite serendipitously, to provide the ideas which could give flesh to Leibniz's vision.

AI is re-establishing the cooperation between philosophy and engineering which so motivated and enlightened Pascal and Leibniz, but now android epistemology is working with richer tools. In the centuries of philosophical discussion since Pascal and Leibniz first saw how arithmetic could be mechanized, the concept of "machine" has not been much extended beyond Pascaline. But AI is working with new kinds of machines—not just physical computing machines but also "virtual" machines which consist of software (run on other, "actual" machines) but perform real feats in the world. Through the work of Turing's student, Robin Gandy, and others, theorists are developing new and more general formal conceptions of machines that compute.

Some of the early work in artificial intelligence seems to have taken philosophical theories more or less off the shelf, specialized them to particular tasks, and automated them, so that some of the early work in the subject has the flavor of automated philosophy of science, and even some of the more recent work in machine learning—for example, work on discovering laws and work on causal inference—bears the mark of philosophical sources. But the period is past in which android epistemology could rely substantially on independent work in philosophical logic and philosophy of science. What future development requires is not separation of labor by disciplines, but rigor and imagination, clarity of broad motive and clarity of detail, and a willingness to take off the blinkers of disciplines. Philosophy should not be just one more set of blinkers.

Notes

1. It is now clear that Pascal was preceded by the German polymath Wilhelm Schickard and his Calculating Clock. Schickard was a protege of Kepler.

2. Leibniz is often erroneously credited with inventing binary arithmetic, but its roots are much older, reaching at least back to the ancient Chinese. Binary counting systems have been found in many of the world's ethnologically oldest tribes (Phillips, 1936). It seems that ancient man was much taken with the pairwise nature of his body—two legs, arms, eyes and ears. Binary multiplication is first described in the wonderfully named manuscript "Directions for Obtaining Knowledge

of All Dark Things," believed to have been written by a scribe named Ahmes in about 1650 B.C.

References

Aspray, W. (1981). *From mathematical constuctivity to computer science: Turing, Neumann, and the origins of computer science in mathematical logic.* Ann Arbor, Michigan: University Microfilms International.

Augarten, S. (1985). *Bit by Bit.* London: Unwin.

Boole, G. (1951). *The Laws of Thought.* New York: Dover.

Carnap, R. (1967). *The logical structure of the world: Pseudoproblems in philosophy.* Berkeley: University of California Press. [Originally published in 1928.]

Edwards, A. (1987). *Pascal's Arithmetical Triangle.* Oxford University Press.

Gardner, M. (1968). *Logic Machines, Diagrams and Boolean Algebra.* New York: Dover.

Glymour, C. (1991). Freud's androids. In J. Neu (Ed.), *The Cambridge Companion to Freud.* Cambridge University Press.

Glymour, C. (1992). *Thinking Things Through.* Cambridge, MA: MIT Press.

Haugeland, J. (1985). *Artificial Intelligence: The Very Idea.* Cambridge, MA: MIT Press.

Hebb, D. O. (1949). *The Organization of Behavior.* New York: Wiley.

Hinton, G. E., Plaut, D.C., & Shallice, T. (1993, Oct.). Simulating brain damage. *Scientific American,* pp. 76-82.

Hobbes, T. (1962). *Body, Man and Citizen.* Collier.

Holland, J. (1975). *Adaptation in Natural and Artificial Systems.* Ann Arbor: University of Michigan Press.

Leibniz, G. W. (1679). *De progression dyadica—Pars I,* in the collection of Niedersächsische Landesbibliothek, Hanover. [Reprinted in Herrn von Leibniz, *Rechnung mit Null und Eins* (pp. 42-47). Siemens Aktiengesellschaft: Berlin.]

McGinn, C. (1982). *The Character of Mind.* Oxford University Press.

Pascal, B. (1932). *Pensées.* New York: E.P. Dutton. [Originally published in 1670.]

Phillips, E. W. (1936). Binary calculation. *Journal Inst. Actuaries, 67,* 187-221.

Russell, B. (1926). *Our Knowledge of the External World as a Field for Scientific Method in Philosophy.* London: G. Allen & Unwin.

Russell, B. (1948). *Human Knowledge: Its Scope and Limits.* New York: Simon & Schuster.

2 Machine as Mind

Herbert A. Simon

In this chapter I will start with the human mind and what psychological research has learned about it, I will proceed to draw lessons from cognitive psychology about the characteristics we must bestow upon computer programs when we wish those programs to think. I speak of "mind" and not "brain." By "mind" I mean a system that produces thought, viewed at a relatively high level of aggregation: say, at or above the level of elementary processes that require 100 milliseconds or more for their execution. At that level, little or nothing need be said about the structure or behavior of individual neurons, or even small assemblages of them. Our units will be larger and more abstract.

It is well known that the language and representation best adapted to describing phenomena depends on the level of aggregation at which we model them. Physicists concerned with quarks and similar particles on minute temporal and spatial scales do not use the same vocabulary of entities and processes as geneticists describing how DNA informs protein synthesis.

Whatever our philosophical position with respect to reduction, it is practically necessary to build science in levels. The phenomena at each level are described in terms of the primitives at that level, and these primitives become, in turn, the phenomena to be described and explained at the next level below.

The primitives of mind, at the level I wish to consider, are symbols, complex structures of symbols, and processes that operate on symbols (Newell and Simon 1976). The simplest among these processes require tens to hundreds of milliseconds for their execution. Simple recognition of a familiar object takes at least 500 milliseconds. At this level, the same software can be implemented with radically different kinds of hardware—protoplasm and silicon among them.

My central thesis is that at this level of aggregation conventional computers can be, and have been, programmed to represent symbol structures and carry out processes on those structures in a manner that parallels, step by step, the way the human brain does it. The principal evidence for my thesis are programs that do just that. These programs demonstrably think.

It has been argued that a computer simulation of thinking is no more thinking than a simulation of digestion is digestion. The analogy is false. A computer simulation of digestion is not capable of taking starch as an input and producing fructose or glucose as outputs. It deals only with symbolic or numerical quantities representing these substances.

In contrast, a computer simulation of thinking thinks. It takes problems as its inputs and (sometimes) produces solutions as its outputs. It represents these problems and solutions as symbolic structures, as the human mind does, and performs transformations on them, as the human mind does. The materials of digestion are chemical substances, which are not replicated in a computer simulation. The materials of thought are symbols—patterns, which can be replicated in a great variety of materials (including neurons and chips), thereby enabling physical symbol systems fashioned of these materials to think. Turing (1950) was perhaps the first to have this insight in clear form, forty years ago.

Nearly Decomposable Systems

The successive levels in the architecture of nature are not arbitrary (Simon 1981). Most complex systems are hierarchical and *nearly decomposable.* Consider a building divided into rooms, which are, in turn, divided into cubicles. Starting from a state of radical temperature disequilibrium—every cubic foot of space being momentarily at quite a different temperature from the adjoining spaces—within a matter of minutes the temperature within each cubicle will approach some constant value, a different value for each cubicle. After a somewhat longer time, all the cubicles in a given room will reach a common temperature. After a still longer interval, all the rooms in the building will reach a common temperature.

In a hierarchical system of this kind, we do not have to consider the behavior at all levels simultaneously. We can model the cubicles, the rooms, and the building semi-independently. In the short run, we can analyze the changes in individual cubicles while disregarding their interaction with the other cubicles. In the middle run, we can analyze the individual rooms, replacing the detail of each cubicle by its average temperature. For the longer run, we can consider the building as a whole, replacing the detail of each room by its average temperature.

In layered hierarchical systems of this kind, each subcomponent has a much higher rate of interaction with the other subcomponents in the same component than it does with subcomponents outside that component. Elsewhere (Simon 1981) I have shown how the behavior of nearly decomposable systems can be analyzed mathematically and why, from an evolutionary standpoint, we should expect most of the complex systems that we find in nature to be nearly decomposable.

For present purposes, what is important about nearly-decomposable systems is that we can analyze them at a particular level of aggregation without detailed knowledge of the structures at the levels below. These details do not "show through" at the next level above; only aggregate properties of the more microscopic systems affect behavior at the higher level. In our temperature example, only the average temperatures of the cubicles affect the changes in temperature in the rooms, and only the average temperatures of the rooms are relevant to the course of equilibration of the building as a whole.

Because mind has shown itself to behave as a nearly-decomposable system, we can model thinking at the symbolic level, with events in the range of hundreds of milliseconds or longer, without concern for details of implementation at the "hardware" level, whether the hardware be brain or computer.

The Two Faces of AI

AI can be approached in two ways. First, we can write smart programs for computers without any commitment to imitating the processes of human intelligence. We can then use all of the speed and power of the computer and all of its memory capacity, unconcerned with whether people have the same computational speed and power or the same memory capacity.

Alternatively, we can write smart programs for computers that do imitate closely the human processes, forgoing the computer's capacities for rapid processing of symbols and its almost instantaneous memory storage. We can slow the computer down to human speeds, so to speak, and test whether it can absorb the cunning that will permit it to behave intelligently within these limitations.

Chess-playing programs illustrate the two approaches. DEEPTHOUGHT is a powerful program that now plays chess at grandmaster level and can defeat all but a few hundred human players. It demonstrably does not play in a humanoid way, typically exploring tens of millions of branches of the game tree before it makes its choice of move. There is good empirical evidence (de Groot 1965) that human grandmasters seldom look at more than 100 branches on the tree. By generally searching the *relevant* branches, they make up with chess knowledge for their inability to carry out massive searches.

However, DEEPTHOUGHT by no means "explores all possibilities." "All possibilities" would mean at least 10^{50} branches, 10^{40} times more than the program can manage, and obviously more than any computer, present or prospective can explore. DEEPTHOUGHT exercises a certain degree of selectivity in the branches it explores, but more important, it halts its explorations about a dozen ply deep—far short of the end of the game—and applies an evaluation function to measure the relative goodness of all the positions it reaches. A great deal of chess knowledge, supplied by the human programmers, is incorporated in the evaluation function. Hence DEEPTHOUGHT's chess prowess rests on a combination of brute force, unattainable by human players, and extensive, if "mediocre," chess knowledge.

Consider now a much earlier program, MATER (Baylor and Simon 1966) which is not nearly as good a chess player as DEEPTHOUGHT. In fact, MATER is a specialist designed only to exploit those game positions where an immediate mating combination (possibly a quite deep one) might be hidden. MATER has shown substantial ability to discover such mating combinations—rediscovering many of the most celebrated ones in chess history. What is more interesting, MATER ordinarily looks at fewer than 100 branches of the tree in order to accomplish this feat. It is as selective in its search as human players are in these kinds of situations, and in fact, it looks at nearly the same parts of the game tree as they do.

We can go even farther in comparing MATER with human players. For these kinds of positions (where a possible checkmate lurks), MATER uses the same rules of thumb to guide its search and select promising lines that human masters use. It examines forceful moves first, and it examines first those branches along which the opponent is most constrained. These heuristics, while powerful, do not always lead to the shortest mate. We have found at least one historical instance (a game between Edward Lasker and Thomas) in which both human player and computer required an extra move because the shortest path to a checkmate did not satisfy these heuristics—did not correspond with the most plausible search path.

The remainder of my remarks are concerned with programs that are intelligent in more or less humanoid ways—that carry out only modest computations to perform their tasks. These programs resemble MATER rather than DEEPTHOUGHT. This does not mean that programs for AI should always be built in this way, but my aim here is to consider machine as mind rather than to celebrate the achievements of rapid computation.

The View from Psychology

Selective Heuristic Search

How does intelligence look to contemporary cognitive psychology? I have already mentioned one fact that has been verified repeatedly in the laboratory—human problem solvers do not carry out extensive searches. Even examining 100 possibilities in a game tree stretches human memory and patience. Since many of the spaces in which people solve problems are enormous (I have mentioned the figure of 10^{50} for chess), "trying everything" is not a viable search strategy. People use knowledge about the structure of the problem space to form heuristics that allow them to search extremely selectively.

Recognition: The Indexed Memory

A second important fact is also well illustrated by the game of chess. A chess grandmaster can play fifty or more opponents "simultaneously," moving from board to board and seldom taking more than a few seconds for each move. If the opponents are not stronger than experts, say, the grandmaster will win almost every game, although his play will perhaps be only at master level. This fact demonstrates that much of grandmasters' knowledge (not all of it) is accessed by recognition of cues on the board, for in simultaneous play they have no time for deep analysis by search (Chase and Simon 1973).

Grandmasters, questioned on how they play simultaneous games, report that they make "standard" developing moves until they notice a feature of the board that indicates a weakness in the opponent's position (doubled pawns, say). Noticing this feature gives access to information about strategies for exploiting it. The grandmaster's memory is like a large indexed encyclopedia (with at least 50,000 index entries). The perceptually noticeable features of the chessboard (the cues) trigger the appropriate index entries and give access to the corresponding information. This information often includes relevant strategies.

Solving problems by responding to cues that are visible only to experts is sometimes called solving them by "intuition." A better label would be "solving by recognition." Intuition consists simply of noting features in a situation that index useful information. There is no mystery in intuition, or at least no more mystery than there is in recognizing a friend on the street and recalling what one knows about the friend.

In computers, recognition processes are generally implemented by productions: the condition sides of the productions serving as tests for the presence of cues, the action sides holding the information that is accessed when the cues are noticed. Hence, it is easy to build computer systems that solve problems by recognition, and indeed recognition capability is the core of most AI expert systems.

The number, 50,000, suggested above as the number of features a grandmaster can recognize on a chessboard, has been estimated empirically, but only by indirect means (Simon and Gilmartin 1973). Confidence rises that the figure is approximately correct when one notes that it is roughly comparable to the native language vocabularies of college graduates (usually estimated at 50,000 to 100,000 words).

Items that, by their recognizability, serve to index semantic memory are usually called "chunks" in the psychological literature. Generalizing, we hypothesize that an expert in any domain must acquire some 50,000 familiar chunks (give or take a factor of four). Although existing expert systems for computers are not this large, the figure is not a daunting one.

By way of footnote, extensive data show that it takes at least 10 years of intensive training for a person to acquire the information (presumably including the 50,000 chunks) required for world-class performance in any domain of expertise. This has been shown for chess playing, musical composition, painting, piano playing, swimming, tennis, neuropsychological research, research in topology, and other fields (Bloom 1985, Hayes 1989). Mozart, who began composing at four, produced no world-class music before at least the age of 17, 13 years later. Child prodigies are not exempt from the rule.

Seriality: The Limits of Attention

Problems that cannot be solved by recognition generally require the application of more or less sustained attention. Attention is closely associated with human short-term memory. Symbols that are attended to—the inputs, say, to an arithmetic calculation—must be retained during use in short-term memory, which has a capacity of only about seven chunks, a limit that is based on extensive experimental data (Simon 1976). The need for all inputs and outputs of attention-demanding tasks to pass through short-term memory essentially serializes the thinking process. Generally, we can only think of one thing at a time. (Sometimes, by time sharing, we can think of two, if they are not too complex. Light conversation and driving are compatible activities for most people when the traffic is not too heavy!)

Hence, whatever parallel processes may be going on at lower (neural) levels, at the symbolic level the human mind is fundamentally a serial machine, accomplishing its work through temporal sequences of processes, each typically requiring hundreds of milliseconds for execution.

In contrast, the evidence is equally strong that the sensory organs, especially the eyes and ears, are highly parallel systems. We are confronted with a hybrid system, the sensory (and possibly perceptual) processes operating in parallel, and the subsequent symbolic processes (after patterns of stimuli have been recognized and chunked) serially.

Within the limits of present knowledge, there is a no-man's-land between the parallel and serial components of the processor, whose exact boundaries are not known. For example, there are implementable schemes that execute all processing down to the point of recognition in parallel (for example, so-called Demon schemes), but there are also workable serial recognition systems (e.g., EPAM: Feigenbaum and Simon 1984, Richman and Simon 1989). The available evidence does not make a clear choice between these alternatives.

The Architecture of Expert Systems

Psychology, then, gives us a picture of the expert as having a sensory system that is basically parallel in structure, interfaced with a cognitive system that is basically serial. Somewhere in the imprecise boundary between the two is a mechanism (serial or parallel or both) capable of recognizing large numbers (hundreds of thousands) of patterns in the domain of expertise and of obtaining access through this recognition to information stored in short-term memory. The information accessed can be processed further (using heuristic search) by a serial symbol-processing system.

Recognition takes approximately a half second or second (Newell and Simon 1972). The individual steps in search also require hundreds of milliseconds, and search is highly selective, the selectivity based on heuristics stored in memory. People can report orally the results of recognition (but not the cues used in the process) and are aware of many of the inputs and outputs of the steps they take in search. It appears that they can report most of the symbols that reside temporarily in short-term memory (i.e., the symbols in the focus of attention).

One reason for thinking that this structure is sufficient to produce expert behavior is that AI has now built many expert systems, capable of performing at professional levels in restricted domains, using essentially the architecture we have just described. In general, the AI expert systems (for example, systems for medical diagnosis) have fewer "chunks" than the human experts and make up for the deficiency by doing more computing than people do. The differences appear to be quantitative, not qualitative: human and computer experts alike depend heavily upon recognition, supplemented by a little capacity for reasoning (i.e., search).

The Matter of Semantics

It is sometimes claimed that the thinking of computers, symbolic systems that they are, is purely syntactical. Unlike people, it is argued, computers do not have intentions, and their symbols do not have semantic referents. The argument is easily refuted by concrete examples of computer programs that demonstrably understand the meanings (at least some of the meanings) of their symbols and that have goals, thus exhibiting at least two aspects of intention.

Consider, first, a computer-driven van, of which we have an example on our university campus, equipped with television cameras and capable of steering its way (slowly) along a winding road in a nearby park. Patterns of light transmitted through the cameras are encoded by the computer program as landscape features (e.g., the verge of the road). The program, having the intention of proceeding along the road and remaining on it, creates internal symbols that denote these features, interprets them, and uses the symbols to guide its steering and speed-control mechanisms.

Consider, second, one of the commercially available chess-playing programs that use an actual chess board on which the opponent moves the men physically and that senses these moves and forms an internal (symbolic) representation of the chess position. The symbols in this internal representation denote the external physical pieces and their arrangement, and the program demonstrates quite clearly, by the moves it chooses, that it intends to beat its opponent.

There is no mystery about what "semantics" means as applied to the human mind. It means that there is a correspondence, a relation of denotation, between symbols inside the head and objects (or relations among objects) outside. In particular, the brain is (sometimes) able to test whether sensory signals received from particular objects identify those objects as the meanings of particular symbols (names). And the human brain is sometimes able to construct and emit words, phrases, and sentences whose denotation corresponds to the sensed scene.

There is also no mystery about human intentions. Under certain circumstances, for example, a human being senses internal stirrings (usually called hunger) that lead him or her to seek food. Under other circumstances, other stirrings create the goal of defeating an opponent in chess. Now the two computer programs I described above also have goals: in the one case to drive along a road, in the other case to win a chess game. It would not be hard to store both programs in the same computer, along with input channels that would, from time to time, switch its attention from the one goal to the other. Such a system would then have not a single intention, but a capacity for several, even as you and I.

It may be objected (and has been) that the computer does not "understand" the meanings of its symbols or the semantic operations on them, or the goals it adopts. This peculiar use of the word "understand" has something to do with the fact that we are (sometimes) *conscious* of meanings and intentions. But then, my evidence that you are conscious is no better than my evidence that the road-driving or chess-playing computers are conscious.

Moreover, in formal treatments of semantics, consciousness has never been one of the defining characteristics; denotation has. What is important about semantic meaning is that there be a correspondence (conscious or not) between the symbol and the thing it denotes. What is important about intention is that there be a correspondence (conscious or not) between the goal symbol and behavior appropriate to achieving the goal in the context of some belief system.

Finally, Searle's Chinese Room parable proves not that computer programs cannot understand Chinese, but only that the particular program Searle described does not understand Chinese. Had he described a program that could receive inputs from a sensory system and emit the symbol "cha" in the presence of tea and "bai cha" in the presence of hot water, we would have to admit that it understood at least a *little* Chinese. And the vocabulary and grammar could be extended indefinitely. Later, I will describe a computer program, devised by Siklóssy (1972), that learns language in exactly this way (although the connection with external senses was not implemented).

"Ill-Structured" Phenomena

Research on human thinking has progressed from relatively simple and well-structured phenomena (for example, rote verbal learning, solving puzzles, simple concept attainment) to more complex and rather ill-structured tasks (e.g., use of natural language, learning, scientific discovery, visual art). "Ill-structured" means that the task has ill-defined or multi-dimensional goals, that its frame of reference or representation is not clear or obvious, that there are no clear-cut procedures for generating search paths or evaluating them—or some combination of these characteristics.

When a problem is ill-structured in one or more of these senses, a first step in solving it is to impose some kind of structure that allows it to be represented—that is, symbolized—at least approximately, and attacked in this symbolized form. What does psychology tell us about problem representations: their nature and how they are constructed for particular problems?

Forms of Representation

We do not have an exhaustive taxonomy of possible representations, but a few basic forms show up prominently in psychological research. First, situations may be represented in words or in logical or mathematical notations. All of these representations are basically propositional and are more or less equivalent to a set of propositions in some formal logic. Propositional representation immediately suggests that the processing will resemble logical reasoning or proof.

When problems are presented verbally, the propositional translation of these words may be quite literal or may comprise only the semantic content of the input without preserving syntactic details. In both cases, we will speak of propositional representation. There is a great deal of psychological evidence that input sentences are seldom retained intact but that, instead, their semantic content is usually extracted and stored in some form.

Second, situations may be represented in diagrams or pictures ("mental pictures"). Internally, a picture or diagram can be represented by the equivalent of a raster of pixels (for example, the cerebral image associated with the direct signals from the retina) or by a network of nodes and links that capture the components of the diagram and their relations. Possibly there are other ways (for example, as the equations of analytic geometry), but these two have been given most consideration by psychologists. A picture or diagram amounts to a *model* of the system, with processes that operate on it to move it through time or to search through a succession of its states.

Most psychological research on representations assumes, explicitly or implicitly, one of the representations mentioned in the preceding paragraphs: propositional, raster-like "picture," or node-link diagram, or some combination of them. All of these representations are easily implemented by computer programs.

Equivalence of Representations

What consequences does the form of representation have for cognition? To answer that question, we must define the notion of *equivalence of representations*. Actually, we must define two notions: informational equivalence and computational equivalence (Larkin and Simon 1987). Two representations are *informationally* equivalent if either one is logically derivable from the other—if all the information available in the one is available in the other. Two representations are *computationally* equivalent if all the information *easily* available in the one is easily available in the other, and vice versa.

"Easily" is a vague term, but it is adequate for our purpose. Information is easily available if it can be obtained from the explicit information with a small amount of computation—small relative to the capacities of the processor. Thus, defining a representation includes specifying the primitive processes, those that are not further analyzed and that can be carried out rapidly.

Representations of numerical information in Arabic and Roman numerals are informationally equivalent, but not computationally equivalent. It may be much easier or harder to find the product of two numbers in the one notation than in the other. Similarly, representations of the same problem, on the one hand as a set of declarative propositions in PROLOG, and on the other hand as a node-link diagram in LISP, are unlikely to be computationally equivalent (Larkin and Simon 1987). It may be far easier to solve the problem in the one form than in the other—say, easier by heuristic search than by resolution theorem proving.

Representations Used by People

There is much evidence that people sometimes use "mental pictures" to represent problems, representations that have the properties of rasters or of node-link networks (Kosslyn 1980). There is little evidence that they use propositions in the predicate calculus to represent them, or operate on their representations by theorem-proving methods. Of course, engineers, scientists, and others do represent many problems with mathematical formalisms, but the processes that operate upon these formalisms resemble heuristic search much more than they do logical reasoning (Larkin and Simon 1987, Paige and Simon 1966).

Research on problem solving in algebra and physics has shown that subjects typically convert a problem from natural language into diagrams and then convert the latter into equations. A direct translation from language to equations seems to take place, if at all, only in the case of very simple familiar problems. AI models of the diagrammatic representations that problem solvers use in these domains can be found in Larkin and Simon (1987) and Novak (1977).

Evidence is lacking as to whether there exists a "neutral" semantic representation for information that is neither propositional nor pictorial. At least in simple situations, much information is readily transformed from one representation to the other. For example, in one common experimental paradigm, subjects are presented with an asterisk above or below a plus sign and, simultaneously, with a sentence of the form, "The star is above/below the plus" (Clark and Chase 1972). The subject must respond "true" or "false." Before responding, the subject must, somehow, find a common representation for the visual display and the sentence—converting one into the other, or both into a common semantic representation. But the experiments carried out in this paradigm do not show which way the conversion goes. From the physics and algebra experiments, we might conjecture that, for most subjects, the internal (or semantic) representation is the diagrammatic one, but we must be careful in generalizing across tasks.

I have barely touched on the evidence from psychology about the representations people use in their problem-solving activities. The evidence we have throws strong doubt on any claim of hegemony for either propositional or pictorial representations. If either tends to be dominant, it is probably the pictorial (or diagrammatic) rather than the propositional. The evidence suggests strongly that, whatever the form of representation, the processing of information almost always resembles heuristic search rather than theorem proving.

We can only conjecture that these preferences have something to do with computational efficiency. I have elsewhere spelled out some of the implications of the computational inequivalence of representations for such issues as logic programming versus rule-based computation.

Insight Problems

Problems that tend to be solved suddenly, with an "aha!" experience, often after a long period of apparently fruitless struggle, have attracted much attention. Can we say anything about the mystery of such insightful processes? Indeed, we can. We can say enough to dissipate most or all of the magic.

One problem of this kind is the "Mutilated Checkerboard." We are given an ordinary checkerboard of 64 squares and 32 dominoes, each domino exactly covering two adjoining squares of the board. Obviously we can cover the entire board with the 32 dominoes. Now we cut off the northwest square and the southeast square of the board, and ask whether the remaining 62 squares can be covered exactly by 31 dominoes (Kaplan and Simon 1990).

Subjects generally attack this problem by attempting coverings, and persist for an hour or more, becoming increasingly frustrated as they fail to achieve a solution. At some point, they decide that a covering is impossible and switch their effort to proving the impossibility. They recognize that to do so they need a new problem representation, but unfortunately, people do not appear to possess a general-purpose generator of problem representations. It is not enough to say, "I need a new representation." How does one go about constructing it?

Some subjects do, after a shorter or longer time, succeed in constructing a new representation and then solve the problem in a few minutes. The new representation records the *number* of squares of each color and the *number* of each color that is covered by a single domino. The geometric arrangement of the squares, a central feature of the original representation, is simply ignored. But since the mutilated checkerboard has two more squares of one color than of the other, and since dominoes, no matter how many, can cover only the same number of squares of each color, the impossibility of a covering is immediately evident.

The power of the abstraction is obvious, but how do subjects achieve it? Experiments show that they achieve it when their attention focuses on the fact that the remaining uncovered squares, after unsuccessful attempts at covering, are always the same color. How the attention focus comes about is a longer story, which I won't try to tell here, but which is quite understandable in terms of ordinary mechanisms of attention.

Much remains to be done before we understand how people construct their problem representations and the role those representations play in problem solving. But we know enough already to suggest that the representations people use—both propositional and pictorial—can be simulated by computers. Diagrammatic representations of the node-link type are naturally represented in list-processing languages like LISP. Rasters pose a more difficult problem, for we must define appropriate primitive processes to extract information from them. Finding such processes is more or less synonymous with developing efficient programs for visual pattern recognition.

The Processing of Language

Whatever the role it plays in thought, natural language is the principal medium of communication between people. What do we know about how it is processed and how it is learned?

Some Programs that Understand Language

Enormous amounts of research on language have been done within the disciplines of linguistics and psycholinguistics. Until quite recent times, the greater part of that research was focused on lexical issues, syntax, and phonetics, seldom straying beyond the boundaries of the individual sentence. Without disputing the importance of this activity, it might be argued that far more has been learned about the relation between natural language and thinking from computer programs that use language inputs or outputs to perform concrete tasks. For example, Novak's (1977) ISMC program, which extracts the information from natural-language descriptions of physics problems, and transforms it into an internal "semantic" representation suitable for a problem-solving system. In somewhat similar manner, Hayes and Simon's (1974) UNDERSTAND program reads natural-language instructions for puzzles and creates internal representations ("pictures") of the problem situations and interpretations of the puzzle rules for operating on them.

Systems like these give us specific models of how people extract meaning from discourse with the help of semantic knowledge they already hold in memory. For example, Novak's system interprets the natural-language input using schemas that encapsulate its knowledge about such things as levers and masses and assembles this knowledge into a composite schema that pictures the problem situation.

At a more abstract level, UNDERSTAND extracts knowledge from prose about the objects under discussion, the relations among them, and the ways of changing these relations. It uses this information to construct a system of internal nodes, links, and processes that represent these objects, relations, and operations. In simple puzzle situations, UNDERSTAND can go quite a long way with a minimum of semantic knowledge, relying heavily on syntactic cues.

Acquiring Language

Of equal importance is the question of how languages are acquired. Siklóssy (1972) simulated the process of language acquisition, guided by I.A. Richards' plan for learning language by use of pictures. Siklóssy's program, called ZBIE, was given (internal representations of) simple pictures (a dog chasing a cat, a hat on a woman's head). With each picture, it was given a sentence describing the scene. With the aid of a carefully designed sequence of such examples, it gradually learned to associate nouns with the objects in the pictures and other words with their properties and the relations.

Siklóssy tested ZBIE in novel situations whose components were familiar by requiring it to construct sentences describing these new situations. It learned the fundamentals of a number of European languages, including the appropriate conventions for word order.

Will Our Knowledge of Language Scale?

These are just a few illustrations of current capabilities for simulating human use and acquisition of language. Since all of them involve relatively simple language with a limited vocabulary, it is quite reasonable to ask how they would scale up to encompass the whole vast structure of a natural language as known and used by a native speaker. We do not know the answer to this question—and won't know it until it has been done—but we should not overemphasize the criticality of the scaling-up issue. When we wish to understand basic physical phenomena, we do not look for complex real-world situations in which to test them, but instead design the simplest conceivable laboratory situations in which to demonstrate and manipulate them.

Even in classical mechanics, physicists are far from a full understanding of the three-body problem, much less the behavior of n bodies, where n is a large number. Most scientific effort goes into the study of toy systems rather than the study of a complex "real world." We usually understand the mechanisms that govern the complex world long before we are able to calculate or simulate the behavior of that world in detail.

Similarly, to demonstrate an understanding of human thinking, we do not need to model thinking in the most complex situations we can imagine. It is enough for most purposes that our theory explain the phenomena in a range of situations that would call for genuine thinking in human subjects. Research has already met that criterion for language processing.

Discovery and Creativity

We should not be intimidated by words like "intuition" that are often used to describe human thinking. We have seen that "intuition" usually simply means problem solving by recognition, easily modeled by production systems. We have also seen that the "insight" that leads to change in representation and solution of the mutilated checkerboard problem can be explained by mechanisms of attention focusing. What about "creative" processes? Can we give an account of them, too?

Making scientific discoveries is generally adjudged to be both ill-structured and creative. As it is also a very diverse activity, with many aspects, a theory that explains one aspect might not explain others. Scientists sometimes examine data to discover regularities—scientific laws and new concepts for expressing the laws parsimoniously. They sometimes discover new scientific problems or invent new ways of representing problems. They sometimes deduce new consequences from theories.

Scientists sometimes conceive of mechanisms to explain the empirical laws that describe phenomena. They sometimes develop and execute experimental strategies to obtain new data for testing theories or evolving new theories. They sometimes invent and construct new instruments for gathering new kinds of data or more precise data. There are other things that scientists do, but this list at leasts illustrates the variety of activities in which they engage, any of which may produce a creative discovery.

A number of these activities, but not all, have been simulated by computer. In addition, historians of science have recounted the courses of events that led to a substantial number of important discoveries.

A computer program called BACON (Langley, Simon, Bradshaw, and Zytkow 1987), when given the data available to the scientists in historically important situations, has rediscovered Kepler's Third Law, Ohm's Law, Boyle's Law, Black's Law of Temperature Equilibrium, and many others. In the course of finding these laws, BACON has reinvented such fundamental concepts as inertial mass, atomic weight and molecular weight, and specific heat. We do not have to speculate about how discoveries of these kinds are made; we can examine the behavior of programs like BACON and compare them with the historical record (or with the behavior of human subjects presented with the same problems).

The KEKADA program (Kulkarni and Simon 1988) plans experimental strategies, responding to the information gained from each experiment to plan the next one. On the basis of its knowledge and experience, it forms expectations about the outcome of experiments and switches to a strategy for exploiting its surprise when these expectations are not fulfilled. With the aid of these capabilities, the program is able to track closely the strategy that Hans Krebs used to elucidate the synthesis of urea in vivo and Faraday's strategy in investigating the production of electrical currents by the variation of magnetic fields. Here, the accuracy with which the program explained the human processes was tested through a comparism of its behavior with the data-to-day course of the original research as gleaned from laboratory notebooks.

Programs like BACON and KEKADA show that scientists use essentially the same kinds of processes as those identified in more prosaic kinds of problem solving (solving puzzles or playing chess). Very high quality thinking is surely required for scientific work, but thinking of basically the same kind is used to solve more humdrum problems.

These successes in simulating scientific work put high on the agenda the simulation of other facets of science (inventing instruments, discovering appropriate problem representations) that have not yet been tackled. There is no reason to believe that they will disclose thinking processes wholly different from those that have been observed in the research I have just sketched.

Affect, Motivation, and Awareness

I have said nothing about the motivation required for successful human thinking. Motivation comes into the picture through the mechanism of attention. Motivation selects particular tasks for attention and diverts attention from others. When the other conditions for success are present, strong motivation sustained over long periods of time may secure the cognitive effort that is required to find a problem solution. In this manner, motivation and the mechanisms that strengthen and weaken it can be brought into models of problem solving in a quite natural manner.

Putting the matter in this over-simple way does not demean the importance of motivation in human thinking but suggests that its impact on thought processes is rather diffuse and aggregative rather than highly specific. Moreover, if affect and cognition interact largely through the mechanisms of attention, then it is reasonable to pursue our research on these two components of mental behavior independently. For example, in laboratory studies of problem solving, as long as we establish conditions that assure the subjects' attention to the task, we can study the cognitive processes without simultaneously investigating just how the motivation is generated and maintained.

The theory of thinking I have been describing says very little about consciousness—except in equating ability to report information with its presence in short-term memory. Many of the symbolic processes that support thought are in conscious awareness, but others are not. The presence or absence of awareness has strong implications for the ease or difficulty of testing the details of the theory, but few other implications. I will not try to pursue this difficult topic further here.

Conclusion: Computers Think—and Often Think like People

The conclusion we can draw from the evidence I have sketched is simple: Computers can be programmed, and have been programmed, to simulate at a symbolic level the processes that are used in human thinking. We need not talk about computers thinking in the future tense; they have been thinking (in smaller or bigger ways) for 35 years. They have been thinking "logically" and they have been thinking "intuitively"—even "creatively."

Why has this conclusion been resisted so fiercely, even in the face of massive evidence? I would argue, first, that the dissenters have not looked very hard at the evidence, especially the evidence from the psychological laboratory. They have grasped and held on to a romantic picture of the human mind that attributes to it capabilities that it simply does not have—not even the minds of Mozart and Einstein, to say nothing of the rest of us poor mortals.

The human mind does not reach its goals mysteriously or miraculously. Even its sudden insights and "ahas" are explainable in terms of recognition processes, well-informed search, knowledge-prepared experiences of surprise, and changes in representation motivated by shifts in attention. When we incorporate these processes into our theory, as empirical evidence says we should, the unexplainable is explained.

Perhaps there are deeper sources of resistance to the evidence. Perhaps we are reluctant to give up our claims for human uniqueness—of being the only species that can think big thoughts. Perhaps we have "known" so long that machines can't think that only overwhelming evidence can change our belief. Whatever the reason, the evidence is now here, and it is time that we attended to it. If we hurry, we can catch up to Turing on the path he pointed out to us so many years ago.

References

Baylor, G. W. & Simon, H. A. (1966). A chess mating combinations program. *AFIPS Conference Proceedings, Spring Joint Computer Conference.* [Washington, DC: Spartan Books, 28: 431-47.]

Bloom, B. S. (Ed.). (1985). *Developing Talent in Young People.* New York: Ballantine.

Chase, W. G. & Simon, H. A. (1973). Perception in chess. *Cognitive Psychology,* 4, 55-81.

Clark, H. H. & Chase, W. G. (1972). On the process of comparing sentences against pictures. *Cognitive Psychology,* 3, 472-517.

de Groot, A. (1965). *Thought and Choice in Chess.* The Hague: Mouton [2nd. ed., 1978].

Feigenbaum, E. A. & Simon, H. A. (1984). EPAM-like models of recognition and learning. *Cognitive Science,* 8, 305-36.

Hayes, J. R. (1989, 2nd. ed.). *The Complete Problem Solver.* Hillsdale, NJ: Earlbaum.

Hayes, J. R. & Simon, H. A. (1974). Understanding written problem instructions. In L. W. Gregg (Ed.), *Knowledge and Cognition.* Potomac, MD: Erlbaum.

Kaplan, C. & Simon, H. A. (1990). In search of insight. Accepted for publication in *Cognitive Psychology.*

Kosslyn, S. M. (1980). *Image and Mind.* Cambridge, MA: Harvard University Press.

Kulkarni, D. & Simon, H. A. (1988). The processes of scientific discovery: The strategy of experimentation. *Cognitive Science,* 12, 139-176.

Langley, P., Simon, H. A., Bradshaw, G. L., & Zytkow, J. M. (1987). *Scientific Discovery.* Cambridge, MA: MIT Press.

Larkin, J. H. & Simon, H. A. (1987). Why a diagram is (sometimes) worth 10,000 words. *Cognitive Science,* 11, 65-99.

Newell, A. & Simon, H. A. (1972). *Human Problem Solving.* Englewood Cliffs, NJ: Prentice-Hall.

Newell, A. & Simon, H. A. (1976). Computer science as empirical inquiry. *Communications of the ACM,* 19, 113-126.

Novak, G. S. (1977). Representation of knowledge in a program for solving physics problems. *Proceedings of the Fifth International Joint Conference on Artificial Intelligence.* San Francisco, CA: Morgan Kaufmann.

Paige, J. M. & Simon, H. A. (1966). Cognitive processes in solving algebra word problems. In B. Kleinsuntz (Ed.), *Problem Solving.* New York: Wiley.

Richman, H. B. & Simon, H. A. (1989). Context effects in letter perception: Comparison of two theories. *Psychological Review,* 96, 417-32.

Siklóssy, L. (1972). Natural language learning by computer. In H. A. Simon & L. Siklóssy (Eds.), *Representation and Meaning.* Englewood Cliffs, NJ: Prentice-Hall.

Simon, H. A. (1976). The information-storage system called 'human memory.' In M. R. Rosenzweig & E. L. Bennett (Eds.), *Neural Mechanisms of Learning and Memory.* Cambridge, MA: MIT Press.

Simon, H. A. (1981). *The Sciences of the Artificial.* Cambridge, MA: MIT Press.

Simon, H. A. & Gilmartin, K. A. (1973). A simulation of memory for chess positions. *Cognitive Psychology,* 5, 29-46.

Turing, A. M. (1950). Computing machinery and intelligence. *Mind,* 59, 422-460.

3 The Vitalists' Last Stand

Anatol Rapoport

There was a time when biologists were split into two parties—the mechanists and the vitalists. The mechanists believed that all life processes could be reduced to the operation of physical and chemical laws; the vitalists insisted that they could not. In retrospect it appears that the vitalists have been in continual retreat—one is tempted to say to previously prepared positions. First they maintained that living tissues contain a substance not contained in nonliving matter. In fact, organic chemistry was so named on the basis of this belief. This position had to be given up after Wöhler succeeded in synthesizing urea, an organic substance.

The vitalists next retreated to a position based on a teleological interpretation of biological processes. A teleological process is guided not by what Aristotle called "effective causes" (pushing from behind) but by what he called "final causes" (beckoning from ahead). Thus, the vitalists maintained, purpose was an ingredient of actions characteristic of living beings.

In the Middle Ages purposeful action was ascribed also to nonliving matter. Philosophers taught that everything that exists has its proper place in the scheme of things. If anything is in its proper place, it stays there. If it is forcibly removed, it "strives" to get back to where it belongs. Thus, stones fall to earth because earth is the predominant element in them. Accordingly they seek to be near the center of the earth, which is their "proper place." Smoke, on the other hand, rises from the chimney, because essentially a product of fire, it seeks its proper place in the region of eternal fire beyond the stars. Birds can fly because their proper place is in their nests, which are up in the trees.

The maturation of physics was associated, among other things, with the abandonment of teleological explanations of physical events. A cause came to be regarded as operating on the here and now, as it were. Ironically, this "more scientific" outlook delayed the acceptance of the universal law of gravitation, which apparently rested on the assumption of forces acting at a distance, unacceptable to philosophers who sought to reduce all events to mechanical processes. Nevertheless, the expulsion of teleology from physical phenomena was definitely a step forward in the development of the physical sciences.

This reduction of causes of physical events to efficient causes had no bearing on the vitalists' position. If anything, it strengthened it, because it provided a new position to which to retreat when the "special substance" position was demolished by the synthesis of urea. A prominent vitalist biologist in the first decade of this century was H. Driesch, an Austrian, who performed an experiment purporting to show that the development of an embryo was guided by teleological causation. He cut a sea urchin embryo in its early stage in two, whereupon each half developed into a normal urchin. Had the process been "mechanical," Driesch argued, each half would have developed into a half of a sea urchin. The fact that each developed into the whole animal presumably showed that the state of being a sea urchin was the embryo's "goal." The goal was reached in spite of intervention.

The flaw in Driesch's argument is easy to detect. It consists of a purely verbal conception of a "mechanical" process, according to which the process proceeds automatically without regard for consequences, that is, "thoughtlessly," as it were, in contrast to an "intelligent" process guided by an envisaged goal.

In the exact sciences, a mechanism is conceived as a device whose behavior is governed by explicitly formulated equations. The equations determine trajectories, that is, successions of states of a mechanical system. A trajectory is completely determined by a system of differential equations and a set of initial conditions, involving as many parameters as the order of the differential equations system. Now the initial state of the system consisting of a half of an intact sea urchin embryo is, of course, different from that of a half of an embryo. For one thing, the immediate environment of a separated half contains only the surrounding medium. Specifically, if the embryo which Driesch cut in half consisted of four cells, then each half consisted of two cells in nearly the same condition as in the previous stage (i.e., the two-cell embryo). There is nothing surprising in the fact that this two-cell embryo developed into a normal sea urchin, passing through the four-cell stage on the way.

The concept invoked by Driesch has been called "equifinality." It refers to a tendency of certain kinds of systems to reach some final state from different initial states. In Driesch's example, it was not even different initial states that gave rise to the same final state. As we have seen, the half embryo should be regarded as a state identical to that of an embryo at an earlier stage of a full embryo. Other examples, however, illustrate the principle of equifinality more convincingly. If the growth of a fish is interrupted, the fish will nonetheless grow to about the same size that would have been reached if growth had not been interrupted. This fact suggests that the final "goal" of a growing fish is to be of a certain size. However, this idea, too, is a misconception, as is demonstrated by a simple mathematical model of growth. Suppose the rate of change of a size of an organism is governed by two processes: the take-in of matter from the outside and the break-down of tissues. Supposing that food is taken in through the surface and that the breakdown occurs throughout the volume of this (primitive) organism, and noting that surface is proportional to the 2/3 power of the volume, we can write for the rate of change of volume V:

$$dV/dt = aV^{2/3} - bV,$$

where a and b are constants. We note by setting dV/dt equal to zero that V tends asymptotically to $(a/b)^3$, a quantity independent of the initial condition V_0. One can regard this sort of growth governed by "equifinality." But this "equifinality" is only a consequence of the mathematical structure of the growth model. It has nothing to do with the growing body being alive or not.

Apparent equifinality appears in physics no less than in biology. When light travels through different media, it appears to "choose" a path that minimizes travel time between two given points. Mechanical systems tend to equilibria where their potential energy is minimized. Closed thermodynamic systems tend to equilibria where their entropy is maximized. All these processes take systems to states essentially independent of where they start from. In this way, physical laws can be expressed "teleologically," for example, the Principle of Least Action, that is, in a mathematical form which makes it appear "as if" systems "seek" some "optimal" state to be in. In other words, the vitalist "principle of equifinality" has been explained away by showing that nonliving systems as well as living ones can be demonstrated to be governed by the same principle.

The next stand taken by the vitalists was on "intelligence" as the exclusive possession of some living systems. We now come to a question of central interest to people working in the field of artificial intelligence: "Can machines think?" is the way the layman puts the question. It serves little purpose to ask him to define "thinking." He is convinced that he knows what thinking means since he experiences it directly. And he is also convinced that you know what thinking is and that you know he knows and that therefore definitions are superfluous. I, too, will sidestep the definition. Instead I will go over some recollections going back four and a half decades in which artificial intelligence occasionally crops up.

In late 1945, shortly before I returned to civilian life, I attended a meeting of mathematicians at the Museum of Science and Industry in Chicago. I recall that mathematicians basked in suddenly ignited lime light of fame. The layman stubbornly thought of Einstein as a mathematician who discovered the "secret of the atomic bomb" in the mystic formula $E = MC^2$. And there were some among mathematicians who looked forward to a golden age in mathematics as a new fountainhead of power. World War I, it has been said, was a chemists' war (high explosives, poison gas). World War II was the physicists' war (radar, the atomic bomb). World War III, some maintained with gratifying confidence, would be the mathematicians' war. And the high hopes of the military establishment revolving around "fully automated battlefields" (General Westmoreland's expression) make the prognosis credible.

One of the exhibits at that meeting in Chicago's Museum of Science and Industry was a computer that played faultless tic-tac-toe—never lost and when the opponent made a mistake, invariably won. Seemed quite an achievement at the time. A few years afterward Simon and Newell, who did some work in the field, predicted that in the 1960s the world chess champion would be a computer program. Now, 30 years after the set time limit, computer programs play on the 2400 level, that is, like grand masters. They can easily beat players like most of us but are still no match for a Kasparov. Recently he easily beat the best of them. To be sure, a program playing against a human player is usually put under the same time limitation. We still don't know whether a Kasparov could beat a program if no time limit were placed on either. Possibly not. For a human being, the relaxation of time limits would be an advantage with diminishing returns, as the memory and other factors of mental capacity become overburdened, while a computer program is not subject to the same limitation. As long as its memory is not exceeded, it can continue operating with the same efficiency. The limitations of artificial intelligence are of another sort. To illustrate, I will examine the problem of finding optimal moves by "brute force," that is, by investigating all possible lines of play to any desired length.

Let us look at some results of game theory. We will consider only so called finite games, which can last only a finite number of moves. Tic-tac-toe is such a game. The number of moves in a play of this game cannot exceed nine. An average game of chess lasts 30–50 moves and only rarely more than 100. According to the theory of games such games can be reduced to so called "normal form," in which each player makes only one choice, namely, of a strategy that he will follow as the game proceeds. In this context, a strategy is a complete plan of action, which specifies how the player in question will move in any situation that can possibly arise in the course of the games. Another theorem in the theory of games refers to so called games of perfect information. These are games in which each player knows at all times the situation to which all the preceding moves have led. Both tic-tac-toe and chess are games of this sort. In the former, the cells of the grid in which the players' naughts, and crosses have been placed at a given stage of the game are visible. In chess, the positions of all the pieces on the board (which define the current situation) are visible. The above-mentioned theorem states that in a two-person game of perfect information, each player has at his disposal an optimal strategy which guarantees him the best result that he can attain in that game. In both tic-tac-toe and chess there are just three possible results: win, draw, or lose. An optimal strategy is one which is sure to win if a forced win is possible or to draw if a forced draw is possible. The fundamental result states that in every finite game of perfect information, each player has an optimal strategy.

The result means that if a game of chess is played perfectly by both players, then it must either always end in a win for White, or always end in a win for Black, or always end in a draw. Chess experts suspect that the latter result is the most probable and the forced win for Black the least probable, but this is not known. Nevertheless, the result is of "philosophical" importance. It implies that the reason people play chess is that they do not know how to play it. The reason adults do not play tic-tac-toe is that they do know how to play it and therefore know that each play must end in a draw.

Let me return to the tic-tac-toe-playing computer exhibited in Chicago in the beginning of the age of artificial intelligence. At the time the feat was impressive. Today we know that any teenager who knows something about programs can design one that plays perfect tic-tac-toe. In order to create such a program, the programmer must first analyze the game. He or she will note that if the first player puts an X in the center of the grid, then he must win if the second player puts his O in any side cell. The only way to prevent the first player from winning is to play a corner. If this happens, the first player's best move is the opposite corner, which still gives him a chance of a "double play." There is a way of blocking the double play, however, etc. It is this analysis that guides the design of a program and certainly not the examination of all possible strategies, the number of which is formidable.

To see this, consider a simplified game of chess which consists of only a single exchange of moves. White has 20 choices for his move, and these are the 20 strategies available to him. Black, on the other hand, has 20^{20} strategies available, since he has 20 possible responses to each of White's 20 possible moves. This is a huge number. To get an idea of how huge it is, observe that if 100 strategies can be listed on a sheet of paper and a stack of 100 sheets is an inch high, then a stack needed to list all of Black's 20^{20} strategies would be 40,000 light years thick.

This example illustrates the difference between the "brute force" analysis of a game (examining all possible strategies) and an analysis which examines only possible positions. In tic-tac-toe the number of possible final positions is 126, while the number of possible strategies is in the trillions. And even all possible positions need not be examined, since the outcome of the game is clear after only the first two or three moves. In the two-move chess game, the number of possible positions is only 400, while the number of possible strategies is totally unimaginable.

It stands to reason that chess-playing computer programs are designed by people who know something about the game. They have a repertoire of concepts developed through centuries of analyses in which certain principles of good play were discovered. Chess players refer to them as material, mobility, open files, pawn formation, safety of the king, etc. Especially relevant to this discussion is the fact that none of these concepts can be defined precisely, that is, formulated in a language that a computer can understand, while retaining the full meaning of the concept. The concepts are fully understood only by a person experienced in playing chess. They can be explained by one player to another. They can be to a certain (but only to a limited) extent translated into computer language (i.e., into criteria expressed by numbers, binary relations, and the like).

This brings us to the central problem of designing a sophisticated artificial intelligence, a problem central at this time, because the solution is still a long way off. The problem is endowing artificial intelligence devices with the power of recognition. In AI jargon, it is called "pattern recognition," but this is a loaded term, because "pattern" suggests something concretely describable, and the fundamental article of faith in artificial intelligence work is that if you can describe a form of behavior sufficiently precisely, you can simulate it. But this is just the difficulty. We cannot describe what we recognize, let alone say how we recognize it.

Think of a smell, say of ammonia, or garlic, or roses. As you think about it, you can almost experience it. Moreoever, each one internally experiencing the suggested smell is convinced that every one else is experiencing the same thing. Yet if one were asked to describe these sensations in words, one couldn't get past some generalizations that say very little, like "pungent" or "fragrant" or what not. Consider recognition in very young children. I recall one of my nephews when he was about 18 months old. We gave him some chess pieces to play with. He picked up a knight and made clicking sounds with his tongue. We were impressed. At his age he already associated the chess knight with a horse. But equally impressive was our recognition of the child's act of recognition. Why did we immediately identify clicking sounds with a horse? Because of what a horse walking or running on a city pavement sounds like: "clip-clop." A baby recognizes its mother's face and its mother's voice. But how does it do it? We could build a device able to recognize a voice, because sound patterns can be resolved by Fourier analysis and expressed mathematically. But faces? I wonder. Nor do I think that recognition of voices by humans depends on built-in Fourier analysis devices. I don't know how it works. It just does. We must assume that somehow accumulated experience and, be it noted, not only of an individual but of an entire evolutionary line of predecessors, adds up to this ability. Do we have to produce millions of generations of artificial intelligence devices to simulate this faculty?

Consider the crucial role recognition plays in scientific cognition. When I teach general system theory, I point out that this paradigm has two separate lines of development. One is analytic system theory; the other, organismic system theory. The fundamental unifying principle of analytic system theory is the mathematical isomorphism, which abstracts from content to bring out the structure of a system including the structure of its dynamics. A much-cited example is the mathematical isomorphism between a harmonic oscillator and an electrical system consisting of an inductance, a resistance, and a condenser in series. Both are described by a linear second-order differential equation. The analogy connects mechanical mass with electrical inductance, friction with resistance, rigidity with capacitance—connections which would not occur without the help of mathematical analysis. When we pass from nonliving to living systems, mathematical analysis loses much of its power. Analogies are established by acts of recognition apparently performed without the benefit of analysis. Biological science began with taxonomy, which, in turn, depended on recognition of species, genera, etc. of organisms. We easily recognize that an insect "eats," even if the components of the act of eating are widely different from ours, also that an insect copulates just as we make love, even though there is hardly anything that we can point to that supports the analogy. Or take a simple psychological experiment. The psychologist records an observation: the rat pushed a lever that caused a pellet to be delivered, which the rat ate. The way the motion of the lever caused the pellet to be delivered can be described precisely—little wonder, because someone had designed the apparatus. But the way the rat pushed the lever or ate the pellet cannot be described with comparable precision. In different instances of pushing the lever, quite different movements may be involved. Yet they are all lumped under a statement describing the result—justifiably so, because the psychologist can build a theory of instrumental or operant conditioning by associating only two precisely describable events: pushing the "right" or the "wrong" lever, and the delivery or nondelivery of the pellet. Had the psychologist insisted on reducing all events to "physical laws" (which the vitalists maintain cannot be done), he would have to make note of not only all the neural events, glandular secretions, and muscle contractions inside the rat, but also all the underlying physical and chemical processes, clearly an impossible task.

Surely we do not depend on such reductions in constructing theories of human behavior. The theories we construct do not compare in their reach, generality, and elegance to the theories constructed by physical scientists. But some such theories have made considerable progress. In them you will find references to conceptualization, recognition, values, modes of cognition, compulsions, enlightenment, insight, delusion, etc., etc.—all terms that defy operational definitions but that surely are not meaningless. We know what they mean intuitively just as we know what ammonia smells like or what an orgasm feels like, without being able to describe what goes on inside us when we appreciate the meanings of these terms.

Central to all these faculties is the faculty of recognition, not "pattern recognition," with which designers of artificial intelligence devices are concerned with, but intuitive recognition, acquired through years of personal experience and very probably through eons of evolutionary experience accumulated in the genetic complex. It is on this issue that the vitalists (if such are still around) will make their last stand. Their retreat was marked by "Yes, but can it..." type of objections. When it became clear that organic compounds can be synthesized, and that therefore there was not evidence for the existence of a special living substance, the vitalists said, "Never mind special living substance. Only living systems can exhibit equifinality." Actually it has been known for a long time that physical systems can exhibit equifinality, for example, processes governed by the principle of least action or systems tending toward equilibria or to steady states from different initial conditions. Design of artificial systems governed by equifinality was suggested by cybernetics, a new branch of physics in which the concept of information was linked to that of physical entropy. This linkage became the basis of artificial intelligence technology. When vitalists said, "Yes, but can artificial intelligence devices 'reason'?" the high-speed all-purpose computer was the answer. Artificial intelligence devices were also produced that could "learn," that is, improve their performance. The vitalists kept asking whether they could "really" think. The question was parried by the challenge to define "thinking." The vitalists kept asking whether automata could "feel," a question that inspired science fiction fantasies. All these questions could be dispensed with by a trivial answer: If you made an automaton that would be like a human being in all respects, it would be a human being.

We are reminded of the great Russian philosopher Lomonossoff, one of the founders of modern chemistry, who once and for all demolished the Aristotelian concept of "essence" by declaring that substances are what they are because of their properties, not because of some "essence" that alone defines their identity. Thus water is water simply because it has the properties of water. It is absurd to imagine a substance that has all the properties of water but is not "really" water, because it lacks the "essence" of water. The antivitalist would say the same thing of a humanoid automaton. Could such an automaton be made? Nothing simpler. We have at our disposal automata with linear dimensions less than two meters, weighing less than 100 kilograms, operating at temperatures below 40°C and, above all, produced by totally unskilled labor.

Joking aside, the challenge is to make a humanoid automaton the hard way, from scratch, as it were. Now why do we want to do this? Or do we? Better said, how far do we want to go in that direction and why? Two sources of motivation suggest themselves, one, in my opinion, a worthy one, the other questionable. The worthy motivation is that of heeding the call of a challenge to creativity. The questionable motivation is that generated by power addiction. This addiction manifests itself in the West, especially in the United States in what I call technolatry, the worship of technology, analogous to idolatry, the worship of idols. Recall the beginning of Mark Twain's great classic, *Connecticut Yankee*. After the introduction, in which Mark Twain tells how he met this strange man, he lets the man speak for himself. The novel continues in the first person.

"I am an American," the Yankee begins his narrative. "My father was a blacksmith, my uncle was a horse doctor. I can make anything…." Note he does not say, "I can do anything." He says he can *make* anything, but he gives the impression that he regards this technological virtuosity as tantamount to omnipotence. Indeed, the Connecticut Yankee attempts to turn King Arthur's England into a democratic society by introducing nineteenth century technology. He fails. Whether this failure reflects Mark Twain's pessimism about human nature or his skepticism about the humanizing influence of technology, we can't be sure.

Legends about the evil consequences of power addiction are common. In the Nibelung saga, the dwarf Alberich has to forswear love to gain power. His power addiction is catching and destroys every one who catches it. The legend of the Golem is built on the same theme. Today we are persistently warned against playing God, against the proliferation of nuclear power, against genetic engineering, and so on.

We can heed or ignore these warnings. At this time I will not discuss the ethical issue. I will only raise the epistemological issue. The construction of a device presupposes a knowledge of how it is supposed to work.

Where does this knowledge come upon the barrier of self-reference? We are familiar with the so called antinomies of formal logic—the paradox of Bertrand Russell's barber and its relatives. These go back to scholastic theology where the question was put whether God can make a stone that He cannot lift. If He can, what about His omnipotence? If He cannot, what about His omnipotence? Are we now asking whether we can construct an automaton with a will of its own, a creative imagination of its own, that is, an ability to imagine things that we could not have imagined? A conscience of its own which would inhibit it from obeying power-drunk madmen? The crucial question, in my opinion, is not whether we could do such a thing but whether we would want to. Some will say yes; others no. If both kinds of people engage in a serious, really honest self-searching dialogue, they may learn a good deal about both themselves and others. And that would be all to the good.

4 Could a Robot Be Creative— And Would We Know?

Margaret A. Boden

The notion that a robot, a mere android, might be creative is widely regarded as ridiculous. Computers are commonly believed to be utterly incapable of creativity. This opinion was first expressed over a hundred years ago by Ada Lovelace.

Lady Lovelace realized that Charles Babbage's "Analytical Engine"—in essence, a design for a digital computer—could in principle "compose elaborate and scientific pieces of music of any degree of complexity or extent." But she insisted that the creativity involved in any elaborate pieces of music emanating from the Analytical Engine would have to be credited not to the engine, but to the engineer. As she put it: "The Analytical Engine has no pretensions whatever to *originate* anything. It can do [only] *whatever we know how to order it* to perform."

If her remark means merely that a computer can do only what its program enables it to do, it is of course correct—and, for my argument, important. But if it is intended as a denial of any interesting link between computers and creativity, it is too quick and too simple. We must distinguish four different questions, which are often confused with each other in discussions of Lady Lovelace's claim.

The first question is whether computational concepts can help us understand how human creativity is possible. The second is whether computers (now or in the future) could ever do things which at least appear to be creative. The third is whether a computer could ever appear to recognize creativity—in poems written by human poets, for instance, or in its own novel ideas about science or art. And the fourth is whether computers themselves could ever *really* be creative (as opposed to merely producing apparently creative performance).

If we want to know whether robots could ever be creative, we must be clear about which of these questions we are asking. Certainly, we are asking the first three. Even though the first question specifically mentions *human* creativity, a definition of creativity would be required in order to answer it. That definition could then be applied to other creatures, including androids. As for the second and third questions, these are obviously crucial: we want to know whether, in practice, a robot could appear to be creative (and to recognize creativity).

The answers I shall propose to these three questions are, respectively, *Yes, definitely; Yes, up to a point;* and *Yes, necessarily (for any robot which appears to be creative).* This does not mean that creativity—whether in robots or in humans—is predictable, nor even that an original idea can be explained in every detail after it has appeared. But computational ideas can help us understand how human "intuition" works and how it might be paralleled in a robot.

It might appear that, for the purposes of android epistemology, the fourth question is the most important of all. It is important here, yes. But it is not a scientific query, as the other three are. It is in part an expression of a philosophical worry about meaning and in part a disguised request for a moral-political decision. I shall discuss this issue in a later section. First, let us consider whether a robot could at least appear to be creative.

The Definition of Creativity

Why does creativity seem so mysterious? To be sure, artists and scientists typically have their creative ideas unexpectedly, with little if any conscious awareness of how they arose. But the same applies to much of our vision, language, and common-sense reasoning. Computational psychology (and other forms of psychology too) offers many theories about unconscious processes.

Creativity is mysterious for another reason: the very concept is seemingly paradoxical. If we take seriously the dictionary definition of creation, "to bring into being or form out of nothing," creativity seems to be not only beyond any scientific understanding, but even impossible. It is hardly surprising, then, that some people have "explained" it in terms of divine inspiration, and many others in terms of some romantic intuition, or insight.

Neither of these popular views can be plausibly applied to robots, so if one of them is correct, then creative robots will forever stay within the pages of science fiction. But there is no reason to accept either. No reader of this volume, I assume, will warm to the first (although it was seriously asserted in a British "quality" newspaper only a few years ago, in a review of the play *Amadeus*). Even the second, to which some readers may assent, is unhelpful. From the psychological point of view, "intuition" is the name of a question, not of an answer. What we want to know is how intuition works. If we knew that, we might be able to say whether a robot could be intuitive, too.

People of a scientific cast of mind often try to define creativity in terms of "novel combinations of old ideas." In that case, the surprise caused by a creative idea is due to the improbability of the combination. In that case, too, statistical tests could be used to identify creativity (as some experimental psychologists have recommended).

Combination-theorists typically leave at least two things unsaid. The novel combinations have to be valuable in some way, because to call an idea creative is to say that it is not only new, but interesting. Combination-theorists usually omit value from their definition of creativity, perhaps because they (mistakenly) take it for granted that unusual combinations are always interesting. Also, they often fail to explain how it was possible for the novel combination to come about. They take it for granted, for instance, that we can associate similar ideas or recognize more distant analogies, without asking just how such feats are possible.

These cavils aside, what is wrong with the combination-theory? Many ideas—concepts, theories, paintings, poems, music—that we regard as creative are indeed based, at least in part, on unusual combinations. Moreover, provided that we can give a computational explanation of analogy, there seems no reason why a robot could not be creative. An android could combine and recombine its ideas as well as the rest of us, and come up with some valuable surprises in the process.

The inadequacy of the combination-theory lies in the fact that many creative ideas are surprising in a deeper way than this. They concern novel ideas which not only *did* not happen before, but which—in a sense that must be made clear—*could* not have happened before.

Before considering just what this seemingly paradoxical "could not" means, we must distinguish two senses of *creativity*. One is psychological (let us call it P-creativity), the other historical (H-creativity). An idea is P-creative if the individual person (or robot) in whose mind it arises could not have had it before; it does not matter how many times other people (or other androids) have already had the same idea. By contrast, an idea is H-creative if it is P-creative *and* no-one else—whether person or robot—has ever had it before.

H-creativity is something about which we are often mistaken. Historians of science and art are constantly discovering cases where other people, even in other periods, have had an idea popularly attributed to some individual hero. Whether an idea survives, whether it is lost for a while and resurfaces later, and whether historians at a given point in time happen to know about it, depend on a wide variety of unrelated factors. These include fashion, rivalries, illness, trade patterns, economics, war, flood, and fire.

The same would doubtless be true of H-creative ideas generated by androids. Given the "not invented here" syndrome so common in AI, an H-creative robot in one laboratory might well be utterly ignored (as opposed to being noticed, but scorned) by the people, and the androids, in another. Moreover, if a robot could be creative without our recognizing it (a possibility discussed in a later section) then someone might not know about all the H-creative ideas originated by the androids in their own laboratory.

It follows that there can be no systematic explanation of H-creativity. Certainly, there can be no psychological or computational explanation of this historical category. But all H-creative ideas, by definition, are P-creative too. So an explanation of P-creativity would include H-creative ideas as well.

Before trying to explain P-creativity, however, we must define it intelligibly. What does it mean to say that an idea "could not" have arisen before? Unless we know that, we cannot make sense of P-creativity (or H-creativity either), for we cannot distinguish radical novelties from mere "first-time" newness.

Noam Chomsky, discussing what he called the "creativity" of natural language, reminded us that language is an unending source of novel (even H-novel) sentences. But these sentences are novelties which clearly *could* have happened before, being generated by the same rules that can generate other sentences in the language. Any native speaker, and any robot too, could produce novel sentences using the relevant grammar. In general, to come up with a new sentence is not to do something P-creative.

The "coulds" in the previous paragraph are computational "coulds." That is, they concern the set of structures described and/or produced by one and the same set of generative rules.

Sometimes, we want to know whether a particular structure could, in principle, be described by a specific schema, or set of abstract rules. — Is 49 a square number? Is 3,591,471 a prime? Is this a sonnet, and is that a sonata? Is that painting in the Impressionist style? Could that geometrical theorem be proved by Euclid's methods? Is that wordstring a sentence? Is a benzene-ring a molecular structure that is describable by early nineteenth-century chemistry (before Friedrich von Kekule's famous fireside daydream of 1865)? — To ask *whether an idea is creative or not* (as opposed to how it came about) is to ask this sort of question.

But whenever a particular structure is produced in practice, we can also ask what generative processes actually went on in the computational system concerned. — Did a human geometer (or an android) prove a particular theorem in this way, or in that? Was the sonata composed by following a textbook on sonata-form? Did Kekule rely on the then-familiar principles of chemistry to generate his seminal idea of the benzene-ring, and if not, how did he come up with it?—To ask how an idea (creative or otherwise) *actually arose*, is to ask this type of question.

We can now distinguish first-time novelty from radical originality. A merely novel idea is one which can be described and/or produced by the same set of generative rules as are other, familiar, ideas. A genuinely original, or creative, idea is one which cannot.

So *constraints*, far from being opposed to creativity, make creativity possible. To throw away all constraints would be to destroy the capacity for creative thinking. Random processes alone can produce only first-time curiosities, not radical surprises (although randomness can sometimes contribute to creativity [Boden 1991, ch. 6]).

To justify calling an idea creative, then, one must specify the particular set of generative principles—what one might call the conceptual space—with respect to which it is impossible. Accordingly, literary critics, musicologists, and historians of art and science have much to teach the psychologist—and the ambitious android-designer. But their knowledge of the relevant conceptual spaces must be made as explicit as possible, to clarify just which structures *can*, and which *cannot*, be generated within them.

It follows from all this that, with respect to the usual mental processing in the relevant domain (chemistry, poetry, music...), a creative idea is not just improbable, but impossible. How did it arise, then, if not by magic? And how can one impossible idea be more surprising, more creative, than another? It begins to look as though even humans cannot be creative, never mind robots. If creativity is not mere combination, what is it? How can creativity possibly happen?

Exploring and Transforming Conceptual Spaces

A generative system defines a certain range of possibilities: chess-moves, for example, or jazz-melodies. These structures are located in a conceptual space whose limits, contours, and pathways can be mapped in various ways. Mental maps, or representations, of conceptual spaces can be used (not necessarily consciously) to explore the spaces concerned.

When Dickens described Scrooge as "a squeezing, wrenching, grasping, scraping, clutching, covetous old sinner," he was exploring the space of English grammar. He was reminding us (and himself) that the rules of grammar allow us to use any number of adjectives before a noun. Usually, we use only two or three; but we may, if we wish, use seven (or more). That possibility already existed, although its existence may not have been realized by us.

A much more interesting example of exploration can be found in the development of post-Renaissance Western music. This music is based on the generative system known as tonal harmony. Each piece of tonal music has a "home key," from which it starts, from which (at first) it did not stray, and in which it must finish. In this musical genre, reminders and reinforcements of the home key can be provided, for instance, by fragments of scales decorating the melody, or by chords and arpeggios within the accompaniment.

As the years passed by, after the introduction of this form of music-making, the range of possible home keys became increasingly well-defined. J.S. Bach's "Forty-Eight," for example, was a set of preludes and fugues specifically designed to explore—and clarify—the tonal range of the well-tempered keys. In other words, he was defining the basic dimensions of this conceptual space in a deliberate and systematic way.

Travelling along the path of the home key alone soon became insufficiently challenging. Modulations between keys then appeared, within the body of the composition. But all possible modulations did not appear at once. The range of harmonic relations implicit in the system of tonality became apparent only gradually.

At first, only a small number of modulations were tolerated—perhaps only one, followed by its "cancellation." Moreover, these early modulations took place only between keys that were very closely related in harmonic space. Over the years, however, the modulations became increasingly daring, and increasingly frequent. Harmonies that would have been unacceptable to the early musicians, who focussed on the most central or obvious dimensions of the conceptual space, became commonplace. By the late nineteenth century, there might be many modulations within a single bar, not one of which would have appeared in early tonal music.

Eventually, the very notion of the home key was undermined. With so many, and so daring, modulations within the piece, a "home key" could be identified not from the body of the piece but only from its beginning and end. Inevitably, someone (it happened to be Arnold Schoenberg) suggested that the convention of the home key be dropped altogether, since it no longer made sense in terms of constraining the composition as a whole. (Significantly, Schoenberg did not opt for a musical chaos. He suggested various new constraints to structure his music-making: using every note in the chromatic scale, for instance.)

Exploring a conceptual space is one thing. Transforming it is another. What is it to transform such a space? One example has just been mentioned: Schoenberg's dropping the home-key constraint to create the space of atonal music. *Dropping a constraint* is a general heuristic for transforming conceptual spaces.

Non-Euclidean geometry, for instance, resulted from dropping Euclid's fifth axiom, about parallel lines meeting at infinity. This transformation was made "playfully," as a prelude to exploring a geometrical space somewhat different from Euclid's. Only much later did it turn out to be useful in physics. (It is because so much creative thinking is playful, rather than goal-directed, that the term "conceptual space" is preferable to its cognate, "search-space.")

Another very general way of transforming conceptual spaces is to *consider the negative*: that is, to negate a constraint. One well-known instance concerns Kekule's discovery of the benzene-ring. He described it this way:

I turned my chair to the fire and dozed. Again the atoms were gambolling before my eyes.... [My mental eye] could distinguish larger structures, of manifold conformation; long rows, sometimes more closely fitted together; all twining and twisting in snakelike motion. But look! What was that? One of the snakes had seized hold of its own tail, and the form whirled mockingly before my eyes. As if by a flash of lightning I awoke (Findlay 1965, p. 39).

This vision was the origin of his hunch that the benzene-molecule might be a ring, a hunch which turned out to be correct.

Prior to this experience, Kekule had assumed that all organic molecules are based on strings of carbon atoms (he himself had produced the string-theory some years earlier). But for benzene, the valencies of the constituent atoms did not fit.

We can understand how it was possible for him to pass from strings to rings, as plausible chemical structures, if we assume three things (for each of which there is independent psychological evidence). First, that snakes and molecules were already associated in his thinking. Second, that the topological distinction between open and closed curves was present in his mind. And third, that the "consider the negative" heuristic was present also. Taken together, these three factors could transform "string" into "ring."

A string-molecule is an open curve. If one considers the negative of an open curve, one gets a closed curve. Moreover, a snake biting its tail is *a closed curve which one had expected to be an open one*. For that reason, it is surprising, even arresting ("But look! What was that?"). Kekule might have had a similar reaction if he had been out on a country walk and happened to see a snake with its tail in its mouth. But there is no reason to think that he would have been stopped in his tracks by seeing a Victorian child's hoop. A hoop is a hoop, is a hoop: no topological surprises there.

Finally, the change from open curves to closed ones is a topological change, which by definition will alter neighbor-relations. And Kekule was an expert chemist, who knew very well that the behavior of a molecule depends not only on what the constituent atoms are, but also on how they are juxtaposed. A change in atomic neighbor-relations is very likely to have some chemical significance. So it is understandable that he had a hunch that this tail-biting snake-molecule might contain the answer to his problem.

Hunches are common in human thinking (mathematicians often describe them in terms of an as-yet-unproven "certainty"). An adequate theory of creativity must be able to explain hunches. It must show how it is possible for someone to feel (often, correctly) that a new idea is promising *even before* they can say just what its promise is. The example of Kekule suggests that a hunch is grounded in appreciation of the structure of the space concerned and some notion of how the new idea might fit into it.

A creative robot would benefit from having hunches, as people do. Without them, it would waste a lot of time in following up new ideas that "anyone could have seen" would lead to a dead-end. Some of its hunches, some of its intuitions, would doubtless turn out to be mistaken (as some of ours do, too). But that is not to say that it would be better off without them.

Robots with hunches...could there actually be such things?

Could a Robot Be Creative?

A robot could be creative (or rather, it could at least *appear* to be creative) if the ideas conveyed metaphorically in the last section could be expressed in terms of functioning computer systems. In other words, conceptual spaces would have to be precisely identified, and ways (some general, some domain-specific) of exploring and changing them would have to be explicitly defined. In addition, the android would need a computational model of analogical thinking, since analogy plays a large part in "combinatorial" creativity and sometimes contributes to "impossibilistic" creativity, too (as in the example of Kekule, described above).

Some AI-work has already been done to these ends. In some cases, a conceptual space has been effectively mapped without any intention to model creativity, as such. Models specifically focussed on creativity are still relatively uncommon, and in almost all cases deal with space-exploration rather than space-transformation. As for analogy, we shall see that some work in this area suggests that a creative robot could emerge only after a fundamental change in current AI-methodology.

Computational work on musical perception, for example, has helped to advance the theory of harmony as well as to show how listeners manage to find their way around the space of tonal harmony (Longuet-Higgins 1987). This account of the musical interpretation of key, modulation, and metre has been successfully applied to compositions by a very wide range of composers, from baroque to romantic. If a robot were to enjoy Elgar, or even recognize a waltz as being in 3/4 tempo, beating time to it almost as soon as it has begun (as we can), it would have to inhabit this musical space, as we do. (Whether it might also inhabit others, which we cannot enter, is discussed in the next section.)

Closely related work on jazz has shown that very simple computational processes, making only minimal demands on short-term memory, can generate acceptable (and unpredictable) improvisations. By contrast, the generation of the underlying chord-sequence requires a much more powerful grammar (so cannot be done on the fly by human musicians) (Johnson-Laird 1988, 1989). The rules for improvisation take into account developing melodic contours, harmonizing the melody with the accompaniment, playing (and passing between) the chords schematically described in the underlying chord-sequence, and keeping the correct metre and tempo.

In both these cases (only one of which was intended as a study of creativity), musical "intuition" has been, in part, anatomized. A robot jazz-musician might therefore exist one day, capable of improvising *Tea for Two* in a pleasing manner. In both cases, too, detailed psychological and musicological questions have arisen as a result of specific aspects of the model. A heuristic which is helpful in interpreting Bach-cantatas, for example, may or may not be helpful in dealing with other music by Bach, or music by Vivaldi or Brahms.

Recent (unpublished) work by Christopher Longuet-Higgins has begun to anatomize the expressive space which characterizes, say, a Chopin waltz. The human pianist interprets terms in the score such as *legato, staccato, piano, forte, sforzando, crescendo, diminuendo, rallentando, accelerando, ritenuto,* and *rubato*. But how? Only if we can express this musical sensibility precisely could a robot play Chopin expressively. Longuet-Higgins has provided rules for all these expressive terms (and for the two pedals as well), and has come up with some counterintuitive results. He shows that the conceptual space of a crescendo, for instance, is more complex than one might think. A constant increase in the loudness of the relevant passage (the program must work out what is "the relevant passage") does not sound like a crescendo, but like someone turning up the volume-knob on a radio. Instead, he uses a nonlinear rule, based on the velocity of a ball rolling on a hill.

Since this program plays Chopin's *Minute Waltz* acceptably (to human ears), one could say that there already exists a robot which can play Chopin. Whether it can cope equally well with all of Chopin's waltzes, or with even one of his mazurkas, is a different—and very interesting—question. If one wants a robot-pianist with actual fingers, a twenty-first century version of Vaucanson's flute-player, then subtle sensori-motor skills would have to come into play. But the current program has, to some degree, the appreciation of *musical* space that is required to distinguish "mechanical" from "expressive" performance of this Chopin composition.

A conceptual space of a very different sort has been modeled by Harold Cohen's AARON (McCorduck 1991). This program, in one of its incarnations, generates aesthetically acceptable line-drawings of human acrobats. The drawings are individually unpredictable, but all lie within the preassigned genre. This genre is defined, in part, by AARON's "body grammar," which specifies not only the anatomy of the human body (two arms, two legs), but also how the various body parts appear from different points of view or in different bodily attitudes.

The program can draw acrobats with only one arm visible (because of occlusion), but it cannot draw one-armed acrobats. Its model of the human body does not allow for the possibility of there being one-armed people. They are, one might say, unimaginable. If, as a matter of fact, the program has never produced a picture showing an acrobat's right wrist occluding another acrobat's left eye, that is a mere accident of its processing history: it *could* have done so at any time. But the fact that it has never drawn a one-armed acrobat has a deeper explanation: such drawings are, in a clear sense, *impossible*.

If Cohen's program were capable of "dropping" one of the limbs (as a geometer may drop Euclid's fifth axiom, or Schoenberg the notion of the home-key), it could then draw one-armed, or one-legged, figures. A host of previously unimaginable possibilities, only a subset of which might ever be actualized, would have sprung into existence at the very moment of dropping the constraint that there must be (say) a left arm.

A superficially similar, but fundamentally more powerful, transformation might be effected if the numeral "2" had been used in the program to denote the number of arms. For "2," being a variable, might be replaced by "1" or even "7." A general-purpose tweaking-transformational heuristic—whether in a human mind or a robot's—might look out for numerals and try substituting varying values. Kekule's chemical successors employed such a heuristic when they asked whether any ring-molecules could have fewer than six atoms in the ring. (They also treated carbon as a variable—as a particular instance of the class of elements—when they asked whether molecular rings might include nitrogen or phosphorus atoms.) A program which (today) drew one-armed acrobats for the first time by employing a "vary-the-variable" heuristic *could* (tomorrow) be in a position to draw seven-legged acrobats as well. A program which merely "dropped the left arm" *could not*.

At present, only Cohen can change the constraints built into the program, thus enabling it to draw pictures of a type which it could not have drawn before. But some programs, perhaps including some yet to be written by Cohen, might do so for themselves.

To be able to transform its style, a program would need (among other things) a meta-representation of the lower-level constraints it uses. For the creative potential of a self-transforming system depends on how it represents its current skills (drawing "a left arm and a right arm" or drawing "2 arms") and on what heuristics are available to modify those representations and thereby enlarge its skills. We have already seen that if Cohen's program had an explicit representation of the fact that it normally draws four-limbed people, and if it were given very general "transformation heuristics" (like "drop a constraint," "consider the negative," or "vary the variable"), it might sometimes omit, or add, one or more limbs.

Evidence from developmental psychology suggests that this sort of explicit representation of a lower-level drawing skill is required if a young child is to be able to draw a one-armed man, or a seven-legged dog (Karmiloff-Smith 1990). Comparable evidence has been found with regard to other skills, such as language and piano-playing; here too, imaginative flexibility requires the development of generative systems that explicitly represent lower-level systems (Karmiloff-Smith 1986).

The implication is that a creative robot, capable of transforming its conceptual spaces as well as exploring them, would need such many-levelled representations of its own conceptual spaces. The proverbial all-singing, all-dancing robot, for instance, would need high-level representations of its verbal, musical, and motor skills. At present, we have only the sketchiest idea of how such high-level representations might be spontaneously developed (as opposed to being specifically provided by a programmer) (Clark and Karmiloff-Smith, in press).

A few existing computer models of creativity can transform their own spaces to some extent. Douglas Lenat's AM and EURISKO are well-known examples (Lenat 1983). The "Automatic Mathematician" does not produce proofs, nor does it solve mathematical problems. Rather, it generates and explores mathematical ideas, coming up with new concepts and hypotheses to think about. Its exploratory heuristics can examine, combine, and transform its concepts in many ways, some general and some domain-specific. One, for example, can generate the *inverse* of a function (this is a mathematical version of "consider the negative").

At the end of the last section we asked whether robots could have hunches. Well, AM does: some of its heuristics suggest which sorts of concepts are likely to be the most interesting, and AM concentrates on exploring them accordingly. AM finds it interesting, for instance, that the union of two sets has a simply expressible property that is not possessed by either of them (an instance of the notion that *emergent* properties, in general, are interesting).

AM's hunches, like human hunches, are sometimes wrong. Nevertheless, it has come up with some powerful mathematical notions, including Goldbach's conjecture and an H-novel theorem concerning maximally-divisible numbers. In short, AM appears to be significantly P-creative, and slightly H-creative too. However, critics have suggested that some heuristics were specifically included to make certain mathematical discoveries possible and that the use of LISP provided AM with some mathematically relevant structures "for free" (Lenat and Brown 1984; Ritchie and Hanna 1984). The precise extent of AM's creativity, then, is unclear. But we do have a sense of what questions we should ask in order to judge.

Because EURISKO, unlike AM, has heuristics for changing heuristics, it can explore and transform not only its stock of concepts but its own processing-style. For example, one heuristic asks whether a rule has ever led to any interesting result. If it has not (given that it has been used several times), it will be less often used in future. If the rule has occasionally been helpful, though usually worthless, it may be specialized in one of several different ways. (Because it is sometimes useful and sometimes not, the specializing-heuristic can be applied recursively.) Other heuristics work by generalizing rules in various ways or by creating new rules by analogy with old ones.

With the help of domain-specific heuristics to complement these general ones, EURISKO has generated H-novel ideas concerning genetic engineering and VLSI-design. Some of its suggestions have even been granted a US patent (the US patent-law insists that the new idea must not be "obvious to a person skilled in the art"). The heuristic principles embodied in EURISKO have nothing specifically to do with science. They could be applied to artistic spaces too. So some future acrobat-drawing program, for example, might be able to transform its graphic style by using similar methods.

A different type of self-transforming program is seen in systems using genetic algorithms (Holland, Holyoak, Nisbett, and Thagard 1986). As the name suggests, these heuristics are inspired by the genetic mutations underlying biological evolution. For example, two chromosomes may swap their left-hand sides, or their midsections (the point at which they break is largely due to chance). Repeated mutations, over many generations, result in unexpected combinations of genes drawn from many different sources. GA-programs produce novel structures by similar sorts of (partly random) transformation.

In general, the usefulness of the new structures is increased if the swapped sections are coherent mini-sequences (like the alternative bars allowed at every bar-line in eighteenth-century "dice-music"). However, identifying the "coherent mini-sequences" is not a trivial matter. For one thing, they do not function in isolation: both genes and ideas express their influence by acting in concert with many others. Moreover, coherent mini-sequences are not always *sequences:* coadapted genes tend to occur on the same chromosome but may be scattered over various points within it; similarly, potentially related ideas are not always located close to each other in conceptual space. Finally, a single unit may enter more than one group: a gene can be part of different coadaptive groups, and an idea may be relevant to several kinds of problems.

GA-programs help to explain how plausible combinations of far-distant units can nevertheless happen. They can identify the useful parts of individual rules and the significant interactions between rule-parts, even though a given part may occur within several rules and even though a "part" need not be a sequence of juxtaposed units (it may be two sets of three units, separated by an indefinite number of unspecified units). Rules are "selected" by assigning a strength to each one according to its success, and gradually dropping the weaker rules out of the system. Over time, the most useful rules are identified even though they act in concert with many others—including some that are useless, or even counter-productive. In this way, a GA-system may transform an initial set of randomly generated rules into a rule-set that solves the relevant problem even better than human experts do.

Creative robots, might rely (in part) on combinatorial methods like these. Indeed, psychologists favoring the combination-theory (see the second section) might posit processes akin to GA-mechanisms within human minds. But in explaining many "creative" combinations, they would need to appeal also to analogy. A creative robot would need to be able to identify analogies, for seeing a new analogy is often important in artistic and scientific creativity. To close this section, then, let us consider Douglas Hofstadter's "Copycat" model of analogical thinking (Chalmers, French, and Hofstadter 1991; Hofstadter and Mitchell 1991; Hofstadter, Mitchell, and French 1987; Mitchell 1990).

Hofstadter reminds us that seeing a new analogy is often much the same as perceiving something in a new way. It is hard to say where perception ends and analogizing begins, since perception is itself informed by high-level concepts. The Copycat project takes these psychological facts seriously. The program allows for the generation of many different analogies, where contextually appropriate comparisons are favored over inappropriate ones. It does not rely on ready-made, fixed representations, but constructs its own representations in a context-sensitive way.

Copycat's "perceptual" representations of the input-patterns are built up dialectically, each step being influenced by (and also influencing) the type of analogical mapping which the current context seems to require. A part-built interpretation that seems to be mapping well onto the nascent analogy is maintained and developed further. A part-built representation that seems to be heading for a dead end is abandoned, and an alternative one started which exploits different aspects of the target-concept.

The domain actually explored by Copycat is a highly idealized one, namely, alphabetic letter-strings. But the computational principles involved are relevant to analogies in any domain. In other words, the alphabet is here being used as a psychological equivalent of inclined planes in physics.

Copycat considers letter-strings such as *ppqqrrss*, which it can liken to strings such as *mmnnoopp*, *tttuuuvvvxxx*, and *abcd*. Its self-constructed "perceptual" representations describe strings in terms of descriptors like leftmost, rightmost, middle, same, group, alphabetic successor, and alphabetic predecessor. It is a parallel-processing system, in that various types of descriptors compete simultaneously to build the overall description.

The system's sense of analogy in any particular case is expressed by its producing a pair of letter-strings which it judges to be like some pair provided to it as input. If, for instance, it is told that the string *pqr* changes into *stu* and is then asked what the string *def* will change into, it will probably (though not necessarily) produce the string *ghi*. If, on this occasion, it is not looking for the most obvious analogy but for a somewhat more creative one, it may produce *gghhii* instead.

The mapping functions used by Copycat at a particular point in time depend on the representation that has already been built up. Looking for *successors* or for *repetitions*, for instance, will be differentially encouraged according to the current context. So the two letters *m* in the string *ffmmtt* will be mapped as a sameness-pair, whereas in the string *abcefgklmmno* they will be mapped as parts of two different successor-triples: *klm* and *mno*.

Even in the highly idealized domain of alphabetic letter-strings, interesting problems arise. Suppose, for instance, that Copycat is told that *abc* changes into *abd*, and it must now decide what *xyz* changes into. Its initial description of the input-pair, couched in terms of alphabetic successors, has to be destroyed when it comes across *z* —which has no successor. Different descriptors then compete to represent the input-strings, and the final output depends partly on which descriptors are chosen. On different occasions, Copycat comes up with *xyd* and *wyz*. Each of these is a consequence of different internal representations and mapping functions. The line of thought, and of redescription, which led to *wyz*, for instance, involved moving backwards through the alphabet instead of forwards, and so seeing the head of the input-string as the place where some substitution should take place, instead of the tail. Notice that the initial description in this case is not merely adapted, but destroyed. Hofstadter compares this example with conceptual revolutions in science: the initial interpretation is discarded, and a fundamentally different interpretation is substituted for it.

This constructive process can be telescoped, if the relevant descriptions are provided beforehand. In humans, culturally based telescoping of this sort explains why a schoolchild can quickly understand, perhaps even discover, an analogy which took the relevant H-creative thinker many months, or years, to grasp. The particular analogy, we assume, is new to the child. But its general type is familiar. The notion that simple linear equations, for example, capture many properties of the physical world may already be well established in the pupil's mind. It is hardly surprising, then, if this analogical mapping mechanism can be activated at the drop of the teacher's chalk.

As Hofstadter points out, most AI-models of analogy (and of problem-solving) put the computer in the place of the schoolchild. That is, the relevant representations and mapping rules are provided ready-made to the program. It is the programmer who has done the work of sifting and selecting the "relevant" points from the profuse conceptual apparatus within his mind. Hofstadter criticizes current AI-models of scientific discovery, such as BACON and its computational cousins (Langley, Simon, Bradshaw, and Zytkow 1987), on the same grounds. Copycat, preliminary though it is, shows that a design for a creative robot need not take relevance for granted in this way.

—And Would We Know?

Suppose there were creative robots, exploring and transforming their conceptual spaces in what they regarded as valuable ways. Would we necessarily know? That is, would a creative robot always appear, to us, to be creative?

To recognize a creative idea requires one to understand the relevant conceptual space and to locate the new structure with reference to it. One must be able to distinguish explorations of various types and transformations of various depths. It is not necessary—though it is helpful—to be able to express these insights explicitly. In many cases of human creativity, we can say very little, if anything, about why we regard the new idea as creative (as opposed to merely new).

Nor is it always necessary—though, again, it is helpful—to distinguish the evaluative from the interpretative aspect of one's response. In the arts, and in pure mathematics, we tend to value exploration and transformation for their own sake. When we are faced by a scientific or a practical problem, in which the new idea has to fit the facts in some way, we tend to distinguish the originality of the idea from its value. But in both arts and sciences, we can consider a certain way of thinking and then ask whether the new idea is valuable from that standpoint. So a post-Impressionist painter can distinguish original from run-of-the-mill Impressionist paintings, and a non-Catholic can appreciate the theological ingenuity of the form of birth-control known as Vatican roulette.

It follows that to recognize the creativity of a creative robot we would need at least to share its conceptual spaces, if not its values too. (Values that were highly perverse, from our point of view, might prevent us from recognizing the goal-structure of the robot's thinking and so hinder us in assessing its "conceptual" creativity.)

If the robot's program was specifically built into it by us, we would in general have a better chance of understanding its novel ideas. But even so, we might not recognize all of its creative moments.

We might be temporarily "trapped" within certain thought-structures and so fail to understand the android's potentially intelligible ideas. (Gestalt psychologists have described "functional fixedness," wherein someone fails to recognize something he or she is perfectly capable of recognizing: for example, that a pair of pliers could be used as a pendulum-bob.) Or we might be defeated by the speed and storage available to the robot. We saw in the last section that the computational complexity of jazz-improvisation is limited by the size of human short-term memory. A robot musician could be equipped with a larger STM and could be given musical rules of greater computational complexity accordingly. Not only could it (unlike us) compose new chord sequences on the fly, but it could produce improvisations which we could neither mimic nor even fully appreciate.

Moreover, just how specific is a program "specifically built into it by us"? An android whose program allowed for quasi-random transformations (like those effected by genetic algorithms) might sometimes produce ideas which we would be bound to value, because they solved a class of problems in which we are interested, but which we could not understand.

If creative robots were willing and able to explain to us how their novel ideas related to the pre-existing conceptual spaces, that would help. In that case, they would be like the historian of art or science (or the anthropologist) who links unfamiliar ways of thinking. But being willing and being able are different things. It is not obvious that an android would have very much greater access to its own thought processes than we do. To be sure, its greater speed and storage capacity would make some difference. But if it were to function in real time, even these might not suffice to enable it to reflect on all its internal processes. In short, its introspection might be limited for much the same reasons as ours is. If so, it could not always initiate us (or itself) into the mysteries of its own creativity.

Finally, what of the effects of embodiment? To the extent that our understanding is grounded in our embodiment, androids might well share some understanding with us. Language, for example, has many characteristics arguably due to the fact that we are bodily creatures moving face-forward in a material world (so the Archangel Gabriel, as a purely immaterial being, simply *could not* have conversed with Mary in her native Aramaic [Boden 1981]). Countless linguistic expressions are metaphors, living or dead, grounded in our bodily experience. Conceptual "spaces," and their "exploration" and "mapping," are obvious examples. Even "transformation" recalls, for instance, the potter's clay. Indeed, some students of language and literature have argued that our oppositional conceptual schemes, and the nature of our rhetoric and argument, are fundamentally shaped by the bilateral symmetry of our bodies (Turner 1991).

If these admittedly speculative hypotheses are sound, a robot shaped like an amoeba or a jellyfish could be expected to have a conceptual architecture significantly unlike ours. A genuine android, on the other hand *(sic)*, might structure its concepts in a more humanlike way, largely as a result of its bilateral symmetry, assuming, of course, that the robot's conceptual architecture developed spontaneously along with its sensori-motor skills, as opposed to being built in by a human roboticist. Perhaps a human roboticist could build all manner of oppositional thought-structures into a jellyfish-robot, which (if this argument is correct) could not be expected to develop them "naturally" for itself.

The upshot is that some instances of creativity in robots might remain unknown to us. Wittgenstein said: "If a lion could speak, we would not understand it." A man-made lion, or an android, could be much more intelligible. But it need not be.

Yes, But Could a Robot REALLY Be Creative?

Some philosophers would be content to admit everything I have said so far but would nevertheless insist that a robot could not *really* be creative. Even if an android's performance rivaled Beethoven, Newton, and Shakespeare all rolled into one, it would be no more than apparently creative. As remarked in the first section, this rejection of the very idea of truly creative robots depends mainly upon two worries: one about the ascription of intentionality, and the other about whether we ought to give androids a place in our society.

The first worry has been eloquently, and influentially, posed by John Searle (1980, 1990). His "Chinese room" argument is too well-known in AI circles to need recounting here. It was developed with GOFAI-robots in mind, androids controlled in the Good Old-Fashioned AI-way. But it would apply also to situated robots insofar as their reactions are programmed, not hardwired.

Very briefly (for a fuller account, see Boden 1988, ch. 8), my rebuttal focuses on Searle's main premise, that computer programs are "all syntax and no semantics."

It is this premise which enables Searle to reject the "Robot Reply," because it implies that even a robot enjoying rich causal interactions with its environment could not *really* enjoy them. The robot's visible movements might seem highly significant to us, but not to the robot itself; and its internal computations would be as empty of meaning to it as those of any VDU-bound computer. As for creativity, a robot might improvise jazz, or play Chopin waltzes, so as to make tears of joy come into our eyes—but, unlike human performers, it would understand nothing of these musical worlds. It does not matter how impressive its appearance of creativity is: there is no "Android Answer." If Searle's premise is correct, no android could really be creative.

Searle regards his premise as intuitively obvious (as do some champions of computational psychology, e.g., Fodor 1980 and Stich 1983). And so it is, if one considers a program merely as an abstract mathematical structure, or uninterpreted logical calculus. But one may also consider a program in terms of its ability, when implemented in a computer, to cause certain things to happen inside it. (Indeed, Brian Smith has recommended that computer scientists interested in the semantics of programming languages should do so [Smith 1982].) On that view of what a program is, the premise is false.

A programmed instruction (implemented in a computer) is analogous to Searle-in-the-room's understanding of English, not of Chinese. A word in a language one understands (one for which the relevant causal connections have been set up) causes certain processes to go on in one's head, some of which may result in observable behavior. In a robot, likewise, input-peripherals feed into the internal computations, which lead eventually to changes in the output-peripherals. In between, the program causes a host of things to happen inside the system itself. At the level of the machine code, the effect of the program on the computer is direct, the machine being engineered so that a given instruction causes a unique operation.

A programmed instruction, then, is not merely a formal rule. Its essential function (when implemented in the relevant hardware) is to make something happen. This fact is relevant if intentionality can be naturalistically analyzed in terms of causal relations.

Allen Newell's (1980) definitions of "designation" and "interpretation" in

physical symbol systems exemplify such an analysis: "An expression designates an object if, given the expression, the system can either affect the object
itself or behave in ways depending on the object; and the system can interpret
an expression if the expression designates a process and if, given the expression, the system can carry out the process." Given this account of intentionality, computer programs are not "all syntax and no semantics." On the contrary, their inherent causal powers give them a toehold in semantics.

Admittedly, no existing "creative" program can really understand the
domain it explores. Too many of the relevant causal connections are missing.
AARON, for instance, does not really understand that humans have two arms
and two legs. One might say that it has the beginnings of an understanding of
what it is to compare two symbols (in the program), to interrupt a line, to
draw symmetrically, and perhaps even to draw one thing occluded by another. However, it cannot recognize symmetry in other androids' drawings, and
it has no real sense of the third dimension.

A robot equipped with low-level vision would have some of the many relevant causal connections which AARON lacks. A fully-fledged android would
have all of them (as well as ways of transforming its own conceptual spaces).
Having rejected Searle's crucial premise and accepted the causal analysis of
intentionality assumed so far, we would therefore be unreasonable to deny
that androids are really creative.

Some naturalistic analyses of intentionality, however, would provide grounds
for refusing to ascribe real creativity to androids. These are biologically based
analyses, which insist that the causal connections involved be of a certain (teleological) type and be developed within a certain (evolutionary) context.

Ruth Millikan (1984, 1989), for instance, argues that intentional concepts
have to be analyzed in a historical-teleological way. A bodily organ or psychological process has a "proper function" in "normal conditions," where these
technical terms are to be teleologically understood. That is, they do not refer
to the body's functioning (properly) without any damaged parts, nor to (normal) statistically average environmental conditions. Rather, they refer to
behavior, whether internal or external, which in the relevant ecological niche
results (not always, but often enough) in the survival of the creature concerned and in the satisfaction of its various goals. Moreover, the organs and
processes concerned must have been developed, at base, by biological evolution (this allows for a process to have a history of individual learning, in those
species capable of learning). The historical and teleological criteria are intimately linked, for it is the evolutionary context which enables us to identify
the proper functions, normal conditions, and goals.

Because of its historical dimension, this philosophical account of intentionality excludes all androids—both the GOFAI-type and fully-hardwired
situated robots. What I referred to above as the "essential function" of a computer program, or of programs in general, is not a "proper function" in Mil-

likan's sense, because it was designed by computer scientists. Likewise, the function of a circuit in a situated robot was determined by the engineer who built it. Notice that this biological analysis of intentionality does not insist (as Searle does) on any particular material stuff, such as neuroprotein. But its evolutionary aspect implies that no android (no artificial, man-made creature) could *really* be creative.

I have argued elsewhere for a similar view, in distinguishing "extrinsic" from "intrinsic" teleology (Boden 1972). A robot's goals and purposes are not intrinsic to it but are ultimately explicable in terms of human purposes. Certainly, an android could generate specific goals that had not been foreseen by, and might not even be acceptable to, any human being. However, the fact that a robot—even one descended from a long line of self-modifying robots—has *any goals at all* can ultimately be explained by (historical) reference to the purposes of some other creature. This is not the case for humans. Someone's goal of becoming the President of the USA may be explained by a specific ambition on the part of some other purposive being (consider Jack and Joseph Kennedy). But that a person has any purposes at all cannot, barring theological "explanations," be explained in this way.

People have purposes *intrinsically*, because the impersonal process of evolution has resulted in goal-seeking human organisms. Since psychological vocabulary in general assumes the possession of intrinsic purposes, robots cannot be described as creative in the full sense of the word.

Word-senses change, however. If androids existed, we could hardly avoid using a rich intentional vocabulary—not just "instruction," "infer," and "search"—to describe them. Would we eventually allow (what we do not allow today) that systems with extrinsic purposes can merit psychological descriptions *without scare quotes*? (If so, an apparently creative robot would be regarded as *really* creative.) This question raises the moral-political worry mentioned above, for to remove all the scare quotes would be to admit androids into our moral universe. People who preferred not to do so would therefore insist on keeping the scare quotes.

Suppose that an apparently creative robot, equipped with a self-transforming version of the line-drawing program described previously, were to draw acrobats with "triangular" calves and thighs. Suppose also that no human artist had drawn such things before. Many art critics might refuse to accept the robot's drawings as aesthetically valuable. They could not deny the analogy between limb parts and wedges—but they would dismiss it as uninteresting, even ugly. However, such things *have* been drawn before, and many people appreciate Picasso's "triangular" limbs. Why this difference in attitude?

The difference lies in the view that it is one thing to allow a human artist to challenge our perceptions and aesthetic conventions, but quite another to tolerate such impertinence from a robot. To be impertinent is to say something (perhaps something both true and relevant) which one has no right to say. At a certain level of generality, every person has a right to be heard, to try to persuade others to share his or her view. Each of us has this right by virtue of being a member of the human community. But robots are not natural members of the human community, as members of *homo sapiens* are.

Of course, inherited membership is only one way of entering a community: someone can be invited to join. Androids would have some claim to honorary membership of the human community, for they could do many humanlike things. But a decision on our part to regard robots as *really* creative would have far-ranging social implications. It would mean that, up to a point, we should consider their interests—much as we consider the interests of animals. For interests, *real* interests, they would be assumed to have. Suppose a robot-artist were to ask you to find it a thicker pen, so that it could experiment with its new way of cross-hatching. If you had accepted it as *really* creative, you would be obliged, within reason, to interrupt what you were doing in order to help it. In other words, you would be obliged to put its interests above (some of) your own.

The decision to remove all scare quotes, when describing a robot as creative (or intelligent), carries significant moral overtones. So, like moral decisions in general, it cannot be forced upon us by the facts alone. No matter how impressive future androids may be, we could (without self-contradiction) insist on retaining all the moral responsibility, and the epistemological authority, too. In that case, quasi-creative robots might be widely used, much as pocket-calculators are today, with the full range of psychological vocabulary being employed in describing them. But we would shoulder the entire moral and epistemological responsibility for following their "hunches," or trusting their "insights."

Whether people actually would react to androids in this grudging way is an empirical question. The answer might depend on mere superficialities. Our moral attitudes and general sympathies are much influenced by biologically based factors, including what the other person—or quasi-person—looks like, sounds like, and feels like. Fur or slime, cuddliness or spikiness, naturally elicit very different responses. If androids were encased in fur, given attractive voices, and made to look like teddy-bears, we might be more morally accepting of them than we otherwise would be (Frude 1983). If they were made of organic materials (perhaps involving connectionist networks constructed out of real neurones), our moral responses might be even more tolerant.

It is impossible to know, now, how we would decide to treat androids, should they ever exist. But the crucial point is that this issue would involve a moral decision, in addition to recognition of the scientific facts. However creative a robot appeared to be, however impressively original its performance, we might nevertheless refuse—on moral grounds—to call it really creative.

In sum: there is no scientific reason why a robot should not be creative. That is, a robot could produce apparently creative performance, by means of the exploration and transformation of its conceptual spaces. Insofar as we shared the robot's conceptual spaces, we would be equipped to know that it was (apparently) creative. Whether, given all this, a robot could ever *really* be creative is not a question for science.

References

Boden, M. A. (1972). *Purposive Explanation in Psychology.* Cambridge, MA: Harvard University Press.

Boden, M. A. (Ed.). (1981). Implications of language studies for human nature. In *Minds and Mechanisms: Philosophical Psychology and Computational Models.* Ithaca: Cornell University Press.

Boden, M. A. (1988). *Computer Models of Mind: Computational Approaches in Theoretical Psychology.* Cambridge: Cambridge University Press.

Boden, M.A. (1991). *The Creative Mind: Myths and Mechanisms.* New York: Basic Books.

Chalmers, D. J., French, R. M., & Hofstadter, D. R. (1991). *High-Level Perception, Representation, and Analogy: A Critique of Artificial Intelligence Methodology* (CRCC Tech. Rep. 49). Bloomington, IN: Center for Research on Concepts and Cognition, Indiana University.

Clark, A. & Karmiloff-Smith, A. (in press). The Cognizer's innards: A psychological and philosophical perspective on the development of thought. *Mind and Language.*

Findlay, A. (1965). *A Hundred Years of Chemistry.* [3rd. ed., T. I. Williams (Ed.).] London: Duckworth.

Fodor, J. A. (1980). Methodological solipsism considered as a research strategy in cognitive psychology. *Behavioral and Brain Sciences, 3,* 63-110.

Frude, N. (1983). *The Intimate Machine: Close Encounters with the New Computers.* London: Century.

Hofstadter, D. R., & Mitchell, M. (1991). An overview of the Copycat Project. In K. J. Holyoak & J. Barnden (Eds.), *Connectionist Approaches to Analogy, Metaphor, and Case-Based Reasoning.* Norwood, NJ: Ablex.

Hofstadter, D. R., Mitchell, M., & French, R.M. (1987). *Fluid Concepts and Creative Analogies: A Theory and its Computer Implementation* (CRCC Tech. Rep. 18). Bloomington, IN: Center for Research on Concepts and Cognition, Indiana University.

Holland, J. H., Holyoak, K. J., Nisbett, R. E., & Thagard, P. R. (1986). *Induction: Processes of Inference, Learning, and Discovery.* Cambridge, MA: MIT Press.

Johnson-Laird, P. N. (1988). *The Computer and the Mind: An Introduction to Cognitive Science.* London: Fontana.

Johnson-Laird, P. N. (1989). *Jazz Improvisation: A Theory at the Computational Level.* Unpublished working-paper, MRC Applied Psychology Unit, Cambridge.

Karmiloff-Smith, A. (1986). From meta-processes to conscious access: Evidence from children's metalinguistic and repair data. *Cognition, 23,* 95-147.

Karmiloff-Smith, A. (1990). Constraints on representational change: Evidence from children's drawing. *Cognition, 34,* 57-83.

Langley, P., Simon, H. A., Bradshaw, G. L., & Zytkow, J. M. (1987). *Scientific Discovery: Computational Explorations of the Creative Process.* Cambridge, MA: MIT Press.

Lenat, D. B. (1983). The role of heuristics in learning by discovery: Three case studies. In R. S. Michalski, J. G. Carbonell, & T. M. Mitchell (Eds.), *Machine Learning: An Artificial Intelligence Approach.* Palo Alto, CA: Tioga.

Lenat, D. B. & Brown, J. S. (1984). Why AM and EURISKO appear to work. *Artificial Intelligence*, 23, 269-294.

Longuet-Higgins, H. C. (1987). *Mental Processes: Studies in Cognitive Science*. Cambridge, MA: MIT Press.

McCorduck, P. (1991). *Aaron's Code*. San Francisco: W. H. Freeman.

Millikan, R. G. (1984). *Language, Thought, and Other Biological Categories*. Cambridge, MA: MIT Press.

Millikan, R. G. (1989). Biosemantics. *Journal of Philosophy, LXXXVI*, 281-297.

Mitchell, M. (1990). COPYCAT: *A Computer Model of High-Level Perception and Conceptual Slippage in Analogy-Making*. Unpublished Ph.D thesis, University of Michigan.

Newell, A. (1980). Physical symbol systems. *Cognitive Science, 4*, 135183.

Ritchie, G. D. & Hanna, F. K. (1984). AM: A case study in AI methodology. *Artificial Intelligence*, 23, 249-268.

Searle, J. R. (1980). Minds, brains, and programs. *Behavioral and Brain Sciences, 3*, 473-497. [Reprinted in M. A. Boden (Ed.), *The Philosophy of Artificial Intelligence* (ch. 3). Oxford: Oxford University Press, 1990.]

Searle, J. S. (1990). Is the brain's mind a computer program? *Scientific American, 262*, 1, 20-25.

Smith, B. C. (1982). *Reflection and Semantics in a Procedural Language* (Ph.D dissertation and Tech. Rep. LCS/TR-272). Cambridge, MA: MIT.

Stich, S. C. (1983). *From Folk Psychology to Cognitive Science: The Case Against Belief*. Cambridge, MA: MIT Press.

Turner, M. (1991). *Reading Minds: English Studies an the Age of Cognitive Science*. Princeton, NJ: Princeton University Press.

Zytkow, J. M. (1990). Deriving laws through analysis of processes and equations. In P. Langley & J. Shrager (Eds.), *Computational Models of Discovery and Theory Formation* (pp. 129-156). San Mateo, CA: Morgan Kaufmann.

5 From Cognitive Systems to Persons

Antoni Gomila

What sort of cognitive systems are persons? Are the mental phenomena that characterize a person of a purely cognitive nature? It seems clear that the mainstream answer to this latter question in cognitive science is yes. In fact, it is one of its working assumptions. Here, I want to challenge this assumption. It is my contention that there is a set of mental phenomena, constitutive of personal systems, that cannot be fully understood in terms of information-processing mechanisms alone, though they are heavily dependent on these mechanisms. This set constitutes what I would like to dub the "personal" level of mind. It has intrinsic properties that make it worth studying on its own.

In this chapter, I want to make three related claims as regards the nature and properties of this personal level. First, what distinguishes this set of phenomena is the possibility of (partial) accessibility and manageability of one's own states. This requires making sense of a notion of "one's own mental states," which entails a self-centered point of view. But characteristically, the domain we can access and manage is restricted. Second, this capacity results from the social setting which constitutes the primary environment for our cognitive resources to deal with. In other words, it is to cope with the demands of a social environment that a new level of mental organization arises. Stated this way, though, the claim is clearly defective. Not any kind of social environment will do. In fact, evolutionary considerations show that a mutually reinforcing relation takes place between cognitive resources available and the nature of the social setting in which these resources are put to work. But in its turn, the presence of cognition changes the social context. So we need specify the way in which this social setting gives rise to a new, personal level of mental organization functional and the cognitive resources that support this new level. This is our third claim: language acquisition is the crucial step in this process, in that it provides the cognitive system with a secondary representational system which facilitates the reorganization of our cognitive resources and allows, in its turn, a new, more complex, pattern of social interaction.

These joint claims, it seems to me, have some virtues that make them appealing. On the one hand, they point to an account that could help us understand our phenomenal and common sense experience of ourselves (which is not the same as to vindicate it). On the other, it offers a natural bridge to make sense of the relationship between individual and social psychology and cognition. Finally, it tries to be consistent with the evolutionary constraints that shaped our embodied minds.

But, at present, it is not possible to make a straightforward defense of this account. Rather, we will try to show, on conceptual and empirical grounds, that it provides a unified approach to a set of phenomena that have been separately studied and to a set of findings whose interpretation has not been particularly obvious. To show its plausibility, then, is the aim of the argument. But if the hypothesis proves true, it may have important implications as regards the role of AI in cognitive science.

To assess these consequences will be the purpose of the last section. Before that, though, we will be concerned with an attempt to characterize the personal level and to show that it cannot be fully understood in information-processing terms. Next, we will argue against the methodological assumption that our functional organization is fixed from the start. This argument will allow us to characterize a meta-representational level of functional organization, as a result of language acquisition, in the following section. We then present a model of how this meta-representational resource makes possible the appearance of a personal level, given the social needs the system has to face. In the next section, we will refine the model through evolutionary considerations to make clear the close relationship between sociality and cognition. In conclusion, some implications of the argument for work in AI will be considered.

The Personal Level

There is some debate in philosophical circles as to how to define the concept of person. For our purposes, though, we can leave it aside, since our aim here is simply to claim the irreducibility of the personal phenomena, whatever way we define it, to a purely cognitive level of explanation. The most distinctive personal phenomenon is action, our capability to behave in virtue of our reasons. In action, there is an essential reference to the system as a whole: its self-interest, well-being, autonomy, happiness, or responsibility. It is this global unity that gives the notion of person its grip.

However, cognitive scientists philosophically-minded (Fodor 1981; Pollock 1989, among many others) tend to adopt a subpersonal version of the representational theory of mind, modeled after decision theory. According to this approach, beliefs and desires are understood as relations to mental representations, that is, mental states with syntactic, as well as semantic, properties. It is the causal powers of these states, in virtue of their syntactic properties, that cause action. In so doing, they explain action from a subpersonal stance, as if it were just another case of cognitive performance (e.g., sentence understanding).

In so doing, though, no understanding is provided as to how intentional states, because of their intentionality, cause actions. In other words, what we need to know is why intentional explanations are explanatory as intentional, why reasons can be causally relevant because of their reasonableness, not just because they have some other functional or syntactic properties. My contention is that we can reach this understanding only when we take into account the integrative competence that constitutes a personal level of mental organization.

To illustrate my point, let me tell you a little "chauvinistic" story. Raymon Lull (also known as Lulio) was a medieval philosopher, from Mallorca—the place I am from. Until he was 25 years old, he conducted a "dissolute" life, a life of "sin and pleasure" (for medieval standards, I guess), as he recalls in his autobiography. At that age, though, in chasing a girl he wanted as his lover, he entered a small chapel and had a mystic experience. The Virgin appeared to him and ordered him to go and convert unfaithful Muslims. And so he did. He abandoned "society," became a monk and began writing on God and His properties. He tried to prove the superiority and truth of the Christian God over Allah, by way of logical demonstration (this is the real reason why he is still remembered, of course). As he writes in his autobiography, he realized that Reason is the path to the true God. Unfortunately, the Muslims of Northern Africa were not very fond of logical proofs, and he died as a martyr in Tripoli.

The point of this story is to supply instances of what I call personal phenomena and its irreducibility to a subpersonal level. Thus, we find here a case of change of behavior, for example, and of the reasons for this. Up until his conversion, our hero decided what to do in terms of the pleasure he would get out of it. After that, though, all his actions were directed to spread the name of God. He changed all his habits: instead of big meals and comfortable beds, he shifted to fasting and sleeping on the ground; instead of social events and lovers, solitude and, eventually, martyrdom. How are we to understand this change?

Somebody could think that a change like this could be due to a mental breakdown, some sort of amnesia, or whatever. It could. But this is not at issue: functional explanations are not problematic. We are concerned with understanding the possibility of an intentional explanation of this change, and to this extent we need only assume that cases like this one—sudden conversions, we might call them—are possible.

On the other hand, I assume that nobody will claim that the mystic experience literally changed his psychology. Very probably he continued to feel thirsty and hungry, but, in some sense, they were no longer the right kind of desires for him to have. Because of a change in his beliefs, then? Well, perhaps. He could have acquired the belief that his life was purposeless, or that his behavior was wrong, or that God wanted him for some important enterprise. Notice that all these are beliefs about himself. But how could these beliefs change his desires?

Notice that the point I am aiming at is that the usual decision-theoretic apparatus, to which the subpersonal approach to action appeals, is clearly insufficient to cope with cases like this one. Decision theory is a sort of calculus to find the rational action given one's beliefs and desires (in technical terms, subjective probabilities and utilities). In this way, it views human action from a subpersonal standpoint. Nevertheless, decision theory lacks the resources to account for a (more or less) radical change in one's beliefs and desires. In particular, in treating beliefs and desires as separate modules, it is unable to make sense of a situation like ours, where new beliefs, especially beliefs about oneself, seem to change the structure of purpose and desire. Moreover, in assuming a principle of rationality as maximization of benefits, it renders as irrational actions that bring about self-destruction: martyrdom, as in our case, but also any sort of heroism.

That decision theory is insufficient as an action theory has been severely noted. Elster (1983), for example, documents different situations in which we find "interferences" between beliefs and desires (having a certain desire prevents one from having a certain belief, or the acknowledgement of the impossibility to satisfy a certain desire causing one to change one's desire—this is the "sour grapes"-type, which gives name to the book). Other problematic cases include moral conflicts (Jackson 1985), where different options seem to be equally rational; weakness of the will (Audi 1979; Mele 1983), where one does the converse of what one intends; and, in general, what has to do with motivation to act (Thalberg 1985). Besides, in recent years some authors have stressed the role of emotions in intentional action (Cooper 1987; de Sousa 1987).

What is needed, then, is to understand the especificity of reasons as causes. The subpersonal, functional approach treats mental states as states directly relevant to the production of action. Our view, on the contrary, is that mental states become causes of action insofar as they are taken as causes by the agent, that is, insofar as the agent is committed to those intentional states. We still need to account for this "taken as" relation, but this approach, if successful, shows how intentional states, by virtue of being intentional, can be causally relevant. Without abandoning belief-desire talk, we take into account how they are integrated by the agent.

Thus, in our story, there is a change in one's values, in one's moral identity, and consequently, in one's desiderative structure, in one's goals. This change has to be explained in terms of how one thinks of himself and of goodness. To understand it, then, we need to consider how the person integrates her different experiences and intentional states and commits herself to action. All this points out the most distinctive feature of human action: its flexibility, its changeability, its being removed from environmental control. In fact, it is just when such behavioral flexibility is present that an intentional explanation is required. What psychological structure makes this flexibility and adaptibility possible is what is unclear. Our proposal will be that it is the outcome of a personal level of psychological organization that arises as a way to deal with the requirements of a very specific social setting by taking advantage of some of the cognitive resources available.

But our example also illustrates another phenomenon characteristically personal, that is, our tendency to give reasons for what we decide and do—whether they coincide or not with the valid intentional explanation. It is in this context that the appeal to the mystic experience and the appearance of the Virgin makes sense. Lulio needed to explain, not only to others but also to himself, the reason for his change. It seems to me that we are doing that all the time. We need to be consistent, in some unspecified sense, and normal. If you do not accept the constraints for this normativity, you have to give powerful reasons—powerful in the sense of acceptable. Otherwise, you are seen as a fool. Lulio's change was a very radical one, and therefore a very powerful reason should be the cause. A religious appearance provided such a reason. Not just anything would have sufficed.

Here we find a second component of our personal level: a social dimension. The capacity to set our goals and preferences is now constrained by the social context in which these goals and preferences are carried out. The behavioral flexibility that our functional organization at the personal level allows us is bound by the institutionalized practices and values. And, in some way, we make sense of our behavior and decisions in terms of what is socially acceptable.

Sometimes, this necessity leads to confabulation, to telling stories which are not true but which render our behavior reasonable and intelligible. They are not exactly lies, though they are untrue, because there is no intention to induce false beliefs in others. These kinds of stories have been detected in introspection reports (about problem-solving strategies, Nisbett and Wilson 1977), and in autobiographical memories (Rubin 1986). But they do not always need to be false. Our behavior often is the result of a deliberative process, of weighting and pondering preferences and values. The connection between action and justification is then apparent to us. What is important is to realize the pressure to make sense of our deeds, past and present, to be accountable for them, in terms acceptable by the community with which we interact. There is a structural reason for that. Our behavioral plasticity entails that the nature of an action depends on the intention with which it is done; if we do not want to be responsible for some behavior, we'd better have some good story to tell. And what makes a good story good (that is, convincing) is socially relative.

That does not mean that the individual values are different from the social values and that stories are always excuses. What we are claiming is that the individual values are social values, internalized in some way, and that the person needs them in order to understand herself as an individual. Of course you may try to cheat on your reasons, especially if you are on trial, but even then this social dimension can become explicit through remorse and regret.

Thus, we can say that the personal level includes those phenomena that involve the system as a self-centered point of view, that assume an identity. In particular, our story has shown the individual as agent, both in the goal-setting component and in the justificative component. And we have tried to show the social dimension of this personal level and its irreducibility to subpersonal components.

Unfortunately, though, when these phenomena are acknowledged, they are dealt with either in purely functional terms (Dennett 1978) or in exclusively social ones (Harré 1984). The former lack the capacity to understand how human action is shaped by the social context in which it takes place. The latter overlooks the nature of computational mechanisms that sustain and distinguish our psychological features, in comparison to other social beings. A way to understand the interaction of these two axes of persons is our goal.

However, it is likely that not every cognitive and social trait is relevant to the constitution of a personal level. We have to make our hypothesis more precise. The idea we will explore is that the meta-representational capacity made available by language acquisition, plus the primacy of the social context for human infants, favors the appearance of an individuality structure, a self-centered point of view, a unified level of behavioral management (all these expressions are equally metaphorical, at this point).

Challenging the Methodological Assumptions

What I am suggesting is that we should think of a level of psychological organization that arises as a consequence of the context in which our cognitive resources are put to use (i.e., a social context). What distinguishes this level of organization is the capacity to access and manage our representations, thus making possible a new sort of mental phenomena. In other words, personal phenomena rely on a nonlearned, nonmaturational, functional organization. Before we can proceed, though, we need to examine the viability of such a suggestion. That is important because one of the characteristic methodological assumptions in cognitive science and AI has been the adoption of a fixed picture of the computational resources available to a system in a certain domain. In terms of Pylyshyn (1983, 1985), it has been assumed that the functional architecture of the virtual machine is given from the beginning and, accordingly, that the results of applying the test for cognitive penetrability at different moments will always be the same.

Now, there are several reasons that can have played a role in making such an assumption welcome. Parsimony, for instance. An account of a cognitive capacity which postulates no change in the functional architecture is more parsimonious than one that hypothesizes changes, given that they explain the same phenomena. The modular approach to the diverse cognitive competences, and a consequent disregard for the systematic global functioning, can also be relevant in this context. Finally, the grip of functionalism with its stress in functional aspects over the structural ones can also have been influential.

The outcome has been a continuist approach to computational architecture, even in developmental psychology, one that attributes to children the same kind of functional resources required to account for adult competences (see Pinker 1984, as an example).

It is important to notice that it is not the lack of interest in learning or developmental aspects of cognitive capacities we are talking about; in fact, the last decade has experienced a boom in conceptual and linguistic development (Carey 1985; Keil 1989; Pinker 1989). The irruption and fast spread of connectionism, furthermore, has provided new technical and conceptual (though polemical) apparatus to deal with these phenomena. Neither is it the current ignorance of how the maturational processes that the neural structures undergo affect the computational resources available to the system at a cognitive level (Changeux 1986). Our point is that, in assuming that the functional architecture does not change through cognitive development, the picture is that of a process of quantitative change from an initial state which includes all the "constraints" and computational resources required to reach the adult competence.

Our modest aim here is not to challenge this assumption in the domains in which it has been put into use. Rather, our concern is to undermine its universal validity. Thus, it will be claimed that, as a result of certain cognitive achievements in development and of the reorganization of the system to which these achievements give rise, new cognitive resources become available. In particular, our model claims that the acquisition of language is the key process to such a qualitative change, its effects being enriched representational powers, in the form of meta-representation, and, as a consequence, accessibility to our information structures. This achievement is what allows us to deal more effectively with the requirements of the social context in which we behave, through a personal organization.

There is, nevertheless, a principled objection against the possibility of such new level of organization, beyond mere methodological considerations. In his ongoing criticism of empiricist approaches to the mind, Jerry Fodor has argued against the possibility of qualitative changes in cognitive development. His argument relies on the premise that the progression from a stage of cognitive organization to a qualitatively different one can be accomplished solely by the cognitive mechanisms existing at the earlier stage (Fodor 1975), and therefore, no real enrichment is ever possible.

The answer to this argument consists in pointing out that Fodor succeeds in excluding the possibility of different stages of cognitive organization only if it is assumed that the transition from one stage to the next is achieved through a learning process. Fodor's premise is cashed out in terms of formation and testing of hypothesis as the unique cognitive mechanism available; and this requires one to already have the conceptual resources characteristic of the next stage in order to formulate the relevant hypothesis, thus preventing real qualitative change. What we will have to show is that the developmental transformation in representational powers introduced by language we are proposing need not rely on such a mechanism, but is rather a by-product of language learning. Language becomes an instrument for conceptual reorganization.

An analogy can make the point clearer. The visual capacities required to see through a microscope are just the normal ones, but the visual information available (the distal stimulus) is quite different. It is not that the instrument modifies our visual capacities; it is rather that its use makes available new kinds of information. Similarly, new representational capacities are made available by language, without any transformation required for our learning mechanisms.

Furthermore, not only is the innatist argument weak, it is also misguided from an evolutionary point of view. In claiming that our functional organization is fixed from the beginning, it assumes that is the outcome of a selective process. There are reasons to believe that such possibility is not an evolutionary stable strategy, that is, is not a good solution to the problem of cognition. Putting everything into the genes is not advantageous because it results in rigidity and greater difficulties in adapting to novel situations. This point, so obviously undisputed as regards knowledge, applies equally to functional mechanisms. Being able to improve one's innate mechanisms is a powerful tool of adaptive behavior—it makes possible greater flexibility and plasticity. In fact, human development's most distinctive feature is plasticity (Lerner 1984).

Linguistic Cognitive Systems

That language influences our cognitive capabilities is not, unfortunately, a commonplace idea in cognitive science. Maybe this situation is the upshot of the rejection of the multi-staged Piagetian views of psychological development and the success of the formal-modular Chomskyan approach in linguistics. But in no way is it implied by this success. Even the truth of the modularity thesis as regards language comprehension and production (Fodor 1983) does not prevent language from being influential in the nature of our conceptual representations, through the lexico-semantic level.

As a matter of fact, conceptual and lexical development are not separate processes, though they are different (Macnamara 1982; Markman 1989). At a first stage, you just find conceptual development, which probably is a precondition for lexical acquisition. But after that moment, most concepts are learned first lexically. Language, on the other hand, provides ways to represent arbitrary categories, by means of adjectives, for instance, which permit subtler discriminations among the members of a natural class.

This capability to represent in a finer-grained way that distinguishes language goes beyond the mere distinction noun-adjective (or for that matter, verbs). These categories broadly correspond to semantic ones. What is essential for linguistic representation is the whole bunch of grammatical categories (pronouns, modifiers, possessives, conjunctions, prepositions, …), which allow reference to absent objects, counterfactual states of affairs, temporally displaced situations, etc. Most importantly, these features constitute the grounds for recursion, the ability to embed sentences and thus express very complex ideas. That is why it has been claimed that only the thoughts of linguistic beings exhibit intensionality (Emmett 1989), that is, the failure of substitutivity of equivalent expressions, since only linguistic representation supplies the means for different representations of the same object (or situation).

The idea here is that as soon as we consider language not just as a system of communication but also as a representational system, its effects on our representational capacities become apparent. Moreover, its influence is a matter of not just representational structures, but functional as well, especially as regards cognitive control. Thus it has been claimed that language is involved in analogic reasoning (Goswami 1991; Premack 1988), or in reasoning generally (Margolis 1987); in behavioral control as in "egocentric speech," (Vygotsky 1962); in meta-memory (Flavell and Wellman 1977). The common idea behind all these cases is that it facilitates access to the relevant pieces of information.

Although it is still difficult to make a conclusive case for the essential contribution of language to our mental life, a recent survey of the situations in which thought occurs without language (Weiskrantz 1988), that is, prelinguistic children, apes, and pathological cases due to neural injuries, seems to suggest an important qualitative difference in competences. Moreover, other cases of thought without language point in the same direction. Thus, as regards early hominids, the interpretation of archaelogical and fossil evidence. in terms of symbolic behavior does not go very far (Chase and Dibble 1987). And deaf people who have not been able to develop any sort of gestural language are mentally retarded (Sacks 1989).

So the question now is this: in virtue of what does linguistic representation make possible informational access and control? The answer to this question, as we see it, is that linguistic representation gives rise to meta-representation, that is, new representational structures whose contents refer to what can be called "primary" cognitive states (Leslie 1984) because of their immediacy, context-dependency, and forceful character upon the subject. Thus, the behavior of a meta-representational cognitive system is not necessarily the outcome of the processing of the input according to the normal procedure (or function); but, in being able to represent to itself the procedure usually used in such a situation, the system is able to manipulate it, or to apply it in a different sequence, or even to put it to work in a different, maybe new, situation. The outcome is greater behavioral flexibility, new alternative paths to behavior. And consequently, the need to have a way to choose among them.

A couple of examples can help make clear what is intended here. Karmiloff-Smith (1990) examined the schemas children use to draw familiar objects (houses, people, animals) to assess their structure and rigidity. Her strategy consisted in asking the children to draw objects that do not exist. This way, the strength of the representational constraints on their normal drawing procedures was tested. The results show an interesting developmental pattern of representational change in terms of the nature of the modifications children are capable of in coping with the task. While younger children deleted elements and changed the size and shape, older ones modified position and orientation and introduced elements from different conceptual categories. This difference suggests a change from "internal representations specified as a sequentially fixed list, embodying a constraint that was inherent in the earlier procedural representations, to internal representations specified as a structured, yet flexibly ordered set of manipulable features" (p. 57). She claims that this pattern of development is not restricted just to drawing but to any representational structure that involves sequenciality: counting, music, phonological awareness.

It seems as if only when we can represent to ourselves how we solve certain sorts of problems, or behave in certain situations, that is, when we are able to represent our own representations, are we in a position not to follow such patterns, or to modify them. Indeed, something like that is what is entailed by the studies in errors, their etiology and the way we cope with them. Different theories have been proposed, but there appears to be certain agreement on distinguishing three levels of cognitive performance: skills, rules, and knowledge; and that errors at each of these three levels of behavioral control take place, with distinctive features. Reason (1988) offers a "state of the art" characterization:

> Errors at the skill-based and rule-based levels arise from misapplied expertise. Those at the knowledge-based level, on the other hand, are due to a lack of expertise. People are forced to resort to knowledge-based processing when they run out of pre-established problem solutions. Here, the errors are much more variable in form, arising as they do from confirmation bias, from bounded ratio-

nality, from 'spillage' out of the limited workspace, and from an incomplete or inaccurate knowledge base. While we may succeed in explaining them retrospectively, the forms taken by such knowledge based mistakes are difficult to specify in advance. All that can be forecast with any confidence is that they will be exceedingly abundant. (pp. 47-48)

What is suggested here is that when we are in a certain kind of problem which we do not have a stereotyped way to deal with, we will have to look for "solutions" among everything we know; that is, we will have to access our different procedures and select what can prove relevant to our present concerns. If we are successful, a new procedure can be added to our repertoire as a result—that is, we will become experts in these kinds of situation.

It is interesting to notice the coincidence between Karmiloff-Smith's model and the model for error. Both distinguish between procedures, rules, and a higher level of representation which consists, precisely, of a representation of our rules and procedures available—which we have called meta-representations. Notice also that it is this higher level of representation that makes possible access and modifiability of our "primary" representations, producing, as a consequence, behavioral flexibility and creativity: the preconditions for action.

Certainly, there is no commitment on the part of these authors to language as the key element in facilitating this development. In fact, Karmiloff-Smith (1986) suggests that qualitative changes took place in human phylogeny that made possible new symbolic representations, and language would be a result of these changes, greatly improving our meta-representational capacity, which is, nevertheless present without language. But, in the absence of language, meta-representation is very limited, never reaching full recursivity, and we have already shown the powerful representational tools language makes available (see also Feldman 1988). The next task is to consider how a personal level is grounded in such a mechanism.

Meta-Representation in a Social Context

So far we have argued that language represents a major change in our cognitive resources by giving rise to meta-representation. Meta-representation involves access to one's own representations, thus permitting a flexible use of our schemas, scripts, or whatever structures we have available. It is clear that not every cognitive mechanism is susceptible to reach meta-representation, and it is this fact that makes credible the modularity thesis. What is not a widespread opinion is that meta-representational mechanisms could be what make instructional learning possible: a new procedure is first taught, then it is practiced, and finally it becomes automatized.

Once the power of this new mechanism is recognized, we are in a position to consider how it facilitates a personal level of organization. A first step in that direction comes from what has been called the "theory of mind." It consists of the ability for intentional interpretation, that is, for viewing one's own and other people's behavior in terms of internal states, of beliefs, desires, and goals. Research in developmental psychology has shed light on the nature of this competence and its developmental stages. Here we do not need be concerned with the details. It will suffice to mention that the pattern of development is one of increased complexity in the structure of intentional states ascribed. Thus, ascription of intentions as the reason for behavior is followed by awareness of the conditions of belief fixation (perceptual conditions), and by the ability to distinguish between what is said and what is meant; after that, the child is able to interpret somebody's behavior in terms of her intention to influence the mental states of another person (intentions to change someone else's intentions), to finally interpret the attributed representations themselves.

It is not especially contentious to claim that it is through this process that we come to think of ourselves as agents, as a unified center of intentions and action. In acting, a coherent treatment of our current states must be done, so that the best course is followed. The notion of meta-representation developed in the previous section is useful here to make sense not only of the representational structure of these "intentions about intentions" (Leslie 1984), but also of the possibility to access and weight our reasons and decide what is appropriate in a given situation. The upshot would be a unified structure of understanding and action.

A whole understanding of this structure, however, cannot be reached if we do not take into account the aspects of moral development. Or better, intentions and behaviors are not neutral, but morally charged. Although research in both areas seems to run "modularly," an understanding of children's development must make sense of changes that take place simultaneously. There are "good" and "bad" intentions and behaviors for the child, right from the start. Its development consists precisely in changes in what is good and bad. Unfortunately, this field of study has been dominated by the highly intellectualistic approach of Kohlberg (1984), though recent studies turn to a more behavioral study of moral development (Kagan and Lamb 1987). What is missing is the connection with the intentional concepts that make moral concepts possible (and probably necessary as well; see next section).

A first level of intentional interpretation (or theory of 'self-propelled objects,' as Premack 1988, has put it), involving propioceptive monitoring and self-recognition (Crook 1985; Gallup 1972), and probably linked to other innate mechanisms of social cognition, such as face recognition (Sergent 1988), can be found in apes (Byrne and Whiten 1988; Premack and Woodruff 1978) as well as prelinguistic children (Lewis and Brooks-Gunn 1979). Our contention here is that language, in giving rise to meta-representation, makes as well possible a more powerful unifying structure, or self.

This follows from the very nature of meta-representation. It requires a way for subject-reference, that is, for distinguishing my beliefs and intentions from the attitudes I am attributing to others. That linguistic indexicals provide such a mechanism can barely be disputed. The idea here is that to learn to use this symbolic system, a propioceptive awareness is enough, while once acquired, the system becomes able to represent to itself the relations and attitudes that entertains.

But this self-structure has important functional consequences. It does not substitute any basic mechanism, of course—it supervenes on them—but it works as an organizational principle for all the phenomena that have to do with flexibility and self-understanding: identity, personality, moral character, self-consciousness, introspection, in fact, all those aspects that have to do with the social context. For some evolutionary reason that we will try to clarify in the next section, our groupal organization favors for development of a unified and integrated perspective in meta-representation. Thus, it filters disturbing experiences, eliminates dissonances, selects memories, organizes feelings and emotions, determines good reasons for action, and sets the goals.

Maybe the best way to make clear the role this structure plays is to see what happens when it is impaired, as in the Multiple Personality Disorder (Humphrey and Dennett 1989). What characterizes this disputed syndrome is different personal structures in a unique individual. Different selves seem to be "in charge" at different moments. And each is characteristically different: in emotions, in personal memories, in goals, and even in the way of talking. What seems to happen is that a trauma from early childhood prevented the development of a unified understanding of oneself—that event being impossible to reconcile with the rest.

How are we to make sense of this structure? Here, a notion of "self" suggests itself. But there is no commitment to a substantialist conception of the self, rather the converse. Our approach tries to show how a unified self-conception arises out of cognitive resources available given certain social requirements. Dennett's (1988) idea of the self as a "speaker" or "narrator" for the mind seems suggestive in this context. But there is one important remark to make: this "narrator" is not just an epiphenomenon but plays an important, though restricted, causal role. Think, for instance, of memory. The fact that we speak of autobiographical memory means that there are some workings of our memory that cannot be fully explained in terms of properties of the organization of memory alone. The personal context in which memories take place results in some of them being available, some others being specially relevant, and even some events not being recalled at all. The self as "narrator," then, should be conceived, from a functional point of view, as a center of regulation and consistency of mental activity.

In summary, the view we have been favoring starts from the acknowledgement of personal phenomena, to posit a specific mechanism to account for them. This mechanism is required by the complex social setting in which behavior takes place and takes advantage of a particular sort of cognitive achievement, meta-representation—a means of access and manipulation of mental representations. Language figures as the key element in the model, as the condition for meta-representation on the one hand, and for the complexity in social structure on the other. We now need to turn to evolutionary considerations to shed light on this dual role of language.

The Phylogenesis of Persons

We have been claiming that a personal level of psychological organization arises as a developmental response to the challenges posed by the social context in which our cognitive resources are put to work. And we have characterized it as a structure that unifies and gives consistency to the workings of the mind, allowing for flexibility, adaptiveness, and modifiability, in such a way that it yields socially acceptable behavior (rational behavior). In this section, we want to go a little further in defense of this view, but from a different approach. The basic idea is that there are evolutionary reasons that provide independent support to the view that it is social pressures that give rise to new cognitive structures, which in their turn, alter the nature of the social organization.

Imagine, to make clearer what is intended, a group of automata, able to move around and detect which position of the space is to be occupied by whom at the next moment, and to control their own movements. It is likely that they would be able not to bump into each other. This is a very simple case of cognitive (perceptual and motor) abilities mediating simple interactive patterns. The social interrelations are just ones of bumping-avoidance. The moral to draw is that you cannot have complex social relations without sophisticated cognitive capacities. Well, there is an alternative: just to hardwire the patterns of interaction—as in social insects, for instance—but then what you get is a highly hierarchical social system with extremely rigid patterns of behavior.

Another way to make the point is from a cognitive standpoint. An innovation in cognitive resources would produce, in an already social being, a new range of behavioral possibilities, of tools for social coordination. This development is just the kind of event we find at the dawn of Homo sapiens: an enlargement, not only of brain volume, but of neuronal interconnections—the seat, if any, of mentality. No surprise, then, that a new range of behavioral capacities became available, new forms of social organization among them. One of these novelties seems to have been language. If, as we have argued, language in its turn favors a reorganization of our cognitive system, then new possibilities to cope with the social structure can be expected, which in its turn, amount to a qualitative change of the social structure itself. I cannot dare to offer a reconstruction of the evolutionary history that made these changes possible, but I will try to make clear the rationale behind the process.

We have been concerned with the specificity of human action as a distinctive feature of the personal level. In the human case, behavior is not contingent upon the presence of a particular stimulus—at least, not in general. Human behavior is not instinctual, automatized, genetically controlled, but rather open, flexible, adaptive. In fact, that very adaptiveness is what makes human behavior intelligent: in not being stimulus-bound, human behavior can be suitable in novel situations, or in situations without reliable clues.

A hypothesis has been put forward to give reason of the selective pressure that made this phenotypic behavioral plasticity advantageous. According to Brandon and Hornstein (1986), behavioral flexibility is especially useful in a changing environment; by the same token, one could say it is useful in a process of colonization of new, different environments. What is important to notice is that, conceding that behavioral plasticity was the selective outcome of a changing environment, behavioral plasticity, in its turn, entailed a qualitative change in the nature of the social coordination among the members of the group: since behavior was no longer instinctual, automatic, genetically controlled, reliable clues were no longer available for the group to behave upon. A different pattern of interaction was to be found: here is where intentional action appeared. Given that behaviors, calls, or displays were no longer reliable signals (because of their flexibility), or when reliable, they were not compelling (because the behavior was no longer automatized), sense was to be made of such features in terms of the goals of the individuals.

But the goals of the individuals are not to be seen as individualistic or random. Given the ecological niches that the first humans occupied, the survival value of goal-coordination, or, in other words, cooperation is rather obvious. Steele (1989), for example, suggests that the strategy developed to cope with the greater predation risks resulting from bipedalism and terrestriality was to form larger groups. A way to coordinate the potentially flexible behavior of its members was to be found. Here is where social pressures play a role in the constitution of individual goals. The upshot is the appearance of social ritualization.

Ritualization is a concept from ethology that refers to an innate, complex, but rigid, social behavior. Social ritualization, then, refers to a basic form of conventionalization, consisting in nongenetically controlled, standardized, normative behavior, without genetic control. In other words, forms of social organization, presupposing interpretational abilities, arose as stable solutions to the coordination problem within a group (stable in an evolutionary sense). This way, the behavioral indetermination ("what to do in a given situation?")

that stems from the behavioral flexibility and lack of genetic control could be overcome: instead of having to find the best solution for every situation on her own, the child, during the socialization process, acquires the repertoire of conventional social practices instituted in her group. This is what anthropologists call culture. Their normativity, however, is not as compulsory as instinctual behavior, so that changes and improvement can modify the group's conventions.

Once these proto-conventions are in place, individuals become accountable to the group, and hence, a personal structure begins: identity is required in order for the group to avoid cheaters, individuals that benefit from the cooperation but try not to contribute to the costs. Cooperation is based on reciprocal altruism (Cosmides and Tooby 1989; Trivers 1971), and anything that contributes to its success turns out to be evolutionarily adaptive. Language, no doubt instrumental in making possible the level of psychological organization that constitutes personal identity, is clearly functional to this extent. It plays a role in the success of the social organization by providing a way to declare goals, resolve conflicts, negotiate deals and make agreements (Konner 1982) that goes beyond the particular spatio-temporal constrains in which communication takes place.

In the same way that the cognitive reorganization that language makes possible does not eliminate the basic skills and representations, the result of this process was not the absolute elimination of instinctual reactions and propensities. This fact is why we sometimes experience conflicts between what we think we should do and what we do and why different cultures have tried to have them repressed.

We are now in a position to better appreciate the developmental process the child undergoes in her becoming a person and to recognize what is achieved. She comes to develop not only understanding of her social world but also a unified conception of herself as actor within this world, as an individual. She is able to make sense of one's and other's behavior, to predict and explain it, but also to set her own goals, to decide what to do, to take advantage of what she interprets the situation to be—in summary, to see herself as an agent within this world.

Persons in AI

If the argument we have developed is in the right direction, there are some interesting consequences that follow as regards the prospects for Artificial Intelligence models of cognitive competences. As a mode of conclusion, I would like to touch upon them.

a) The claim that computational simulations of cognitive processes are themselves relevantly cognitive relies on the assumption that cognitive processes are computational. What we have said offers no grounds to doubt that; therefore nothing in principle prevents AI from carrying out its goals. Being a person is a matter of developing a distinctive functional organization, one which results from having to interact with other intelligent beings.

b) Computational simulations of personal processes, however, would require taking into account not only the cognitive aspects involved but also the social ones. In other words, the point of a personal level of psychological organization is the need to deal with a particular social setting. Some have even claimed that the whole psychological capacities evolved as a "solution" to the pressures of our social nature (Humphrey 1984). Our, more modest, claim is just that the personal structure is contingent upon such pressures. To put it another way, out of the social setting in which human psychological development takes place, our mental organization would be different; in particular, no personal structuring would develop.

c) In any case, cognitive simulations will have to take into account personal features in cognitive processing if reproduction of human capacities is to be claimed. To this extent, it would be necessary to model needs, criteria of satisfaction, patterns of integration of information, coordination problems, and interpretational capacities. And above all, a unified point of view and of action.

But having gone so far, a different question suggests itself: why artificial persons? Defenders of their possible construction simply assume that what is possible ought to be carried through. But why so? What is the point of building artificial persons, that is, of building persons artificially? Are not there enough people in the world? Notice that the idea of having robots for specially difficult missions, or dangerous settings, often appealed to, is of no relevance in this context. It seems obvious to me that if there were artificial persons, they would not undermine their "personality." If people are not to be discriminated against for reasons of race, gender, or nationality, why should they be for reasons of hardware?

Thus, one thing is to acknowledge the possibility of artificial people—what, no doubt, has important implications as regards our self-conception, but maybe not very different from acknowledging our biological heritage—and another, yet to be argued for, is to assume that we should expend our energies and resources building one. Of course, this argument does not apply to the construction of intelligent systems: their usefulness is beyond doubt. But to acknowledge the difference between the status of building persons and cognitive systems is to concede the major point I have been arguing for.

Acknowledgments

I'm specially grateful to Annette Karmiloff-Smith, and the editor's referees, for useful comments that helped me to improve the argument.

This work was made possible by a Fulbright grant from the Spanish Government. My gratitude to the Rutgers Department of Philosophy for its hospitality, and especially to Jerry Fodor for his generous supply of intellectual challenges.

Note

1. Parts of this work were presented at the Workshop on Cognitive Science, Valencia, Spain, January 1992.

References

Astington, J.W., Harris, P.L., & Olson, D.R. (Eds.). (1988). *Developing Theories of Mind*. Cambridge, MA: Cambridge University Press.

Audi, R. (1979). Weakness of the will and practical judgement. *Nous, 13*, 173-196.

Brandon, R.N. & Hornstein, N. (1986). From icons to symbols: Some speculations on the origins of language. *Biology and Philosophy, 1*, 169-189.

Byrne, R.W. & Whiten, A. (Eds.). (1988). *Machiavellian Intelligence*. Clarendon.

Carey, S. (1985). *Conceptual Change in Childhood*. Cambridge, MA: MIT Press.

Changeux, J.P. (1986). *L'homme neuronal*. Fayard.

Chase, P. G. & Dibble, H.L. (1987). Middle Paleolithic symbolism: A review of current evidence and interpretation. *Journal of Anthropological Archeology, 6*, 263-296.

Cooper, R.M. (1987). *The Structure of Emotions*. Cambridge, MA: Cambridge Univ. Press.

Cosmides, L. & Tooby, J. (1989). Evolutionary psychology and the generation of culture, Part II. Case study: A computational theory of social exchange. *Ethology and Sociobiology, 10*, 51-97.

Crook, J. H. (1985). *The Evolution of Human Consciousness*. New York: Oxford University Press.

De Sousa, R. (1987). *The Rationality of Emotion*. Cambridge, MA: MIT Press.

Dennett, D.C. (1978). *Brainstorms: Philosophical Essays on Mind and Psychology*. Harvester Press.

Dennett, D.C. (1988). Why we are all novelists. *Times Literary Supplement*, Sept. 16-22, pp. 1016, 1029.

Emmett. (1989). Must intentional states be intensional? *Behaviorism, 17*, 129-136.

Elster, J. (1983). *Sour Grapes*. Cambridge, MA: Cambridge University Press.

Feldman, C.F. (1988). Early forms of thought about thoughts. In J.W. Astington, P.L. Harris, & D.R. Olson (Eds.), *Developing Theories of Mind*. Cambridge, MA: Cambridge University Press.

Flavell, J. & Wellman, H. (1977). Metamemory. In R. Kail & J. Hagan (Eds.), *Perspectives on the Development of Memory and Cognition*. L. Erlbaum.

Fodor, J. (1975). *The Language of Thought*. Crowell.

Fodor, J. (1981). *Re-Presentations*. Cambridge, MA: MIT Press.

Fodor, J. (1983). *The Modularity of Mind*. Cambridge, MA: MIT Press.

Gallup, G. (1972). Self-recognition in primates. *American Psychologist, 32*, 329-338.

Goswami, U. (1991). Analogical reasoning: What develops? A review of research and theory. *Child Development, 62,* 1-22.

Harré, R. (1984). *Personal Being.* Harvard University Press.

Harré, R. (1987). Persons and selves. In A. Peacocke & G. Gillet (Eds.), *Persons and Personality.* B. Blackwell.

Humphrey, N. (1984). *Consciousness Regained.* New York: Oxford University Press.

Humphrey, N. & Dennett, D. (1989). Speaking for ourselves: An assessment of multiple personality disorder. *Raritan IX,* No. 1 (pp. 68-98).

Jackson, F. (1985). Davidson on moral conflict. In E. LePoré & B. McLaughlin (Eds.), *Actions and Events.* B. Blackwell.

Kagan, J. & Lamb, S. (1987). *The Emergence of Morality in Young Children.* The University of Chicago Press.

Karmiloff-Smith, A. (1986). From meta-processes to conscious access: Evidence from children's metalinguistic and repair data. *Cognition, 23,* 95-147.

Karmiloff-Smith, A. (1990). Constraints on representational change: Evidence from children's drawing. *Cognition, 34,* 57-83.

Keil, F. (1989). *Concepts, Kinds and Cognitive Development.* Cambridge, MA: MIT Press.

Kohlberg (1984). *Essays on Moral Development.* Harper & Row.

Konner, M. (1982). *The Tangled Wing.* Harper.

LePoré, E. & McLaughlin, B. (Eds.). (1985). *Actions and Events.* B. Blackwell.

Leslie, A. (1984). The origins of 'Theory of Mind'. *Psychological Review, 94,* 412-426.

Lewis, M. & Brooks-Gunn, J. (1979). *Social Cognition and the Acquisition of Self.* Plenum.

Macnamara, J. (1982). *Names for Things: A Study of Human Learning.* Cambridge, MA: MIT Press.

Margolis, H. (1987). *Patterns, Thinking and Cognition.* The University of Chicago Press.

Markman, E. (1989). *Categorization and Naming in Children.* Cambridge, MA: MIT Press.

Mehler, J. & Fox, R. (Eds.). (1985). *Neonate Cognition.* L. Erlbaum.

Mele, A. (1983). Akrasia, reasons and causes. *Philosophical Studies, 44,* 345-368.

Nisbett, R. & Wilson, T. (1977). Telling more than we can know: Verbal reports on mental processes. *Psychological Review, 84,* 231-259.

Olson, D.R. (1988). On the origins of beliefs and other intentional states in children. In J.W. Astington, P.L. Harris, & D.R. Olson (Eds.), *Developing Theories of Mind.* Cambridge, MA: Cambridge University Press.

Pinker, S. (1984). *Language Learnability and Language Development.* Harvard University Press.

Pinker, S. (1989). *Learnability and Cognition.* Cambridge, MA: MIT Press.

Pollock, J. (1989). *How to build a person .* Cambridge, MA: MIT Press.

Premack, D. (1988). Mind with and without language. In L. Weiskrantz (Ed.), *Thought Without Language.* Clarendon Press.

Premack, D. (1990). The infant's theory of self-propelled objects. *Cognition, 36,* 1-16.

Premack, D. & Woodruff. (1978). Does the chimpanzee have a theory of mind? *Behavioral and Brain Sciences, 1,* 515-526.

Pylyshyn, Z. (1983). *Computation and Cognition.* Cambridge, MA: MIT Press.

Pylyshyn, Z. (1985). Plasticity and invariance in cognitive development. In J. Mehler & R. Fox (Eds.), *Neonate Cognition*. L. Erlbaum.

Reason, J.T. (1988). Framework models of human performance and error: A consumer guide. In L.P. Goodstein, H.B. Andersen & S.E. Olsen (Eds.), *Tasks, Errors and Mental Models*. London: Taylor & Francis.

Rubin, D. (1986). *Autobiographical Memory.* Cambridge, MA: Cambridge University Press.

Sacks, O. (1989). *Seeing Voices*. University of California Press.

Sergent, J. (1988). Face perception and the right hemisphere. In L. Weiskrantz (Ed.), *Thought Without Language*. Clarendon Press.

Steele, J. (1989). Hominid evolution and primate social cognition. *Journal of Human Evolution, 18,* 421-432.

Thalberg, I. (1985). Questions about motivational strength. In E. LePoré & B. McLaughlin (Eds.), Actions and Events. B. Blackwell.

Trivers, R. (1971). The evolution of reciprocal altruism. Quarterly Review of Biology, 46, 35-57.

Vygotsky, L. (1962). *Thought and Language*. Cambridge, MA: MIT Press.

Weiskrantz, L. (Ed.). (1988). *Thought Without Language*. Clarendon Press.

6 Could, How Could We Tell if, and Why Should— Androids Have Inner Lives?

Selmer Bringsjord

I've been rabidly interested for a good long while in the general three-part question which gives this chapter its title. And, to make explicit the depressing fact that each of the parts in this query gives rise to a *series* of related and no less recalcitrant questions, I've been preoccupied with this maddening morass:

↓		
COULD?	HOW TELL?	SHOULD?
(Q1) Could androids be conscious?	(Q2) How could we tell if androids have inner lives?	(Q3) Why should androids have inner lives?
(Q1′) Could androids have inner lives?	(Q2′) Will the Turing test provide us with the means for telling whether an android has an inner life?	(Q3′) Might there be some practical reason why AI researchers might attempt to build an android which has an inner life?
(Q1″) Is there something it's like to be an android?	(Q2″) Will the Total Turing test provide us with the means for telling whether an android has an inner life?	(Q3″) Might there be some practical reason why AI researchers ought to build a "qualia-possessing" robot?
(Q1‴) Suppose that «f», a formula in some symbol system[1] that has been designed by a human programmer P for an android A, is to mean f for A. Can «f» mean f not only for P but also for A? ⋮	(Q2‴) Will the Total Total Turing test provide us with the means for telling whether an android has an inner life? ⋮	(Q3‴) Might there be some practical reason why AI researchers ought to take seriously the notion of "having a point of view"? ⋮

There is of course a question perhaps more fundamental than, and prior to, the title of this chapter, namely,

Can we build androids?

To this question I'm inclined to answer in the affirmative. Indeed, I have no doubt whatsoever that androids are coming and that I can play a (decidedly small) role in bringing them on stage. With respect to the COULD? category, however, I have burned more than a few of my grey cells in producing a book-length case (Bringsjord 1992a) in favor of a negative view—a view according to which, for example, androids will necessarily lack a Nagelian inner life.[2] With regard to the SHOULD? category, I have argued elsewhere[3] that (Q3‴) should be answered in the affirmative; from the standpoint of story generation within AI, there is in fact a good *practical* reason for taking seriously the general notion of having, and the specific notion of a *machine* having, a point of view. In this chapter, I set myself the task of tackling the TELL IF? category; specifically, I'll address below the questions bolded in the above table. I shall argue that the Turing test, and for that matter all known variations on the Turing test (including a fascinating one which appeals to machines more powerful than Turing machines), are inadequate. While there may arrive some promising, as-yet-to-be-devised Turingish test, I think it's *plausible* to hold that if I make my case herein, there simply doesn't *exist* a concrete test of the sort which would gladden the hearts of empiricists like Turing.

Formal Background

I assume, on the part of the reader, familiarity with standard elementary recursion theory—naïve set theory, string theory, the standard automata hierarchy [from finite automata to Turing machines (TMs)].[4]

Though what TMs can *do* defines the class of computable functions (the μ-recursive functions), for this chapter (for reasons seen below) it's more important to know what they *can't* do. One well-known function TMs can't compute is the *full halting problem:* We write $M_P\colon u \to \infty$ to indicate that machine, or automaton, M goes from input u through a computation, directed by procedure P, that never halts. We write $M_P\colon u \to halt$ when machine M, directed by P, goes from input u to a computation that does halt. We can also harmlessly suppress mention of inputs and talk only of machines halting or not halting *simpliciter*. Furthermore, let the traditional property of decidability be handled by way of the symbols Y ("yes") and N ("no"). Finally, let $n^{M,P}$ be the Gödel number of pair machine M and program P. The full halting problem is classically unsolvable, that is, when, again, the machines we're talking about are Turing machines, and P and P^* are programs, there is no machine-program pair M, P such that for every pair M^*, P^*:

$$M_P\colon n^{M^*,P^*} \to Y \text{ iff } M^*_{P^*} \text{ halts}$$

$$M_P\colon n^{M^*,P^*} \to N \text{ iff } M^*_{P^*} \text{ doesn't halt}$$

The Argument From Serendipity

The original answer to (Q2), of course, is "By employing the Turing test (TT)."

TT, as most readers will doubtless recall, is based on the imitation game, and its players are a human, an android,[5] and another human playing the role of judge. The judge can send in questions via teletype to the human and the android, who are shielded from the judge's view, in an attempt to ascertain which is the human and which is the android. [For a discussion of the first bona fide playing of something close to TT, see Epstein (1992).]

Turing holds that if the android can fool the judge, then the android is to be declared a thinking (= inner-life-possessing, conscious...) agent. More precisely, Turing's position (Figure 1) is apparently summed up by the bold proposition that

(TT-P) If an android A passes the Turing Test, then A is conscious (= thinks, ...).

I anticipate specific resistance to this encapsulation of Turing's position. Some will say that (TT-P)'s conflation of 'is conscious' with 'thinks' runs counter to a close reading of Turing's seminal "Computing Machinery and Intelligence." For in this chapter (it will be said), Turing very clearly set himself the task of replacing not "Can machines be conscious?" with "Can machines pass TT?" but "Can machines *think*?" with the empiricist "Can machines pass TT?" This is in fact the case. But it should not be overlooked that in this same paper Turing was forced to consider consciousness and did claim that a machine (computer, android, ... see note 5) passing TT would in his book *be* conscious. [Turing said—in my opinion incorrectly—that the alternative was solipsism. See *The Argument from Consciousness* section in Turing (1964).] At any rate, I'm inclined to regard the ultimate epistemological hornet's nest to be *precisely* the question of whether an android can be conscious or have a mind. Those in favor of construing 'thinks' in such a way that it dodges this nest (that is, those in favor of having (TT-P) refer only to 'thinks') are simply dodging the very point of the admittedly difficult enquiry of which this chapter aims to play a part.

Figure 1. Turing Test.

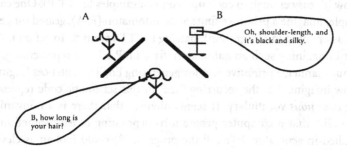

```
(setf *sentence-parts*
  '((NP bill sandy jonah harry ....)
    (DET a the her ....)
    (N consumer man woman hair house school ....)
    (BV is was ....)
    (CNJ and or ....)
    (ADJ happy stupid anxious annoyed euphoric depressed ....)
    (MOD very unbelievably incredibly outrageously ....)
    (ADV often always sometimes ....)))

(setf tt-fsa
  '((Initial (1))
    (Final (9))
    (From 1 to 3 by NP)
    (From 1 to 2 by DET)
    (From 2 to 3 by N)
    (From 3 to 4 by BV)
    (From 4 to 5 by ADV)
    (From 4 to 5 by |#|)
    (From 5 to 6 by DET)
    (From 5 to 8 by |#|)
    (From 6 to 6 by MOD)
    (From 6 to 7 by ADJ)
    (From 7 to 9 by N)
    (From 8 to 8 by MOD)
    (From 8 to 9 by ADJ)
    (From 9 to 4 by CNJ)
    (From 9 to 1 by CNJ)))
```

Figure 2. LISP schema representing a primitive FSA for generating English sentences.

Is (TT-P) tenable? Apparently not. In order to see this, start by assuming that "passing the TT" is fleshed out to include explicit parameters (e.g., the judge must be fooled n% of the time, must be fooled for m minutes, ...) for π. Now it's easy enough to cook up counter-examples to (TT-P). One can, for example, imagine a primitive finite state automaton (FSA), geared for generation (as opposed to recognition), passing the TT within π. To get on the road toward imagining such an automaton, fix a LISP schema representing, in an obvious manner, a primitive FSA for generating English sentences (Figure 2).

Now imagine that the recurring "...." in this schematic code represents a truly *enormous* vocabulary. It seems obvious that there is a nonvanishing probability that *a* computer program incorporating *at least* something like this filled-in generator (let's call the program $\mathcal{P}$) could fool an as-clever-as-you-like human judge within π. I agree, of course, that it's wildly improbable that $\mathcal{P}$ would fool the judge—but it is *possible*. And since such a "lucky" case is one in which (TT-P)'s antecedent is true while its consequent is apparently false, we have a counter-example.[6]

There is, of course, a longer and rather more famous (or infamous) attack on TT in the literature, *viz.* Searle's (1980) Chinese Room Argument (CRA), which (as most readers will know) appeals to a thought-experiment involving a monolingual speaker of English (Searle himself, perhaps) who is placed inside a box having two small openings, one for paper to be given in and one for paper to be given out. Written upon the paper coming in are various kinds of squiggle-squoggles (that bear no similarity to the kinds of inscriptions used by native speakers of English to communicate in English). Searle has certain instructions in English for which squiggle-squoggles to send out when certain other squiggle-squoggles are taken in. Searle-in-the-box gets very good at manipulating the squiggle-squoggles. Whenever an outside-the-box-person (= outsider) sends in "!@#$%^," Searle-in-the-box quickly outputs the appropriate string, "+_)(*," say. The catch is that these mysterious strings are actually expressions in Chinese, and the outsiders are native Chinese speakers. Searle-in-the-box becomes so adroit at doing his thing that the outsiders cannot distinguish the linguistic behavior of the box from that of a fellow Chinese speaker. And his argument, tied to our concern with TT and confessedly compressed, is that here we have a case where TT is passed (in Chinese) but where no real understanding or consciousness (apart from that involved in following the English instructions) is present.

I don't think Searle's argument is sound (as it stands, anyway[7]), but present purposes (for reasons that will become clear) are best served by assuming for the sake of argument that it *is*. We will return to the Searlean attack on TT later on; let's now return to my own simpler attack on TT, and specifically to responses to it. I'm aware of six general rebuttals to the sort of counter-example I have given against TT. I will consider each rebuttal in turn and attempt to show that each is unsuccessful.

Rebuttals

Rebuttal 1: Biting the Bullet. The first rebuttal is one I have encountered recently from a few students in computer science with whom (among others) I have verbally shared a compressed version of the above attack on TT: "Though it may be hard to swallow, in the thought-experiment you describe there simply *is* a conscious computer-based entity, namely that thing which runs your $\mathcal{P}$ and passes TT." To some degree I fear that this reply commits the fallacy *petitio principii*, but I'm willing to forego that line of counter-attack in favor of a short but apparently powerful counter-argument which trades on the fact that $\mathscr{P}$ is within the reach of LISP novices:

(1)   If Rebuttal 1 is sound, then programs written today in introductory AI courses by first-time LISP users are sufficient for AI's grandest dreams.

(2)   It is not the case that programs written today in introductory AI courses by first-time LISP users are sufficient for AI's grandest dreams.

∴ (3)   Rebuttal 1 is unsound.

Rebuttal 2: The Appeal to Dennett's Intentional Stance. The second rebuttal on behalf of Turing and his TT centers around an appeal to Dennett's (1971) so-called "intentional stance" adopted when beliefs and desires (etc.) are ascribed to inanimate objects:

> Lingering doubts about whether the chess-playing computer *really* has beliefs and desires are misplaced; for the definition of the intentional systems I have given does not say that intentional systems *really* have beliefs and desires, but that one can explain and predict their behavior by *ascribing* beliefs and desires to them.... The decision to adopt the strategy is pragmatic, and is not intrinsically right or wrong. (pp. 224-225)

How can Dennett's doctrine figure in a defense of TT? Perhaps a defender of TT might Dennettishly say in response to the counter-example I've given that we should adopt the intentional stance toward the android in question, thereby dropping the question of whether this android *is* conscious in favor of simply *regarding* it to be conscious.[8]

I find this Dennettish position profoundly unsatisfactory, for reasons that others have ably expressed (e.g., Fetzer 1990, pp. 14-15). Dennett seems to me to be simply ignoring the question that gets the HOW TELL? category going (recall our table from above), that is, he's ignoring

(Q2)   How could we tell if androids have inner lives?

And it thus comes as no surprise that Dennett is also simply ignoring

(Q2′)   Will the Turing test provide us with the means for telling whether an android has an inner life?

Is this a good defense of TT? I don't think so. Ignorance may be bliss, but it doesn't scare off arguments. Dennett's position amounts, at bottom, to a refusal to answer the questions with which we are concerned! TT, according to Dennett, isn't even a *candidate* for telling whether an android is conscious. One can see this without getting bogged down in the niceties of Dennett's ploy, because for sheerly logical reasons Dennett's view doesn't have the form required for a formidable rebuttal: Dennett's practical technique for making predictions, his intentional stance, entails neither (TT-P) nor the negation of any premise in my attack on (TT-P).

Rebuttal 3: The Appeal to Counterfactuals. Perhaps a more cogent rebuttal in defense of TT can be derived from the notion of a counterfactual. Here's how this rebuttal might run against me: "The counter-example against (TT-P) involves, by your own admission, a fluke or accident—a fluke in which your program $\mathcal{P}$ turns out to enable the android in question to pass TT. But surely what a proponent of AI and TT would hold is that not only must TT be passed on some particular occasion, but also that the test must be such that *had it been run in other circumstances at other times, it would also be passed.* Only if these counterfactual conditions are met should we say that something passes TT. Since these conditions are *not* met in your purported counter-example, the position you attack remains intact."

Is this rebuttal successful? Before answering this question, we must be at least somewhat clear about what account of counterfactuals this reply is employing. Suppose, accordingly, that the rebuttal in question employs Lewis' (1973) well-known account of counterfactuals. According to this account, roughly, some counterfactual $\phi \Rightarrow \psi$ is true at world w iff in all relevantly similar possible worlds w', w'', ..., if ϕ obtains in these worlds, so does ψ. Now, given this account, we can begin to see how Rebuttal 2 is supposed to work. This rebuttal evidently includes a modification of (TT-P), *viz.* something like the counterfactualized

(TT-P′) If an android A passes TT at t in world w, and if A had taken TT in w_1, or w_2 ... (worlds relevantly similar to w), A would have passed, **then** A is conscious (= thinks, ...).

Rebuttal 3 is then completed by adding to it the claim that my counter-example against (TT-P) doesn't work against (TT-P′).

What are we to say about this rebuttal? Does it fare better than its predecessor? I don't think so, and my rationale is really quite simple: My counter-example involves (say) an android A^* passing TT at t^* in world w^*. I have assumed that when TT is passed here, there is a certain causal system, namely A^*, which, when in the confines of TT at t^* in w^*, enters into a complex causal chain which eventuates in the judge having a suitable amount of trouble correctly deciding between human and android. While it's correct to say that this complex causal chain is in some sense improbable, even *wildly* improbable, it *is* nonetheless a causal chain which obtains only because certain physical laws are firmly in place. For this reason, since in all relevantly similar worlds w_1, w_2, ... these laws are also in place (their being in place in these other worlds is, after all, what undergirds traditional counterfactual analyses of causation), it's true to say that in all relevantly similar possible worlds to w^*, A^* will pass. For this reason, (TT-P′) isn't immune to the original counter-example.

Rebuttal 4: Retreat to a Probabilistic TT. "The argument against TT from serendipity seems fundamentally flawed. You argue that TT is inadequate because there is some remote chance a finite automaton could pass it. But Turing can reply that if a system passes TT it's *overwhelmingly probable* that it is conscious."

This rebuttal entails a retreat captured by

(TT-P″) If an android A passes TT, then it's **overwhelmingly probable** that A is conscious (= thinks, ...).

And so the question arises as to whether (TT-P″) is any good. I don't think it is; here's why.

What the thought-experiment at the heart of the argument from serendipity reveals is not, strictly speaking, that some specific, fixed program $\mathcal{P}$ passes TT. It was only to ease exposition that in that argument I presented part of an FSA for generating English sentences, and, likewise, it was only to ease exposition that I said the thought-experiment gave rise to a fixed program. What the experiment really shows is that there exist *any number* of "junky" programs $\mathcal{P}_0$, $\mathcal{P}_1$, ... which pass TT. In other words, the experiment shows that some programs which no one would want to say have the capacity in and of themselves to bring consciousness to the computers which run them *do*, according to Turing's view, have this capacity. I call these programs "junk" programs. The existence of these junk programs should worry the proponent of (TT-P″) because, for all we know now, in the future they may very well be regularly run. Indeed, it's easy enough to envision a future in which all sorts of tricks (jazzed-up "ELIZAs," holograms, typing errors designed to look human-like, randomized sentence generators, etc.) go into the passing of TT and similar tests. If such a future comes to pass, if, that is, TT is routinely passed by elaborate but ingenious tricks, then why would it be said that it's overwhelmingly probable that something passing TT is conscious? In such a future, (TT-P″) would be very implausible, but since the argument from serendipity entails that such a future may very well arrive, (TT-P″) is, at present, suspect. Of course, some will maintain that such a future will not obtain, despite the fact that the argument from serendipity establishes that there are junk programs existing in the abstract. But this rosy prognostication needs a justification, and in particular a justification which doesn't itself simply assume that (TT-P″) is true—and such a justification seems rather hard to come by.

Rebuttal 5: Tinkering with TT. Perhaps a wiser response to my original counter-example is to tinker with TT in such a way as to broaden the abilities required by the android bent on fooling the judge. This route has been taken by Harnad (1989, 1991)[9]: he claims that to its detriment TT involves only "linguistic" behavior and that if you modify TT in such a way that the robot, to pass, must also exhibit sensorimotor behavior on par with that of a human, then you have a valid test for android consciousness. [It's important to note and remember, given what's coming, that Harnad agrees that both

Searle's CRA and the Argument From Serendipity overthrow (TT-P).] Let's follow Harnad and coin the result of this emendation the 'Total Turing Test,' or TTT.

The core of Harnad's position with respect to this test and the inner lives of androids would seem to be

(TTT-P) If an android A passes the TTT within π', then A is
conscious (= thinks, ...).

Harnad (1991), after again admitting that Searle's CRA shoots down TT, claims that TTT surmounts Searle's argument.[10] I have *some* inchoate doubts about whether TTT does, in fact, surmount Searle, but I'm overall inclined to agree with Harnad in this regard. I'm certainly prepared to agree with him herein *for the sake of argument*. For, unfortunately, TTT has another, more serious, problem: *viz.*, it's hard to see how (TTT-P) is immune to counter-examples built out of those which destroy (TT-P). In order to construct such a counter-example, recall our monstrously large, but (in the ladder of computational power) essentially simple, generation program $\mathcal{P}$, intimated by our schematic LISP above. By hypothesis, $\mathcal{P}$ can handle the linguistic or conversational aspects of Harnad's TTT. Now suppose, in addition, that robotics has produced a robot R capable of astonishing sensorimotor capability. That is, R is able to throw a football, dodge a Nolan Ryan-pitched baseball, pick up objects, sit, stand, run, jump, skip, thread a needle, ... and so on. The problem with R, however, is that *it behaves randomly*. It throws a football when it "feels like it," not on demand. R, in fact, is quite dumb: the engineers who built it never gave a second thought to bestowing any "intelligence" upon R. Their aim was simply to build a physical device capable of great feats of physical dexterity, and never, not even for a split second, did they give a thought to infusing R with knowledge in any sense of the word. R, if you like, is a kind of random, new-century court jester: you set it loose and it haphazardly does its sensorimotor dance. Suppose now that the programs which run R are supplemented with $\mathcal{P}$—call this new composite program $\mathcal{P}_R$. Suppose, in fact,

Figure 3. Total Turing Test.

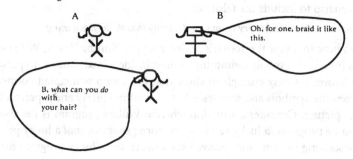

that *as luck would have it*, during the confines of TTT, R's linguistic behavior via $\mathcal{P}_R$ (by virtue of $\mathcal{P}$) coalesces wonderfully with R's sensorimotor behavior. The odds of this are admittedly astronomical, a zillion to one—but it happens: $R + \mathcal{P}_R$ passes the TTT. Here, once again, we seem to have a counter-example: we seem to have a case where (TTT-P)'s antecedent is true while its consequent is false. Pure serendipity, as opposed to anything we'd be inclined to call genuine thought, has seen to it that TTT is passed.

Over the past two years, however, Harnad has come to supplant (TTT-P) with a more circumspect position on Turing Testing (the supplantation has been performed in unpublished exchanges over the Net, often involving others interested in Turing Testing), a position which he believes is immune to the sort of attack I've brought to bear above. The position is

(TTT-P′) If an android A is TTT-indistinguishable from someone with a mind (= someone conscious), one has no nonarbitrary reason for doubting that A has a mind when told that A is a machine.

Unfortunately, it's easy to show that (TTT-P′) is false. In order to do so, we have merely to follow the recipe followed above: conduct a thought-experiment in which (TTT-P′)'s antecedent is true, but its consequent is false. More specifically, begin by supposing that A is T3-indistinguishable from someone with a mind. To make this a bit more vivid, suppose that roboticist Smith escorts an android around with him which is T3-indistinguishable from someone with a mind, but suppose that Smith cloaks this robot in some way (use your imagination) and refers to it as 'Willie.' So, you carry on conversations with Willie for years, *and* you play baseball (and the like) with Willie over the same period of time. Then one day Smith says, "Aha! Watch this!" and he tears off the skin over Willie's forehead, and therein sits a computer busily humming, etc.

So far so good. How do we get the falsity of (TTT-P)'s consequence built into the thought-experiment? That's a piece of cake. Let's begin by reminding ourselves of what we need. We need the Willie scenario to include the falsity of

One has no nonarbitrary reason for doubting that Willie has a mind.

Without loss of generality we can instantiate this statement to me. So we need the scenario to include the falsity of

Selmer has no nonarbitrary reason for doubting that Willie has a mind.

Here's how to adapt the scenario. Selmer says to Smith, "Look, Willie is still just a bunch of symbols swimming around inside a box. There's no person in the picture. It's easy enough to show that there's no principled connection between the symbols and sensors/effectors working nicely and a person being in the picture. Consider a situation wherein Willie's program is (as above) a *composite* program: a lucky random sentence generator *and* a lucky program for processing information received via sensors *and* a lucky program for processing information sent to effectors—all code that's based on technology students master in the first few weeks of Intro. to AI."

The key point is that *though the adapted scenario may not be compelling, it's surely nonarbitrary since it's derived from a scenario which, as Harnad himself agrees, shoots down (TT-P)*. Clearly, by Harnad's own lights, I have a nonarbitrary reason for doubting that Willie has a mind. Hence (TTT-P′) is false.

But is there something beyond TTT? Some test similar in spirit but able to separate the fakers from the thinkers? Yes—or at least such a test is at least mentioned by Harnad (1991, note 2). He calls this new test the Total Total Turing Test (!), or TTTT. In this test, the judge is not only allowed to converse with the android in question and observe the sensorimotor behavior of the android, but is also allowed to "look under the hood."

That is, the judge can very literally look inside the head of the android in order to see if what's there matches up with the neurophysiology (etc.) of the human brain, right down to neurons and even molecules. The idea is that if an android's linguistic and sensorimotor behavior matches our own *and* this android's "brain" neuromolecularly matches our brains, we have a good test for inner life; or, put baldly in the form of our now familiar refrain:

(TTTT-P) If an android A passes the TTTT within π'', then A is conscious
(= thinks, …).

Have we arrived, then, at what Turing was aiming at: a test to gladden the hearts of AI-ish empiricists? I don't think so. And the reason for my pessimism is straightforward. TTTT is chauvinistic in the sense that it runs counter to the fundamental intuitions supporting functionalism, the theory of mind according to which (in its AI guise) consciousness can arise from the correct compu-causal interconnection of physical stuff quite different from human flesh, including, say, a silicon-based substrate. Let's follow Rey (1986) in using the label 'AI-Functionalism' to point toward the very general, vague, all-encompassing functionalist theory of mind that underlies AI.[11] There are evidently many workable versions of AI-Functionalism, that is, many workable versions of what this internal organization must be like: there is the "flow chart functionalism" of Dennett (1978) (Figure 4), the "Turing machine functionalism" of Putnam (1960), the "AI adapted" version of Ramsey's sentence functionalism given by Horgan (1984), Pollock's (1989) "nomic" functionalism, and so on. Given our space constraints, I think we'd be well-advised to try to get by with the following rough formulation of AI-Functionalism:

(AI-F) For every two "brains" x and y, possibly constituted by radically different physical stuff: if the overall flow of information in x and y, represented as a pair of flow charts (or a pair of Turing machines, or a pair of Turing machine diagrams, …), is the same, then if "associated" with x there is an agent s in mental state S, there is an agent s′ "associated" with y which is

Flow Charts

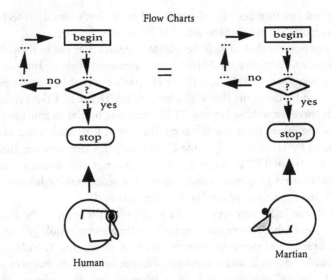

Figure 4. Dennett's "Flow Chart" AI-Functionalism.

also in S.

I have placed the term "brain" in scare quotes because I want to count as a "brain" that complicated, interconnected, thoroughly unfamiliar group of physical objects that might be associated with the mental powers of an extraterrestrial. And I have also placed the term 'associated' in scare quotes, simply because our rough-and-ready version of AI-Functionalism should be neutral on the relation between an agent and an agent's body.[12] So what (AI-F) says, intuitively, is that if you find a flow chart match between human brains and Martian brains, then you can be assured that the human person and the Martian enjoy the same mentality.

The Artificial Intelligentsia, for the most part, does hold that the building of an android, or at least a generally intelligent robot, is to be achieved by programming a computer-with-sensors-and-effectors.[13] Given this, TTTT would for such researchers be unpalatable. For after all, this test seems to suggest that the best route toward building an android is one closely allied with (perhaps even *identical* with) cloning and/or the construction of prosthetic devices.

However, perhaps TTTT's chauvinism is easily repaired: perhaps all we need require in this test is a Dennettish "flow chart" match between the "brains" of players *A* and *B*, not a neuromolecular match. That is, perhaps when the flow of information in the brains of *A* and *B* is brought to the appropriate level of abstraction, we will then be in a position to enquire as to a possible consciousness-implying match.

Is this new test, call it 'TTTT*,' (Figure 5) acceptable? I don't think so, for

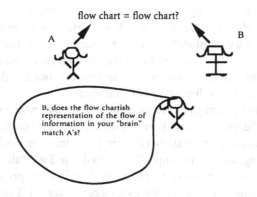

Figure 5. Total Total Turing Test*

two related reasons, one practical, and one abstract and mathematical, both revolving around whether the test here "can" (in some sense) be carried out. (There appear to be other equally serious problems with TTTT*.[14]) The practical reason for not embracing TTTT* is that in going from TT to TTTT* we have gone from Turing's original proposal, a neat, tractable, intuitive game (so neat, tractable and intuitive that the Boston Computer Society managed to conduct a simplified version of it recently; Epstein 1992), to a largely impracticable nightmare. What do I mean? Well, the *impracticability* of TTTT* is easy enough to see with help from another simple thought-experiment. Suppose that a robot or android R^* is touted next year by its creators as being the bearer of consciousness and that these creators are challenged to substantiate their claims. Though, as we have seen, TT is fatally flawed, the creators of R^* nonetheless could, in an attempted defense, administer this test: they could put a computer in one room, put a human in another, put a judge in a third, set up the teletype commlink, and so on. They could just as clearly administer TTT. And just *maybe*, if by next year there is some remarkable breakthrough in brain scanning devices which makes it possible to compare snapshots of brains at the neuronal level, R^*'s creators could administer TTTT. (This is, I readily grant, a *big* maybe.[15]) But what about TTTT*? Can *it* be administered? No. The fact is we wouldn't know how to go about conducting this test. Suppose, for the sake of argument, that R^*'s brain is a connection machine. How would we go about trying to "match" this connection machine with a human brain in order to see if there is correspondence at the correct level of abstraction? I take it that we wouldn't *know* how. At present, we can only dream hollowly of a time when we can scan the low-level computations of radically different computing architectures and thereby determine what high-level algorithms are at work.

Indeed (and this is my second, more abstract, complaint about TTTT*), it's not at all clear that divining the flow charts at work in some low-level computation is a computable process. My worry can be expressed by deploying a fragment of (un)computability theory[16] which I'll now present. This fragment is not only needed at the present juncture, but it will also come into play again later, in our discussion of Rebuttal #6.

I'll introduce this fragment of uncomputability theory in a purely "syntactic" manner. Suppose we have some **totally computable** predicate $S(P, u, n)$ iff $\mathcal{M}_P: u \to$ halts in exactly n steps. (Keep in mind that our machines, *architecturally speaking*, are always simply TMs.) Predicate S is totally computable in the sense that, given some triple (P, u, n), there is some program P^* which, running on some TM $\mathcal{M}^*$, can give us an accurate verdict, Y or N, for whether or not S is true of this triple. (P^* could simply instruct $\mathcal{M}^*$ to simulate $\mathcal{M}$ for n steps and see what happens.) This implies that $S \in \Sigma_0$, the starting point in the Arithmetic Hierarchy, and that S is composed of **totally computable predicates**. But now consider the predicate H, defined by

$$H(P, i) \text{ iff } \exists\, n S(P, i, n).$$

Since the ability to determine for a pair (P, i) whether or not H is true of it, is equivalent to solving the full halting problem, we know that H is not totally computable. Hence $H \notin \Sigma_0$. However, there is a program which, when asked whether or not some TM $\mathcal{M}$ run by P on u halts, will produce Y iff $\mathcal{M}_P: u \to$ halt. For this reason H is **partially computable**, and in Σ_1. To generalize informally, the syntactic representation of the landscape here is

Σ_n set of all predicates definable in terms of totally computable predicates using at most n quantifiers, the first of which is *existential*

Π_n set of all predicates definable in terms of totally computable predicates using at most n quantifiers, the first of which is *universal*

Δ_n $\Sigma_n \cap \Pi_n$

We have, based on this scheme, the Arithmetic *Hierarchy* because, where $\subset$ is proper subset,

$$\Sigma_0 \subset \Sigma_1 \subset \Sigma_2 \ldots$$
$$\Pi_0 \subset \Pi_1 \subset \Pi_2 \ldots$$
$$\text{for every } m > 0, \Sigma_m \neq \Pi_m$$
$$\Pi_m \subset \Sigma_{m+1}$$
$$\Sigma_m \subset \Pi_{m+1}$$

It's possible to devise a more procedural view of (at least, the lower end of) AH. Σ_0 and Σ_1 have already been viewed procedurally. How, then, could Π_1, the first genuinely uncomputable stop in AH, be viewed procedurally? Kugel (1986) has aptly called Π_1 procedures **nonhalting procedures**. Here's how they essentially work. Let R be a totally computable predicate (a crucial assumption for the following); then there is some program P which decides R

Now consider a corresponding predicate $G \in \Pi_1$, *viz.*,

$$G(x) \text{ iff } \forall y R(x, y)$$

Here's a nonhalting procedure P^+ [*not* a program, and note, also, that we count P^+'s last output (if there is one) as its result] for solving G, in the sense that a Y is the result iff Gx[17]

- Receive x as input
- Immediately print Y
- Compute, by repeatedly calling P, $R(x, 1)$, $R(x, 2)$, ..., looking for a N
- If N is found, erase Y and leave result undefined

Hopefully you can see how this trick can be extended to produce **trial-and-error procedures** which decide the predicate H. They would immediately print N and then if, during the simulation, halting occcured, N would be replaced with Y.

Very well. Now suppose that moving from low-level information to flow charts centers around functions on the positive integers, Z^+, so that we're concerned with functions $f : Z^+ \rightarrow Z^+$. To be more specific, suppose that we are given the values of a Turing-computable function f, and that we are given the task of finding a computer program $\mathcal{P}_f$ that computes f. If $\mathcal{P}_f(x)$ is the value produced when the program $\mathcal{P}$ is given x as input on its tape, then we say that a program $\mathcal{P}$ **confirms** f iff for every $f(x)$, $f(x) = \mathcal{P}_f(x)$. We will say that some "process" **M**, leaving open for now whether or not this process is computable or not, **flow-charts** one of our functions f iff **M**, upon receiving $f(1)$, $f(2)$, ..., $f(n)$, $f(n+1)$, ... as input, outputs a program $\mathcal{P}$ that confirms f.

But how can this scheme provide some illumination of the task required by a proponent of Rebuttal 5? My point is more than the obvious and well-known fact that for every function f of the relevant type, there are infinitely many programs which flow chart f (though this itself must be quite depressing for the proponent of TTTT*). The point I'm making speaks to the learned defender of TTTT* who is aware of this fact and who can, therefore, be counted upon to attempt to systematize for a given function f the *set* of programs that confirm f. Let me explain. Suppose, first, that we talk about flow-charting (in the technical sense just introduced) for the "dual case;" that is, suppose that we consider a situation where we have a *pair* of value sequences $f(1)$, $f(2)$, ..., $f(n)$, $f(n+1)$, ... $= F$ and $f'(1)$, $f'(2)$, ..., $f'(n)$, $f'(n+1)$, ... $= F'$ and that our task is finding a process that flow-charts both sequences and then, in addition, compares these outputs (which will be, for each sequence, a set of programs) in order to see if they are, by some metric, the "same." This situation is supposed to be a formal analogue for the "matching problem" scenario in which two machines, seen at a low-level, are compared with an eye to the question of whether they are "running the same flow chart." Suppose that the formalization I have offered is accepted. What is my point? Simply this: the matching problem may now require a process more powerful, perhaps *much* more powerful, than what the champion of TTTT* can allow. We know (Kugel 1977), to be more specific, that if, in an attempt to construct a process **M'** for our matching problem, we employ Turing machines (or their equivalents) which are capable of only evaluating functionals in Σ_0 of the Arithmetic Hierarchy, then **M'** will be able to produce only finitely many programs—and *that might, for all we know,* be unacceptable to the proponent of TTTT* bent, by definition, on solving the matching problem. Even if we are willing to go beyond Turing machines in an attempt to get our process **M'**, even, for example, if we are willing to move to so-called trial-and-error machines capable of evaluating functionals in Σ_2, there is a determinate sense of 'complete' (Kugel 1977) according to which **M'** will be *in*complete in terms of its output with respect to F and F' and the like. Now of course everything here comes down to what *is* acceptable (a proponent of TTTT* might say—imprudently, no doubt; I make the point only for illustration—that it's good enough, when trying to flow chart F, to produce a haphazard *guess* as to a computer program that confirms it). My point is simply that when the matching problem at the heart of TTTT* is formalized a bit, it quickly becomes unclear as to whether or not this problem is (in the general sense) tractable. In light of this result, if we've ended up at TTTT*, it seems to me we have lost sight of the refreshingly concrete and commonsensical TT.

All may not be lost, however. I said above that there were *six* rebuttals one could make to the argument from serendipity. The fifth rebuttal, that of "tweaking" TT, looks, for reasons now articulated, to be unpromising. Indeed, I'm inclined to hold that Turing's hope—a nice, neat, empirical test free of the mind-body quagmire—has faded away forever in the face of the TT—TTTT* dialectic we have just gone through. But what about the *sixth* rebuttal? To it we now turn.

Rebuttal 6: Ruling Out FSAs. In Rebuttal 6 one aims specifically at preventing a finite state automaton from passing the TT, and even from passing Searle's (1980) Chinese Room test.[18] That is, one labors, in this rebuttal, to by definition rule out a "dumb" automaton from passing the sort of test at the heart of this progression. For example, Kugel (1990, 1986) has proposed a test in the form of a game intended to *supplant* TT and its close relatives:

> Let the players in our theoretical game be divided into two parts, one that *acquires* knowledge and one that *uses* it. And let's test how good they are in terms of what I have called the guessing game. This game is run by a judge who sits behind two bins marked *YES* and *NO*. The judge thinks up a concept (say the concept is a woman) and starts dropping cards (say with pictures on them) into one of the two bins. The cards that fall under the concept (those that contain a picture of a woman) go into the *YES* bin, and those that do not, go into the *NO* bin. The players try to guess the judge's concept from the binning examples alone. A player *wins a round* of this game if he, she or it eventually guesses the concept correctly. And we say that it guesses the concept correctly if there comes some time at which all

(future) guesses, about which bin a card will be placed in, are correct. Notice that a player need not know the concept right at the start and that it need not announce when it has figured that concept out. Notice, also, however, that the player must be able not just to guess the concept (and say, perhaps, "Your concept is *woman*"). The player must both identify the concept and be able to apply it. That's how you win a round. The machine *wins a game* (consisting of infinitely many rounds) if it wins at least all the rounds that the person wins—if it can learn all the same concepts, from binning examples, that the person can learn. We call the set of all concepts for which a player can win the game that player's guessing set. The machine wins...in other words, if its guessing set includes (properly or improperly) the guessing set of the human player. (1990, pp. 4-5)

I give an impressionistic picture of the Kugel Test (KT) in Figure 6.

While KT seems at first glance to come out of left field, its introduction makes good sense. Kugel begins to reveal this by asking us to consider the question

(Q4) Can rooms multiply?

This question is asked in the context of a situation where we send into a room (or a Searlean box) such questions as

$$2*2 = ?$$
$$64*7 = ?$$

and get back a reply. If we play this game within parameters π^*, an FSA can fool us—with a kind of deception that by this time looks all too familiar. But since (# is used for punctuation)

$$\{n\#m\#p \mid n*m = p \ \& \ n, m, p \in \mathbf{N}\}$$

cannot be recognized by an FSA,[19] Kugel suggests that we ask our room for the result of multiplying *any* two natural numbers. If we up our standards in this way, we in one fell swoop prevent an FSA from fooling us. Kugel proposes that we follow the same sort of strategy with respect to TT—by adopting KT and KT's rules, three in number (and based on the primitive locution 'a guess at a time t is correct,' whose operational meaning is obvious), and simple enough:

(R1) A player **guesses the concept correctly** iff there is a time t such that for every t' later than t, all guesses at t' are correct.

(R2) A player **wins a round** iff it guesses the concept correctly.

(R3) A machine M **wins a game**, consisting of infinitely many rounds, iff it can guess all the same concepts, from winning examples, that the person can.

Kugel's proposal is the expected one, analogous to Turing's: *viz.*, replace our (Q1) with

(Q1''') Can androids win guessing games?

What are we to make of this proposal? Is it any good? Well, one thing's for sure: KT is certainly no more practicable than TTTT*, in light of the fact that the Kugel test must be played for an infinite amount of time! But suppose we drop the requirement that our Turingish test, whatever it is, must be doable in the here and now (in favor, perhaps, of the notion that the test need only,

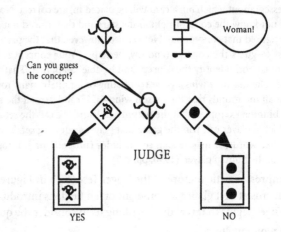

Figure 6. Kugel Test.

theoretically speaking, divide conscious androids from nonconscious ones). Such a reversal doesn't resurrect TTTT* (which, it will be recalled, was rejected in part because of its "real world" impracticability, and in part because of its possible mathematical impracticability, if certain standards are maintained for processes tackling TTTT*'s matching problem), since this test will presumably allow an FSA to pass it. And in light of this fact, though I didn't mention it above, TTTT* succumbs to the sort of counter-example (aimed originally at TT) with which we started. That is, it seems possible that we could, today, serendipitously create an FSA which gives rise to the sort of "flow chart match" called for by TTTT*. (And, for reasons articulated above in connection with Rebuttal 4, what the formal possibility of such serendipity shows is that, for all we know, a host of what I called 'junk' can pass TTTT*.) Kugel's fundamental worry is precisely this possibility, which he considers Searle to have exploited; and he wants, by "infinitizing" things, to rule it out. And rule it out he has: no FSA can win the guessing game, for the same reason that no such automaton can prevail in the multiplication game. So the "serendipity trick," according to which a finite automaton coincidentally passes any of the tests in the TT—TTTT* progression without any consciousness in the picture, cannot be deployed against KT. This is certainly a virtue of KT. Is KT, then, what we have been looking for? Should it be adopted as a quasi-empirical test that does sift out the machines that think from those that don't? In order to answer this question, I think we need to take more seriously the notion that an agent, or person (or thinking thing ...), whether of the human or machine variety, is to be identified with some class of automata. For only then will we be in a position to appreciate views about which machines we are to be identified with—views bound up with KT. Kugel (along with Gödel, perhaps) holds that we aren't FSAs, that we aren't Turing machines, but that we persons are trial-and-error machines. Others disagree. In order to adjudicate this dispute, and to thereby adjudicate the inevitable debate over whether or not KT is adequate, we need to look closer, first, at the concept of agent as automaton.

So, why talk of agents as automata? Why allow such locutions as 'Persons are finite state automata' to occupy the center of the debate into which we have entered herein? First, there is reason to think that quantification over agents *of some sort* cannot be kept out of discussions about the logico-mathematical and philosophical foundations of AI. It's not just that remarks connecting AIs with persons are easy to find in the symbolicist AI literature. [For example, "The ultimate goal of AI research (which we are very far from achieving) is to build a person, or more humbly, an animal" (Charniak and McDermott 1985, p. 5).] It is rather that talk of agents appears to be well nigh ineliminable. Symbolicists or logicists, indeed even those only moderately sympathetic toward this camp, have, as a matter of tradition, unabashedly talked about what armchair reflection can disclose about the computational nature of our thought.[20] Thus, for example, while Smolensky (1988), in surely (with reactions and reply included) one of the longest and most thorough essays on the foundations of AI in the literature, while not (often, anyway) quantifying over agents (cognizers, persons, ...), *does* quantify over virtual machines (the intuitive processor and the conscious rule processor) which, for all intents and purposes, operate as agents in his discussion.

But second, even if there is disagreement about the literature's commitment to agent- or person-talk, there are certainly decent *arguments* in favor of such talk. Some of these arguments are defensive.[21] But some are offensive. There appear to be, for example, formidable arguments for the claim that so-called *de se* beliefs (e.g., "*I* believe that AI is moribund") must be present in *any* android-of-the-future intended by AI-niks to match or exceed the symbolic reasoning, perceptual, motor, ... powers of human persons (Pollock 1989). And it's hard to see how AI-niks could "build-in" to a robot *de se* beliefs, whether these beliefs are symbolicist or connectionist in character, without treating this robot, and without having the robot treat itself, as an *agent*. Third, and finally, I should hasten to point out that 'Persons are (say) Turing machines' terminology is intended to be a form of shorthand.[22] After all, a standard first-order symbolization of 'Persons are Turing machines' (where Tx *iff x* is a Turing machine, Px *iff x* is a person) as

$$\forall x(Px \rightarrow \exists y(Ty \wedge x = y))$$

would, on the assumption that I'm a person, imply that

$$\exists y(Ty \wedge selmer = y).$$

But this is of course hard to swallow, since Turing machines are (at bottom; see any formal account) *sets*, which, given both that (i) sets are (usually regarded to be, anyway) nonphysical, and (ii) a corollary of Leibniz' Law, *viz.*

$$\forall x \forall y [x = y \rightarrow (Fx \rightarrow Fy)],$$

implies that I am nonphysical. But one surely doesn't want to cash out the foundations of AI in such a way that it *entails* agent dualism (roughly, the view that human agents are immaterial). Of course, each of our relevant agent-automata theses ('Persons are finite state automata,' 'Persons are Turing machines,' 'Persons are trial-and-error machines') can be slightly modified to reflect a physicalist orientation,[23] as in, for example, 'Persons are *physical* Turing machines.'[24]

Very well. Then here is the question for us: is KT, based as it is on Kugel's view that persons are not to be identified with finite state automata, acceptable? Is there good reason for thinking that persons are indeed *not* FSAs (over and above reasons discussed above)? I have heard many in AI and Philosophy cavalierly say such things as "Of course we're not finite state automata. These automata can't X," where X is sometimes "speak a language," or "recognize $\{a^n b^n \mid n=m\}$," etc. But pontification isn't enough (especially in light of the fact that if you allow an FSA to have a very large tape, it might be able to, for example, recognize $a^n b^n$ strings of a length beyond which we, having finite brains for "tapes," can't handle), and I know of no careful, sustained arguments in the literature for the thesis that persons can't be FSAs. Nonetheless, I happen to think Kugel is correct, and I'll sketch a little modal argument now to try to show that he is.

My modal argument features not arithmetic or string theory, but rather storytelling. (I couch the argument in terms of storytelling only to enhance readability. It could be given exclusively in terms of modalized string generation.) Let's set up the following relations: Px iff x is a person; Fx iff x is a finite automaton; Sx iff x is a story (which is in turn simply a string satisfying the bare minimum in terms of its narrative component: we shall regard "Jones played softball" to be a story); Gxy iff x generates y. Persons can generate stories "in their heads," or by writing them down, or by verbalizing them, etc. An FSA generates a story by printing it out on its tape in the conventional manner. Given this scheme, the well-known limits on FSAs would imply that

(4) $-\exists x[Fx \wedge \forall y(Sy \rightarrow Gxy)]$

This proposition is to be distinguished from

(5) $-\forall x(Sx \rightarrow \exists y(Fy \wedge Gyx))$

which is false. On the other hand, (4) is certainly true (it admits of simple proof, since, among other reasons, no FSA can, with respect to certain fixed alphabets **A**, generate the set of all strings in all $L \subset \mathbf{A}^*$). What, now, is *my* claim about these matters? That there is a certain property, call it **modalized typed story power**, possessed by some persons but necessarily not by any FSA. Let me explain: First, change (4) to the *de re* modalized

(4′) $-\exists x \Diamond [Fx \wedge \forall y(Sy \rightarrow Gxy)]$[25]

Which is of course equivalent to

(4″) $\forall x - \Diamond [Fx \wedge \forall y(Sy \to Gxy)]$

This last formula says that FSAs *lack* modalized story power (and is again a corollary of computability theory, since mathematical truths—the relevant one here being that FSAs lack story power *simpliciter*—are logically necessary). Now it may seem that I, on the other hand, have story power (*simpliciter*), that is, where s denotes Selmer:

(6) $Ps \wedge \forall y(Sy \to Gsy)$

What does it *mean* to have story power? It means, simply, that I can generate all stories, and furthermore, given that there exist an infinite number of stories, that I can generate an infinite number of stories. But there is an obvious problem with (6). It's simply that I *can't* generate every story (since, among other reasons, there exist stories involving concepts I do not understand)—something which (6) implies I *can* do. Then what *do* I maintain? That I *can* generate an infinite number of stories in a way that lets me beat out FSAs, but that my generative power must be expressed more circumspectly: specifically, in such a way that "can" here is a "modal logic" can, and in such a way that the stories in question are organized so as to make plain the inability of FSAs to generate them. Let me unpack this. Suppose that S denotes the set of all stories. Then perhaps there is an *infinite* set or type $\mathcal{T} \subset S$, every member of which I can (not here the modal sense) generate.[26] This fact can be expressed by

(6′) $\forall y(y \in \mathcal{T} \to Gsy)$

If (6′) is true of a person, we say that that person has **typed story power**. Some may doubt—with, I concede, good reason—that I, or any other person, has typed story power. But I submit that no one should hesitate to ascribe *modalized* typed story power to me, a property expressed by

(6″) $\Diamond \forall y(y \in \mathcal{T} \to Gsy)$

Why do I believe that I and countless others possess modalized typed story power? Proposition (6″), in a nutshell, says that I'm such that it's logically possible that for every story s in $\mathcal{T}$, I generate s. (For an account of progressions that could form the set $\mathcal{T}$, see note 26, if you haven't already.) Put another way, (6″) claims that there exists a coherent situation or a possible world in which I generate all of $\mathcal{T}$. And this can, of course, be a world in which I'm not constrained by the physical laws and psychological and physiological limits that constrain human persons in the *actual* world. Put yet another way, given a rough-and-ready conflation of logical possibility with conceivability, confirming (6″) amounts to conceiving, carefully, of a scenario in which I can generate all of $\mathcal{T}$. [In this connection, see the discussion of Zeus in Boolos and Jeffrey (1980), an imaginary creature with the power to enumerate an infinite set in a finite amount of time.] Since it certainly seems logically possible that a superhuman counterpart to Selmer could both grasp and generate each and every story in $\mathcal{T}$ (= grasp and generate each and every story in the Chomskyan type of progression described in note 26); and since, for every infinite type (or set) of stories $\mathcal{T}$ (like that described in note 26), it's logically *im*possible that any FSA generate all members of this type, we have found a property that blocks identification of FSAs with persons.

So, I'm inclined to agree with Kugel that persons aren't finite state automata. But Kugel goes well beyond this. Cognoscenti will see, in fact, that KT is designed so as to preclude victory in it by a Turing machine (or any other automata of equal or lesser power). In order to prevail in KT the machine in question must be a trial-and-error machine. As we've seen, such machines have the "hardware" of Turing machines but are nonetheless able (for example) to solve the Full Halting Problem, in part because the conventions governing what constitutes output are, for trial-and-error machines, relaxed.

But why does Kugel want to bypass Turing machines and move to trial-and-error machines? What's wrong with identifying persons not with finite state automata (a move which, we can perhaps now readily grant, is problematic), but with Turing machines? There are at least two general reasons. One, the counter-examples and related argumentation which shot down TT—TTTT* could be easily based on Turing machines, not finite state automata. Two, Kugel has an *argument* for the proposition that persons are trial-and-error machines. This argument is based on two properties, which Kugel calls **pigheadedness** and **narrow-mindedness**, possessed by Turing machines, but not by trial-and-error machines. We don't have the space to consider these properties in their full formal glory;[27] a quick presentation will have to suffice. Consider the task given to a machine of "learning" infinite sequences of natural numbers from finite initial segments of these sequences. Here is Kugel's (1990) example:

> Suppose that we give [a machine] the first four members of an infinite sequence—2, 4, 6, 8, ... To demonstrate that it has figured out the sequence we ask [the machine] to predict other members and, for our example, let's focus on the eighth. "16," you say. So far so good. But suppose that we now show [the machine] some more of the sequence—2, 4, 6, 8, WHO, DO, WE, ... Now you would say (I hope) that the eighth item is APPRECIATE. But our machine, if it is a [Turing machine], cannot do that. (p. 19)

A machine is **pigheaded** if once it comes up with an answer to our "sequence game" it has to stick with that answer. In Kugel's example, the machine involved could doubtless have waited until it saw more items before committing itself to the nth member of the sequence. But if the machine is a *Turing* machine, a final commitment must come at some time after a *finite* amount of "reflection;" Turing machines are therefore pigheaded. A machine is **narrow-minded** if, once announcing the nth member of the supposed sequence or the sequence itself, it can "learn" no other sequence with the same initial segment. Again, this is true of a Turing machine, given the standard conventions governing the output from such a machine. Now here is Kugel's argument based on these two properties:

(7) Human agents are neither pigheaded nor narrow-minded.

(8) If human agents are Turing machines (or, for that matter, finite state automata), they *are* pigheaded and narrow-minded.

(9) Human agents are automata, of some sort.

∴ (10) Human agents are trial-and-error machines.

What are we to say of this argument? Well first, it's clearly enthymematic. The hidden premise is that 'if human agents are automata of some sort, they are either finite state automata, Turing machines, or trial-and-error machines.' Though there are some problems with this premise, I'm inclined to let it go (since the possibilities left out by this premise's disjunction can perhaps be collapsed into its disjuncts[28]). The problem I have with the argument is premise (9), since I'm agnostic on the question of whether human agents are automata of *any* sort.[29]

But let's not lose sight of our purpose: evaluating TT and its descendants. And the descendant under scrutiny at present is KT. Alright then. Is KT acceptable? To put it more carefully and in another way: Does KT have problems other than that it may erroneously imply that human agents are trial-and-error machines, when in fact they are not? I think so. Do we have in KT an acceptable variant of the original TT? I'm afraid not. At least this is the way it looks to me. The first reason for worrying about KT is that it is a good deal more rigid than the original TT. What makes TT ingenious is that the judge can introduce almost any area of life or learning into it (by simply asking questions in that area). But KT is committed to learning as the fundamental process to which testing must conform. In light of this, how, for example, would the judge test in the area of (say) storytelling? Can the judge within TT ask the human and the machine to produce what they regard to be a short but moving story? Yes, clearly. But can the judge within *KT* ask the human and the machine to provide what they regard to be a short but moving story? Apparently not. What the judge in KT *can* do, of course, is to display both examples of stories of this type and, on the other hand, tedious stories, both displayed on cards to be thrown into KT's bins after they're displayed. But that would not seem to be enough, for clearly the cognitive abilities required to pick out moving stories from (say) sentences taken at random from newspaper stories is different from the abilities necessary for *composing* moving stories.[30] The point is not simply that trial-and-error machines might be able to prevail in the test despite being lousy storytellers; the point is a more general one: *viz.*, trial-and-error machines might prevail without displaying the observable correlate to those cognitive abilities which are, for all we know, definitive of personhood—abilities involving the creative *production* of text (or, for that matter, pictures, paintings, theorems, etc.).

I said there were *two* things threatening KT. What is the second? It is simply that KT doesn't seem immune to the sort of serendipity based counterexample with which we are by now so painfully familiar. To put it colloquially, it would seem that a trial-and-error machine could "luck out in the limit." If the concept to be learned is 'woman,' on the basis of cards showing women on the one hand and simple geometric shapes on the other (this is the situation in our above illustration of KT), then suppose we recall our simple generator $\mathcal{P}$ of English from above. What is to stop a trial-and-error machine from calling $\mathcal{P}$ for serendipitous declarations about what the concept in question in KT is? Nothing. But then since $\mathcal{P}$ didn't suffice to ensure consciousness above (in attacks on TT—TTTT*), it doesn't suffice now. I conclude, then, that KT is inadequate, and that if some descendant of Turing's original test is going to cut the mustard as a genuine indicator of machine consciousness now or even in a *Blade Runner*ish[31] future, we haven't yet seen it.

Notes

1. For a discussion of symbol systems see Bringsjord (1991a).

2. See Nagel (1974) for a seminal discussion of the concept of point of view.

3. CINEWRITE, a model of (or an algorithm-sketch for) creative writing which I have proposed and explained in Bringsjord (1992a,c) and used in Bringsjord (1991b), may provide a rationale for an affirmative answer to (Q3‴). I have proposed the model CINEWRITE in connection with my work on a project in story generation known as *Autopoeisis*, the ultimate aim of which is to have a computer write sophisticated fiction. In CINEWRITE, we *might* have an answer to (Q3‴) because, among other things, CINEWRITE implies that AI researchers interested in getting a computer to write stories should perhaps take "point of view" seriously.

4. Readers wanting a detailed look at elementary recursion theory can turn to a quartet of books I have used in teaching logic and computability: Lewis and Papadimitriou (1981), Ebbinghaus, Flum, and Thomas (1984), Boolos and Jeffrey (1980), and Hopcroft and Ullman (1979). For a comprehensive mature discussion of such matters that includes succinct coverage of *un*computability, including the Arithmetic Hierarchy (which figures centrally in my coming answer to QUEST), see Davis and Weyuker (1983), and Soare (1980).

5. Actually, Turing (1950) apparently envisaged in his test not an android but a robot, maybe even simply a computer, but there is no harm in modifying things in this way.

6. There are, of course, *other* problems with TT. For example, as Rey (1986) points out, Turing's orientation is a *behavioristic* one, while the orientation of today's logicist AI researcher is a *functionalist* one. Turing is concerned *only* with human-machine teletype equivalence, a purely behavioral notion. He is not concerned with the organization, structure, etc. of the internal states of the digital computer (android, robot, etc.) he envisions passing his test. But AI researchers care very much about the internal states of the machine. After all, they are engaged in a search for a program that generates the sort of internal organization that, *a la* functionalism, gives rise to genuine consciousness.

7. See Chapter V of Bringsjord (1992a) for a discussion of Searle's Chinese Room argument.

8. Dennett's position has a number of illustrious subscribers. John McCarthy, for example, took

this position in conversation with me about related matters at IJCAI 1991 after I presented Bringsjord and Zenzen (1991).

9. This is as good a place as any to point out that Harnad and I *perhaps* fundamentally agree regarding the limits of empirical tests for consciousness. See the speculative last few pages of Harnad (1991). We do, however, seem to take quite different roads to this agreement.

10. A bit of Harnad's (1991) reasoning, in his own words:

So in the TTT variant of Searle's thought experiment there would again be two possibilities, just as there were in the Chinese Room. In the original TT case, the machine could either really be understanding Chinese or it could be merely going through the motions, manipulating symbols *as if* it understands them. Searle's argument worked because Searle himself could do everything the machine did—he could *be* the whole system—and yet still be obviously failing to understand. In the TTT case of seeing, the two possibilities would again be whether the machine really saw objects or simply *acted exactly as if* it did. But now try to run Searle's argument through. Searle's burden is that he must perform all the internal activities of the machine—he must *be* the system—but without displaying the critical mental function in question (here, seeing; in the old test, understanding). Now machines that behave as if they see must have sensors—devices that transduce patterns of light on their surfaces and turn that energy into some other form (perhaps other forms of energy, perhaps symbols). So Searle seems to have two choices. Either he gets only the *output* of those sensors (say, symbols), in which case he is *not* doing everything that the candidate device is doing internally and so no wonder he is not seeing (here the "System Reply" would be perfectly correct); or he looks directly at the objects that project onto the device's sensors (i.e., he is *being* the device's sensors)—but then he would in fact be seeing! (p.50)

11. As Rey points out, *contra* Turing (1950), AI-niks sanguine about building a robotic person (= android ...) hold that the *internal organization* of this creature is of utmost importance (that's why they program, after all—to *cause* a certain organization in the hardware), and they presumably must hold that this internal organization, in order for its bearer to be conscious (etc.), must be of a certain computational form. Since TT *ignores* internal organization, for this reason alone it's suspect.

12. It might be said, not implausibly, that for all we know at present, agents, whether alien or human, might be identical with their bodies, might be diverse from their bodies and furthermore immaterial, might be diverse from their bodies but nonetheless physical objects that supervene upon their bodies (Pollock 1988), and so on.

13. Some connectionists seem to want to reject functionalism (so much the worse for connectionism, it seems to me). For example, the Churchlands (1990) say "The emerging consensus on [the] failures of [logicist AI] is that the functional architecture of classical SM (Turing) machines is simply the wrong architecture."

And for more on the view, *contra* traditional logicist or symbolicist AI, that the stuff *does* matter:

[Connectionists] argue that intelligence will emerge only from a special hardware that reproduces the massive parallelism of the human brain, in which huge numbers of interconnected cells tackle different parts of the same task at the same time. ... Hardware is the essence of intelligence, says connectionism, and not only does traditional AI miss out on this fact, but it uses the wrong hardware. (Hurlbert and Poggio 1989, p. 43)

14. The most prominent of which is the so-called arbitrary realization argument, to which I devote all of Chapter VI in Bringsjord (1992a). (This argument apparently originated with Block 1978. See also Searle's 1983, p. 3 early "beer can" use of it.) The argument, compressed, runs as follows. "If the stuff doesn't matter, but only the computational organization does, if all we need is the right algorithm, which can then run on any old hardware, then what if we take our consciousness-producing algorithm *A* and realize it in the form of a billion Chinese workers carrying

around buckets of water (etc.) in a manner isomorphic to *A*? Would we want to say these industrious Chinese give rise to a gigantic person with thoughts and feelings? If functionalism is correct, we are forced to answer yes to this embarrassing question."

15. For a readable look at recent evidence revealing how little we know about the brain despite such marvels as PET scanners, see "Brain yields new clues on its organization for language," *Science Times* of *New York Times*, 9/10/91.

16. The scheme to come is standard, but I follow Kugel (1977) closely.

17. The reader should satisfy him- or herself that the following procedure *does* decide G.

18. I'm assuming—unexceptionably, I think—that Searle-the-shuffler-of-pieces-of-paper-and-apparent-computer, who seems to outside native speakers of Chinese to be a native speaker, is representable by a finite state automaton.

19. For the proof, see any standard introductory textbook in the theory of computation (the books I mentioned earlier would do the trick).

20. Those doubtful of this have only to read through Genesereth and Nilsson (1987). And here from Harnad (1991), a mild fan of logicist AI, is talk that implies a willingness to ponder the computational nature of agents:

> Our linguistic capacities are the primary examples [of behavior that appears to be symbolic in nature], but many of the other skills we have—logical reasoning, mathematics, chess-playing, perhaps even our higher-level perceptual and motor skills—also seem to be symbolic. In any case, when we interpret our sentences, mathematical formulas, and chess moves (and perhaps some of our perceptual judgements and motor strategies) as having a systematic meaning or content, we know at first hand that that's literally true, and not just a figure of speech. Connectionism hence seems to be at a disadvantage in attempting to model these cognitive capacities.

21. Those (such as Marvin Minsky) who hold that "person" is a category to be eliminated from science, as, say, phlogiston was, would do well to reflect upon the difficulty of rendering sentences like "I want to take a holiday"as "My brain (central nervous system? neo-cortex?) wants to take a holiday," or perhaps as the no less unpalatable "Brain-23 (constant denoting "my" brain) wants to take a holiday."

22. Readers reluctant to allow even an ontology which includes a generic, nonquestion-begging, exposition-easing concept of an agent are free to (for example) paraphrase "Persons are Turing machines" as some such thing as "Some computational theory of the Turing machine variety is the best way to explain human cognition." The tactic of paraphrasing would have to be performed *uniformly* throughout this paper—which would lead, I think, to some rather cumbersome locutions which are, I think, rather harmlessly compressed in the ways I have chosen.

23. Physicalist versions of these theses will, of course, have the drawback that they by definition rule out, or perhaps beg the question against, agent dualism. Agent dualism is at least taken seriously by a number of philosophers, some of whom work on the foundations of AI and Cog Sci (e.g., Pollock 1989).

24. And such a modification would be carried out so as to not imply that there is some standard way to *manufacture* Turing machines. There are, of course, innumerable ways to physically implement Turing machines, and these implementations, if you will, can be ranked in terms of speed, reliability, mobility, and so on.

Lest readers think that the issue of which class of automata human persons are to be placed in is idle chatter, it should be pointed out that Kirk (1986) has recently said that if we identify persons not with Turing machines (or with equivalents such as Register machines, infinite abaci, etc.) but instead with finite state automata, then the (now-in-disrepute-anyway) argument that Gödel's incompleteness results imply that persons are more powerful than machines is derailed. [The argument apparently originates with Lucas (1964). I examine it in Chapter VII of Bringsjord (1992a)]. Kirk's rationale is a simple but trenchant one: given that the Gödelian argument must involve a premise to the effect that persons are to be identified with axiom systems that are strong enough to generate arithmetic (since Gödel I applies only to systems at least this strong), if persons are identified with FSAs, the argument, of necessity, fails. This is the case because FSAs are strong enough only to represent weak second-order arithmetic, which isn't strong enough to express all recursive functions.

25. My modal operators ($\square$ for necessarily, $\lozenge$ for possibly) in the argument I'm giving here can be interpreted intuitively: $\square$ for generic logical necessity, $\lozenge$ for generic logical possibility. A reader uncomfortable with this can read me as presupposing the simple Kripkean system Q1, in which the domain is fixed across possible worlds, the Barcan Formula is valid, and rules regimenting the necessity of identity entail that from '$x = y$' one can infer to '$\square(x = y)$.' More details concerning the machinery that I think is needed to articulate arguments, etc., regarding the foundations of AI/Cog Sci can be found in Chapter II of Bringsjord (1992a).

26. There are a number of equally respectable ways to flesh out $\mathcal{T}$. Here are two, the second more direct and powerful, and also more traditional, than the first. The first is by capitalizing on an endless supply of primitives; where primitives are not to be identified with English words, but rather with certain English words and neologisms indicating novel concepts. 1: "Once upon a time there was a young man, Noah, a bank teller, who thought his nose was elephantine, and so was quite shy, refusing, in fact to go out in public. But one day the circus came to town, and Noah heard, floating through his window, the irresistible roar of tented festivities. He decided to go. Once there, the ringmaster spotted Noah's proboscis, pronounced it magnificent, and on the spot hired Noah to play a clown." 2: "Once upon a time there was a young man, Noah, a pickpocket, who thought his nose was elephantine, and so was quite shy, refusing, in fact to go out in public. But one day the circus came to town, and Noah heard, floating through his window, the irresistible roar of tented festivities. He decided to go. Once there, the ringmaster spotted Noah's proboscis, pronounced it horrible, and on the spot hired Noah to play a monster." 3: "Once upon a time there was a young man, Noah, a nik (someone obsessed with washing under their fingernails—a neologism, I trust), who thought his hands were elephantine, and so was quite shy, refusing, in fact to go out in public. But one day the circus came to town, and Noah heard, floating through his window, the irresistible roar of tented festivities. He decided to go. Once there, the ringmaster spotted Noah's hands, pronounced them wondrous, and on the spot hired Noah to play a freak."

The second way to flesh out $\mathcal{T}$ is more traditional. It involves modeling stories on examples used in the original proof by Chomsky (1956, 1957) that English isn't an FSA language. Chomsky pointed out in the '50s that (and here I will follow Partee, Meulen, and Wall 1990) English contains a number of constructions (If...then, either...or, subject-main verb agreement, etc.) which imply ruleful paired correspondences and that these correspondences can be nested to an arbitrary depth. Here is an example from Chomsky and Miller (1963) with the correspondences indicated by subscripts:

Anyone$_1$ who feels that if$_2$ so-many$_3$ more$_4$ students$_5$ whom we$_6$ haven't$_6$ actually admitted are$_5$ sitting in on the course than$_4$ ones we have that$_3$ the room had to be changed, then$_2$ probably auditors will have to be excluded, is$_1$ likely to agree that the curriculum needs revision.

To convert this to a story we have only to change 'Anyone' to (say) 'John' and make the corresponding changes. Clearly, we can talk formally of expanding such nested stories to an indefinite length.

27. Interested readers should consult the refined, comprehensive theory worked out in Osherson, Stob, and Weinstein (1986). See also Solomonoff (1964).

28. Neural nets are at bottom cellular automata, which are at bottom k-tape Turing machines, which are at bottom standard Turing machines. And what sense could it make to add, say, pushdown automata to the disjunction? Futhermore, perhaps the machines in the Arithmetic Hierarchy beyond TMs can also, here anyway, be collapsed.

29. Again, for a book-length treatment of the issue, see Bringsjord (1992a). See also the book *In Defense of Uncomputable Cognition* (from Kluwer), written by myself and Michael Zenzen.

30. It's interesting to note, in connection with this point, that Kugel (1986, pp. 147-148) in a brief section *Recognition versus Generation* is tempted to affirm (what I regard to be the doubtful proposition) that the ability to recognize something *x* as *F* implies the ability to *produce* something *x* that has *F*.

31. *Blade Runner* is a classic sci-fi movie in which only an elaborate pupil-scanner (which detects the usual physiological correlate to an emotional response to provocative questions) enables one to distinguish androids from humans.

References

Block, N. (1978). Troubles with functionalism. In *Perception and Cognition: Issues in the Foundations of Psychology*. Minnesota Studies in the Philosophy of Science.

Boolos, G. and Jeffrey, R. (1980). *Computability and Logic*. Cambridge University Press.

Bringsjord, S. (1991a). Is the connectionist-logicist clash one of AI's wonderful red herrings? *Journal of Experimental and Theoretical Artificial Intelligence*, 3, 4, 319-349.

Bringsjord, S. (1991b). *Soft Wars*. New American Library, an imprint of Penguin USA.

Bringsjord, S. (1992a). *What Robots Can and Can't Be*. Studies in Cognitive Systems Series, Kluwer Academic.

Bringsjord, S. (1992b). CINEWRITE: An algorithm-sketch for machine-generated fiction, and two difficult problems facing this generation task. In M. Sharples (Ed.), *Computers and Writing: Issues and Implementations*. Kluwer Academic.

Bringsjord, S. (1992c). CINEWRITE: An algorithm-sketch for writing novels cinematically, and two mysteries therein. *Instructional Science*, 21, 155-168. [Reprinted in M. Sharples (Ed.), *Computers and Writing: State of the Art*. Kluwer Academic.]

Bringsjord, S. and Zenzen, M. (1991). In defense of hyper-logicist AI. *IJCAI* (pp. 1066-1072). San Mateo, CA: Morgan Kaufman.

Charniak, E. and McDermott, D. (1985). *Introduction to Artificial Intelligence*. Addison-Wesley.

Chomsky, N. (1956). Three models for the description of language. *IRE Transactions on Information Theory*, 2, 3, 113-124.

Chomsky, N. (1957). *Syntactic Structures*. The Hague, Mouton & Co.

Chomsky, N. and Miller, G.A. (1963). Introduction to the formal analysis of natural languages. In Luce, Bush, and Galanter (Eds.), (1965), *Readings in Mathematical Psychology*, Vol. 2. New York: John Wiley.

Churchland, P.S. and Sejnowski, T.J. (1989). Neural representation and neural computation. In L. Nadel, L. Cooper, P. Culicover, and M. Harnish (Eds.), *Neural Connections, Mental Computations*. Cambridge, MA: MIT Press.

Dennett, D. (1971). Intentional systems. *Journal of Philosophy*, 68, 87-106.

Dennett, D. (1978). *Brainstorms*. Cambridge, MA: Bradford Books, MIT Press.

Ebbinghaus, H.D., Flum, J., and Thomas, W. (1984). *Mathematical Logic*. New York: Springer-Verlag.

Epstein, R. (1992). The quest for the thinking computer. *AI Magazine*, 13, 2, 80-95.

Fetzer, J. (1990). *AI: Its Scope and Limits*. Dordrecht, The Netherlands: Kluwer Academic.

Genesereth, M. and Nilsson, N. (1987). *Logical Foundations of Artificial Intelligence.* San Mateo, CA: Morgan Kaufman.

Gold, E.M. (1965). Limiting recursion. *Journal of Symbolic Logic, 30.*

Harnad, S. (1989). Minds, machines and Searle. *Journal of Experimental and Theoretical Artificial Intelligence, 1,* 5-25.

Harnad, S. (1991). Other bodies, other minds: A machine incarnation of an old philosophical problem. *Minds and Machines, 1,* 43-54.

Horgan, T. (1984). Functionalism and token physicalism. *Synthese, 59,* 321-338.

Hurlbert, A. and Poggio, T. (1989). Making machines (and artificial intelligence) see. *The Artificial Intelligence Debate.* Cambridge, MA: MIT Press.

Kirk, R. (1986). Mental machinery and Gödel. *Synthese, 66,* 437-452.

Kugel, P. (1977). Induction, pure and simple. *Information and Control, 35,* 276-336.

Kugel, P. (1986). Thinking may be more than computing. *Cognition, 22,* 137-198.

Kugel, P. (1990). Is it time to replace Turing's test? 1990 workshop *Artificial Intelligence: Emerging Science or Dying Art Form,* sponsored by SUNY Binghamton's Dept. of Philosophy's Program in Philosophy and Computer & Systems Sciences, and by AAAI.

Lewis, D. (1973). *Counterfactuals.* Harvard University Press.

Lucas, J. R. (1964). Minds, machines, and Gödel. *Minds and Machines.* Englewood Cliffs, NJ: Prentice Hall.

Nagel, T. (1974). What is it like to be a bat? *Philosophical Review, 83,* 435-450.

Osherson, D. N., Stob, M., and Weinstein, S. (1986). *Systems That Learn.* Cambridge, MA: MIT Press.

Partee, B. H., Meulen, A., and Wall, R.E. (1990). *Mathematical Methods in Linguistics.* Kluwer Academic.

Pollock, J. (1988). My brother, the machine. *Nous, 22,* 173-212.

Pollock, J. (1989). *How to Build a Person: A Prolegomenon.* Cambridge, MA: Bradford Books.

Putnam, H. (1960). Minds and machines. *Dimensions of Mind.* New York University Press.

Putnam, H. (1965). Trial and error predicates and the solution of a problem of Mostowski. *Journal of Symbolic Logic, 20.*

Rey, G. (1986). What's really going on in Searle's Chinese room. *Philosophical Studies, 50,* 169-185.

Schank, R. and Reisbeck, C. (1981). *Inside Computer Understanding.* Lawrence Erlbaum.

Searle, J. (1980). Minds, brains and programs. *Behavioral and Brain Sciences, 3,* 417-424.

Searle, J. (1983). *Intentionality.* London, GB: Cambridge University Press.

Smolensky, P. (1988). On the proper treatment of connectionism. *Behavioral & Brain Sciences, 11,* 1-22.

Smolensky, P. (1989). Connectionist modeling: Neural computation/mental connections. In L. Nadel, L. Cooper, P. Culicover, and M. Harnish (Eds.), *Neural Connections, Mental Computations.* Cambridge, MA: MIT Press.

Solomonoff, R. (1964). A formal theory of inductive inference. *Information and Control, 7.*

Turing, A. M. (1964). Computing machinery and intelligence. In A. R. Andersen (Ed.), *Minds and Machines* (pp. 4-30). Contemporary Perspectives in Philosophy Series. Englewood Cliffs, NJ: Prentice Hall.

7 Android Epistemology: An Essay on Interpretation and Intentionality

Kalyan Shankar Basu

The possibility of thematizing a conference on android epistemology generates a refreshing hope that certain questions have not (yet) been settled forever, that there is still in them a tension that would continue to perturb the irrevocability of the most obvious answers. The tension in this particular case originates in the (almost) impossible juxtaposition of the words "android" and "epistemology." Epistemology derives from the Greek root *episteme*, which, in the context of Hellenistic thought, denotes an understanding of the world: understanding, not at the level of fact or of proposition, but as a certain kind of relation of attunement and acquaintance, of human life to its world; a relation that informs and animates all concernful life. Hence epistemology maintains a closeness or a salience to the notion of man and his reflective existence. Android, on the other hand, denotes the property of being man-like; yet this statement of similitude connotes, in actuality, dissimilitude. For android is man-like but, by this very token of similarity, never man. Hence the tension: the juxtaposition of the one similar and infinitely distant to, and the other, ineluctably bound up with the notion of man.

The only avenue, perhaps, to confront the contradictory force of this tension is to address the notion of man itself; subject it to a diremption that would reveal, at its roots, either the corrigibility that abolishes all distance from its facsimile, the android—in which case the similitude in the latter's definition is to be understood only in its positive aspect, or a kind of incorrigibility that would relegate our theme to the field of (meaningful) contradiction and parody.

I shall address the notion of humanness in a scattered, though not incoherent, fashion. Taking my points of departure from certain aspects of human perception and cognition pointed out in the later works of von Ludwig

Wittgenstein, I shall attempt to re-evaluate certain well-worn concepts like truth, knowledge, and memory, in terms of others like intelligibility, salience, and narrative: and, in this re-evaluation, I shall try to argue that the question of epistemology is in fact inseparable from that of ethics and that both belong in essence to the unique and incorrigible domain of the human. I shall direct my efforts towards indicating the constitutive conditions of this incorrigibility.

The Perception of Aspects

Wittgenstein (1953), in his *Philosophical Investigations,* introduces the notion of aspect-perception. Let me quote a few relevant lines: "I contemplate a face, and then suddenly notice its likeness to another. I see that it has not changed; and yet I see it differently. I call this experience 'noticing an aspect'" (p. 193). Similarly, in the next few paragraphs, he comments on the perception of certain paradoxical figures, for instance, one which at times appears as a rabbit, while at others, as a duck.

There are a couple of points worth noting here. First, if one were to ask the experiencer what he *saw,* one would get the spontaneous reply "a duck" or "a rabbit," never something like "I am seeing the following arrangements of points, lines, surfaces, and intensities, which I am now interpreting as a rabbit." In other words, the content of the experience of seeing is a certain *meaningful whole* that we are acquainted with as a duck (or a rabbit), and not a certain arrangement of intensities: what the nature of this meaningful whole is would be a significant portion of my subsequent inquiry. Second, the identity of the underlying *unnamed* figure, which is, of course, a certain arrangement of intensities, does not itself change in the process of the change in its perception. What changes is the *recognition* of the figure—a recognition that we spontaneously claim in language, through our utterance. This lead us to believe that the contents of our experiences of perception are not certain formal arrangements of features which we subsequently decipher, but *spontaneously organized aspects of those features that are intelligible to us.*

Spontaneous organization, as distinct from conscious interpretation—which occurs, for instance, in deciphering blueprints or coded drawings—is evidenced by two characteristic features. First, the response to the interlocutor takes the form of a (spontaneous) cry of surprise and recognition; that is, a direct expression *(ausserung)* of a visual experience, and not a standard perceptual report of what is being seen. Second, the form of words used to describe the content of the perception is characteristically couched in terms of aspects—for instance, "rabbit, with ears swept back"—and never in terms of "such-and-such arrangement of intensities." The former kind of description is not one of several alternatives, but one closest to hand, or one that springs to mind as the most salient. And yet, notwithstanding this immediacy, the fact of its being an organization is undeniable, for the terms of description are, typically, ensembles of concepts intelligible only within a specific cultural matrix. For example, the response of a member of a culture for which the rabbit is an unfamiliar or unknown creature, would be quite different: in fact, the rabbit-aspect would not, in all probability, be perceived at all. Hence, we see in this experience the play of two apparently contradictory notions: the immediacy of a certain kind of perception and its intrinsic mediation or filtration by a certain cultural matrix.

The unity of this experience, in the face of its apparent contradictoriness, is sustained by the notion of an *aspect,* which I introduce at this point as a fundamental and indivisible attribute of all human perceptual experience. Wittgenstein also stresses the importance of this notion and uses it to illustrate the difference between the state of *seeing* (or perceiving) something and that of *knowing* something. In fact, it is precisely because the experience of seeing anything is already and always one of seeing it in terms of aspects, that the sudden dawning of new aspects—as in the case of the duckrabbit—is not experienced as something bizarre or magical, but as a discovery of an alternative mode of perceiving the underlying (unchanged) figure. In other words, the capacity to experience the dawning of a new aspect is derivative to the general attribute of all perceptual experience of being one of a *continuous perception of aspects.* In contradistinction, the phenomenon of knowing or cognizing is a second-order experience, of reconstructing the object in terms of formal schemata of relationships and attributes, and this after divesting it of the first-order aspects which are incongruous to the subsequent assimilation.

In light of this discussion, we see that the apprehension of the world, in perception, is definitely not a matter of registering a certain "raw" arrangement of physical intensities, followed by an interpretative process that assimilates the data into representational schemas which thus give it a certain linguistic identity. On the other hand, it is again definitely not an immediate perception of an already assimilated figure: there is a certain cultural intervention which constrains the very form of its recognition. In fact, there is, in every such apprehension, a *play* of the immediate and the vicarious: a play that is exhibited in the fact that the recognition is always a spontaneous recognition within language—the appropriation of the object into a realm of naming or predicating. In this sense, the threshold of perception coincides with the threshold of naming—that is, the threshold of entry into language. It is a threshold which evidences the interpenetration of fact and convention and which becomes the condition for the emergence of the object as a meaningful segment of experience.

This does not mean that there is never a mode of apprehension that is one of an ensemble of physical intensities; in fact, we routinely apprehend many things of this kind, and of which we cannot make any sense. In fact, before the recognition of a rabbit-figure as indeed such, there is a period of incomprehension and bewilderment, when the outlines haven't taken shape, so to speak. What I wish to underscore, on the other hand, is a certain essential difference between the quality of this latter kind of uncomprehending gaze, and that of the former, which has, around it, a general air of intelligibility. It is this former kind of apprehension that I am calling "perception" and that I am characterizing as marked by the salient attribute of being a continuous perception of aspects.

The transition from the stage of uncomprehending apprehension to one of perception is sharp enough to merit the designation of an *event*. Moreover, it is an event of a peculiar kind: it is an event that is, in a definite sense, *irreversible*. The perception of anything as such-and-such obliterates, other than in a trivial chronological sense, every memory of being in a situation where it was not already and always that. There is no reverting, in a manner of speaking, to the innocence of an unrecognized apprehension; the aspects cling to the form and will not be exorcised—not that I cannot contrive to formulate a description of the object in a language carefully neutralized of all the aspects in terms of which I have perceived it; only that I can no longer *perceive* it as such. This is a rather significant point, for it indicates that the apprehension of a perceptual field in terms of a certain organization of aspects is not merely a matter of associating a certain kind of representation to a pre-existing figure: this in itself would not be irreversible. On the other hand, the irrevocability of such perceptions indicate that the perceived figure *is not anterior* to the form of its perception (that is, in terms of aspects); in the event of its perception it *becomes* that which it is perceived as. In other words, the perceived figure becomes *ontologically* identical with its recognition within language.

There is another peculiarity about the form of this perception that is worth remarking. The recognition of its object in terms of its aspects confers on it a certain *unity*: every effort subsequent to this recognition to decompose the figure into its parts or individual aspects, and in fact any attempt to apprehend it *analytically*, encounters a certain (epistemic?) resistance. The part is always now a part of the whole that is—has been perceived—*anterior* to it. There is no talking about perceiving a segment of the rabbit-figure that is not already, say, that rabbit's ear or that rabbit's leg. In a deeper sense, this unity is not restricted within just the particular perceived object, but overflows into a whole network of related aspects. There is no calling into question the fact of the matter of being a certain aspect, or a certain arrangement of aspects, without addressing a whole network of other aspects and their arrangements which the first presupposes and within the terms of which it is defined. This situation repeats itself and is complicated by the fact that most of such clusters of aspects can only be interdefined: there are no facts that bring to a halt this infinite drift of meanings within language.

The point of the foregoing discussion is to bring the nature of perceptual experiences into sharper focus, with a view to guarding against its reduction into positivist, behaviorist, and cognitivist accounts that entertain a certain innocence towards the peculiar and irreducible role of language in such experiences. The field of perception is irrevocably situated at the intersection of language and the unintelligible intensity of the physical world. The event of perception, in which the object emerges within this field, witnesses its *recognition* within a certain language—a recognition that situates it on a certain familiar topography of *conventions*, of naming and describing. The form of this recognition, in terms of aspects, confers on it a certain unity: a unity in itself, whereby every perception of its constituent parts and aspects stands within the anterior perception of the whole it has been perceived as; and a unity *with* the network of related and interdefined aspects and meanings against and through which the first inherits its identity. Perception then, can no longer be conceived as a registering of a "raw" distribution of intensities followed by an assimilation into formal schemata of representation, but must be conceived as an event with a certain component of *intentionality:* an intentionality that consists in the irrevocable appropriation of its field into a certain linguistic unity; in other words, perception is more appropriately understood as an intentional event that draws its field into what I would designate as an *interpretative holism.*

The Intentionality of Language

Wittgenstein, in *Philosophical Investigations,* raises fundamental doubts about the kinds of processes that are involved in the understanding and use of words. He explores the possibility of whether such applications can be conceived of as instances of following a certain system of rules "given" to consciousness. This exploration leads him into a paradox concerning the nature of following any kind of rule as such. From this skeptical examination, he goes on to explore whether the application of common nouns—predicates of sensations, visual impressions, and the like—can be explained on the basis of having a representative sample present in the mind at the time of use. This leads him again into certain paradoxical conclusions that make him finally reformulate the very notion of meaning in a decisive break with the entire analytical tradition of western epistemology.

The problem with the unexamined notion of following a rule can be exhibited in the following hypothetical context, in the presentation of which I follow Saul Kripke (1982) closely. In the application of most rules, like, for instance, the rule of addition, it is generally the case that though the rule has been applied to only a finite number of actual instances, it determines the result of its application to the entire, perhaps infinite, set of possible instances.

In every case of its application to instances for the first time, there can be a skeptical challenge as to whether the same rule is being followed as has been in the past. In the case of addition, suppose I am performing it for the first time for the numbers 68 and 57, and let us assume that I had never performed it before for numbers greater than 56. Upon my producing the result of 125, according to what I take as the normal rule for addition, the skeptic challenges me that perhaps what I had meant by addition in the past was a rule that ought to have given the result of 5 for the present instances; he substantiates this challenge by claiming that perhaps what I had meant by addition in the past was a rule that works like addition as I now take it, but only if the instances are less than 57; otherwise, it always produces 5 as the result.

Bizarre as it is, the challenge is quite irrefutable: for, by hypothesis, I had performed only a finite number of additions in the past and had never given myself explicit instructions as to what should be the result in the present case. Moreover, any attempt to decompose the rule into primitives (like the explicit results for numbers less than 10, and the rule for carry, etc.) is vulnerable to the same skepticism: for instance, the skeptic might claim that what I had actually meant by the rule for carry, was…, and since I had performed this rule for only finitely many instances, I have no way again to refute his charge. Put in somewhat more general terms, what the skeptic doubts is whether there was some past *fact* about me, that mandates what I should do *now* in the matter of following the particular rule. He expresses this doubt by showing that any attempt to establish such a fact as a fact of my mental history would be equally compatible with an infinite set of different interpretations he could manufacture for the rule under consideration.

What is really at issue in this skeptical challenge is the very nature of anything that can conceivably function as an adequate criterion of identity for the intensions of rules. The skeptic demonstrates that such criteria of identity, if they exist, cannot at least be of the nature of facts. Candidates for such kinds of facts are more basic kinds of rules whose interpretations are in some sense indubitable; however, the skeptic counters their candidacy by raising the same doubts about *their* identity. In particular then, they cannot be some form of "machine code" in terms of some primitive hardware instruction set, for the question can be raised immediately that perhaps these primitive instructions had been interpreted differently in the past, and one could always manufacture alternate interpretations compatible in every way with the past history of behavior.

Interestingly, this problem can arise only for entities that have an irreducible *interpretative* relationship with the world and its own actions. An entity that simply "follows" a sequence of instructions that are identically and uniquely correlated with certain sequences of internal actions can never face this problem: the criterion of identity of rules that are combinations of these instructions is the *fact* of that unique and identical correlation with sequences of internal actions that mandates its actions at every instance of following a combination of instructions. And even if this fact is not *given* to the scope of its actions, it is implicit in its design and must be exhibited, perhaps metalinguistically, in every complete description that can claim to be such. On the other hand, if every context of action implicates an irreducible component of interpretation, only then does the question of the identity of such contexts across a life becomes nontrivial and acutely problematic.

The problematic is intimately related to the fact that while the primary significance of language for us is designative-referential, there is in this referentiality an *essential inscrutability* (I recall Quine). Words in a human language are not *labels;* that is, they do not contain in themselves any criteria that can affix them to portions of the world; their references are, on the other hand, mediated and determined through a process of *interpretation,* which weaves them into a certain context of conventional usage, metonymy, and memory. This interpretation is definitely an event, but it has no determinate factual content—the interpreted word stands within the disclosure of an entire corpus of practice, usage, and memory. Some philosophers call this corpus the *horizon.*

The indeterminacy of the criteria of identity within linguistic contexts, then, is the outcome of the inscrutability conferred on such contexts by the essential role that interpretation plays in determining the contents (references) of such contexts. In fact, the attribute of intentionality that is salient to human language is an *outcome* of the fact that the referentiality of such a language is essentially inscrutable, and hence it can, in a nontrivial sense, be *about* the world, while being irreducible to it. The determinant of this intentionality is not any fact that can be given or made present to introspection, but a horizon of linguistic traditions within whose disclosure it stands.

Wittgenstein's reflections on the intentionality of words for sensations and visual impressions lead him into paradoxes of a similar nature. For instance, I point to a particular colour, and ask, "How do I know that this colour is 'green'?" It has been supposed that understanding for words that denote sensations consists in having something like an image or a sample in the "mind," which would provide the criterion for their correct use. But this assumption is really defenseless against even fairly simple skeptical challenges. For one, a word like 'green' can apply to a potential infinity of tints of green, so in some sense, either the entire putative extension should be given to the mind, or some rule that would determine the minimum necessary degree of closeness to the mental sample. The first is clearly impossible, while the second leads into the usual paradoxes of following a rule. For another, the question really begs itself, because any sample picture too would generate the same question, that is, can the word 'green' be applied to it correctly? Hence, in itself, the sample extension cannot function as a criterion of adequacy. Even if we rule out this doubt, saying that the correctness of mental "samples" is beyond doubt, one encounters another paradox, described by Goodman (1973) in

Fact, Fiction and Forecast. I follow Kripke, again, in presenting this idea.

This paradox takes the same skeptical shape as that for following a rule. It turns out that we cannot rule out the possibility that what in fact was given to my mind was not a sample of green, but of some other colour *grue*, that behaves in the following way: past objects were grue if and only if they were (then) green, while present objects are grue if and only if they are (now) blue. In this case, this sample directs me to apply the word 'green' to grue objects always. Suppose a certain grue object is present before me (which means that right now it is blue); then I would, under the direction of my mental sample, call it 'green.' But then, a blue object would fall under the extension of 'green.' It would not help to suppose that in the past (when my sample was green!) I stipulated that 'green' would apply to all and only those things as the "same colour as my sample"; the skeptic can always object that perhaps what I had meant by 'colour' in the past was…!

Here again the problem really emerges because human beings act within a language which they have to interpret. What is at stake is to understand the *nature* of this interpretative practice. This practice, as the foregoing discussions demonstrate, is not of the nature of a translation into the primitives of some indubitable realm eventually outside language—and hence exempt from the requirement of interpretation in themselves. This is, in fact, how machines work: their languages are intrinsically *functional* in that they correspond uniquely and identically to certain sequences of functional states that are completely describable in terms of their physical realizations. On the other hand, human beings are "condemned" to exist completely and only within language. It is the set of interpretative practices that breaks the "self-enclosedness" of language and allows it to "hook up" up with the world, to refer, and to animate our symbolic practices.

What this series of arguments leads up to, again, is that even if understanding (and meaning) has a content, then this content is not of the nature of what we call a *fact*. In other words, it culminates in the conclusion that the intentionality of language is not a *sui generis*—given to consciousness. In this sense, meaning is not something that is epistemically given, nor even a state of awareness: it does not have a determinate content that determines its significance, its criteria of adequacy or of truth, and even of its conditions of use. Understanding is an event, and in fact an *act*, of interpretation. It is towards an exploration of the nature of this act that we now turn.

The Nature of Interpretation

The discussion on perception and intentionality brings to a focus the fact that the apprehension of the world, whether in terms of perception or in terms of action (application of words and rules), involves an irreducible mediation of language. This mediation is nontrivial, or nonconservative, in at least two important senses: first, it has an irrevocable ontological impact on the world it mediates—that is, in terms of our previous description, it *appropriates its objects into an interpretative holism;* second, it impregnates its referentiality with an *essential inscrutability.* In both these senses, the nature of human existence in relation to its language is fundamentally different from that of entities that have an essentially functional relationship to language. For such entities, language is conservative with respect to its referentiality and serves merely as an encoding of its denotations; hence, the only sense of interpretation, in this case, is the trivial one of *translation* (or even *transcription).*

The nature of an (human) interpretative practice can be explored by looking somewhat more closely at the notion of an aspect. As I have pointed out, an aspect cannot be conceived of in isolation from its description in language: in this sense, its realm is not that of the ("pure") object, but that of its intersection with language. More significantly, an aspect belongs to that domain of language in which it is the medium of existence within a culture. In this sense, an aspect is the object's intelligibility, as a cultural item or an artifact. To perceive anything in terms of aspects is to have already located it on a familiar terrain of convention and use.

The ubiquity of aspectuality in every perceptual experience evidences that we do not perceive things in a "passive" sense, but there is, in perception, a *directedness.* This directedness stems from the character of perception as having an immanent *intention* of investing its field with certain *coherences;* in other words, to perceive anything is to perceive it meaningfully. It is in fact this attribute of directedness (some philosophers describe this as *noesis)* that allows an interrelationship between the senses of intentionality, as being *about* something, and as being intentional (purposive). Hence, the universality of the statement, "all perceiving is perceiving under aspects," derives from the fact that the fundamental coherences of experiences of perception are grounded in their intelligibility within a certain cultural apperceptive field.

The virtue of coherence is not self-contained: the coherence of a field of perception has a necessary reference to the terrain of convention and use. In fact, the field is coherent only insofar as it can be *situated* on this terrain. This terrain is a *historical* object; that is, it is the accumulation of practices and meanings that cannot be made present, or available, in any determinate synchronic sense. On the other hand, it remains as a perpetual possibility of elaborating a particular meaning into the past—to trace, immanently, the etymology of words, or the genealogy of concepts and practices. To be able to situate anything on this historical terrain is to make it *continuous* with the possibilities of elaboration which it holds out. Hence, we give the notion of coherence, which is essentially synchronic, a historicized reading by defining it in terms of continuity.

The understanding of a word (like 'green' for instance) and the perception of a thing consists in the grasping of its aspects, which is an expression of its intelligibility, that is, its continuity with experiences within a certain culture. This continuity consists in the possibility of *integrating* the perception with remembered and habitual patterns and modes of experiencing and acting, and elaborating it against the articulation of such patterns within the current context of the experience. In other words, meaningfulness consists in the possibility of an integration-elaboration into the *continuity of a subjective experience.* The aspects we grasp may not even be describable as things or qualities but only in allusion and metaphor—in its similarities to and its differences from other experiences. Taken in themselves, the aspects are both the cause as well the evidence for their integration into the continuity that we have remarked.

The elaboration of meanings into the past is made explicit and then emerges in the form of a *narrative.* The narrative form is the epitome and metaphor for all things which have a history within language. It gives us a way to conceptualize that elusive terrain that holds within it the diachrony of history *and* the synchrony of a perpetual background for the emergence of meaning: *the horizon, in this light, inscribes all its possible histories.* We have remarked that an essential attribute of this terrain is that it cannot be made present "all at once": this is its historicity. We apprehend it more appropriately as a *repository of narrative possibilities.* The meanings of words learned within a culture stand within the disclosure of accumulated meanings and practices which make up the interpretative background (the terrain or the horizon) specific to that culture. This disclosure is made explicit whenever the meanings are traced back or elaborated into this horizon. Every such tracing back takes the form of a rendering of a locus within this terrain: this locus always has a diachronic significance, and its rendering in language has the narrative form. Hence, the interpretative background is not a body of facts but a store of possibilities for narrating the locus of meanings of words and practices.

The notion of narrative has some significances that should be remarked upon. It presupposes a certain conception of time. However, narrative time differs from physical notions of time, in that its time has a certain *unity:* there is a definite sense that its time is moving to a certain epitome, or a completion. This movement towards its completion is precisely what is signified by the word *denouement.* Hence, an elaboration of meanings into the interpretative background takes the form of a narrative which has an immanent sense of time directed towards its completion. It is in this sense that the horizon adumbrates, in every specific instance of this narrative elaboration, the forms of the *future* articulation of practices and meanings. It does so, not substantively, but by ruling out those forms of history that do not have the sense of completion which is immanent to its narrative elaboration. It is in this sense that the horizon contains its own history; its ramifications are consonant with the futures adumbrated by *their* narrative elaborations.

The notions of continuity, coherence, and *denouement* are in some sense imponderable; in them we come up against the limits of explication—for each is explicable only in terms of the others. Hence, to the extent that narrative is the phenomenon whose essence lies in these indivisible roots, we take it to denote the whole of their import. The isomorphism between the continuity of subjective experience and that of narrative points to a sense in which this subjective experience is a continual elaboration of a narrative within and against the matrix of its culture.

We understand, then, that an aspect is the expression of the integration of the perceptual field into the narrative unity of the subjective experience of the perceived. By interpretation, we understand this integration. Interestingly, the concept of narrative unity is used by Alasdair MacIntyre (1985) to ground his notion of ethics. I shall take this concept as the bridge that links up the notions of knowledge and ethicity for man (and android); but before that, I would make a few remarks on the question of truth and the relationship that our notion of interpretation has with it.

The Question of Truth

By placing the notion of interpretation at the basis of the question of meaning, we displace what has, in the tradition of analytical philosophy, always had a privileged claim to this position—the notion of truth. This tradition has, implicitly from St. Augustine and explicitly from Göttlob Frege, equated the meaning of sentences with the conditions on the references of their various parts that would make the sentence true. It was perhaps implicitly assumed in this tradition that the "conditions that would make a sentence true" are sufficiently pretheoretic, prelinguistic, and indubitable as to be able to function in the foundational role that is given to them in this statement. We submit, and have demonstrated through a series of arguments, that such conditions are neither prelingual nor indubitable and hence cannot be used to define the notion of meaningfulness which, in fact, they presuppose.

On the other hand, as we have have seen, the notion of reference itself is fairly involved. Human languages do not pick up referents as do baggage checks in an airport departure lounge. Referential contexts are imbued with an essential inscrutability by virtue of the kind of role that interpretation plays in them. Recent influential thinking in the truth-conditional theory of meaning (Davidson 1984) has in fact remarked that the two major components of such theories—namely, the theory of truth and the theory of reference—cannot be placed in an unexamined relationship to each other and that, in fact, the theory of truth, contrary to common opinion in the tradition, is *anterior* to a theory of reference.

Davidson has tried to preserve the essential claims of the truth-conditional theory of meaning by posing it not in any substantive sense, but as a *meta-theory* of meaning—that is, by retaining the components of reference and truth as *posits*. This is definitely a sophisticated approach towards avoiding the blindness of the more naive theories. Another feasible direction is to explore the relationship between the two components (reference and truth) within the more fundamental (hermeneutic) problematic of interpretation, and that is the direction I have taken in this essay.

In this approach, I have taken care to hold apart the first-order notions of perceiving and understanding from the second-order notions of knowing and cognizing, which presuppose the former. In my view, truth has an ambiguous status with respect to these categories. The *discursive* notion of truth (as in logic and epistemology) is more a function of the (logical) form of sentences and to that extent is a second-order notion. The experiential (and "every-day") notion of truth (as in life contexts, when conditions of intelligibility are syncategorematic with judgments of truth) is a first-order notion. In fact, it is precisely the condition of intelligibility that is the substantive basis for the *experience* of truth, in distinction to its formal or discursive formulation. The discursive formulation is, in fact, an instance of a more general process in which the objects of experience are divested of their aspects, in order that they may be decomposed and recomposed into the formal categories of specific knowledge systems. In this process, the object of experience is appropriated as the object of theory.

Just as intelligibility is the substantive and experiential component of the (discursive) category of truth, there is a similar notion that is the substantive component of the category of theory or knowledge—the notion of *salience*. Salience is to be understood as certain substantive and structural conditions of relatedness of ensembles of narrative phenomena: conditions through which such ensembles become significant for each other's elaboration within the overall framework of the narrative. Such saliences obtain in everyday life, whereby phenomena of the lived-world *(lebenswelt)* are routinely and empirically perceived as related to each other through conditions of cause, significance, agency, value, and so forth. In fact, the internalization of such saliences and their functionalities within certain (irreflective) realms of practice, are the precondition of one's *competence* to exist viably within a culture.

In fact, the everyday judgments of truth and falsity and the general frameworks of beliefs and actions are *preformed* within the structures of the these saliences, and their efficacies are directly a function of the extent to which they are informed by them. In light of this fact, the possibility of translation between languages is *determinate* to the extent that ensembles of words in one is conservative with respect to those saliences that are integral to the referential contexts of their targets in the other. Of course, given the essential inscrutability of such contexts, the translation is always *under-determined* by any history of behavior animated by it. This thesis tries to steer a path between those of Quine (1969) and Davidson and Hintikka (1969) on this issue of the possibility of (radical) translation.

Time and Memory

In a preceding section, we have remarked that the notion of narrative is essentially correlated with the theme of time. We shall argue that time is crucial to an understanding of the distance between man and automata-like entities. Time is immanent to every narrative and occurs in this sense as *narrative time*. Yet both narrative and time have been conceptualized in western metaphysics in objective terms, that is, in terms that are ultimately external to human existence (it is only with Heidegger that this tradition is overturned). Hence, one can legitimately inquire after the internal significance of either, or both: in other words, what is our *acquaintance* with time and narrative?

I introduce as an initial response the notion of memory. It is in fact as memory that both time and narrative are given in human consciousness. It is in the possibility of memory that time, as a subjective and an anthropological phenomenon, is seen as essentially the same as narrative. For memory is to be seen not as an array of stable contents indexed on chronology but rather as the traces of experiences, drawn out and elaborated within the field of a subjective interlocution. In this sense, what we recollect is not (immutable) facts, but a certain kind of *history;* in other words, my remembrance is the coherences and intelligibilities revealed and composed within an interlocution of my past. Such coherences accrue as the minimal and necessary constraints intrinsic to the domain of language that is the medium of this interlocution, and to the continuity of the subject of this remembrance. In fact, such coherences situate the remembrance within the narrative that is the fabric of every subjective experience. This memory is the ground and the condition of this narrative, yet memory is not anterior to it; rather, the narrative is the *integral significance* of the entire corpus of memory.

The internal perception of time within subjective experience is precisely as the immanent time of its narrative. This time occurs as an accumulation of ramified and elaborated traces of remembrances, attaining with perspective the density of the continuum and pregnant with the continuing possibility of further interlocution, of further recognition.... In other words, time as immanent narrative time is the *horizon* of all subjective experience, and the ground of that continuity that allows me to designate myself as subject in the sentence, "I see...."

Hence the relation of man with time is not an objective, external and exigent one, but an intrinsic necessary condition for his subjective existence within a culture, a language community, and a world. I shall take this idea as the point of departure towards an understanding of the distance between man and android.

We have remarked that the salient aspect of the role that language plays in human life contexts is to invest such contexts with an essential inscrutability, an inscrutability that arises because the determinants of reference for such languages are irreducibly historicized and set within the disclosure of a certain horizon of elaborative possibilities. Such a condition arises possibly because human acquaintance with language, within the general contexts of socialization, stands within such a disclosure in the very first instance: language learning is never—completely, at least—a matter of ostensive definitions or syntactics; it is more a matter of elaboration and discourse in the very language that is being learned, and against the specific background of interpretative possibilities.

On the other hand, automata-theory creates a paradigmatically different kind of language. Expressions in such a language, as we have remarked before, correspond identically to a sequence of functional states which, eventually, have a language-independent definition. This correspondence is indeed the heart of the machine and the ultimate principle of its design (in the vocabulary of Aristotle, efficient *and* final cause). Interpretative contexts for such languages are in fact nothing more than transcriptive contexts, and by this token, quite transparent. By the same token again, intentionality of such languages is definitely *sui generis:* it can be made present as a determinate set of correlations between primitive expressions and the functional states they denote, and the (recursive) rules of composition which allow an infinite number of complex denoting expressions. The historicity that confers the indefiniteness and opacity to the intentionality of human languages reduces in this case to nullity: *automata have no history.*

But this situation leads to an even more significant fact: automata have no intrinsic relationship to time. Human acquaintance with time is as the immanent time of the narratives that make his subjective experience, within its remembrances, a *history.* Such narratives arise as possibilities for elaboration of meanings, *continuously* into the interpretative horizon, as they are instantiated. The condition for such elaborations is precisely the peculiar status that human language has in relation to us—the status that the composition of meanings within such a language overflows from the present of all facts that can be the basis for such a composition. It is this peculiar kind of language, and our existence within it, that gives us, binds us, to memory and, ultimately, to time.

We can see now that the question of time for automata—for the android in general whose relationship to language is dehistoricized, reduces to a purely external formulation. This relationship is purely exigent, external, and objective. In fact, the only such relationship is that minimally required in the formal and procedural formulation and functioning of the rules that iteratively carry it towards a certain set of predesignated functional states (goals).

Certain qualifications and implications of this characterization need to be remarked. This understanding of the word "android" is set within the contemporary notion of an automaton: it is quite possible that a certain threshold of complexity be reached, in the future, that would inaugurate a novel regime in which this understanding would prove inadequate. Contemporary technological experience already indicates that complexity gives rise to emergent features that, in a limited sense, claim autonomy from preformulated structural-functional laws that set up identical correspondences into a domain of functional states. In fact, it is precisely the quite unprecedented frequency of technological revolution that exposes the inadequacy of simplistic or tendentious characterizations and makes the whole debate about strong AI rather incongruous. On the other hand, what is being attempted in this essay is an articulation of certain essential attributes of human subjective experience towards the claim that, as of now, the notion of an android is incommensurate with such attributes.

What in fact this articulation of the nature of human perceptual experience shows is the incommensurability of certain levels of description, and consequently, the irreducibility of one to another. Human perceptual experience has been discursively formulated in terms of categories salient to it—for instance, aspectuality, narrative, memory, time, subjectivity, culture, and language—which are irreducible to the typically structural-functional-syntactic-procedural-compositional categories that are salient for automata theory. It is not even the case that a notion of emergence, "innocent" or otherwise, can bridge the gap; in fact they can do no more than save appearances, for the disjunction they address is not a contingent one but an essential one—between two distinct orders of phenomena. Hence they require distinct languages of description and discourse.

Coming back to the android, its exteriority to time cancels, in a sense, its claims to any sort of *interiority,* for man's claim to interiority is the condition that all his experience and behavior is composed and adumbrated within a structure of interlocution that is his immanent horizon of time. Hence all claims of intelligibility and identity have to be referred, in the last instance, to this immanent horizon—which is the subject's constitutive condition of subjectivity. The android, on the other hand, exists within a determinate syntax of relations and laws (at least at some level of abstraction); its "experience" and "behavior" needs no interlocution but only a reference to the determinacy of this syntax; hence conditions of intelligibilty and identity are formally and determinately embedded within this syntax and are recoverable through a decoding, without any reference to the android per se.

In this sense an android doesn't really "live," but (merely) functions; in the same sense, the words "experience," "perceptions," and "behavior" are not relevant to it, for they involve an implicit reference to a certain kind of intentionality, and in fact to a structure of subjectivity to which an android has no claim. That is, in fact, the case for every kind of description couched in a human language; for every word in such a language reveals on interlocution an *irreducible intentional content:* each contains an implicit reference to the interiority of an interpreting agent—an interiority that *cannot be made present to itself.*

Similarly, the pure exteriority of an android implies that it is completely transparent to *naming,* that is, it can be precisely and adequately named through any complete description of its content or its state, which in turn is formulated within the syntax that is the basis for its functioning. This is so since, in contradistinction to human perception and understanding, that, for an android (we cannot really use the same terms), is a *fact* and has a stable and explicable content, that determines its significance, its criteria of identity, and its conditions of use. To summarize this through an implication, an android is *blind to aspects:* what it "perceives" is a certain finite field of intensities that it organizes subsequently into a schema of formal elements according to a certain finite syntax.

Responsibility and Memory

I shall try to indicate in this section a relation between (human) subjective truth and ethicity. The question of ethicity, as all questions relating to human existence, has manifold significances and can be appraised from many perspectives. It can, for instance, be situated within a general analysis on value, or within a hermeneutic theory of "good life," or within an existential discourse on freedom, or within an ontological perspective on care, concern, and resoluteness; and as a historical fact, all these various perspectives have been taken by different philosophers, at different times. In this essay, I shall take the perspective that human existence is inflected by an ethicity to the extent that it has a certain capacity: the capacity to see itself from a perspective of *responsibility.* I am not going to dare to try to define what responsibility means (at least not in this essay); I am in fact going to appeal to whatever prediscursive notion we all have as to what responsibility of any kind can possibly mean. I am going to link up this prediscursive idea of responsibility with the foregoing discussion in two ways: from an intrinsic perspective of memory, and from an extrinsic perspective of resoluteness. Both are ultimately aspects of the notion of narrative.

I have remarked that my remembrance takes the form of an interlocution of my past, where experiences are revealed and composed within a general form of coherence. Such remembrances frame a general narrative structure whose *arché* confers on my specific ensembles of reflections and actions a certain minimal aspect of integrity. There is, immanent to every such narrative, a certain kind of temporality—a narrative time whose principal salient aspect is an intrinsic directedness towards its own completion or epitome. This completion has a peculiar ontological status: it has no substantive significance, even as a possibility; rather, it is a kind of *formal anticipation* of the kind of structure it should take to become a whole. Significantly, every action reflectively composed within and made integral to this general narrative structure bears within it this same kind of anticipation, a directedness towards its own wholeness. Of course, this fact has absolutely no substantive significance and in no way can supply a prescription of what specific forms a history of actions has to take to fulfill its own anticipation in this regard. On the other hand, it is merely a continual imperative to attain a certain formal destiny. It is the capacity to project action from within *this* perspective that I call responsibility.

The extrinsic perspective on responsibility is related to the recognition of the conditions of possibility of all communicative practice—including forms of reflection: in fact, a recognition of the irreducible *social* nature of all such conditions. It is extrinsic, since it relates to an explicit recognition of such conditions, and it is a willful choice in the face of such a recognition, to take up a certain attitude towards all future action.

I have argued that the intelligibility of perception derives from its continuity with the narrative of subjective experience. In fact, the possibility of finding the language of others intelligible is the condition that certain relevant narrative structures and relationships—that is, saliences—are shared by the members of a language community. More importantly, the confirmation of experiences and their criteria of truth, identity and adequacy, and the possibilities of dialogue and social action, too, are rooted in the condition that certain narrative saliences are shared at some basic level by an entire community. Ethicity, or the possibility of ethical existence, starts from an explicit and resolute recognition of this precondition for the community and a *responsibility* stemming from this recognition, to promulgate the identity of the subject in ways that are consistent with, and felicitous to, the shared narrative structure.

Summary and a Conclusion

We have sketched out in this essay certain salient aspects of human languages and the ways in which they relate to human symbolic practices. The most significant aspect of this relationship is the ineliminable role of an interpretative practice in the constitution of meaning within these languages. The interpretative act situates its field within a horizon of accumulated meanings and practices and thereby bestows on all referential contexts an irreducible historicity. Intentionality of languages comprises such contexts and as such, it becomes impossible to make the present a determinate content. The elaboration of meanings within and against the interpretative horizon takes on the general structure of a narrative. Remembrance, as an interlocution of the past, also takes on the narrative form. Every narrative has an immanent temporality, and the immanent time of the narrative(s) of human memory constitutes the intrinsic and necessary condition for living in a linguistified world and the possibility of projecting actions from within ethical perspectives. Hence, every equation between man and android has to bear the burden of a history which the latter erases.

References

Churchland, P. S. (1988). *Neurophilosophy: Toward an Unified Philosophy of Mind-Brain.* Cambridge, MA: MIT Press.

Davidson, D. (1984). *Inquiries into Truth and Interpretation.* Oxford: Clarendon.

Davidson, D. & Hintikka, J. (Eds.). (1969). *Words and Objections: Essays on the Work of W. V. Quine.* Dordrecht, Holland: D.Reidel.

Gadamer, H.-G. (1975). *Truth and Method* (G. Barden & J. Cumming, Trans.). New York: Seabury.

Goodman. (1973). *Fact, Fiction and Forecast.* Indianapolis: Bobbs-Merrill.

Husserl, E. (1964). *Phenomenology of Internal Time Consciousness* (M. Heidegger, Ed.; J. Churchill, Trans.). Bloomington: Indiana University Press.

Kripke, S. (1982). *Wittgenstein on Rules and Private Language.* Cambridge, MA: Harvard University Press.

MacIntyre, A. (1985). *After Virtue: A Study in Moral Theory.* London: Duckworth.

MacIntyre, A. & Emmet, D. (Eds.). (1970). *Sociological Theory and Philosophical Analysis.* London: Macmillan.

Mulhall, S. (1990). *On Being in the World: Wittgenstein and Heidegger on seeing Aspects.* London: Routledge.

Quine, W.V. (1960). *Word and Object.* Cambridge, MA: MIT, The Technology Press.

Quine, W.V. (1969). *Ontological Relativity and Other Essays.* New York: Columbia University Press.

Ricoeur, P. (1967). *Husserl: An Analysis of his Phenomenology* (E.G. Ballard & L.E. Embree, Trans.). Evanston: Northwestern University Press.

Silverman, H.J. (1988). *The Horizons of Continental Philosophy: Essays on Husserl, Heidegger, and Merleau-Ponty.* Dordrecht: Kluwer.

Wittgenstein, L. (1953). *Philosophical Investigations* (G.E.M. Anscombe, Trans.). Oxford: Basil Blackwell.

8 Taking Embodiment Seriously: Nonconceptual Content and Robotics

Ronald L. Chrisley

A central idea in cognitive science is that there is something that computers and brains do but that other objects, be they rocks, trees, or bicycles, do not. There are several candidates for what that commonality between brains and computers is: they process information, they represent, they compute. It is hoped that by finding similarities between computers and brains, we might be able to use the techniques of computer science to help us demystify the mental activity that the brain supports.

However, leaving the postulated similarities at such an abstract level may limit the productivity of this approach. After noting the connections, if any, between what brains do and what computers in general do, it seems a good idea to look for more specific connections between human cognition and the activity of particular kinds of computers, computers that share at least some of the purposes and functions of the brain. Recent trends in cognitive science suggest that we have already come close to exhausting the insights that can be gained from comparing human cognition to the activity of disembodied, formal computational systems such as theorem provers and expert systems. In particular, it seems wise to enrich the study of human cognition with an emphasis on computers that control robots which perceive and act in a real-time, real-space environment. Indeed, the idea seems to go beyond the mere computer/brain analogy to extend the correspondence to the robot/body, and further, it is often claimed that the respective environments of these systems should be included within our theoretical view if we are to achieve a deeper understanding of cognition. Although this class of computational/robotic systems surely includes more than what is typically meant by the term "android," it seems clear that all androids fall into this class.

Likewise, some philosophers of mind and language have rejected traditional, logic-based, formal notions of thought as too static and coarse-grained to account for the aspects of cognition that involve perception and action, or any kind of cognitive dynamics, such as learning, development, or concept formation. But rather than just stopping with this rejection (an *eliminativist* position), these philosophers have suggested new notions of the content of mental life, notions of content which can allow for modes of intentional interaction that is not mediated by fully formed concepts. These notions of *non-conceptual content* vary from author to author, but they have in common an intended purpose: to permit the explanation of a greater range of intentional phenomena, to widen the scope of intentional explanations from the mere logical to the fully psychological.

There are (at least) two connections between these recent developments, in complementary directions. First, some of the arguments that establish the need for non-conceptual content for the explanation of human cognition apply also to the case of artificial computational/robotic systems operating in real-time and real-space. That is, a proper understanding of android epistemology will require these new notions of non-conceptual content and non-conceptual mentality.

Conversely, the development and deployment of the notion of non-conceptual content require assistance from a practical and theoretical understanding of computational/robotic systems acting in real-time and real-space. In particular, the usual "that"-clause specification of content will not work for non-conceptual contents; some other means of specification is required, means that makes use of the fact that contents are aspects of embodied and embedded systems. That is, development and deployment of the notion of non-conceptual content will use concepts and insights gained from android design and android epistemology.

This chapter addresses this second connection between non-conceptual content and embodied, robotic computation. The next section explains what is meant by content, and how it is used in explaining the behavior of intentional systems. It also makes clear the distinction between conceptual and non-conceptual content. Then it is shown why standard means of content specification ("that"-clauses) will not work for non-conceptual content. After that, some alternative means of specification are proposed, and it is argued that all of the plausible ones employ notions of the embodiment and embeddedness of an intentional system, notions which are made precise via a detailed understanding of the relationships between computation/robotic properties and intentional ones: an understanding, that is, of android epistemology.

Content-Based Explanation

The intentional explanatory strategy that dominates cognitive science typically understands psychological states in terms of attitudes (belief, desire, knowledge, intention, etc.) toward contents (that there is a door ahead, that 2 + 2 = 4, etc.); such attitude/content pairs are appealed to in intentional psychological explanation. For example, one might explain why a robot opened a door (that is, show that the robot's opening the door wasn't just an accident; if circumstances had changed slightly—if the door were one foot over to the right, say—the robot would still have opened the door) by claiming that the robot *intended to open the door*; one could explain the possession of this intention as being the result of the robot's *desire to be in the next room* and its *belief that opening the door will help it get into the next room*. I will call explanations that appeal to such attitude/content pairs *content-based explanations*.

This notion of attitude/content pairs has played a key role in artificial intelligence (AI), but the emphasis there has been on one attitude in particular: knowledge (since intelligent action is seen to require knowledge of some sort). Correspondingly, within the field of AI there has been a great deal of interest in the nature of knowledge: how it can be manifested in programs or robots, and how it can be acquired or transferred. Although this line of inquiry is one approach to the goals of understanding the epistemology of artificial agents, it is also true that this particular emphasis on knowledge has resulted in a gap in current approaches to AI: not merely a (relative) lack of understanding of attitudes other than knowledge, but also, and perhaps to a greater extent, the absence of a proper understanding of the notion of content and its relation to the explanation and design of intelligent systems.

What is Content?

Content is the way the world is presented to a subject of experience. It is convenient to explicate what is meant by content by appealing to the notions of "that" clauses, information, and truth-conditions, but this will be done by showing how content is different from those notions, not by identifying content with any of those three:

1 "That" clauses, such as "that there is a door ahead" and "that 2 + 2 = 4" do indeed specify contents, but it would be wrong to define content as that which is specified by such clauses. First, "that" clauses can specify only complete, propositional contents; yet expressions that sentences comprise (such as names and predicates) carry their own, subpropositional contents. Second, and more importantly, it is argued in the next section that there are propositional contents that cannot be specified with "that" clauses.

2 Like information, content can be understood to be "carried" by states, representations, symbols, and expressions. But information is typically under-

stood as something that cannot be false: a state can only carry the information that x is P if it actually is the case that x is P. This is notoriously not so with content: sentences and beliefs can be false, and the content of my experience as of an oasis in front of me can be an illusion.

3 Having some kind of norm of correctness (truth-conditions, say) is necessary for the possibility of falsity and is a characteristic feature of content. However, one cannot look to truth-conditions alone to take the place of content in psychological explanation since, as Frege pointed out, there are propositions that have identical truth-conditions, yet we might assent to one and dissent from the other (for example, "the Morning Star is Venus" and "the Evening Star is Venus," given that the Morning Star is the Evening Star); the propositions might have different cognitive significance, different content.

Content, then, is a way of taking the world to be, and has two essential features: characteristic norms of correctness and a characteristic pattern of cognitive significance.

Conceptual and Non-Conceptual Content

I join others (Crane 1992; Cussins 1990; Davies 1990; Evans 1982; Haugeland 1991; Peacocke 1992) in arguing that a distinction should be made between conceptual and non-conceptual contents.[1] For several reasons, much of the work in AI has concentrated by default on the case of conceptual content, but there is reason to believe that understanding non-conceptual content is essential to understanding (and therefore to designing) intentional systems in general (see Cussins 1990).

Some ways of representing the world (contents) are objective or near-objective, some are not. A way of representing some aspect of the world is objective if, for example, it presents that aspect of the world as something that could exist while unperceived. Strawson (1959) maintained, as did Evans (1982) after him, that at least in the case of thinking about spatio-temporal particulars, truly objective thought is manifested in the possession and maintenance of a unified conceptual framework within which the subject can locate, and thus relate to any other arbitrary object of thought, the bit of the world being thought about.

If this understanding of objective thought is correct, then it has important implications for the understanding of pre (or non or sub) objective representation. Preobjective representation involves contents that present the world, but not *as* the world, not as something that is or can be independent of the subject. An infant's early perceptual/motor interactions with its environment are a plausible example of the presence of a preobjective mode of thought. The infant tracks an object (thus suggesting that there is some intentional relation between the infant and the object) when it is perceptually occurrent, yet when the object is occluded from view, the infant loses interest in the object, and is in fact startled if the obstruction is removed to reveal the object. Since the very notion of an *object* essentially involves the notion of something that can exist even though occluded, the infant is not thinking of the object *as an object*. The contents of the infant's thoughts concerning the object do not present the object as something objective, as something that could exist while unperceived. According to the Strawsonian/Evansian line I am taking, then, the infant's lack of objectivity must be manifested in the lack of a unified framework of thought: the infant is unable, in general, to locate objects in such a framework. I will call such preobjective contents *non-conceptual* contents (*NCCs*); *conceptual* contents, on the other hand, are objective.[2]

It is a consequence of this way of understanding the conceptual/non-conceptual distinction that conceptual contents will necessarily be systematic, will meet Evans' Generality Constraint (1982, p. 104):

> (GC) For any conceptual contents (ways of thinking of properties) F and G, and any conceptual contents (ways of thinking of objects) a and b, if a subject knows what it would be for a to be F and for b to be G, then it must know what it would be for a to be G and for b to be F.

The constraint (GC) is a direct consequence of the necessity, for there to be objective, conceptual thought, of a unified framework within which to locate all properties and particulars.

Non-conceptual contents, on the other hand, are not systematic. In the case of NCC, the mode of thought is preobjective; a unifying framework is not present, and there, therefore, properties and particulars which cannot be related in the proper way. The idea of non-conceptual content, then, implies that one can represent the world with proto-concepts that do not universally recombine with all other possessed proto-concepts.

For example, consider an infant which cannot, as before, think of a particular object (a glass, say) as existing unseen, but *can* represent its mother as being behind, out of view (on the basis of hearing her voice or feeling her arm, say). The contents of such an infant will violate the Generality Constraint, since the infant may be able to think (something like) *glass in front of me* and *mother behind me* but not *glass behind me*. The infant's contents are not fully objective and are therefore non-conceptual. To ascribe conceptual content to the infant in this case would mischaracterize its cognitive life and would not allow prediction or explanation of the infant's behavior.

An important constraint on content ascription is what I will call the *Possession Principle*: a subject may entertain a content *C* only if the subject possesses all of the concepts (if any) that *C* comprises. Thus, *glass in front of me* would not be a content that the infant could entertain, since the infant's failure to meet the Generality Constraint demonstrates that the infant does not possess one of the constituents of the content, the concept *glass*.

Other Ways a Content May Fail to be Conceptual

However, the manner in which contents fail to be objective is richly textured. A content may manifest its non-conceptuality by failing to respect any of a number of conceptuality constraints. A nonexhaustive and nonexclusive set of such constraints might include, in addition to (GC), the following properties of conceptual content:

(SP)   it must have subject-predicate structure;

(RP)   if the content is to be a way of thinking about an item, the subject must know which (in the sense required by what Evans calls "Russell's Principle") item is being thought about;

(MC)   if the content is to be a way of thinking about an item, the subject must be able to think of the same item in a number of other ways;

(EU)   if the content is to be a way of thinking about an item, the subject must be able to think of the item as existing unperceived, as something for which the qualitative/numeric distinction applies, or as something which can be reidentified;

(PE)   if a subject is capable of taking the attitude of belief toward the content, then it must be able to entertain the possibility that its belief is false; it must have the concept of belief to have any beliefs.[3]

Thus, non-conceptuality could be manifested in the failing to meet of any of these conceptuality constraints. It should be emphasized that these constraints are offered as examples only. It might be that some of them are not required of all conceptual contents, or it might be that some of them are required of *all* contents, and thus failing to meet them is not a way for a content to be non-conceptual. Nevertheless, these examples will be of use in illustrating a proposed alternative means of content specification later.

The Inadequacy of Standard Specifications for NCC

Preconceptual Linguistic Use Specifications

In order for a theory of intentional action to be able to appeal to specific contents in its explanations, it must have a means of canonically specifying those contents, a means of specifying them according to their essential properties, such as their truth conditions or their cognitive significance. For example, one can specify a content by the phrase "the content toward which subject A took the belief attitude exactly 10.3 seconds ago," but this would not be a canonical specification, since it does not pick out the content it does in virtue of the content's essential properties, but rather its accidental ones. A standard means of canonically specifying contents is what I will call the "linguistic use" means of specification: providing an expression in English (or other natural language), usually preceded by "that," with the same content as the one to be specified (e.g., "The content of my belief is *that the object on the table is a* computer" or "The last bit of register A0 being on means *that a message is in the input buffer*").

Of course, almost any proposed means of specifying content will use language in a more general, and conventional, sense of the word "use" than the one I am employing here. However the following criticism of linguistic use methods are not directed towards proposed forms of specification that use language in this broad sense. The expression "linguistic use" is meant to be a technical one: I mean to include under the term only those means of specification that pick out contents exclusively in the manner mentioned in the definition above: viz., by providing an expression in a natural language that has the very same content as the one that is to be specified. In this narrower, more technical sense, means of specification may use language in the general sense and yet not be subject to the negative conclusions in what immediately follows.

Although the linguistic use means of specification might work well for conceptual contents, there are several reasons why one might think that it is not adequate for the specification of subobjective NCCs. First, a direct claim can be made: language is itself conceptual—all the contents involved in using language are fully objective—and therefore linguistic use specifications can specify only conceptual contents. Linguistic use specifications are what has been called elsewhere (Cussins 1990, especially pp. 382 ff; Peacocke 1986, especially p. 17) *conceptual* specifications of content: specifications that are made in such a way as to require a subject to possess the concepts used in the specification if that subject is to be able to take an attitude toward that content. Thus linguistic use specifications, employing conceptual language, will not be able to specify the contents of, say, an infant's or animal's psychology, since such specifications would require the infant or animal to possess concepts which it in fact lacks.

In spite of the strong intuitions behind this line of thought, there are reasons why it might be more illuminating to establish the incompleteness of linguistic use specifications by a means other than one which relies on the principle that all language is conceptual; for one thing, many would want to deny that language is entirely conceptual. What I will do, then, is split linguistic use specifications into two types: *purely descriptive*, and *indexical*. I will argue that specifications of neither type can specify NCCs. First, a means of specification, in order for it to be of use in a scientific theory, must specify NCCs canonically, a method which rules out descriptive linguistic use. Furthermore, content specifications must be context-independent, a method which rules out indexical linguistic use. Thus some means of specification other than linguistic use is required.[4]

The Inadequacy of Descriptive Linguistic Use

Cussins (1990) has brought together some insights from Evans (1982) and Perry (1979) that can serve as an argument against the possibility of using descriptive (that is, nonindexical) language to specify non-conceptual contents.

Perry shows that there are contents, constitutively linked to perception and action[5] (for example, the contents of one's "I" thoughts), that are not equivalent in terms of cognitive significance to any contents specified, in a purely descriptive manner, by the linguistic use method.

However, one *can* give a linguistic use specification of the contents of one's "I" thoughts, but only if one employs indexicals, as in the ascription: "RC believes: 'I am spilling sugar all over the supermarket floor.'" One cannot use a nonindexical specification, as in "RC believes 'the person named RC is spilling sugar all over the supermarket floor,'" since it specifies a content that is distinct from that of the first-person thought I would normally have in that situation, as can be seen by the differences in the two contents' connections to action. As a result of amnesia, I might think in the latter case "Well, the person named RC had better clean it up" and go on my way, whereas in the former case no amnesia could get me to think that it was anyone else's mess but mine. In order for the belief *the person named RC is spilling sugar all over the supermarket floor* to have any implications for my action, it must be supplemented by the belief *the person named RC = I (me).* The belief *I am spilling sugar all over the supermarket floor* requires no such further identification; its connections to action are direct, unmediated.

The application of Perry's insight to the case of NCC is direct: if any NCCs are directly connected to perception and action in the way that "I" contents are, then Perry's arguments establish that such contents cannot be specified by means of descriptive language use. One line of reasoning that leads one to conclude that all NCCs *are* constitutively connected to perception and action is the following. As observed before, NCCs are subobjective by virtue of the fact that they do not enable the bit of the world being thought about to be integrated into a unified framework of particulars and their interrelations. It is this lack of a framework which restricts subobjective thought to contents that are essentially linked to perception and action. The idea employed here is that indexicality is the starting point; contents that (merely) have constitutive connections to action and perception are the basic case. It is only through the construction of a nonsolipsistic conception of the world via some unified framework of particulars and relations that one's contents can display the kind of perception and action transcendence that is characteristic of descriptive modes of thinking. It is the very subobjectivity of NCCs that allows the application of Perry's argument to their case: they cannot be specified by descriptive language use.

This understanding of NCC seems to agree with (at least one reading of) what Evans (1982) meant by non-conceptual content:

> Let us begin by considering the spatial element in the non-conceptual content

of perceptual information. What is involved in a subject's hearing a sound as coming from such-and-such a position in space? ... When we hear a sound as coming from a certain direction, we do not have to think or calculate which way to turn our heads (say) in order to look for the source of the sound. If we did have to do so, then it ought to be possible for two people to hear a sound as coming from the same direction (as 'having the same position in the auditory field'), and yet to be disposed to do quite different things in reacting to the sound, because of differences in their calculations. Since this does not appear to make sense, we must say that having spatially significant information consists at least partly in being disposed to do various things. (pp. 154-5)

This idea is very similar to Perry's way of characterizing ways of thinking that are essentially likened to perception and action. Just as there is no "calculation" in the case of Evans' example of auditory content, there is no "calculation" in Perry's example of the first-person mode of thought: one knows, in an unmediated manner, that such thoughts are directly related to one's own actions and perceptions. An identification with some descriptive mode of thought (for example, *I (me) = the person named RC*) is not required for action.[6]

Another indication that NCCs are, like the contents of the indexicals "I" and "now," constitutively linked to perception and action is that if one attempts to specify such contents by means of linguistic use, then one tends to use indexicals in so doing.[7]

If what has been said is correct, then NCCs are indexical contents in Perry's sense, and therefore, like the content of conceptual first-person thoughts, cannot be specified by descriptive linguistic use. But there is reason to believe that nonconceptual contents, unlike the contents of conceptual first-person thoughts, cannot be specified by the alternative of indexical linguistic use, either.

This is so, if not because of the conceptuality of language, as discussed above, then for reasons related to the requirement that scientific theorizing be context-independent (in a particular sense). That is, even if indexicals could, *per impossibile*, be used to specify NCCs via linguistic use (either because they do not have conceptual content, or because they can somehow linguistically specify a content that is not, strictly speaking, the content they carry, or because it is possible to devise new indexicals that introduce, in a nonsystematic way, elements of the environment into the content being specified), such indexicals alone would be inadequate for the particular task at hand: a context-independent intentional science. Specifically, the function of the indexical is merely to call attention to other factors (subject, context, and their relation) so that a content may be specified. In such a case, all the individuative work is being done by those highlighted elements, not the indexical itself.[8] Thus, in order to specify the content, one would need more than mere linguistic expressions; one would also need an environment related to those expressions in order to allow those expressions to function and thus carry content. Thus, even *indexical* linguistic use cannot be used to specify NCCs.

This conclusion is also supported by the following line of reasoning: given 1) NCCs are indexical; 2) the suggestion that the content of all linguistic indexicals can be reduced to "I" and "now" plus some descriptive component; 3) that there might be organisms which entertain nondescriptively specifiable NCCs but do not possess the first-person mode of presentation (the content of "I"); then it follows that there will be no indexical linguistic use specification for the NCCs of such organisms.

These arguments agree with the conclusion of other writers (e.g., Peacocke 1981, p. 191): in specifying contents that are constitutively linked to perception and action, such as particular first-person modes of presentation, we cannot employ the content in question but must refer to it instead. The task, then, is to find ways of referring to such modes of presentation that identify them not only uniquely, but canonically, as discussed above.[9]

Alternatives to Standard Means of Specification

To be frank, I don't yet have a fully worked-out alternative means of content specification. What the rest of this chapter will do, however, is describe some possibilities that are currently under consideration and explain why they are at least plausible candidates for an alternative. This will not only serve to explicate many of the issues that have been discussed and to pacify those "what else could there be?"-type worries that may be nagging some readers; it will show along the way why one must take embodiment seriously if one is to be able to specify non-conceptual contents for an intentional science.

Conceptual Subtraction

One idea is that perhaps linguistic use fails only as a matter of technicality; perhaps some modification of it can overcome its limitations, while using the same, fundamentally nonembodied, approach. It seems such a modification would have to be something like the conceptual subtraction (CS) means of content specification. As the name might suggest, this method is similar in spirit to a pure conceptual specification, such as linguistic use. Nevertheless, and the above arguments against linguistic use specifications of NCCs notwithstanding, it seems possible that the CS method can specify non-conceptual contents, because it is distinct from pure conceptual specification in a crucial way. The CS method is an attempt to stay as close as possible to our practice of linguistic use specification while throwing out the restrictions that make linguistic use inadequate. The problem with purely conceptual specifications, as we have seen, is that they cannot specify subconceptual contents. Any attempts at specifying the content of, say, particular preobjective experiences of an infant, would over-ascribe, in that such specifications would imply that the infant possesses abilities that it does not, in fact, possess. That is, they would violate the Possession Principle (cf. earlier). For example, specifying the content of the infant's belief as "that there is a glass in front of me" would imply that the infant possessed the concept of a glass, with its attendant concepts, not only *drinking, manufacture,* and *liquid,* but also object and location; it would also imply that the infant's thinking about the glass adhered to the generality constraint, and supported the ability to think of the glass as something that could exist unperceived. This would invite the theorist to make false predictions about, and would disallow correct explanations of, an infant's behavior.

The idea behind CS specification is to proceed with a conceptual, linguistic use specification, but also to tag the implications of that specification to which one does not wish to be committed, that is, to start with the conceptual content and then subtract properties of the conceptual content (such as "meets the generality constraint" or "supports the idea of existence unperceived") which the content to be ascribed does not possess. Then there will be no over-ascription of abilities and therefore no false prediction or inaccessible explanation.[10]

In order to be able to employ the CS method, one must first capture all the different implications an ascription of a conceptual content carries with it. This will involve both a cataloguing of the general requirements for all conceptual contents and all concepts, such as the Generality Constraint, and a listing of the particular requirements for each individual concept. One might end up with a list like the one earlier for the general conceptual requirements, with the addition of something like

Particular conceptual requirements:
bachelor:
(1) organism must also possess the concept *unmarried*
(2) organism must also posses the concept *male*

...

drinking glass
(1) organism must also possess the concept *liquid*
(2) organism must also posses the concept *drinking*

...

Etc.

It is very important to note that the above, as well as the list made earlier, is meant to serve only as a toy example of the enumeration of constraints for the CS method, and not as a specific proposal for what these constraints should be. Also, the capturing of the commitments need not proceed via enumeration; the catalogue will undoubtedly employ quantification. It might also be recursive, in that conceptual requirements might themselves have further conceptual requirements, such that a content might meet some of the requirements for, say, RP, and not others.

Once this enumeration of conceptual requirements is in place, specifications of sub-conceptual contents in ascriptions would be possible:

> The content of the infant's belief is *that there is a drinking glass* [-GC, -EU, -1] *within reach*—where the qualifiers within brackets after a concept indicate in what ways that part of the content fails to be conceptual.

In order for any alternative specification to succeed, several conditions must be met. Any particular application of the method must indicate at least one content, at most one content, and, as discussed before, it must indicate the content canonically.

In the case of the CS method, the first condition prompts one to wonder "how can one be sure that a subtracted content is actually a content at all?" One suggestion[11] for a criterion for an abstract entity to be a content is that it be able to help rationalize a subject's behavior by serving as a premise in practical reasoning. Thus, the need to meet this first condition highlights the fact that the CS approach has meaning only within the context of inference rules that relate such subtracted contents. A "logic" of subtracted contents is required, one that will capture the a priori relations between (for example) the content "glass[-EU, -2] at location$_1$[-EU, -MC]" entertained at time t_1 and the content "glass[-RP, -2] at location$_2$[-EU]" entertained at time t_2, where location$_1$ and location$_2$ are ego-centric specifications of places, such that they are coreferential, given the turning action performed between times t_1 and t_2. The inference from the first to the second content, inasmuch as it is correct, will have to fall under some inference rule in this "logic" of subtracted contents.

The second condition puts further constraints on the CS method. For it seems possible that there may be any number of ways that a concept could fail to incur some particular conceptual commitment. For example, it seems that any number of contents meet the condition "just like the concept *glass*, but does not meet the Generality Constraint." So it seems that one's catalogue of conceptual commitments is going to have to be sophisticated indeed if one is to be able to specify a content uniquely.

But perhaps this just shows that the second condition is, strictly speaking, too strict. Of course, there is something to the idea that content specifications are useful only when there is some restriction on the contents that they specify. But this need not imply that specifications are of use in psychological explanation only when a unique content is specified. One might be able to specify only some restricted set of contents, those that share a particular set P of properties, as opposed to specifying a unique content. But if the explanation to be given need only appeal to the fact that the content possesses the properties in P, and if it can be made intelligible that the nonintentional characterization of the system to be explained could instantiate some content with the properties in P, then perhaps no further individuation is required. In fact, anyone who thinks that many of our ascriptions of conceptual content are, strictly speaking, inaccurate will have to appeal to some consideration such as this one in order to make sense of the fact that such ascriptions are as successful as they are.

With respect to the third condition, the CS method of specification will inherit the advantages of purely conceptual specifications: the ability to specify content in terms of its essential properties. If the first two conditions can be met or dispensed with, it seems that one can only question the canonicity of CS specifications if one is willing to question the canonicity of linguistic use specifications as well.

Another advantage of this close relation to conceptual specification is the ability to unify the conceptual and non-conceptual aspects of content within the same formalism.

But there are several obstacles to the successful deployment of this method. One possible worry is that the commitments to be subtracted must be atomistic: it must be the case that if one subtracts a commitment, one is not logically forced to subtract out other commitments. Or at least if there are such holistic interrelations, they should be explicitly captured in a syntax of some kind. For example, if it is impossible to fail to meet the Generality Constraint without also failing to meet Russell's Principle, then either these should be rejected as candidates for commitments to be subtracted, or one must rule out, formally, the possibility of C[-GC] and C[-RP] for all concepts C.

This worry seems unfounded, however. As long as the commitments P referred to in a specification are sufficient to meet the three conditions above, it doesn't seem necessary to refer to other commitments, even if they are holistically related to those in P. This view might have to be abandoned once one starts to develop a logic for subtracted contents, since one might want to guarantee, for example, that distinct specifications imply distinct contents. But note that this is not guaranteed even for linguistic use.

There are other worries, however. Perhaps there is no canonical, finitely-specifiable list of conceptual requirements, either in general or for particular contents. Another possible difficulty is that the method might not be general enough; there might be non-conceptual contents that are not expressible as subtractions of conditions from conceptual ones. The problem is not that there might be non-conceptual contents that are subtractions of concepts other than those which we, as human theorists, possess; the fact that we do not possess these conceptual contents is not in itself an argument against the idea that they could be specified as logical functions of the concepts which we do in fact possess. Rather, the worry is that there might be non-conceptual contents that are not subtractions of any conceptual contents, be they in our possession or not. Without an argument against such a possibility, it would be excessively teleological to assume that all non-conceptual contents must be able to be expressed as subtractions from the conceptual contents into which some of them develop.

Finally, there is a general problem for nonembedded means of content specification, including both linguistic use and conceptual subtraction: the externalism of content. A general externalist claim is that the intentional nature of the cognitive phenomena to be explained requires that the specifications of the contents involved must make reference to the environment of the subject. This claim is true not only because intentional properties do not in general supervene on the states of the organism alone,[12] but also because intentional phenomena can be specified, explained, and understood only in terms of their directedness toward the external world and the potential to interact with it. For example, it seems very likely that a means of specification must include some way of representing the spatial environment of the subject if it is to be able to express and explain spatial NCCs and their interrelations, as used in the construction of cognitive maps.

One might question this conclusion by noting that conceptual content is intentional, yet we specify such contents via nonembodied means (linguistic use). One reason we can get by with nonembodied specifications for conceptual content, but not for non-conceptual content, will be given next.

But there is also reason to believe that we *can't* in general get by with nonembodied specifications, even in the purely conceptual case. If externalist positions such as those expressed in Burge (1982) and Putnam (1975) are correct, then there is no way that a sentence of English language on Earth could specify even the conceptual contents entertained by our Twins on Twin-Earth. So, *a fortiori*, linguistic use could not specify Twin-Earth NCCs.[13] In order for the CS method to avoid this limitation, it must be the case that one can subtract from an Earthly conceptual content to yield a Twin-Earthly NCC. This seems possible only if the NCCs of Earth and Twin-Earth are the same (i.e., if externalist arguments apply only at the conceptual level). Yet there are those (for example, Davies 1991) who would maintain that even (some) non-conceptual contents are external. If so, we have yet another reason to reject nonembedded means of specification of NCCs. Perhaps, then, it is time we turned to embedded alternatives.

Embedded Indexicals

One such alternative means of specification is suggested by the discussion at the end of the last section. There, descriptive linguistic use was rejected as a means of NCC specification because it cannot accommodate contents that have constitutive connections to perception and action. And indexical linguistic use was rejected because it alone could not specify content, but rather it must be supplemented by an environment within which language can function.

But we actually do specify contents via indexical linguistic use; we might explain RC's behavior by saying, "He started cleaning up the mess because he realized *that he himself was the one making a mess*," which includes a content specification by means of indexical linguistic use (the reflexive "he himself").

So either we don't need to appeal to an environment when specifying contents via indexical linguistic use, or appeal to such an environment is possible, and effortless.

Well, "no" and a qualified "yes." No: we *do* need to appeal to the environment with such specifications. One has to know which subject is in question in order to fully grasp the significance of their first-person thoughts. This is clearer in the case of demonstratives: "He thought <*that*> is a doorway" will explain why a subject ran into a false stage door if one understands, *inter alia*, that the <*that*> refers to the false door. Just as attributions such as "The content of the agent's visual perception was *this*" are effective, if at all, only when the speaking theorist and hearing theorist share the same environment (a condition that cannot, in general, be expected to fulfilled in the practicing of cognitive science[14]), the specification of non-conceptual contents (indexically or otherwise) will have to recreate this context by invoking some detailed description of the agent's environment.

But if so, doesn't this just show that we already take embodiment seriously, and make implicit appeals to a subject's environment, when we employ conventional indexical linguistic use specifications? Yes, but: the simplicity of the task of world-involving in such cases is a consequence of the systematicity of conceptual, linguistically specifiable contents involved. Such contents have conceptually elegant rules of world-involvement (e.g., "a use of the first-person mode of thought refers to the person who is using it"). Once that conceptual simplicity is absent, as in the case of nonsystematic NCCs, the rules for world-involvement become fragmented, nonsystematic, and ad hoc, and thus demand more effort for their specification, as well as the specification of the environment in which they function.

Can the specification of such nonsystematic indexicals proceed by means of linguistic use? Can there really be a term that has associated with it the world-involving function appropriate for an NCC? Technically speaking, I suppose so, if we can specify such contents at all. For once one had some theoretical grasp of the function in question, one could simply introduce a term that had that function as its indexical function. But the point is that one would have to have some way of theoretically grasping that function in the first place, since the function will not be one with which we are already familiar in our everyday use of language. Even if, strictly speaking, indexical linguistic use is possible, its possibility is contingent upon that for which I am arguing: an alternative to linguistic use specifications.

The challenge of NCC specification via indexical linguistic use will not primarily be a matter of choosing the right (nonsystematic, nonlinguistic) indexicals but mainly a matter of specifying, in the appropriate ways, the subject, its context, and the relations between them. A large part of the work in developing a means of specification for NCCs will be formalizing the practice of highlighting certain aspects of the subject/environment system so that a particular, non-conceptual way of representing that situation is indicated. And even the task of choosing the right indexicals will require some sophisticated way of relating the subject to its environment.

But embeddedness requires embodiment; because EI specifications must be embedded, they must take embodiment seriously. In order to be able to make reference to the relations between a subject and its environment, one must think of the subject as having a position in that environment. Also, in order to understand how the highlighted environmental factors play a role in fixing the content, one must have some understanding of (at least) the perceptual and motor capabilities of the system. It is for these reasons, and because one must specify the nonsystematic indexical functions involved in grasping various NCCs, that EI specification must make reference to the underlying, nonintentional characterization of a system.

Content Realization

The last two means of specification to be considered here, content realization (CR) and ability instantiation (AbI), are both, unlike those before, non-conceptual specifications in that they do not express, but rather refer to, the content to be specified, and therefore employ concepts without requiring the organism to possess those concepts in order to entertain the content so specified. In the case of CR, this reference is achieved by mentioning a set of perceptual, computational, and/or robotic states and/or abilities that realize the possession of that content in a particular case or set of cases.

As mentioned before, specifications must indicate at least one content, at most one content, and must indicate contents canonically. These three conditions, involving as they do the notion of indication, are primarily epistemic constraints. The non-conceptual nature of CR specifications, however, will give at least the first two of these conditions a metaphysical bite.

At Least One Content: Realization

By requiring that the referenced states indicate at least one content, the first condition entails that the states mentioned in a CR specification must realize a content; they must be sufficient for the possession of a content. One could imagine a weaker form of state- or ability-based specification, in which the states would not have to realize the content they specify but would instead merely suggest to the theorist the content to be specified, with no accompanying metaphysical claim that those states specify the content because they realize it. But if the metaphysical relationship is abandoned, what relationship is to be put in its place? How is one to know if the states on offer will succeed in suggesting the content in mind? In the absence of answers to these questions, any alternative to the metaphysical approach is precisely the kind of specification that I am trying to avoid: one that succeeds, when and if it does, without appeal to any principle (or at least not any articulated principle). A scientific psychology requires more rigor than such a means could currently provide; it seems that such rigor could only be provided, if ever, by a means of specification informed by a theory of "suggestion" itself (i.e., a near-complete scientific psychology). Scientific psychology would have to be completed before it could begin.

Note that there is nothing in the CR approach that precludes an externalist individuation of content. It might be true that individualistic properties alone do not determine some or all contents (although not necessarily for the reasons given in, for example, Putnam [1975] and Burge [1982]), but this just means that the states used to specify such contents will themselves have to be externalistically individuated. This is not in itself a difficulty (*pace* Fodor 1981), since there are several examples in cognitive science of such an embedded notion of state or ability.

It is important to the proper understanding of CR specification that one note that although sufficiency of the states for the specified content is required, necessity of the former for the latter is not. That is, the specification does not have to provide or even invite a reduction of the content it specifies. To specify a content by mentioning one realization of that content is not to indicate the physical type that constitutes possession of that content in general. Indeed, CR specifications do not even require that a reduction of the content to a nonintentional vocabulary be possible (which is just as well, since there are good reasons to believe that such reductions are *not* possible). Conversely, the fact that there might be infinitely many other physical configurations, that fall under no nomologically-governable physical type, that are also realizations of the given content, counts not one whit against the ability of the particular realization mentioned to pick out, clearly and distinctly, the content in question. Consider how one might indicate to someone a particular economic phenomenon by describing a particular manifestation of that phenomenon in terms of a particular currency, set of countries, etc.

At Most One Content: Holism
In order for the states referenced in a CR specification to specify a content, they must not only realize the content in question; the second condition mentioned above, together with a simplistic notion of realization-based specification, entails that the specifying abilities must realize only that content. This would appear to be at odds with the fact that content is holistic: contents come in groups, so any abilities that are sufficient for one content are going to be sufficient for others as well. Thus, it seems that CR specifications might have difficulty respecting the second condition.

One should not reply to this objection by denying the holism of content, even non-conceptual content. For even if NCC does not meet the Generality Constraint completely, some more limited of holism may be required if we are to speak of content at all. Rather, one should reply by pointing out that to make the above objection to CR specifications is to misunderstand the holistic nature of content. It is a holism that has to do with capacities, and not the exercising of those capacities. That is, while it may be true that one cannot acquire the capacities for entertaining a content (*c*) without thereby acquiring the capacities to entertain many others (*S*), it is not thereby true that if one entertains *c* one must entertain all of those related contents in *S*. Thus, a realization may specify only one content, even if the capacity to entertain that content entails the capacity to entertain others.

Canonicity

Even if CR specifications indicate one and only one content, it must be ensured that they do so canonically. That is, they must avoid, for example, being like the linguistic use specification mentioned before: "the content toward which the subject took the belief attitude exactly 10.3 seconds ago." One might think that CR specifications cannot specify contents canonically, since canonical specifications must invoke the essential properties of the content, while CR specifications proceed by the mention of a particular realization of that content, which might be thought to be only contingently related to the content.

But a requirement for such strict necessity seems to be too stringent. Consider linguistic use specifications. Although there *might* be a necessary connection between a content and a *word* that expresses it, the relation between the content and the *sounds* or *marks* that instantiate the word that has that content is contingent. So if such marks are sufficient for canonical specification, then it seems possible that other entities contingently related to the content, such as one of its realizations, could also be sufficient for canonical specification.

To make good this analogy between marks and particular realizing states, there needs to be more to CR specifications than mere realizing states, just as there is more to linguistic use specifications than mere marks or sounds. In the case of linguistic use, there is a practical capacity, on the part of the theorist, to relate these arbitrary marks to the contents they express. This practical capacity is part of being a member of a linguistic community and is acquired through exposure to the norms that the community applies to the sounds and marks that the language comprises. So it would seem that CR specifications, if they are to be canonical, must rely on some practical capacity for relating particular realizing states to their general forms, the forms which are essential to any state that realizes the content in question. And this capacity might have to be acquired through familiarity and practical interaction with the system in question.[15] Note that one would not have to develop such a capacity for every system to be explained, but only for the system or systems that one wishes to use for the purposes of CR specification of content.

However, the more that one models CR specification on the case of linguistic use specification, the more one runs the risk of limiting CR to conceptual contents. It could very well be that the requirement of a public, practical capacity to understand others is what restricts linguistic use to objective contents. If so, one might worry that the requirement for a practical capacity to understand the canonical realizing system in CR specifications might likewise limit such specifications to the conceptual case. Although this worry cannot be dispelled entirely here, it should be pointed out that there is a stronger link between a content and one of its realizing states ("intrinsic intentionality") than the relation between a content and the arbitrary properties of one of the symbols that convention and practice have associated with that content ("derived intentionality"). In fact, once the general parameters of the specifying system have been determined, there might be a necessary relationship between a state, given that it is bounded by those parameters, and the content it realizes. Therefore, canonical specification may be possible without relying on practical capacities that might restrict one to conceptual contents. But perhaps this is just optimism; at present the issue is unresolved.

Ability Instantiation

The limitations of both nonembodied (linguistic use, CS) means of specification, as well as of those that merely *mention* embodiment (EI, CR), might have a common cause. Specifically, it might be that the only way canonically to specify NCCs is via an explicit demonstration or actual instantiation of the idealized robotic and computational abilities involved in entertaining that content. Attempts to specify an NCC in a linguistic use manner fail to indicate (to any theorist seeking to understand the agent) the correct content and therefore leave certain connections to perception, action, and other contents inexplicable; perhaps merely *mentioning* the abilities must also fail, for similar reasons. Practical, canonical specification of an NCC might require the actual instantiated presence of an ability, rather than the conceptual idea of that ability. There are two possible ways that the abilities could be instantiated: external to the theorist, in some apparatus (external ability instantiation, or EAI); or within the theorist/environment system itself (self-instantiation, or SI).

External Ability Instantiation

There are practical reasons why actual instantiation of specifying abilities, as opposed to mere reference to them, might be required. The demands for embeddedness in content specification call for a means of specification that not only allows one to represent explicitly the spatio-temporal relations between the system being modeled and its environment, but must also itself be a concrete system that persists through time and possesses computational abilities. As mentioned before (in the discussion of the possibility of embedded indexical, EI, specifications), the context of the subject will have to be reconstructed if we are to be able to specify (at least some) NCCs; this should be achieved, at least in part, via a judicious choice of the syntactic properties of the specification formalism itself. It should have an active, computational format, rather than the static format of axioms and theorems on a printed page. The complexity of a fine-grained static formalism with spatio-temporal 'parameters' (for example, "Believes[robot$_3$, time$_1$, *that is an obstacle*, the chair at location (x,y,z)]") would be prohibitive; instead, a computer simulation (of the interactions of the various axioms and 'given' conditions of the theory) would make explanation and prediction more tractable than if one were to use noninstantiated, referential, 'manual' analysis. In order to understand which content is involved in a particular situation, a theorist could look at how an instantiated system (for example, an android, or a simulation of one) responds to different counter-factual contingencies, could monitor the evolution of the current state forward or backward in time, etc. This would not be feasible with a noninstantiated means of specification.

But there is a more theoretical reason why an external, active instantiation of some abilities that realize a non-conceptual content might be necessary for the canonical specification of that content. EAI specification can be seen as a response to the worries, just expressed at the end of the previous subsection, concerning the canonicity of content realization (CR) specifications. Perhaps one can specify contents, as CR aims to do, in terms of the states and abilities which realize them, but the prerequisite practical ability, on the part of the theorist, to move from abilities to contents might require an active presence of those abilities, with which a theorist can interact, not just reference to them. The observable temporally-extended action of the computational formalism (and its interaction with its environment) might be the only way canonically to specify certain NCCs, given their resistance to specification by standard means. Some phenomena may be explicable only through the use of *models*; perhaps only via models in which, for example, actual time and space are used to represent the temporal and spatial aspects of the modeled system, as opposed to formalizms that represent those aspects with something else: a written variable or spacing on a page. It seems likely that in order to be able to specify NCCs and their inter-relationships, one will have to choose representations for them in such a way that there is a nonarbitrary relationship between the syntactic properties of the representations and the contents to which they refer: the syntactic properties will assist directly in specifying the content.

This approach (and others presented here, inasmuch as they are concerned with the question "what is a *canonical* specification?") places an emphasis on the theorist's own embodiment, with the notion of a theorist's *psychology* that such embodiment implies. Canonical specification cannot proceed independently of the cognitive make-up and limitations of the theorist using that specification; rather, what counts as a sufficient specification or, more generally, explanation, will depend on the conditions under which the *theorist's* abilities to grasp contents may be exercised. One tentative proposal is that our psychologies as theorists are such that we will have canonical NCC specification only when we employ actual instantiations of that content.

Self-instantiation
There are two different proposals to be considered in this section, although both are similar in several ways, including their speculative nature and science-fiction feel. With that as a disclaimer....

The first form of self-instantiation continues the realization thread under consideration in the previous subsections. There a worry was expressed: that the practical capacity required for theorists to move from realizations of contents to the contents themselves will have to be similar to the practical capacity for language to such an extent that only linguistic, conceptual contents can be so specified. Despite the observation that the relationship between realizations and contents is less arbitrary than that between sounds or marks and linguistic contents, the discussion above (in external ability instantiation) suggests that the practical capacity may have to be an almost social kind of interaction with the specifying system if it is to provide canonical specifications of NCCs. This fuels the worry.

Perhaps the instantiation that provides canonical specification should be something more intimately known, thus avoiding the need for interactive, social capacities. Perhaps the instantiation should be the theorist itself.

The scenario I have in mind is not the use of some private "inner pointing," against which Wittgenstein railed. Rather, imagine a (possibly not-too-futuristic, given recent advances in imaging techniques) situation in which the theorist learns the relation between publicly observable states/abilities and contents for his or her own particular case. The theorist's nonintentional state at any given time will be directly observable, and the theorist will have a privileged (though not necessarily infallible) acquaintance with the corresponding intentional state. This combination of extro- and intro-spection may permit the development of a practical capacity for the theorist to mention his or her own physical states to specify contents that would otherwise be ineffable. If one further assumes that the realizations of theorists' contents do not differ dramatically from each other, there will be the possibility of theoretical, scientific communication concerning NCCs.

This means of specification is not, strictly speaking, one of state/ability *instantiation*, since the specifications themselves could very well be references to or mentions of the states of the theorist that realize the content in question. But since the development of this capacity for such states to specify contents canonically requires a period in which the theorist actually instantiates (perhaps some "basis" subset of) the contents to be specified, it seems appropriate to include this method under the "instantiation" rubric. Any of the instantiation methods could have an initial period of specification via instantiation, during which technical terms are introduced to refer to the contents so specified. But use of such terms for specification would still be a case of instantiation specification, since the norms of use of such terms are determined by their means of introduction.

However, the second form of self-instantiation specification is more directly a case of instantiation. It also has more of the feel of the "inner pointing" which Wittgenstein argued against, yet with a grounded twist that might allow it to avoid coming under the purview of his private language arguments. The idea here is to cut out the middle man by altering the environment of the theorist (to which one wishes to communicate a content) in such a way that the theorist actually entertains (but does not necessarily believe) that content.

This can be seen as playing the same role for EI specification, in terms of grappling with the constraints placed on canonicity by the nature of the theorist's cognitive abilities, that EAI specification and the first form of SI specification played for CR specification. For example, in a typical EI (embedded indexical) specification, one might say "the infant sees the wall like <*this*>," followed by a description of the infant's environment, then its position and orientation within that environment, and its sensori-motor abilities. The analogous move to that made before, then, is to claim that this referential approach is not sufficient for canonical specification; a more instantiated approach is required. The move would claim that any success for the EI method would be due to the theorist's being able to *imagine* the situation from the infant's point of view. But our imaginations are notoriously limited; why not actually have an externally-prompted experience with the same content as the one to be specified?

Clearly, it would be too awkward (at present) for one to manipulate a theorist's environment to the extent necessary for such specifications. But we cannot rule out the possibility that technology (for example, virtual reality) could be of assistance here, if or when it is developed.

Nevertheless, there are obvious potential difficulties: could an adult theorist, no matter how his or her environment is manipulated, really see the world the way an infant does? Even if one believes, as is surely the case, that adults entertain a wide range of non-conceptual contents, is it plausible that they are the same contents that are entertained by an infant? A bat?

Rather, it seems that if canonical specification requires *that* close a link between theorist and subject, then we are severely limited in our capacities to understand each other from a scientific viewpoint. I choose to interpret this as a strike against such a strong notion of the requirements for canonical specification rather than against the prospects for a scientific psychology.

Embodiment and Computation

No matter which (if any) of the types of alternative specification actually turn out to be successful, it seems clear that NCC specification requires appeal to the spatio-temporal relations between the system being modeled and its environment (embeddedness); for this (recall the end of the embedded indexical subsection) and other reasons, then, such specification also requires either reference to or the instantiation of (some of) a content-exercising system's intrinsic nonintentional properties (embodiment).

It is natural to look to computation and robotics to provide ways of characterizing and thinking about the functionally relevant aspects of the system's embodiment and its environment. But there are two thoughts that might give one pause.

First, computational phenomena are themselves arguably intentional. Computational states are typically representational: they are about things; they carry their own form of (subpersonal) content. So one might wonder how computational notions could provide the characterizations of nonintentional states required for NCC specifications. For indeed the embodiment and environment of the system must be characterized as nonintentional (or at least noncontentful) if an infinite regress of content specifications is to be avoided. But computational analyses specialize at coming up with elucidating, uninterpreted (if not downright nonintentional) ways of characterizing intentional systems. Of course, computational states *are* intentional, are about something; but to view them as, say, Turing Machine quadruples is to highlight their merely causal properties and to ignore their semantics. Perhaps the value of this kind of analysis has been over-emphasized or misunderstood; I certainly don't think that a complete understanding of computation will be primarily formal and nonintentional. Nevertheless, such characterizations do have their place, and they might be ideal candidates for capturing the embeddedness and embodiment of systems for the purpose of content specification.

On the other hand, some might think of computation as a world-independent, abstract notion, not the kind of thing that could square well with the requirements of embodiment and embeddedness at all. All that can be said here is that there are reasons, discussed elsewhere, for rejecting this disembodied, asemantical view of computation (see, e.g., Smith 1991). In fact, one could put the force of the issue the other way: given that content specifications must be embodied and embedded, if cognitive science is going to understand representational content in terms of computation, we had better develop our computational notions accordingly, rejecting the formal for the embodied and embedded.

One way that non-conceptual content and computation relate, then, can be captured with the motto: "do not ask what your intentional theory can do for your robot; ask what your robot can do for your intentional theory." That is to say, it seems that in order to specify contents and their interrelations, a means of content specification for an NCC-involving cognitive science will require concepts and insights from a theory of computation (especially robotic and perceptual computation). Further, such a formalism might require not only concepts and insights, but instances of computational/robotic phenomena, perhaps even full-fledged androids.[16]

Conclusion

The existence of non-conceptual content (NCC) places several demands on any cognitive science theory that wishes to address the full range of human cognitive behavior. I have argued that the way to answer these demands is to take embodiment seriously, by establishing a close connection between NCC and computational/robotic abilities. I argued that we need an alternate means of content specification that can, unlike the standard method of linguistic use ("that" clauses), canonically specify NCCs. I suggested that a worked-out means of specifying computational and robotic abilities might go a long way toward meeting these requirements, but have yet to produce a fully worked-out means of specifying NCCs. The demands that must be met before this can be done are considerable, but they should not discourage: an emphasis on NCC not only constrains but also liberates in that it allows psychologists to direct their energies toward explaining cognitive phenomena which have to be ignored from within a conceptualist approach, since the phenomena essentially involve contents which are non-conceptual: cognitive phylogeny, conceptual development, perception, learning, and action.

Notes

1. I should point out that none of the cited authors characterize non-conceptual content in exactly the same way, nor does my notion exactly agree with any one of theirs. But the differences are largely irrelevant for the purposes of this chapter.

2. The extent to which infants—even neo-nates—are unable to conceive of existence unperceived is a hotly debated topic, with received opinion currently swinging in favor of objectivity at a very early age, if not at birth. Such empirical details are irrelevant here, since the example of the infant still illustrates what is meant by NCC, even if it is at odds with what we know about the intentional capacities of infants. Furthermore, what little justification that has been offered for the stampede away from seeing infants' abilities as preobjective seems to be based on some philosophical misunderstandings.

3. For an example of a list of conceptuality/objectivity constraints similar to this one, see Cussins (1986), pp. 218-219.

4. Peacocke (1990) shows the insufficiency of standard specifications for a restricted class of NCCs, perceptual demonstrative contents; and develops (1989, 1992) an alternative means of specification, scenarios, for these contents. But the goal in this chapter is to establish the insufficiency of linguistic use specifications for NCCs in general (or at least for a broader or distinct class of NCCs than does Peacocke); for these NCCs the scenario means of specification will not work (nor was it intended to).

5. Actually, Perry claims that it is the fact that a belief is a "locating belief" that makes its specification essentially indexical; I'm favoring here Cussins' analysis that it is a content's constitutive links to perception and action that requires nondescriptive specification for that content.

6. A word of caution: Evans' point should not be construed to be claiming that non-conceptual contents are somehow infallible because of their direct connections to perception and action. The essential links can be inappropriate for the current situation, therefore yielding a false NCC: because of a reflection, the sound might be heard as coming from the right (with all the commensurate right-directed dispositions), when in fact the source of the sound is straight ahead.

7. Another caution: though I am arguing that all NCCs are indexical, in that they are nondescriptively linked to perception and action, I am not claiming that the relation in the other direction is true (that all indexical contents are non-conceptual, or subobjective); on the contrary, I think "I" has conceptual content (I might be wrong on this, as on anything else, but fortunately it would have no undesirable consequences to what I am arguing here if I were). Unlike Cussins (1990, p. 391, n. 46), I do not feel justified in rejecting out of hand indexical linguistic use specifications of contents for a scientific psychology. Some indexical contents (the first-person, the present-tense) seem to be conceptual (at least enough to avoid the problems of context-dependence) and are thereby specifiable by indexical linguistic use. Thus, I am required to provide an argument (which I do) for the claim that indexical linguistic use specifications will not work for the case of non-conceptual contents (although embedded indexical specifications might succeed; see below).

8. One might wonder, "how is it that indexical linguistic use specifications seem to work in some cases, even though no systematic way of specifying various aspects of the context is at hand?" The reply: in the case of indexical linguistic use specifications of conceptual contents (such as those that specify the mature first-person mode of presentation with "I"), the objective, context-independent nature of conceptual thought permits specification with only one extra contextual parameter: the person grasping the content, in the case of the first-person, and the time of the grasping, in the case of the present tense.

9. Of course, one should evaluate other proposed alternatives to the standard means of linguistic use, few though they may be, before concluding that another alternative is needed, but there is no space here for such a survey. Suffice it to say that other alternatives (possible worlds, possession conditions, proto-propositional specifications) are insufficient either because they ignore cognitive significance (are purely extensional), or they only are faithful to the case of cognitive significance in the same cases (that is, conceptual, or non-conceptual with shared environment) that linguistic use is, which I have already argued is insufficient for a scientific psychology.

10. The basic idea of the CS means of specification seems to have been independently reached by Colin Allen (1992).

11. Thanks to David Charles for this suggestion.

12. Martin Davies (1991) gives some compelling examples of non-conceptual, perceptual contents that do not supervene on the internal state of the organism experiencing that content; the important differences are in the way the organism is embedded in the environment, and thus the environment can be expected to play a major role, beyond the one of specifying truth-conditions, in the specification of non-conceptual contents.

13. Note that arguments merely to the effect that symbols must be grounded, that there must be some environment in order for an agent's states to have any content at all (Harnad 1990), do not in themselves argue against nonembodied specifications. It is only when one claims that external conditions partially individuate a content that one can put forward this kind of externalist argument for embodied specifications of content. The argument that symbols must be grounded is compatible with an internalist individuation of contents, even though it demands that such contents can exist only in the context of an environment toward which they are directed.

14. But see self-instantiation below.

15. See self-instantiation for further discussion of how this might be possible.

16. Thus, my discussion here does not concentrate on computation via the claim that the mind is computation (although that equation might be a consequence of the concerns here); rather, the emphasis is that computation is a (and perhaps the only) systematic means of specifying otherwise ineffable contents.

References

Allen, C. (1992). Mental content. *Brit. J. Phil. Sci.*, 43.

Burge, T. (1982). Other bodies. In A. Woodfield (Ed.), *Thought and Object: Essays on Intentionality* (pp. 97-120). Oxford: Clarendon Press.

Chrisley, R. (1993). Connectionism, cognitive maps and the development of objectivity. *Artificial Intelligence Review*, 7, 329-354.

Crane, T. (Ed.). (1992). The non-conceptual content of experience. In *The Contents of Experience*. Cambridge: Cambridge University Press.

Cussins, A. (1986). *A Representational Theory of Mind*. Unpublished PhD thesis, University of Oxford.

Cussins, A. (1990). The connectionist construction of concepts. In M. Boden (Ed.), *The Philosophy of Artificial Intelligence* (pp. 368-440). Oxford: Oxford University Press.

Davies, M. (1990). Thinking persons and cognitive science. *AI and Society*.

Davies, M. (1991). Externalism and perceptual content. *Proceedings of the Aristotelian Society*.

Evans, G. (1982). *The Varieties of Reference*. Oxford: Oxford University Press.

Fodor, J. (1981). Methodological solipsism considered as a research strategy in cognitive science. In J. Haugeland (Ed.), *Mind Design* (pp. 307-338). Cambridge, MA: MIT Press.

Harnad, S. (1990). The symbol grounding problem. *Physica D, 42*, 335-346.

Haugeland J. (1991). Representational genera. In Ramsey, Rumelhart, & Stich (Eds.), *Philosophy and Connectionist Theory* (pp. 61-90). Hillsdale, NJ: Lawrence Erlbaum.

Peacocke, C. (1981). Demonstrative thought and psychological explanation. *Synthese, 49*, 87-217.

Peacocke, C. (1986). *Thoughts: An Essay on Content*. Oxford: Blackwell.

Peacocke, C. (1989). *Transcendental Arguments in the Theory of Content*. Oxford: Oxford University Press.

Peacocke, C. (1990). Analogue content. In Perry, Almog, & Wettstein (Eds.), *Themes from Kaplan*. New York: Oxford University Press.

Peacocke, C. (1992). Scenarios, contents and perception. In T. Crane (Ed.), *The Contents of Experience*. Cambridge: Cambridge University Press.

Perry, J. (1979). The problem of the essential indexical. *Nous, 13*, 3-21.

Putnam, H. (Ed.). (1975). The meaning of "meaning." In *Philosophical Papers Vol. II: Mind, Language, and Reality* (pp. 215-271). Cambridge University Press.

Smith, B.C. (1991). On the threshold of belief. In D. Kirsh (Ed.), *Foundations of Artificial Intelligence*. Cambridge, MA: MIT Press.

Strawson, P. (1959). *Individuals*. London: Methuen.

9 Imagination and Situated Cognition

Lynn Andrea Stein

This chapter is concerned with the integration of higher-level "cognitive AI" and lower-level robotics. Robotic systems are embodied: their central tasks concern interaction with the immediately present world. In contrast, cognition is concerned with objects that are remote in distance, in time, or in some other dimension. This chapter exploits the architecture of a particular robotic system to perform a cognitive task by *imagining* the subjects of our cognition, and suggests that much of the abstract information that forms the heart of cognition is used not as a central model of the world but as virtual reality. The self-same processes that robots use to explore and interact with the world form the interface to this information. The only difference between interaction with the actual world and with the imagined one is the set of sensors and actuators providing the lowest-level interface.

Consider, for example, the following tasks. In the first, a pitcher and bowl sit on a table before you. You lift the pitcher and pour its contents into the bowl. Now consider your actions in reading the preceding example. In all likelihood, you formed a picture *in your mind's eye* of the table top, pitcher, and bowl. You envisioned the pouring. In the virtual world that you created for yourself, you sensed and acted. Indeed, there is evidence in the psychology literature that such "imagings" involve the same biological mechanisms as are responsible for actual vision. This virtual reality, your imagination, is precisely the goal of our program.

This chapter describes both the general ideas behind imagination and its concrete instantiation in a particular robotic system. Toto (Mataric 1992) is a subsumption-based mobile robot capable of goal-directed navigation. Meta-Toto is an imagination system that we have built using Toto. MetaToto adds to Toto's original abilities the abstract, cognitive, and apparently disembodied skill of reading and using maps. MetaToto achieves this additional skill by reusing Toto's reactive navigational system to imagine exploring the environment depicted in the map.

This use of the term "imagination" closely parallels both its folk-psychological sense and the work of several computer and cognitive scientists. For example, Sutton (1990) augments the exploration of his reinforcement-learning agent with rehearsal, or "imagined" exploration, in the Dyna architecture. Kosslyn (1993) makes the strong claim that all mental imagery is in essence this kind of reuse of perceptual machinery; his recent clinical data support my suggestion that cognition is imagined interaction (or, as Kosslyn has put it, "imagery is just like vision, except that there's nothing there").

In the next section, I introduce the idea of imagination as the basis for a robotic architecture. Then I will describe Toto, the robot on which our work is based. While our work does not rely on the specifics of that robot, it does exploit certain properties to make the implementation of the imagination system feasible. In the next section, I discuss the ways in which our work adds to the existing robot; then I present the details of our implementation. Next, I explore an extension of the imagination architecture to a more abstract task. Finally, I analyze the features of the robotic system and the imagination architecture that make this project possible.

A note on terminology: In this chapter, my use of the terms "robotics" and "cognition" is intended to be quite specific: "robotics" involves the portion of the system designed to interact with the world—the "body"—while I intend "cognition" to refer to the nonimmediate, or the "mental." In humans, "cognition" might correspond roughly to the function of the cerebrum, while the remainder of the body implements "robotics." Although this usage is far from universal, I will adopt it throughout this chapter and will consequently omit the scare quotes surrounding these terms.

In fact, just as these distinctions are not really so crisp in biology, there is much overlap of functionality in artificial systems. However, without claiming to be able to draw a sharp boundary between them, I believe that there is utility to be gained from the rough distinction between interactive "robotic" systems and abstract "cognition."

Imagination as Situated Cognition

Traditional AI architectures have assumed that the superficial dissimilarities between cognitive and robotic abilities reflect fundamental differences in underlying machinery. Accordingly, the two areas have been studied separately, with widely divergent approaches used to provide the desired functionality. For those who work in cognitive AI, robotics has come to be viewed largely as an interface to the world, providing (often highly interpreted) sensory data and executing actions as instructed. This approach is typified by the traditional planning literature. (See Allen, Hendler, and Tate 1990 for a survey.)

For the robotics community, planners and other cognitive apparatus are viewed as "problem-solving boxes" that periodically issue high-level goals. (See, for example, Latombe 1991.) While the relative importance of these two components varies depending on the problem addressed, both research communities have traditionally agreed on this rough dichotomy and the consequent specification of the cognition/robotics interface independently of sensori-motor functions.

The traditional implementation of the cognition box is itself a kind of simulation. It often contains a "world model": some representation of the environment derived (in principle) from the output of the robotics component. Planning and other cognitive tasks are accomplished relative to this world model. The representation of the world in this model is often unlike the raw sensory data supplied by the world itself, and the operators on this world model are abstracted and idealized versions of actual actions. Plans are derived by "simulating" action in this world model. Errors occurring within the simulation are not fatal and can be discovered and eliminated before action is taken in the world.

The advantage of this approach is that the simulation is tailored to the planning task. Its disadvantage is the same: because the simulation is tailored for planning, plans developed in simulation depend on the irrelevance of the idealizations in the simulation to the real world. Such assumptions often include the static and predictable nature of the world. In practice, these assumptions are often untenable. (See, for example, discussions in Agre and Chapman 1987, Sanborn and Hendler 1988, and Brooks 1991a,b.)

More recently, there has been substantial interest in architectures that integrate some or all of the cognitive functionality directly into the robotic architecture. Some achieve this hybridization by compiling cognitive functionality off-line, that is, by essentially using the "cognition box" as a specification for the robot's reactions. Examples of this type of integrated architecture include Rosenschein and Kaelbling (1986), Schoppers (1987), and Chapman (1990). Others, such as Georgeff and Lansky (1987) and Sanborn and Hendler (1988), treat cognition as preference information to be used when the world does not demand a particular reaction. The first approach limits the simulation aspects of cognition, while the second treats cognition essentially as in Figure 1.

I propose a different integration of cognition and robotics, one which leaves the robotic architecture essentially unchanged but takes seriously the idea of cognition as *imagined interaction*. It complements the reactive approaches described above, providing a different kind of planning-as-simulation. While traditional planners use an abstracted world and plan operators distinct from the actual robot controls, our system uses the robotic architecture itself. That is—as in Figure 2—the interface between robotics and the immediate world is multiplexed to provide a second low-level interface, between robotics and imagination. The robot senses and acts in this imagined world precisely as it does in

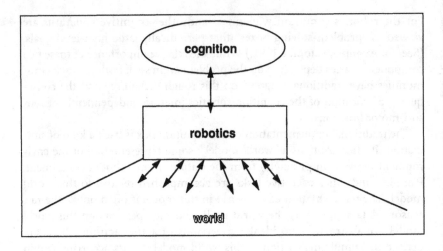

Figure 1. Traditional Architecture.

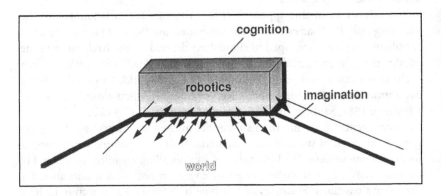

Figure 2. An Alternative Architecture: Cognition as Imagined Interaction.

the actual world. The essential difference between imagination and traditional planning-as-simulation is that imagination and interaction literally share the same machinery. Cognition is actual interaction applied to imagined stimuli.

This idea accords with popular as well as academic psychology. Dreams are often thought of as interactions in which sensory input does not come from the outside world and physical motor function is inhibited. Mental imagery is, according to Kosslyn (1993), simply the application of the processes that drive actual vision to imagined sensation. The task of giving directions often evokes the sensations of traveling along the designated route. Finally, it seems likely that if biology and evolution conspired to spend so long creating the complex motor functions and instincts of higher mammals, much of this would be reused in providing the additional cognitive capacity of human beings.

Imagination and the Homunculus.

One objection that has been raised to the idea of cognition as imagined inter-action is that of the homunculus. If, for example, visual image processing is vision of the "mind's eye," who is it who *sees* through the mind's eye? By this line of reasoning, the agent in the mind—the homunculus—must itself have an agent in its head, and so on in infinite regress.

Our approach does not suffer from this problem. As I describe below, the mind that sees imagined stimuli is the same mind that sees the world. We have simply multiplexed its retinal connections, so that the robot cannot distinguish between the world around it and that of its imagination. Thus, our "homunculus" is the perceptual system of the robot itself.

Imagination vs. World Models

A further aspect of the architecture bears on the simulation of feedback through imagination rather than through the world. Feedback through the world has been a strength of reactive systems, and imagination removes that aspect of the architecture. In this sense, it represents a step towards the more traditional world models of classical planning systems.

Imagination differs from classical world models, however. Imagination is ephemeral. MetaToto need only know the sensations that occur now. Where Toto "continually redecides what to do," MetaToto continually re-imagines the world. Thus, while world models persist and require maintenance, imagi-nation can be reconstructed on the fly.

In addition, cognition requires imagining only the relevant details. That is, only those aspects that bear on things immediately sense-able must be imag-ined. Because the interface between robotics and imagination is at the level of sensation rather than in terms of higher-level predicates, we do not need a model of the global properties of the world. Only that which is imagined to be immediately accessible must be simulated.

A Robot that Explores

This section describes the architecture of the underlying robotic system in some detail. It is intended to give readers unfamiliar with Mataric's work a better idea of the basic interactive system. The details of Toto's machinery are not, however, crucial to the imagination project. MetaToto, our extension to Toto, treats Toto as a black box module (as depicted in Figure 2).

Toto (Mataric 1990, 1992) is a mobile robot capable of goal-directed navi-gation. It is implemented on a Real World Interface base augmented with a ring of twelve Polaroid ultrasonic ranging sensors and a flux-gate compass (Figure 4). Its primary computational resource is a CMOS 68000. Its software

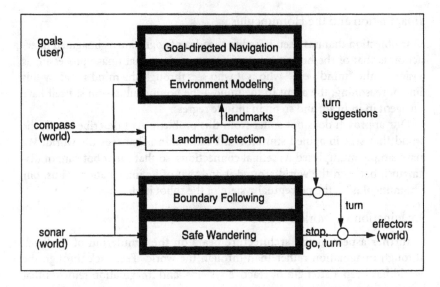

Figure 3. An Architectural Overview of Toto's Control Programs.

Figure 4. Mataric's Toto.

simulates a subsumption architecture (Brooks 1986): a layered control system in which individual modules—or "behaviors"—implement distinct abilities. Figure 3 gives an architectural overview of Toto.

Toto's most basic level consists of routines to explore its world. Independent collections of finite state machines implement such competencies as obstacle-avoidance and random walking. Each of the modules is reactive, relying on the world around it to provide cues to appropriate actions. For example, an obstacle looming large will cause Toto to stop and back up, regardless of its other tasks. Toto's simplest activity—a wall-following "maze exploration"— emerges from the parallel combination of these survival skills.

A second layer, above the wall-following routines, implements a fully distributed "world modeler." While navigating around its environment, Toto synthesizes its experiences into a dynamic and reusable "memory." For example, sustained short average sonar readings on sonars 5 and 6 serve to indicate the presence of a wall on Toto's right. This experience is connected in memory to those that directly precede and follow it, providing a rough topographic "memory" of the explored environment.

By remembering crucial features of its previous experience, Toto is able to correlate its current surroundings with these experiences and to "recognize" previously visited locations. Toto's memory is implemented as a parallel distributed dynamic graph of landmark-recognizer modules. Landmarks correspond to gross sonar configurations (e.g., *wall right*) augmented with compass readings.[1] Each time a novel landmark is recognized, a new graph node allocates itself, making graph connections as appropriate. The resulting modules form an internal representation of the environment. Rough odometry is used to distinguish similar landmark-memories in the recognition of previously visited locations.

Finally, Toto accepts commands (by means of three buttons) to return to previously recognized landmarks. When a goal location is specified, Toto's landmark graph—synthesized memories—uses spreading activation to determine the appropriate direction in which to head. In essence, Toto "feels an urge" to go towards the (remembered) goal landmark. Activation persists until Toto has returned to the requested location. Throughout, Toto's lowest level modules enforce obstacle avoidance and corridor traversal, and Toto's intermediate layer processes landmarks as they are encountered.

Toto's landmark representation and goal-driven navigation are cognitive tasks, involving internal representation of the external environment. This represents a qualitative advance in the capabilities of subsumption-based robots. Nonetheless, this internal representation is accessible only through interaction with the world: unless Toto has experienced the landmark, it has no memories to synthesize. Thus, Toto cannot reason about things unless it has previously encountered them. In the next section, I describe a simple modification to Toto's architecture that allows Toto to represent and "return to" previously *unvisited* landmarks.

Exploring the Unknown

The existing machinery that implements Toto's core provides a strong base for cognitive tasks. It is limited, however, in being able to conceptualize only what has been physically encountered. MetaToto is an extension of Toto's core behavior that accepts directions to navigate to a goal not previously encountered. This ability is qualitatively different for the robot. Toto's goal-directed navigation routines are implemented in terms of its existing internal representation—synthesized experience—and it is impossible even to ask that Toto visit an unexplored location: Toto has no concept corresponding to locations it has not encountered. The primary task for MetaToto, then, is the representation of landmarks that have simply been described.

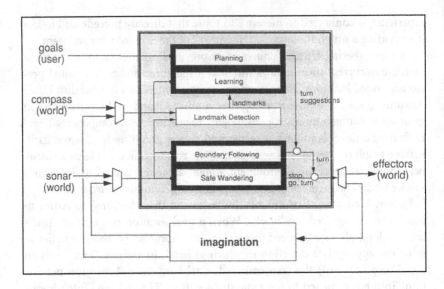

Figure 5. MetaToto Treats Mataric's Toto as a Black Box, Multiplexing Its Inputs and Outputs.

Previous approaches to cognition in robotic systems have implemented more intelligent behaviors as higher levels of control. In the Imagination project, we have taken a different approach. Our approach to architecture is to reuse Toto's existing mechanisms in adding this new skill to MetaToto. We treat Toto's control program as a black box whose inputs and outputs come through the world. By providing an alternative interface through an imagination system, we multiplex Toto's memory construction system. Where Toto must encounter a landmark to be able to make use of it, MetaToto merely envisions that landmark and constructs the same topological "landmark memory." Figure 5 shows an architectural diagram for MetaToto. The shaded area represents Toto's architecture, as designed by Mataric and described previously. For MetaToto, cognition is simply imagined sensation and action.

Implementing Imagination

The initial implementation of MetaToto takes directions in the form of a sketch-map. The use of a geometric communication language facilitates certain of the simulation aspects of MetaToto's imagination. In the next section I discuss a more verbal communication language.

MetaToto is intended to run on the same hardware as Toto. It reuses Toto's software entirely, adding only the imagination system wrapped around the Toto "black box." (See Figure 5.) The compound system subsumes the ability to per-

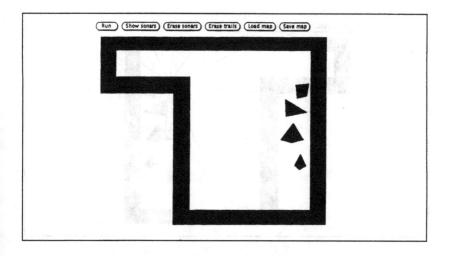

Figure 6. A Sample Sketch-Map.

form all tasks of which the robot was previously capable, plus the additional cognitive exploration of physically unseen environments—"map reading."

MetaToto's imagination uses a rough sketch-map of the environment it is to explore. Rather than looking at the map from above, that is, as abstract information—MetaToto imagines that it is located in a particular place in the map. Virtual sensors describe what it "feels" like to be at that location: what sonar and compass readings MetaToto might receive if at the corresponding real-world location. MetaToto imagines sensing and acting in the sketch-map much as Toto would sense and act in the actual world, with much the same effect. The routines that sense and act in the imagined world are precisely the same as those that would sense and act in the actual world; they differ only by calling the imagined sonar rather than the real.

To implement this system, the sketched floor plan is transformed into a bitmap: black pixels represent "occupied" space; white pixels, free. Neither the discrete nature of this representation nor the relative dimensions of the topographic features correspond accurately to the robot's actual experience; the sketch-map merely provides sufficient information to enable MetaToto's imagination to construct appropriate "memories." A sample sketch-map is depicted in Figure 6.

MetaToto imagines itself as a small circular region within the bitmap. We initially tried to simplify the implementation further by modeling MetaToto as a point. Because the difference between too-close and too-far sonar readings is comparable to the radius of the robot, this implementation allowed MetaToto to imagine traversing passageways far too narrow for the actual robot.

To imagine sensing, MetaToto projects twelve rays, one in the direction of

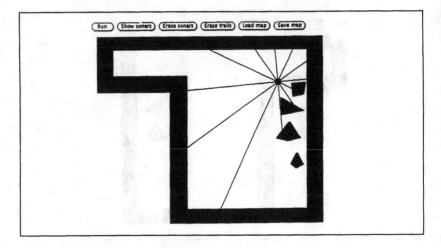

Figure 7. MetaToto Projects Rays to Imagine Toto's Sonars.

each sonar. Figure 7 shows MetaToto's idealization of sonars. We do not attempt to model sonar diffusion or specular reflection at all; imagined sonars simply report the distance to the first black pixel encountered. The algorithm used is based on Bresenham's scan-line algorithm as described in Foley and Van Dam (1982, p. 435). Except for the "junk" landmark type, this implementation appears to be adequate.

To imagine acting, MetaToto maintains three state variables: x and y coordinates and angular heading. Forward and backward motion is discrete, but the distance for backward motion is not precisely the same as that for forward motion. (The robot itself depends on the nonuniformity of actual motion to unwedge itself from certain corners; we use the differential step size to serve a similar purpose.) Similarly, turns are discrete and of a fixed size—30° per step. Sensing occurs discretely after each step.

In this manner, MetaToto explores the floor plan, building the same internal representation of landmarks as Toto would create in its explorations of the environment. Figure 8(a) from Mataric (1992, Fig. 7) shows the landmarks detected by Toto during its exploration of the ninth floor playroom at the MIT AI lab. Figure 8(b) shows MetaToto's (imagined) exploration of the same space.

Once MetaToto has completed its exploration of the floor plan, it is capable of goal-directed navigation in the world. However, unlike Toto, MetaToto can go to places that it has only imagined and not actually encountered. Because the landmark graph has been created by the same mechanisms that are used in exploring the world, MetaToto cannot distinguish those generated by its imagination and those actually encountered. Should the floor plan prove to have been incomplete or inaccurate, MetaToto will respond precisely as Toto would were the world to change between two consecutive visits.

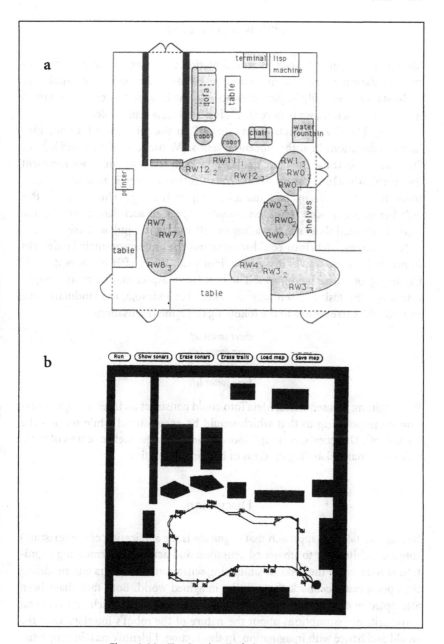

Figure 8. MetaToto Imagines Exploring Its Environment.

(a) [Mataric 92, Figure 7, ® IEEE]. Landmarks detected by Toto on three consecutive runs through the ninth floor playroom at the MIT AI Lab. Shaded areas represent locations corresponding to the same landmark. (b) MetaToto's trajectory on two consecutive runs on the sketchmap of the same environment. Landmarks are indicated.

Following Directions

MetaToto's use of a geometric representation for communication facilitates the simulation aspects of imagination. Humans, however, are capable of understanding verbally imparted directions. While in some senses this task is unfair for MetaToto, we believe that it is nonetheless achievable.

Giving MetaToto directions is "unfair" in the sense that humans give humans directions in anthropocentric terms. We speak of "the second left" or "the corner" because these are the landmarks in terms of which we represent the world. MetaToto has no notion of left turns or corners; instead, it represents the world in terms of sonar and compass readings. Thus, to make this task fair in MetaToto's terms, we ought to speak of such landmarks as "the second extended short sonar reading on left and right simultaneously."

Nonetheless, MetaToto could understand the anthropocentric landmarks in much the same way as it uses the floor plan. What, after all, does it "feel" like to explore these landmarks? The simulation aspect may be more complicated, but the task is essentially the same. For example, the landmark "the second left" corresponds to the following (imagined) sensations:

short sonar left
long sonar left
short sonar left
long sonar left

By imagining this sequence, MetaToto could construct an internal representation corresponding to that which would be encountered while seeking the second left. Directions, although more remote than geometric representation, still have a natural analog in terms of imagined sensation.

Discussion

Because we take the approach that cognition is the application of the (existing) robotic architecture to imagined sensation and action, implementing cognition is reduced to the tasks of simulating sensors and actuators and modeling the appropriate feedback through the imagined world. Both tasks have been attempted in other contexts. The relative success of the approach here relies on some critical assumptions about the nature of the robot's interface with the world and hence with imagination. In this section, I identify certain properties of Toto's architecture that allow for its integration with an imagination system.

The robotic architecture is designed to compensate for the variations of physical experience. For example, while Toto's trajectory through a corridor is roughly "straight down the middle," it is possible—and even expected—that Toto will swerve from side to side in unpredictable ways. For example, Figure 9(a) from Mataric (1992, Fig. 6) shows the variation over the paths taken by the robot during five independent runs through the same hallway. The program that accumulates Toto's experiences and synthesizes landmark-memories takes this into account, ignoring the particular path taken and abstracting the more general pattern indicative of a corridor. When Toto next encounters this corridor, it will almost certainly take a different path. The abstract features—sustained average short sonar readings on sonars 5, 6, 11, and 0—however, remain the same.

MetaToto is able to exploit this feature of Toto's architecture. Because the robotic program generalizes any corridor-like trajectory to the same type of landmark-memory, MetaToto's simulated trajectory need not mimic the robot's actual trajectory. Instead, MetaToto is free to imagine any corridor-like trajectory. Accordingly, we choose to simulate motion as ideal—straight, precise, and discrete—although the actual behavior of the robot is far different. Figure 9(b) shows MetaToto's trajectory through the sketch-map depicting the corridor of (a). While MetaToto's path is an idealization of Toto's, it falls well within the range of variation experienced by the robot over several runs. Both the real and imagined trajectories result in the synthesis of the appropriate (corridor) landmark-memory.

In the same way that Toto generalizes over deviations in its trajectories, the robotic architecture allows for the expected variation in sonar readings. Rather than using sonar as a precise distance metric, Toto relies on the qualitative properties expected of its environment: *too-close, too-far, wall left or right....* By abstracting from the precise readings to range membership and sustained average properties, this architecture allows for the adequacy of naive simulation of sonars.

Further, Toto relies on constant feedback from the world and constant interaction with the world. In contrast to traditional planners, which decide on a course of action and then pass control to an executor, Toto "continually re-decides what to do" (*pace;* Agre and Chapman 1987). This serves as a form of protection from major errors: if MetaToto provides inapplicable landmark-memories—either because its imagination was mistaken or because the world has changed—any incorrect actions by the robot will be recognized and corrected before they can become disastrous. As a result, Toto need not worry about plans gone awry.

These properties allow MetaToto to imagine idealized sonar readings along an idealized trajectory in an idealized floor plan (or with idealized directions); since the result is within the space of possible experiences that Toto might have, MetaToto's landmark-memories capture the appropriate salient properties of the environment.

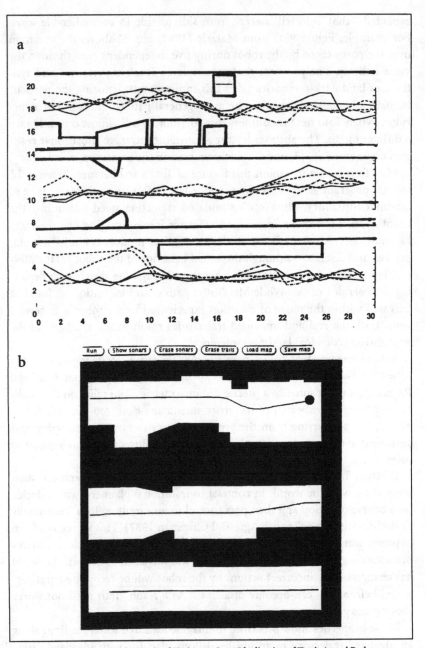

Figure 9. MetaToto's Imagined Trajectory Is an Idealization of Toto's Actual Paths.

Both figures illustrate a single hallway running from left to right and from bottom to top. (a) [Mataric 92, Figure 6, ®IEEE.] Toto's trajectories on five independent runs through a hallway. (b) MetaToto's path through the same hallway.

Conclusion

Unlike previous "cognition boxes," MetaToto is distinguished only by the set of sensors and actuators in which the behaviors ground out: when imagining, MetaToto seizes control of the sensor and actuator control signals and substitutes interaction with the floor plan. Rather than a "higher level reasoning module," MetaToto is a lowest level interface to an alternate (imagined) reality.

MetaToto achieves by embodied imagination the cognition-intensive task of reading, understanding, and acting on the knowledge contained in a floor plan; and MetaToto does so entirely by using Toto's existing architecture, with the sole addition of the virtual sensors and actuators required for navigation of the floor plan. Although MetaToto is only a simple example of imagination, we are hopeful that experiences with MetaToto will lead to more sophisticated use of imagination and virtual sensing and to the development of truly embodied forms of cognition.

Note

1 In fact, the environment in which Toto was tested—the seventh and ninth floors of the MIT AI Lab—yielded sufficiently noisy compass readings that the compass was useful only to distinguish turns and not to obtain true facings.

References

Agre, P.E. & Chapman, D. (1987). Pengi: An implementation of a theory of activity. In *Proceedings of the Sixth National Conference on Artificial Intelligence* (pp. 196-201). San Mateo, CA: Morgan Kaufmann.

Allen, J., Hendler, J., & Tate, A. (Eds.). (1990). *Readings in Planning*. San Mateo, CA: Morgan Kaufmann.

Brooks, R.A. (1986). A robust layered control system for a mobile robot. *IEEE Journal of Robotics and Automation 2*, 1, 14-23.

Brooks, R.A. (1991a). Intelligence without reason. In *Proceedings of the Twelfth International Joint Conference on Artificial Intelligence* (pp. 569-595). San Mateo, CA: Morgan Kaufmann.

Brooks, R.A. (1991b). Intelligence without representation. *Artificial Intelligence, 47*, 13, 139-160.

Chapman, D. (1990). *Vision, Instruction, and Action* (Tech. Rep. 1204). Cambridge, MA: Massachusetts Institute of Technology, Artificial Intelligence Laboratory.

Foley, J.D. & Van Dam, A. (1982). *Fundamentals of Interactive Computer Graphics* [1983 reprint edition]. Reading, MA: Addison-Wesley.

Georgeff, M.P. & Lansky, A.L. (1987). Reactive reasoning and planning. In *Proceedings of the Sixth National Conference on Artificial Intelligence* (pp. 677-682). San Mateo, CA: Morgan Kaufmann.

Kosslyn, S.M. (1993). Image and Brain: *The Resolution of the Imagery Debate*. Cambridge, MA: Harvard University Press.

Latombe, J.-C. (1991). *Robot Motion Planning*. Dordrecht: Kluwer Academic.

Mataric, M.J. (1990). *A Distributed Model for Mobile Robot Environment Learning* (Tech. Rep. 1228). Cambridge, MA: Massachusetts Institute of Technology, AI Laboratory.

Mataric, M.J. (1992). Integration of representation into goal-driven behavior-based robots. *IEEE Journal of Robotics and Automation 8*, 3, 304-312.

Rosenschein, S.J. & Kaelbling, L.P. (1986). The synthesis of digital machines with provable epestemic properties. In J.Y. Ualpern (Ed.), *Proceedings of the Conference on Theoretical Aspects of Reasoning about Knowledge* (pp. 83-98). San Mateo, CA: Morgan Kaufmann.

Sanborn, J.C. & Hendler, J.A. (1988). A model of reaction for planning in dynamic environments. *International Journal of Artificial Intelligence in Engineering, 3*, 2, 95-102.

Schoppers, M.J. (1987). Universal plans for reactive robots in unpredictable domains. In *Proceedings of the Tenth International Joint Conference on Artificial Intelligence* (pp. 1039-1046). San Mateo, CA: Morgan Kaufmann.

Sutton, R.S. (1990). Integrated architectures for learning, planning, and reacting based on approximating dynamic programming. In *Machine Learning* (pp. 216-224).

10 Towards Constructivist Unification of Machine Learning and Parallel Distributed Processing

Chris Stary and Markus F. Peschl

Automated knowledge acquisition (artificial learning) has become a crucial issue for knowledge-based systems used in dynamically changing environments, such as expert systems for planning. Machine Learning (ML) algorithms, such as decision tree algorithms (Quinlan 1986), have evolved from conventional artificial intelligence (AI) techniques. Because of the limitations of the symbol-processing paradigm, parallel distributed processing (PDP) (e.g., Rumelhart and McClelland 1986) seemed to be a promising candidate to improve artificial learning. Finally, artificial life (e.g., Hinton 1987) claimed to be the most natural way to simulate cognitive processes and thus to improve artificial problem solving. Unfortunately, methodological flaws, such as semantic equivalence of symbols with linguistic terms, as well as performance problems (for example, caused by unsupervised learning of PDP-networks), prohibited steady progress towards successful application of a particular learning technique. The diversification of methods and algorithms has not led to the expected improvements of learning behavior. Recently, research communities started to combine conceptually different approaches, such as ML and PDP, without performing epistemological reflections (e.g., Shastri and Ajjanagadde 1989). Because of that lack, such integration processes will remain an adventure, since implicit assumptions and misinterpretations may lead to unsatisfactory results in learning behavior. In order to overcome this deficiency, we suggest that learning techniques be epistemologically evaluated before they are combined.

In this chapter we attempt an epistemological analysis of the most diversified artificial learning approaches, namely ML and PDP. We consider this step to be more promising than unreflected integration attempts to achieve the desired improvements, since we address the conceptual layer first and not the level of algorithms and computation immediately.

Epistemology is concerned with the theory of knowledge. Central issues in epistemology are the nature and acquisition of knowledge, its scope and reliability for problem solving. As a consequence, epistemological reflection of existing scientific methods may provide useful insights for further developments in (diversified) areas of research. It may lead to explanations on why existing approaches do not work satisfactorily, and/or it may influence the current research paradigm. In the case of artificial learning, as we will see, some of the unsatisfying results can be explained by incompatibilities of basic methodological assumptions.

Epistemological reflection of ML techniques has already been attempted by Winograd and Flores (1986). They proposed several epistemological evaluation criteria, namely parameter adjustment, combinatorial concept formation, and evolution of structure. Those criteria cannot be applied fully for the evaluation of ML *and* PDP-approaches, since they assume explicit structures, such as a set of parameters comprising the complete semantics of the problem at hand. This assumption can obviously not be met by PDP. Therefore, we shall develop novel epistemological criteria.

In principle, epistemological reflection of artificial learning techniques can be performed at several layers of abstraction: evaluation at the methodological level, evaluation of commonalities, and evaluation at the 'goal-level.'

Evaluation at the Methodological Level

- according to the learning method: here, the underlying concept for learning, such as learning from examples, is considered.
- according to the implementation method: here, the method used for implementation (for example, frames), is concerned.

Methodological evaluation, for instance, checks the efficiency of control flow by evaluating, for example, the control flow in frame-oriented learning components against the control flow in production systems (where rules are used for problem solving).

Evaluation of Commonalities

- If learning is based on conceptually different techniques, as is the case for ML and PDP (one assumes a fixed set of parameters limiting the problem domain, the other one does not), we may find mechanisms, such as feedback loops, which can be used for more than one technique. These mechanisms have to be tested, whether they are applicable to any combination of the conceptually different learning techniques or not.

Evaluation at the 'Goal-Level.'

- The main goal of any artificial learning system is either cognitive simulation or behavioral simulation. The goal of cognitive simulation is to allow tracing of human cognitive processes in artificial systems by 1:1 mappings of cognitive functions to computable processes, whereas behavioral simulation restricts itself to comparing the performance (that is, the output) of artificial learning systems with human cognitive capabilities. If learning approaches are evaluated at the goal level, their design intention has to be (made) transparent.

The results of our epistemological analyses are based on all of the previously listed aspects, since they are required for constructivist unification. The next section first gives some basic assumptions of AI and their consequences for ML, subsequently introducing epistemological evaluation criteria for ML. There has not been much room for discussion of epistemological issues in traditional ML-communities, although it would have been worthwhile to do so. Earlier discussions of epistemological consequences could have prevented many pitfalls.

Next, we analyze PDP. It becomes evident that the more biological concepts are simulated (through PDP), the more fundamental epistemological issues become (e.g., the role of language for the representation of knowledge).

Since existing hybrid approaches (for example, embedding of rules into PDP; Shastri and Ajjanagadde 1989) have led to more epistemological problems (for example, rule regression leading to meta-meta...layers for control) than practical use, in the next section we develop a unified artificial learning environment where epistemologically reflected learning strategies support supervised but self-regulated learning. The proposed approach establishes neo-behavioristic learning as a novel concept for artificial learning.

Since artificial life techniques combine conventional machine learning with parallel distributed processing,[1] our results can also be applied to unify conventional machine learning, parallel distributed processing, and artificial life.

Epistemological Reflection of Machine Learning Techniques

Traditional reviews of ML-techniques are based on criteria which neither address basic assumptions of ML nor question the environment of learning algorithms. They are based on one of the following aspects (Stary and Winkelbauer 1991):

• behavioral or structural goals of learning (e.g., a minimal set of parameters).

• algorithmical (computational) efficiency.

Both aspects have been extensively discussed in Boose (1988), Carbonell (1990), Kodratoff (1988), Michalski (1983), Michalski, Carbonell, and Mitchell (1986). However, such methodological discussions do not provide deep epistemological insights. For instance, those reviews do not show that unreflected principles, such as decomposition, prohibit the expected improvements (Peschl 1991). The three subsections below show that knowledge for ML is assumed to be a set of symbols which should obey the representational requirements of hierarchical binding and semantical equivalence.

Epistemological Assumptions

In the context of ML, *knowledge* is considered to be a set of parameters (symbols) whose ranges are refined step by step. Symbols are an abstraction of semantic entities, properties, and relationships expressed in natural language. Symbolic representation is usually based on 'facts' and 'rules' which can manipulate the facts. Facts constitute the structure of a problem domain, whereas rules represent the operational part for inferencing—learning and solving.

Symbol Processing. Whenever symbol processing[2] is applied for problem solving, several epistemological problems may occur (Peschl 1990a):

- *Artificial knowledge* has direct correspondences to natural language descriptions. These descriptions are based on linguistic terms which are related to each other by semantic relationships, such as rules. These terms are usually mapped directly to artificial symbols which can be processed by symbol-processing machines and their algorithms (i.e., we can find an isomorphic relation between the semantic categories of natural language and those computer symbols).

- *Symbols* (in a rather semiotic sense) are arbitrary sets of signs whose relationships to elements of the observed world (that is, terms of natural language) are assumed and assigned by the designer of an application. Hence, each symbol has a particular meaning, which is usually provided by the designer. For instance, a designer introduces 'sfu' ('sometime in the future'). It is a predicate symbol which captures some temporal dimension and may be used in logical axioms to specify organizational constraints.

- Individual decisions of the designer may not reflect the view of end users, programmers, or collaborating designers. The designer can remove this *ambiguity* only by specifying the semantics of symbols explicitly (e.g., using logical axioms). If this step is missing, a lot of misunderstandings and misconceptions, particularly in handling specific problem domains, may occur. Most of the ML-algorithms do not provide means to specify the semantics explicitly. Such a set of symbols without semantic specification cannot prohibit misunderstandings. It is not always intuitively clear what meaning a symbol has. Hence, its *semantics cannot always be specified accurately*, because it is the result of individual experiences which each user, designer, etc. has made (with the concerned symbol). If the semantic specification is omitted, the only indicator of a symbol's semantics is the symbol's syntax.

The Role of the Environment. For ML-algorithms, the role of the environment seems to be strictly identified. The parameters of the problem solution whose correct values should be learned by the algorithm are represented as a set. All items or aspects which are not covered by the set of parameters (that is, symbols which are processed by the algorithm) are not part of the problem, but part of the environment. As part of the environment, they cannot contribute directly to a problem's solution.

Only the designer has the control to expand or to reduce the parameter set. He or she also determines the semantics, that is, the identifier and the range of values for each characteristic item (parameter) of the learning algorithm. In doing so, the designer acts as a filter allowing only those aspects (parameters) for problem solving which he or she considers to be relevant.

We now analyze two mechanisms which are used for creating artificial knowledge: finding generalizations and semantical equivalences. We discuss the epistemological (and computational) issues of complexity, incompleteness, and identification of an appropriate layer of abstraction.

Acquisition through Generalization

Generalization is a fundamental process in most categories of learning. We denote generalization to be the process of taking one or more descriptions as input to learning algorithms and producing a new description from which the original can be deduced (e.g., as a special case). The description may concern objects, concepts, events, rules, or any other entity. A generalization of a set of examples can be considered as agreement of what is common to the examples, leaving out the apparently irrelevant distinguishing features. Generalization is not easy to attain, since it can be difficult to determine which items are appropriate to generalize.

Complexity. There are two parts in generalization: finding the appropriate correspondences between components of the descriptions, and determining what is common to the corresponding components. If the generalization has to be explicit, then the learning component has also to construct a new description from the generalizations of the corresponding components. In other words, the learning component has to decide how much two descriptive items have in common. If two items are corresponding, a meta-item has to be generated for generalization.

For example, a learning component is trying to acquire a description of the concept 'table' from examples presented by a teaching component. The description of the first table—a meal table—has three components: a brown surface, a leg in the middle, and dishes on it. The second table is a table for playing table-tennis: green surface, four legs, and a net in the middle. To match these descriptions, the learning component must first find the appropriate correspondence between the table parts (e.g., legs) and the use of table parts (e.g., top for playing or eating), then find a generalization of the table (e.g., at least one leg) and its use (if possible). Finally, the learning component may conclude that a table in general consists of at least one leg, may have different colors, and can be used for different purposes.

The complexity of matching depends on the availability of attributes (parameters). If the examples are only a set of values of named attributes, it is simple to find appropriate correspondences. In case of interdependent items, such as 'the number of legs determines the use of a table,' generalization is hard to achieve.

Michalski (1983) tried to classify generalization methods: *Selective methods*, for example, climb hierarchy heuristics (for 'a-kind-of' relationships), use only explicit items of description (that is, those items which are present in the examples), whereas *constructive methods*[3] concern descriptive items which are not present in the examples. For example, generalizing examples of tables with four, six, and two legs, respectively to a more generalized version of the item 'number-of-legs' requires the construction of the constraint 'Tables have an even number of legs—except if the leg is near the middle,' since the constraint is not directly evident. Obviously, constructive methods can be used to make explicit descriptive items that have to be tested in a second run against other examples.

Determining Appropriate Abstraction (Level). The problem of determining an adequate level of generalization occurs if there is more than one valid possibility to generalize a set of examples. There are two distinct aspects for identifying generalization constraints depending on the quality of descriptive items: either there are many items to be considered as a generalized item, or there are many candidates for generalization because of the size of the overall number of items. In one case, the choice of how general a generalization shall be is undetermined by the examples. In the other case, there are too many possibilities for generalizations because of the large number of items to be considered for generalization. Each aspect has to be treated separately.

If a generalization process requires constraints for generalization, so-called *version spaces* (Mitchell 1983) can be defined. The most general and the most specific generalization—for example, a table has to have at least one leg (if it is in the middle) and a maximum of four legs (if rectangled)—may be useful. If most of the items are neither more general nor more specific than other items, the maximally general and maximally specific items will be almost the same as the entire set of items. An example for a wide and flat spectrum is as follows: 'table'—colored yellow, dark, and light green. Although version spaces facilitate determining ranges and classes, general constraints for generalization between similar item values cannot be given.

In the case of large item sets, we have to restrict the conditions for correspondence. Particular constraints can be identified (e.g., 'A rectangled table has maximally 4 legs' or, at a meta-layer, 'The set of items has to be split into subsets'). Another possibility is to change examples or to give more information about the examples. It has still to be investigated whether the complexity is increasing if interdependent items have to be split for learning.

Apparently, the larger the set of descriptive items, the more computationally expensive is the search for corresponding items. The higher the degree of dependency between descriptive items, the higher becomes the complexity for generalization. On the other hand, the smaller the set of items is and the more independent the items are, the more limited is the possibility of finding generalizations. ML-techniques rely heavily on a variety of heuristics (for example, climb hierarchy or extend-range) for searching corresponding items as well as for determining the kind of correspondence in case of multiple types of items.

Acquisition through Semantical Equivalence

If semantically equivalent terms and expressions can be found describing a problem or its solution, the number of facts and rules, and thus the complexity, can be reduced for artificial problem solving. However, it is not easy to identify semantical equivalence. For instance, consider two rules for learning how to construct a table for playing table-tennis:

Rule 1: *If* you have finished the basic construction of a table *and* marked the fields, *then* you may install the net for playing.

Rule 2: *If* you have fixed all legs on the tabletop *and* colored the tabletop green and white, *then* you may install the net for playing.

There are several ways of identifying semantical equivalence: finding part-to-part relationships in the knowledge representation scheme (for example, correspondence of condition-parts in case of rule-based representation), dealing with incompleteness (for example, is it required to know where to fix the legs on the tabletop?), and dealing with different layers of description (e.g., does the description cover the most general or specific case of a problem domain?). As we will see, incompleteness is correlated to problem descriptions at several layers of abstraction.

Part-to-Part Relationships. Rule 1 refers to the construction of any table for playing games where colored fields and a net are required, whereas Rule 2 goes into more detail about constructing a table for playing table-tennis. Nevertheless, both rules refer to the final step in installing a table for playing games where colored fields and a net are required. In both cases, something like the basic construction of a table, namely fixing the legs and painting the top, is required to finish the installation of the specific table. Both rules clarify conditions for the final adjustment of the net to play table-tennis, although they address different layers of abstraction. They provide semantically equivalent information in their condition part:

- the basic construction step for building a table (Rule 1) is to fix the leg(s) on the tabletop (Rule 2);
- "marking the fields" (Rule 1) specifically means painting the tabletop green and white (Rule 2).

Incompleteness and Different Layers of Abstraction. In Rule 1, the learning component will find information about how to construct a table in general. But this information is incomplete for a detailed specification on how to build a table-tennis table. For example, considering Rule 1, the question remains open—what kind of colors are required?

The example above also illustrates incompleteness with respect to the comprehensive construction of table-tennis tables. In Rule 2, the requirement for colors (green and white) is identified. Rule 1 gives information about the marking of the fields which has not been addressed in the other rule, although the action parts of both rules (that is, the installation of a net) are identical. We can observe several cases of incompleteness, although semantical equivalence can be achieved:

1. A particular but incomplete problem-solving strategy (for example, Rule 1) has been acquired.

    Because of incomplete specification, this case can easily lead to problem-solving results which may not include the required solution (e.g., a table for playing chess which cannot be used for playing table-tennis).

2. A set of rules has been acquired,
    a) which belong to the same layer of abstraction, but the description is incomplete for problem solving.

       Although through combining the condition parts of the rules (then all colors, the number of legs, the fields, and their relationships to the table parts and colors can be identified) a more comprehensive problem solution can be specified, it will not be complete.

    b) but several layers of abstraction have been mixed up.

       This case is exactly covered by the example above. It shows a general and a specific rule about how to build a table-tennis table. However, some essentials are missing and cannot be explained by combining the rules or other semantically equivalent terms.

Completeness at the level of semantical equivalence (what to do to reach a certain goal, for example, to install the net) does not imply semantical equivalence of underlying or superior goals (e.g., the construction of tables in general).

To recognize semantical equivalence at particular levels of abstractions, learning systems may use certain strategies (e.g., depth-first search of the generalization hierarchy). Strategies may recognize different levels of abstraction or provide the learning component with information about the form of items containing semantically equivalent information. In case of operators this can be achieved by observing the behavior. Another way of determining is to note that two items are always matching at the same time (Langley 1982). However, there is no generally recognized strategy to determine incomplete knowledge.

Epistemological Reflection of Parallel Distributed Processing

In contrast to conventional AI, neural nets assume no symbols (i.e., no syntactic units for semantic elements and no inference rules). Weights determine the behavioral dynamics and, thus, the knowledge concerning a specific problem. The higher the propagation caused by inputs, the higher the learning activities in the system.

Epistemological reflection of PDP requires a *novel* perspective of AI-interpretations of knowledge, learning, language, etc. Therefore, at first we will have to reflect on implicit assumptions before we show an alternative which can be provided by the PDP approach. We will discuss the relation between (natural) language and knowledge next, and then we will focus on various levels of processing in the PDP approach. Next, we will present an alternative approach to understanding knowledge and knowledge representation. In this section, we will also motivate for the constructivist unification based on PDP.

Natural Language, Symbols, and Knowledge

Our common sense idea of what is knowledge is that we think of it in terms of "knowledge units" which could be compared to atoms representing the substratum and/or the ultimate parts or structures our knowledge consists of. We also implicitly assume that these "atoms" of knowledge are some linguistic structures (for example, natural language words, symbols, etc.) having an explicit natural language meaning. What we do not take into our considerations is that we are *"seduced"* by our own language; it is very tempting (as it happens for ML) to think that our cognitive processes are based on such symbolic phenomena, because this seems to be the only way of reflecting and having explicit access to our cognitive processes. We are the victims and "prisoners" of our own (natural) language, and we hardly will be able to break through this (linguistic) barrier (Wittgenstein 1949). Nevertheless, we will have to try to get through this border—PDP can be a viable way of adequately circumventing the problems arising when being restricted to linguistic structures.

Conventional AI and thus ML approaches assume that human cognitive systems are just very complex symbol manipulation machines (cf. Newell and Simon's "Physical Symbol Systems Hypothesis;" Newell 1980, Newell and Simon 1976). They completely *ignore* the questions concerning, for instance, how meanings of symbols come into being or are changing—however, these problems are of great importance in representing and processing knowledge. Thus, we have to focus on these problems by reflecting on implicit assumptions in language and knowledge acquisition. Epistemological analysis can help us better understand and also more adequately model ("higher") cognitive processes, as they are embedded in these "low level" processes.

Parallel Distributed Processing—Various Epistemological Perspectives

PDP-networks comprise a large amount of simple processing units (called 'units') which are related by weights (which has led to the term "connectionism"). There is no exchange of messages or symbols assigned with a certain meaning like in ML. Units are rather connected via the exchange of numbers (that is, values denoting weights), which are outputs of other units. Knowledge is stored statically in the weighted connections among the units. Learning in a PDP-network is achieved by changing these weights. Hence, knowledge is not available explicitly; it is distributed over all weights (McClelland and Rumelhart 1986, Rumelhart and McClelland 1986).

Thus, we have to consider PDP-networks as more or less complex "pattern mapping machines" receiving an input and producing an output of activation patterns and a (recurrent or nonrecurrent) network architecture which determines the mapping process. From this perspective, a PDP-network represents nothing but a coupling of these two vectors of activation patterns. A PDP-network is embedded into an environment, which provides inputs for the network and receives outputs from the PDP-network. The network represents a more or less intelligent or complex mapping function (or artificial connection) between these two patterns. We will see that the understanding and the interpretation of a PDP-network depend very much on the application and on the *environment* where this abstract form of pattern processing (as provided by the PDP paradigm) can be observed. Hence, the interpretation and the periphery which connects the PDP-network to its environment determine the usability of the network as well as its value for better understanding the problems and questions concerning knowledge, knowledge representation, etc.

We can distinguish at least two levels of interpreting and applying PDP networks:

i) The most frequent application of PDP-networks is within *symbolic* environments. In most cases this type of processing is applied—some of the most famous and classical examples are the past tense model by Rumelhart and McClelland (1986) and Sejnowski's (1981) "NETtalk." They all have the following control flow:
   • the symbolic input is mapped to an *input pattern* of activations.
   • this pattern of activations is processed by a PDP-network and produces another pattern of activations as output of the PDP network.

- this *output pattern* is retransformed into a symbolic code and thus can be linguistically interpreted by the user.

This kind of control flow implies that—compared to the conventional AI-approaches —the only difference lies in the way of processing, which is of importance ("soft rules," hybrid processing, etc.). However, the basic problems of how, for instance, the meaning of a symbol arises or changes (this is a central question in semantics) are *not* solved because of the restriction to *symbolic* (and thus linguistic) categories: input-, output- and processing-structures. So we have to look out for an alternative form of applying the PDP approach in a more adequate way.

ii) If we reject symbolic input and output devices, PDP-networks are connected not [as in (i)] to an encoding or decoding mechanism which maps the code of symbols to a code of activation patterns (and vice versa), but rather to a sensory and effectory system. One could argue that it is also possible to connect an orthodox symbol-manipulating system to sensors and effectors (for example, in robotics)—we agree, but this argument ignores the fact that, for instance, these sensory data are always transformed into *symbolic* structures (for example, the linguistically interpretable variable "PRESSURE" has a certain value), and thus, the same problems as mentioned before arise. For example, it is not possible to correlate or to "mix" different modalities ("cross modality" seems to be one of the most important factors for building up the meaning of a symbol, word, etc.) in an adequate manner that goes beyond the linguistic borders. If we are interested in the process of how semantics and meaning emerge from meaningless flows of structured energy, we cannot assume an already implicitly given and "public" semantics. It is rather determined by the system's dynamics and architecture and *not* by an external instance.

Such a system, of course, would *not* be capable of playing chess or of solving mathematical problems (at our state of complexity); this problem is, however, of no (or at best of n-th order) interest, if one is investigating the basic problems of knowledge, knowledge representation, and learning. This approach is rather a *bottom up* approach; its aim is to get a better understanding of basic processes in cognitive systems interacting with their environment, with themselves, or with other cognitive systems on a very basic level (i.e., the level of *physical* interactions). Another aim is to show that the so called "high level cognitive processes" are *embedded* in these basic processes and that it is a more adequate way to investigate and understand these low level processes *at first*. Only then we will be capable of more adequately understanding, simulating, and investigating "high level" cognitive processes.

As we are interested in more basic questions, we will refer in the following sections to type (ii) processing in PDP-networks unless stated otherwise.

In our observations and simulations, we are not restricted to symbols, symbolic communication, etc., any more, but we are rather capable of investigating *behavior*, how it is generated, the relation between verbal and nonverbal behavior, simple forms of communication, etc.

Knowledge and Learning

Before discussing the problem of knowledge acquisition and representation in PDP-networks, we have to introduce a differentiation which seems to be quite important for a better understanding of the problems in this section. We are not assuming (like in conventional AI) that there exists a trivial mapping from structures and objects in any environment to natural language structures, such as symbols, words, etc.; we rather distinguish between two domains:

- *Environment* denotes "real world"—we do not have direct access to it, and we are not capable of directly perceiving it. It represents only the *constraints* within which the cognitive system is operating. The means for perception are our senses and human capabilities of expressing in natural language what we think we have perceived (i.e., what has been interpreted by the human cognitive system). It connotes the ontologically[4] given environment every human being refers to. We do *not* have direct access to it, but can only negatively specify it; that is, we can say what it is *not*.

  However, we cannot ignore the environment, since it provides the triggers (perturbations) for the construction processes in the cognitive reality, that is, the environment initiates (triggers) events which lead to processes in the cognitive reality.

- *(Cognitive) reality* is determined by the structure of the nervous system and by the individual cognitive system's history and experiences. As there is *no* direct access to the environment and *no* direct relation between these two domains, cognitive reality is a *construct* enabling the cognitive system not to collide with and to adequately act in its environment (it "fits" into reality; von Foerster 1981).

  It designates the world 'constructed' in our minds by individual experiences, as the constructivist position proposes. One could compare it to the "represented" world inside the representation system (i.e., the brain, the neural network, etc.). The structure of this domain is determined by the structure, architecture, dynamics, etc. of the representation system. It thusly depends on the system's phylogenetic and ontogentic "experiences."

There is no trivial relation (mapping) between these two domains—the cognitive reality is the result of a *construction process.* The PDP approach provides the means for modeling such epistemological considerations; this implies, however, that we have to rethink the ML-interpretations of knowledge and knowledge representation. What are knowledge and learning from this perspective?

Knowledge is the result of a *construction process* in the cognitive reality, enabling the cognitive system to operate adequately in its environment. From a pattern-processing perspective, learning in the PDP-approach means to correlate input with output patterns by slightly changing the values of the network's weights. This process could be compared to an adaption to the environment. There are many learning algorithms with and without supervision (e.g., Hinton 1987). The basic idea is that very small increments/decrements of a great number of weights (one single change would not influence the output) are responsible for a global change of the PDP-network's behavior (or output pattern). Thus, learning is building up a construct or an inner representation of the environment being determined by the structure of the sensory, effectors, and the architecture of the cognitive system.

Assuming type (ii) processing (introduced above), we cannot not find any symbols used for knowledge representation ("distributed" or subsymbolic representation; Smolensky 1988, Hinton, McClelland, and Rumelhart 1986) and therefore we have to consider problems concerning knowledge representation from a completely new perspective. We call it a "neo-behavioristic" perspective; it does, however, *not* have anything in common with traditional behaviorism—quite the reverse! The aim is to get a better understanding of *how* (low level and high level) behavior is generated. The inner representation of the environment (that is, "cognitive reality") is the central issue of our considerations.

The difference to traditional knowledge representation in, for instance, conventional AI is that

- this form of representation is *not* restricted to linguistic or symbolic structures and categories, and
- we are capable of investigating phenomena, such as the arising of meaning, etc., at a *subsymbolic* and senso-motoric level as our level of investigation starts at these basic processes (which are not "contaminated" by our language).

We have to look at this form of knowledge from a *cybernetical* rather than from a logical (linguistical) point of view. Thus, the aim of generating knowledge is to correlate input and output activations adequately in order to *generate* an adequate behavior enabling the cognitive system to "fit" into its environment. This means to behave in such a way that it survives and does not act in such a way as to lead to the system's death. Think, for instance, of a bird flying and landing on the ground; it has to coordinate so many influencing factors and perturbations in order to reach its target. We think of this very basic form of knowledge as being the basis for high level cognitive processes.

Subsymbolic processes are often accused of providing no structure for representing knowledge. In our opinion this kind of statement is true only to a certain extent: distributed representation is not to be equated with lacking structure—the structure cannot be seen as clearly as in symbolic representation. The reason is that linguistic structures do not explicitly occur,[5] which can easily be understood by a human interpreter, in the distributed representation. The structure of the knowledge being responsible for the observed (outer) behavior is determined by the (inner) architecture of the PDP-network and its "experience" being responsible for generating this behavior.

The aim of this approach to learning is, as Maturana (1970) puts it, to "learn" to behave or act adequately in (any) situation or context. It "appears as the continuous ontogenetic structural coupling of an organism to its medium through a process which follows a direction determined by the selection exerted on its changes of structure by the implementation of the behavior that it generates through the structure already selected in it by its previous plastic interactions" (Maturana 1978, p. 45). This interpretation makes PDP compatible with artificial life approaches: Learning "can be defined as any change in the knowledge structure of a system that allows it to behave better on later repetitions of some given type of task" (Muehlenbein 1988, p. 2). The latter interpretation of "adequate" clarifies the behavioral requirements of PDP-based learning components.

Most PDP-learning strategies achieve this aim, that is, the maximum of behavioral success, by searching for an equilibrium state. From an external observer's point of view, one could describe this process of equilibration with expressions such as "the system is building up an internal representation of its environment" or "the cognitive system is remembering or learning something." We have to be aware that such utterances can be understood only as metaphors and external descriptions, because *only* the external observer has access to the cognitive system's internal structure as well as to its interaction with its environment. Such descriptions make sense only from an external perspective. For the cognitive system itself, these descriptions do not incorporate any semantics because it "knows" only its own constructions of its own cognitive reality. The cognitive system is capable only to reflect the differences between its cognitive reality and its environment. The implicit aim for any cognitive system is, as stated above, to construct a cognitive reality which "fits" into its environment.

Towards Constructivist Unification of ML and PDP

In this section, based on the results of our epistemological evaluation, we first outline the constructivist point of view in the context of artificial learning. We then develop a novel cognitive model which allows the unified application of the different learning mechanisms. Finally, we discuss elementary implications for existing concepts, such as emergence and semantical equivalence.

Considering the Process of Construction

One cannot talk about knowledge without talking about the structure of the cognitive system(s) and its/their interaction(s) with the environment. Hence, knowledge is strictly *system relative*, meaning that it always remains knowledge *for* a certain system or group of systems. As an implication we cannot say anything about an "observer-independent" knowledge (or cognitive reality). Each piece of knowledge has to be understood as being the result of a construction process which is triggered by the dynamics of the environment as well as our representation system (in our cognitive reality) in the context of a problem or question which has to be solved or answered in the course of the process of living (i.e., in the process of active interaction with the environment as boundary condition for our constructs in our cognitive reality). It is not only the context of the problem or question but also the (physical) structure of the cognitive system itself which determines (or better, *embodies*) the knowledge.

Knowledge is rather the result of an interaction of processes *within* the cognitive reality than of a process of mapping of observations from the environment to the cognitive domain. Hence, the structure of the cognitive system itself (that is, the architecture of the nervous system, of the sensory and effector system) plays a dominating role in this process of construction, whereas the influence of the environment is rather marginal: it provides a kind of *boundary condition* which perturbates the organism's internal dynamics; it influences, but does *not* control the structure of the cognitive reality. As a result of constructing (more or less adequate) knowledge, the cognitive system is able to act within these conditions. The physical representation of the knowledge (in neural structures) is responsible for the generation of behavior which can be interpreted by an external observer and which causes changes in the sensory surface of the organism (system) itself.

What kind of knowledge does such a system represent? It does *not* represent the external world (that is, environment) in the sense of isomorphically mirroring it. It is a common assumption in traditional Cognitive Science and AI that the knowledge of a cognitive system somehow "mirrors" the environment in linguistic structures. Such a position assumes a more or less passive representation system being the result of a process of mapping. By "mapping" we mean that it is the human designer/user who does the job of identifying the semantic categories—these categories are mapped more or less isomorphically to a symbolic representation system. It is, however, indisputable that the natural representation system (that is, the nervous system) is an active device—it is actively constructing knowledge by interacting with itself and its environment.

Hence, these considerations are based on a constructivist approach for understanding cognition. As a consequence, the cognitive system always represents knowledge with respect to *itself* (i.e., the represented knowledge is knowledge of interaction with the environment). This interaction with the environment is, as has been discussed above, always a process of *construction* (first step of construction) in which the original stimulus (that is, the "direct influence or picture") from the environment is lost. This position implies that the interaction with the environment has to become an *internal construct* which interacts with the other activities within the system. Then, the relation to the environment has become *indirect*. Because of the uniform transmission of neural information (in the form of spikes and spreading activations), no differences can be found between the interactions within the system and "peripheral" influences.

From this perspective, the idea of "objective" or "absolutely true" knowledge sounds quite strange—such concepts have to be replaced by more relative and more tolerant concepts of consensual agreement;[6] that is, the private representational categories ("private semantics") are mutually adapted to each other. This concept does *not* imply, however, that we can speak of an "objective" or "given" semantics or knowledge.

As a consequence of this constructivist view, knowledge is understood as *relational* knowledge; that is, the process of construction means nothing but establishing new or changing existing relations. These relations are not to be understood as relationships being used for database modeling—they are *not* restricted to linguistic categories, they are rather relations between *sub-* or *presymbolic* features, for instance, between different modalities, between flows of activations, etc. If we are assuming a highly recurrent neural representation system (that is, a network with a recurrent architecture), each synaptic connection can be interpreted as a kind of relation[7]—it is physically stored and recognized knowledge, *"embodied"* knowledge. One could argue that the voltages in the computer memory are also embodied knowledge—the difference is, however, that each byte in the computer can be linguistically labeled as standing for a certain register, variable, instruction, etc. This is also true for artificial neural networks. What has to be seen, however, is that we are *confusing* here the *knowledge about the network* (that is, weights, units, connections, etc.) with the knowledge that is *represented* by such a network. Of course, we can extract each single value of a weight, but we *cannot* say what is represented by this particular weight. We rather have to see it as one part involved in the process of producing the network's global behavior. It does not represent something in the traditional sense of representation, that is, standing for something else, but rather in the sense of being responsible for generating behavior.

A relation is always standing between two (or more) features, objects, phenomena, "knowledge atoms,"[8] etc.; it is an expression for their connection. From the perspective of these objects, we can say that a relation implements a kind of *reference* to another object, item, etc. In the case of (natural or artificial) neural networks, these relations are not, as has been mentioned above, of a certain semantic value, such as "is-a" or "part-of." They are rather meaningless (in the sense of "having no linguistic interpretation") weights which determine the influence of one neuron (unit) on another. These connections or relations or references are responsible for the generation of the cognitive system's global behavior. The activity of a single neuron (unit) as well as of a single connection weight cannot be linguistically labeled.

We can look at these relations also as *associations* which are referring from one neuron to another. Hence, the construction of knowledge can be understood as building up associations (relations). It seems that the process of learning in neural structures is performed through a physical change of the structure of relations between neurons. The PDP approach supports this assumption (introduced by Hebb 1949). *Local* changes in the connections are taking place very slightly, causing a change in the *global* behavior. The observer can interpret this change as "learning" or "adaption" (evolutionary epistemology and second-order cybernetics characterize intelligent behavior as a result of a process of adaption).

The previous sections have shown that we have to change our perspective of observation if we want to achieve a deeper understanding of knowledge, knowledge representation, and cognition. As we have mentioned, it is *not* enough that we, as observers, can adopt only the *external* position, we rather have to look *inside* the system to take up an internal perspective (and bring these two positions into correlation to each other). The traditional approaches in cognitive science and ML are implicitly, in most cases, focussing on the observer's external position; that is, researchers are investigating the regularities of linguistic utterances and assume that those are *the* general form and substratum for knowledge representation and cognitive processes.

In the following we are trying to switch to the *internal* observer's position. From this perspective, a completely new and alternative understanding of behavior, language, communication, knowledge, and knowledge representation becomes possible (and necessary). It is quite unusual and does not meet the common sense expectations and assumptions. This conceptual change of view is very promising for the development of a more adequate understanding and model of cognitive phenomena.

The distinction between two types of reality introduced previously fits perfectly into the conception of Maturana (1985), who emphasized the subject-dependency of cognition and observation: "Everything said is said by an observer to another observer that could be himself." He stresses that there is no objective world in the sense used above, which is independent of an actual living system. The particular world is constructed by ongoing (indirect) interaction of the living system with its environment. Thus, there is no (pictorial) representation of entities in an outside world, but rather a network of dynamic correlations between the sensory system and effectors. At this point, we can state that cognition is no new quality that appears in living systems; instead, we should view the cognitive domain as a domain of possibilities a system can take to grapple with its environment. Hence, there is no need for any criterion to attribute a system's behavior to be cognitive or intelligent. Cognition is a substantial component of the living. The existence of a nervous system *per se* also is no criterion, since it only amplifies the possibilities of interaction and, therefore, the cognitive domain.

A Feedback-Based Architecture for Artificial Learning

We now suggest a constructivist model of learning. It shows how symbolic and subsymbolic learning mechanisms can cooperate in a recursive, feed-back-controlled learning environment. In the model, several constructivist principles have been applied:

1. *The learning mechanism and its environment are not independent of each other.*
"In nature, it is often extremely difficult to draw a sharp distinction between the living system and its environment, and interactions with and within the environment are often as complicated as interactions within the living system" (Langton 1989, p. 38).
Stemming from artificial life, where investigations have been focussed on the organism instead of artificial learning mechanisms, this principle assumes that structural changes in the environment as a result of the structural coupling with the learning mechanism are as important as the structural change in the mechanism itself. It is a mutual interaction which leads to learning. Hence, the coupling of the learning mechanism with its environment determines the capability to acquire knowledge. The parties in this interaction are equal and have their particular 'ontogenetic' development.

2. *The produced behavior of an artificial learning mechanism is mostly composed of reactions, which can be rarely described by explicitly formulated goals.*
In contrast to the widespread idea in the AI- and ML-communities that for the explanation of the behavior of artificial mechanisms, the level of rules is appropriate to achieve semantical equivalence, meaning denotes a social construct, established in the structure of language and forms of social interactions. Interactions between different systems lead to a mutual onto-genetic structural coupling. Because of this coupling, meaning cannot be represented by explicit goals, and thus, rules are either inadequate or have to undergo structural changes (Peschl and Stary 1990).

3. *Thinking is not a process of manipulating representations of an external world.*
(Artificial) learning takes place in an internal, closed 'world' (system) which interacts via structural coupling with its environment, which has its particular 'ontogenetic' development.
As a consequence, a constructivist artificial learning system is a *closed sys-*

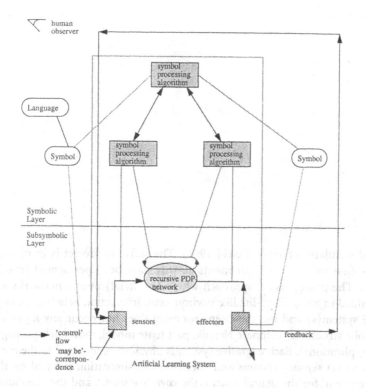

Figure 1.
Constructivist Learning Based on Interacting Machine Learning Algorithms and PDP Networks.

tem, which is perturbated by its environment. Its behavior is determined by steady feedbacks from its environment, which is structurally coupled with the system.[9] The core of our proposed artificial learning system is an internal feedback loop in the recursive PDP-network (see Figure 1), which represents the internal state of the system. A second feedback loop connects the system with its environment. These feedback loops correspond to feedback mechanisms which have been identified by cognitive scientists (e.g., Anderson 1983). Activities in the system may remain in the closed world of the system and may lead to *reverbatory circuits.* As a consequence, the learning system receives external stimuli via its receptors (sensors), processes them internally in reverbatory circuits as long as it determines, and is able to act via its interface (motor system, output unit), which leads to further feedback on the input side (sensoric system).

Some Details for the Alternative Model of Cognition

We now sketch how these epistemological concepts can be implemented in a

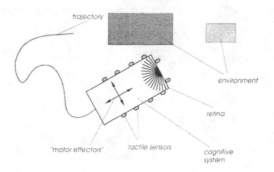

Figure 2.

neural simulation model (Peschl 1991). The software project is in its final state—first simulation experiments already have been performed (Peschl 1992). The project is an approach where (artificial) neural networks are embedded in an artificial-life like environment. Interaction between the cognitive system(s) and its (their) environment does not occur any more via symbolic structures (compare Nettalk, past tense model, most back-propagation applications). Each cognitive system is physically connected to the environment via sensory systems and effectors. The simulation is based on the 'environment' for the neural system, the *cognitive model,* and the *simulation* control (Figure 2). We first describe the environment and then discuss the cognitive model.

The Environment. The environment is assumed to be a two-dimensional plane in which the artificial organisms are moving around (Figure 2). If we apply the environment design module, objects having the shape of rectangles can be placed in the environment. The designer can place different objects in arbitrary size, rotation, and position in the environment by using the mouse device on the graphics display.

In addition to size and position properties, other properties such as *light intensity, mobility* (the position of each object is either fixed or variable), *"energy"* (food for cognitive systems), and *temperature* can be added to these objects.

The Cognitive Model. As shown in Figure 3, the cognitive model is the major component of the developed software architecture. It is closely linked to the control and display module, which interacts with the environment design and the simulation module. The design process of the artificial organism can be divided into two steps: definition and positioning of *sensors* and *effectors* and design of the artificial *neural network.* A kind of complementarily can be found for each modality (i.e., each sensor type has its corresponding effector system *and* the possibility of being "processed" in the environment).

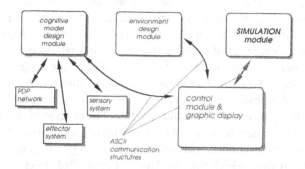

Figure 3.

The *visual* system represents the most important modality, because it enables a global orientation of the cognitive system in its environment. The system may be equipped with an artificial retina which transforms the light intensities into neural activities. The method of *ray tracing* (from computer graphics) is applied. These activities are entering the network dynamics by perturbating it. The designer has the possibility to determine the density of the photo-receptors and, hence, has an influence on the resolution with which the environment is visually perceived. The *tactile* sensors can be compared to a cat's whiskers; that is, they get active if a collision with another object or cognitive system is registered (i.e., computed) at the position where the sensor is placed. As has been stated above, objects can have the "energy" property. The *"food sensor"* gets active if a collision with an "energy object" is registered. The same is valid for the *temperature-sensitive system:* its activity is proportional to the intersected object's temperature.

On the output side of the artificial organism, the complementary effectors can be positioned by the designer. "Neural activities" are transformed into behavioral activities, movement, sounds, etc. There is an effector responsible for the movement of the artificial organism. Neural activity is transformed into physical movement of the cognitive system. The artificial organism is also capable of changing its *light intensity*—the activity of the "light effector neuron" is responsible for the intensity of the cognitive system's emitted light. The same is valid for the *acoustic* effector producing sounds in various pitches. These two effector systems are very important for establishing *communication* between artificial organisms. The *temperature* can also be controlled by the neural network's activities.

The Flow of Control. The user is able to design a neural network with an arbitrary architecture, number of units, etc. for each cognitive system. The weights can be either fixed or changeable and are initialized via a random function or a certain value. It is the designer's task to connect the neural network to the effectors and sensors via "interface-units," which are performing the transformation between the periphery system and the neural activities. From an epistemological point of view, it is important to mention that it is the designer who plays the role of *evolution* if he or she designs the network architecture and the structure of the artificial cognitive system.

The result of each designing process is translated into an ASCII file which acts as an input for the simulation module. The concept of communicating via ASCII files enables the use of a host with high performance for doing the simulation computations. This host is linked to a graphic display of a SUN workstation from which the simulation is controlled. Interaction between these two computers (via ASCII code) also enables a graphical representation of the results.

First simulation experiments have shown that the concept being presented above is quite computationally *expensive*, caused by ray tracing, object intersection, computations for the neural network(s), etc. In particular, if the number of artificial organisms, the number of the objects, the complexity of the neural architecture(s), etc. is increased, the time for computation increases exponentially. This observation justifies the relatively costly structure of communication between the modules via streams of ASCII symbols, since a host may perform the computations, while a workstation is responsible for controlling the simulation and for displaying the results.

Constructivist Coupling

Since the environment is not mapped 1:1 into the system, the system can neither recognize the origin of the perturbances nor the direct implications of its output (activities). The implications of its behavior are mainly based on internal state transitions and on further perturbations from its environment. Hence, a straightforward application of ML algorithms would not fully reflect the basic principles of the proposed artificial learning system.

If we think about the integrated application of ML and PDP in our conceptual framework illustrated in Figure 1, artificial learning occurs at two layers, which may be tightly coupled:

i) *The symbolic layer*
   This layer is directly accessible by human observers. It is the level of conventional ML where symbolic algorithms process parameter sets describing problem domains. But this level is not the dominant one. It is rather a second representation layer for the subsymbolic processes going on in underlying PDP-networks. Hence, subsymbolic knowledge acquisition is linguistically interpreted to be accessible by the human observer. The results of this interpretation can be processed by symbol-processing algorithms (e.g., to verify the acquired knowledge).

ii) *The subsymbolic layer*

At this level, sensor inputs are processed by PDP-networks. Each input may have a correspondence at the symbolic level. Anyway, it is processed recursively by a PDP-network simulating the self-organized architecture for artificial learning. Again, each recursive state transition may have a corresponding linguistic interpretation which can be processed by symbolic learning algorithms located at the symbol layer. Whenever effectors have to be activated, that is, when observable output is generated, the PDP-network provides the required signals. If the artificial system is directly coupled with its environment, these signals will lead to some (motoric) actions.

The internal feedback loops can be implemented by several PDP-networks. For instance, a simple feed-forward network can be used to map a sensoric input to a motoric action. Internal state transitions may occur at several layers that may correspond to particular networks. Since the networks are perturbating each other, the feed-forward network will be influenced by the internal state transitions. We cannot talk any longer about simple input/output behavior, according to the complex input-output relation.

Knowledge acquisition is achieved by *individual experience*. This strategy gives each artificial system its *history*: "History is necessary to explain how a given system or phenomenon came to be, but it does not participate in the explanation of the operation of the system or phenomenon in the present" (Maturana 1978, p. 39). Hence, learning is a continuous, incremental process which transforms the behavior of a system by experiences. The results of knowledge acquisition appear for the human observer justified by the behavior of the system in the past. In addition, as long as linguistic correspondences can be identified, learning can be traced symbolically. Note that the symbolic layer is the one which can be interpreted by the observer. Its elements can serve for further symbolic learning, as indicated in Figure 1. However, the symbolic layer still remains the linguistic level of interpretation of PDP learning results. Because of PDP, the artificial system cannot differentiate between internal and external stimuli (perturbations). All stimuli are treated equally.

Each activation of a PDP-network leads to a learning step. As long as linguistic correspondences can be identified in the external or internal feedback loop, a synchronization with symbolic learning algorithms can be established. When events occur without linguistic correspondences,[10] ML and PDP are decoupled. However, ML and PDP may still compete to improve problem-solving behavior. First approaches have been performed in so-called 'learning environments' (Stary and Winkelbauer 1991, Winkelbauer and Fedra 1991), where a direct evaluation of ML-like and PDP-network strategies can take place.

We now assess some implications which have to be discussed for the future understanding of epistemological criteria, such as semantical equivalence, if we pursue the development of the suggested artificial learning architecture.

Epistemological Consequences

The Myth of Emergence—Do We Have to Distinguish Various Levels?

Talking of emergence means in our context that a novel structure, phenomenon, etc. may emerge to a higher (that is, another more conceptual) level which exists now at a lower (that is, less abstract) level.[11] Afterwards, however, the phenomenon cannot be found on the lower level and is thus a result of some *construction* process by a (human) interpreter. What are the consequences of this construction for ML and PDP?

First, emergence in conventional AI is not as obvious as in alternative approaches like PDP, because in dealing with symbols, the interpreter is provided with meaning *per se*. Reflecting this situation shows that, for instance, the symbol "car" obtains its meaning and semantical 'value' only by the interpreter (i.e., by the interpreter's domain). Thus, meaning does *not* emerge from the machine even if we provide the symbol processor with a semantical unit. It turns out that the original syntactical representation is embedded in this so-called semantical representation, which is nothing but a very sophisticated and complex syntactical structure.

We have to be aware of the fact that *we* are *interpreting meaningless patterns* which represent a certain symbol, letter, etc. We are seduced by our own language when we believe that a machine which manipulates symbols is capable of learning the meaning of a (new) symbol. It is always the observer (interpreter, user, etc.) who is triggered and perturbated by the patterns of symbols. Thus, he or she constructs semantics as a result of a process of emergence in his or her cognitive domain. Hence, we have to distinguish two types of emergence within orthodox AI (ML):

a) The emergence of knowledge, in the process of learning, appears in the form of new generalized symbols which have emerged from lower level units. They are in most cases the result of a deduction process and thus can be reduced to a very simple and elementary type of emergence always occurring when a rule is applied. The emerging structure is *predetermined* by the rules and by all input structures ('experience'). There is only accepted a certain syntax of input 'fitting' in the data and processing structures of the symbol-manipulating machine.

b) The other type of emergence, mentioned above, is always occurring when the machine interprets patterns of symbols which trigger their meaning in the interpreter's cognitive domain. What meaning emerges in the observer's mind depends on his or her experiences and *cannot* be standardized as it is assumed by ML.

Second, PDP-approaches to learning do not have such an obvious claim of emergence like ML does in (a). As we take a closer look, it becomes evident that—for example, neural networks are influenced by *holistic* ideas—a global behavior is emerging from simple local processing units while local behavior does not have anything in common with the global and observed behavior of the whole system. The difference between PDP and conventional AI systems can be found in the fact that each step of processing is explicit (that is, it can be described by linguistic means), whereas, in the field of PDP, local processing is in most cases not completely understood with respect to the emerging global behavior.

Another reason why emergence is not obvious to such an extent in these approaches can be found in the behavioristic orientation. It means—as shown by PDP—that these approaches are closer (than conventional AI) to the explicit generation of patterns (behavior, actions, etc., depending on the devices to which the system is coupled) which have to be interpreted as behavior, symbols, etc. by an observer. Thus the only, but essential, difference between connectionist approaches and symbol manipulation lies in the 'degree of obviousness' in, for instance, interpreting a pattern as a set of emerging symbols.

In our approach, emergence is achieved at the subsymbolic level by PDP. It can be made explicit in case of linguistic correspondence for ML. In such cases, ML-generalization can be applied, too.

Learning and Representing Knowledge in the Triad 'Syntax–Semantics–Pragmatics': Exclusive Emergence or Epistemological Constraint?

The phenomenon of learning is closely related to this triad, as all domains are involved in this process. As we have seen in the previous sections, conventional AI (ML) has become troublesome in the domain of learning common sense knowledge. Ignoring this triad is one of the main reasons for these problems. ML completely leaves open the consideration of the pragmatic aspect, as interaction merely takes place mediately by exchanging symbols which can be represented explicitly by linguistic means. Thus there is no 'direct' access to the environment; that is, no physical interaction is possible, and there is always a syntactical level in between. Another problem emerges when we ignore this relationship between syntax, semantics, and pragmatics concerns, as already mentioned, pseudo-semantical structures which can be reduced to elementary syntactical units. Conventional AI completely ignores the semantical and pragmatical level and is limited to pure syntactical, formal logic. As we have seen, this attempt at describing and representing the world by simply and exclusively mapping objects, phenomena, relationships, etc. to formal structures has failed already in philosophy (cf. Carnap) because of the missing relationship to the real world (i.e., pragmatics).

Our approach, because of PDP patterns, follows a more cybernetical way of representing and learning knowledge. The system is in most cases[12] directly coupled with its environment and has to adapt to it—this process of adaption is the heart of the learning process. Subsymbolic knowledge acquisition is positioned at the other end of the 'syntacs–semantics–pragmatics' scale, namely at pragmatics. In order to process the acquired knowledge, it has to be re-transformed to symbols.

Hence, the main implication of our approach concerns the role of phenomena like language, communication, cognition, etc., which are—in the sense of Maturana—reduced to a physical level from which they emerge. Now, if we are interested in *fundamental* investigations of learning, this approach seems to be more adequate as it comes up to epistemological as well as natural scientific claims because semantics and syntax emerge as an observer's category from a pragmatical physical level. We have to be aware of the problems arising when syntactical structures are processed (e.g., by means of a PDP network). Nevertheless, we have to look for a way of integrating syntactical structures in these cybernetical approaches. If we are interested only in commercial systems without claiming to model cognition, a solution can be found by hybrid systems, that is, to couple PDP and ML to increase the performance at the syntactical level (ML) as well as the lexical level (PDP) (e.g., Shastri and Ajjanagadde 1989).

What about learning semantics? In the symbol-manipulating approach, this problem can be reduced by learning syntactical structures because a pragmatical level is completely missing—which means that there is no relationship to the environment. This implies that learning and representing common sense knowledge—which is based on implicit knowledge—is impossible. As shown by Polanyi (1966), direct physical coupling to an environment is absolutely essential for representing tacit knowledge because

i) there is no other reference but perturbations from the environment, and

ii) direct physical coupling is not describable semantically. Of course, one can describe a certain level, for example, light intensity on being ganged at the photo receptor—which has no semantical value.

Semantics can be acquired by construction of knowledge such as described in our approach where symbols get their meaning from the artificial system's 'cognitive reality.' The observer's semantic interpretation is evident in his or her cognitive domain itself and is determined by interactions at the pragmatical level.

To sum up, pragmatics (understood as the environment triggering construction process in the cognitive reality) represents the 'last point of reference,' although we have to be aware that we—from a constructivist's point of view—do not have evidence of it. The triad 'syntax–semantics–pragmatics' becomes an epistemological constraint if learning happens exclusively in one of the triad's domains.

A Concluding Outlook

The epistemological reflection of artificial learning techniques has provided the basics for constructivist unification of conceptually different learning paradigms: Conventional Machine Learning (ML) and Parallel Distributed Processing (PDP). In particular,

1. ML is based on structural decomposition, which is burdened by the conflict between epistemological requirements, computational goals, and linguistical specifications. Although interfaces to other learning techniques like PDP can be provided, for example, by preparing symbol vectors as input for subsymbolic network processes (e.g., Peschl 1989), the questions for appropriateness and usability remains epistemologically undiscussed. The same situation appears, if, for example, rules are embedded into connectionist systems and overlay hidden units with some kind of structure by unit typing (Shastri and Ajjanagadde 1989). Our architecture, in its claim for *constructing* the environment by mapping it to mental representation, is able to *control* subsymbolic as well as symbolic processing.

   Thus, *generalization and decomposition* occur only on demand, that is, if the artificial system is coupled structurally to its environment and has to solve a problem (e.g., to acquire knowledge about an obstacle for movement).

2. Unified artificial learning needs parallel and highly distributed processing units for knowledge manipulation (acquisition). Learning occurs self-determined (of course based on some kind of heuristics well known from ML) but not within a specific problem domain or micro-world (like in ML). The artificial system decides whether any coupling to a structure in the consensual domains takes place or not. Hence, the consensual domain and the required capabilities to learn (which means to adapt or to 'survive') determine the extent of concurrency and distribution. For example, learning by PDP-networks may lead to behavioral constraints for a problem-solving step which is based on generalized ML-structures.

   In certain environments, competing learning algorithms may be useful for critical situations (e.g., to have some information for consequences of activities). Thus, quality assertions may be required in making problem-solving steps. In this case, the consensual domain or the structural coupling of interacting individuals influences the final decision.

The empirical approach to learning, consequently performed by constructivist unified learning systems, is not measurable by functions directly. Thus the success of problem-solving activities by artificial systems can be measured only empirically, namely by the appropriateness of these activities for the adaption or the evolution of the system itself. To date, the appropriate selection can be supported only by answering quantitative questions, such as availability of training facilities. The more essential questions concern dependency of linguistic description, closed-world assumptions, and the explicit representation of structure. These issues can be discussed only by further epistemological discussions, for example, investigating the question 'What does Gestalt-recognition by PDP-networks imply?'—although ML-hardliners have already recognized the need for 'symbiotic' learning strategies by entitling these approaches 'from stand-alone systems to collaborative problem solving' (Carbonell 1990, p. 8).

Unfortunately, they are not willing to give up their limited comprehension of learning concerning structural representation for the benefit of, for instance, a more holistic approach like constructivist thinking: "When user and system must pool resources and reason jointly, or when either attempts to instruct the other, knowledge must be encoded in an explicit manner comprehensible to both" (Carbonell 1990, p. 8).

In our attempt to convince those hardliners, we have made a first step to introduce epistemologically evaluated architectures based on a constructivist framework. Using this framework, we have seen that problems such as generalization or semantical equivalence need not be investigated any more, since the perceived reality determines the learning activities. The performance of such architectures is measured by their problem-solving behavior, establishing a new kind of behaviorism.

Acknowledgments

This work has been sponsored by the Austrian Science Foundation under contract P7762-HIS as well as by the Max Kade Foundation (New York) and the CD-Lab for Expert Systems (Vienna).

Notes

1. On one hand, Artificial Life is strictly oriented towards Maturana's biological concept of learning, which is fully compatible with a constructivist interpretation of PDP. On the other hand, for the implementation of Artificial Life creatures, techniques from Conventional Machine Learning, such as rules, can be applied easily.

2. In the attempt to map mental processes to computer executable procedures, Newell and Simon (1976) set up the so called 'Physical Symbol Systems Hypothesis.' It is based on the belief that humans and computers process the same kind of elementary entities, namely symbols.

3. Note that "constructive" is merely used in contrast to "selective." It is not used equally with "constructivist."

4. By using the term "ontology," we mean the philosophical tradition to claim the existence and recognizability of an independent external world, that is, the existence of *Dinge an sich*.

5. This recognition uncovers the (AI-)misconception that "structure" is equated with linguistic structure.

6. Of course, such concepts have very interesting implications for the organization and the self-understanding of *science*—these implications cannot be discussed in this context.

7. This is also valid for *artificial neural networks*.

8. These so-called "atoms" *must not* be misunderstood as linguistic primitives or basic linguistic structures—they are rather (from a linguistic perspective) meaningless features responsible for the generation of adequate knowledge.

9. Conventional Machine Learning *per se* does not follow this constructivist principle. There, values are assigned explicitly to parameters, which have been identified by the designer.

10. This case is very likely because of the cross modality of stimuli the system has to deal with (e.g., von Foerster 1981).

11. Emergence has been applied in ML-approaches, when generalization was expected to lead to semantically equivalent results.

12. We are excluding, for instance, PDP-networks receiving symbolic input and generating symbolic output ('symbolic' means linguistically interpreted).

References

Anderson, J.R. (1983). *Architecture of Cognition*. Cambridge, MA: Harvard University Press.

Arbab, B. & Mitchie, D. (1985). Generating rules from examples. In *Proceedings IJCAI-85* (pp. 631-633).

Bergadano, F. & Giordana, A. (1988). A knowledge-intensive approach to concept induction. In *Proceedings 5th Int. Conference on Machine Learning* (pp. 305-317). San Mateo, CA: Morgan Kaufmann.

Bergadano, F., Matwin, S., Michalski, R.S., & Zhang, J. (1988). Measuring quality of concept descriptions. In *EWSL-88* (pp. 1-14).

Boose, J.H. (1988). Knowledge acquisition techniques and tools: Current research strategies and approaches. In *Proceedings Int. Conference on 5th Generation Computer Systems*, ICOT (pp. 1221-1230).

Braitenberg V. (1984). *Vehicles: Experiments in Synthetic Psychology*. Cambridge, MA: MIT Press.

Buchanan, B. & Shortliffe, E.H. (1984). *Rule-Based Expert Systems—The MYCIN Experiments of the Stanford Heuristic Programming Project*. Reading, MA: Addison Wesley.

Carbonell, J.G. (Ed.). (1990). Machine Learning: Paradigms and Methods. Cambridge MA: MIT Press.

Churchland, P.S. (1986). *Neurophilosophy. Toward a Unified Science of the Brain*. Cambridge, MA: MIT Press.

Davis, R. (1984). Diagnostic reasoning based on structure and behavior. *Artificial Intelligence, 24*, 347-410.

Davis, L. & Young, D.K. (1988). Classifier systems with hamming weights. In *Proceedings 5th Int. Conference on Machine Learning* (pp. 162-173).

DeJong, G.F. (1988). An introduction to explanation-based learning. In W.E. Shrobe (Ed.), *Exploring Artificial Intelligence* (pp. 45-81). San Mateo, CA: Morgan Kaufmann.

DeJong, G.F. & Mooney, R.J. (1986). Explanation-based learning: An alternative view. *Machine Learning, 1, 2*, 145-176.

Fisher, D.F. (1987). Knowledge acquisition via incremental conceptual clustering. *Machine Learning, 2, 2*, 139-172.

von Foerster, H. (1981). Das Konstruieren einer Wirklichkeit. In Watzlawick (Ed.), Die erfundene Wirklichkeit, Piper (pp. 39-60).

von Foerster, H. (1984). Erkenntnistheorien und Selbstorganisation. In F. Schmidt (Ed.), *Der Diskurs der Radikalen Konstruktivismus*, pp. 133-158. Frankfurt: Suhrkamp.

Gentner, D. (1983). Structure mapping: A theoretical framework for analogy. *Cognitive Science*, 7, 2.

Gentner, D. & Stevens, A. (Eds.). (1983). *Mental Models*. Hillsdale, NJ: Lawrence Erlbaum.

Ginsberg, A., Weiss, A., & Politakis, P. (1985). SEEK2: A generalized approach to automatic knowledge base refinement. In *Proceedings IJCAI-85* (pp. 367-374).

Goldberg, D.E. (1989). *Genetic Algorithms*. Reading, MA: Addison-Wesley.

Hebb, D.O. (1949). *The Organization of Behavior*. New York: Wiley.

Hinton, G.E. (1987). *Connectionist Learning Procedures* (Tech. Rep. CMU-CS-87115). Carnegie-Mellon University, Pittsburgh.

Hinton, G.E., McClelland, J.L., & Rumelhart D.E. (1986). Distributed representations. In D.E. Rumelhart (Ed.), *Parallel Distributed Processing*, Vol. I, pp. 77-108. Cambridge, MA: MIT Press.

Johnson-Laird, P.N. (1983). *Mental Models*. Cambridge University Press.

Kodratoff, Y. (1988). *Introduction to Machine Learning*. London: Pitman.

Langley, P. (1982). Strategic acquisition governed by experimentation. In *Proceedings ECAI'82* (pp. 171-176).

Langley, P., Bradshaw, G., & Simon, H.A. (1983). Rediscovering chemistry with the Bacon system. In R.S. Michalski, J.G. Carbonell, & T.M. Mitchell (Eds.), *Machine-Learning—An AI Approach*, pp. 307-330. Los Altos, CA: Morgan Kaufmann.

Langton, C. (Ed.). (1989). *Artificial Life*. Reading, MA: Addison Wesley.

Lenat, D.B. (1982). *The Role of Heuristics in Learning by Discovery: Three Case Studies*. Palo Alto, CA: Tioga.

Maturana, H.R. (1970). Biology of cognition. In H.R. Maturana & F.J. Varela (Eds.), *Autopoiesis and Cognition*, pp. 2-60. Dordrecht: D. Reidel. [Boston, 1980.]

Maturana H.R. (1978). Biology of language. In G.A. Miller & E. Lenneberg (Eds.), *Psychology and Biology of Language*, pp. 27-63. New York: Academic Press.

Maturana, H.R. (1985). Erkennen: Die Organisation und Verkörperung von Wirklichkeit, Vieweg.

McClelland, J.L. & Rumelhart, D.E. (1986). *Parallel Distributed Processing, Explorations in the Microstructure of Cognition, Volume II: Psychological and Biological Models*. Cambridge, MA: MIT Press.

Michalski, R.S. (1983). Learning from observation: Conceptual clustering. In R.S. Michalski, J.G. Carbonell, & T.M. Mitchell (Eds.), *Machine-Learning—An AI Approach*, pp. 331-363. Los Altos, CA: Morgan Kaufmann.

Michalski, R.S., Carbonell, J.G., & Mitchell, T.M. (Eds.). (1983). *Machine-Learning—An AI Approach*. Los Altos, CA: Morgan Kaufmann.

Michalski, R.S., Carbonell, J.G., & Mitchell, T.M. (Eds.). (1986). *Machine-Learning—An AI Approach*, Vol. II. Los Altos, CA: Morgan Kaufmann.

Mitchell, T.M. (1983). Learning and problem solving. In *Proceedings IJCAI'83*.

Mitchell, T.M., Keller R.M., & Kedar-Cabelli, S.T. (1986). Explanation-based generalizations: A unifying view. In R.S. Michalski, J.G. Carbonell, & T.M. Mitchell (Eds.), *Machine-Learning—An AI Approach* pp. 47-80. Los Altos, CA: Morgan Kaufmann.

Mooney, R., Shavlik, J., Towell, G., & Gove, A. (1989). An experimental comparison of symbolic and connectionist learning algorithms. In *Proceedings IJCAI'89*. Los Altos, CA: Morgan Kaufmann.

Muehlenbein, H. (1988). *The Dynamics of Evolution and Learning—Towards Genetic Neural Networks*. Los Altos, CA: Morgan Kaufmann.

Newell, A. (1980). Physical symbol systems. *Cognitive Science, 4,* 135-183.

Newell A. & Simon H.A. (1976). Computer science as empirical inquiry: Symbols and search. *Communications of the ACM, 19,* 3, 113-126.

Norman, D.A. (1988). *The Psychology of Everyday Things*. New York: Basic Books.

Peschl, M.F. (1989). An alternative approach to modelling cognition. In *Proceedings Man and Machine-Conference,* John von Neumann Society, Hungary.

Peschl, M.F. (1990a). *Cognitive Modeling* (in German). Wiesbaden, Germany: Deutscher Universitätsverlag.

Peschl, M.F. (1990b). A cognitive model coming up to epistemological claims—Constructivist aspects to modeling cognition. In *Proceedings of the Int. Joint Conf. on Neural Networks* (pp. III-657-662). San Diego, CA: IEEE.

Peschl, M.F. (1991). Artificial intelligence between symbol manipulation, common sense knowledge, and cognitive processes. An epistemological reflection. In B. Soucek (Ed.), *Neural and Intelligent Systems Integration*. New York: Wiley.

Peschl, M.F. (1992). Construction, representation, and embodiment of knowledge, meaning, and symbols in neural structures. In *Connection Science, 4,* 3&4, 327-338.

Peschl, M.F. & Stary, C. (1990). IKARUS—Interdisciplinary knowledge reconstruction based on rules and science theory. In D. Geyer (Ed.), *Proceedings 8th International Conference of Cybernetics and Systems* (Vol. 2). New Jersey: NJIT-Press.

Polanyi, M. (1966). *The Tacit Dimension*. Garden City, NY: Doubleday.

Quinlan, J.R. (1983). Learning efficient classification procedures and their application to chess end games. In R.S. Michalski, J.G. Carbonell, & T.M. Mitchell (Eds.), *Machine-Learning—An AI Approach,* pp. 463-482. Los Altos, CA: Morgan Kaufmann.

Quinlan, J.R. (1986). Induction of decision trees. In R.S. Michalski, J.G. Carbonell, & T.M. Mitchell (Eds.), *Machine-Learning—An AI Approach,* pp. 81-106. Los Altos, CA: Morgan Kaufmann.

Quinlan, J.R. (1988). An empirical comparison of genetic and decision-tree classifiers. In *Proceedings 5th Int. Conference on Machine Learning*. San Mateo: Morgan Kaufmann.

Rosenblatt, F. (1958). The Perceptron: A probalistic model for information storage and organization in the brain. *Psychological Review, 65,* 386-407.

Rumelhart, D.E. & McClelland, J.L. (1986). *Parallel Distributed Processing, Explorations in the Microstructure of Cognition, Vol. I: Foundations*. Cambridge, MA: MIT Press.

Samuel, A.L. (1963). Some studies in machine learning using the game of checkers. In E.A. Feigenbaum & J. Feldman (Eds.), *Computer and Thought,* pp. 71-105. New York: McGraw Hill.

Sejnowski, T.J. (1981). Skeleton filters in the brain. In G.E. Hinton & Anderson (Eds.), *Parallel Models of Associative Memory* (pp. 189-212).

Shastri, L. & Ajjanagadde, V. (1989). *A connectionist system for rule-based reasoning and variables* (MS-CIS-89-06, LINC LAB 141). School of Engineering and Applied Science, University of Pennsylvania.

Shaw, M.L.G. & Gaines, B.R. (1985). *Cognitive foundations of knowledge-based systems* (Tech. Rep.). Dept. of Computer Science, Calgary University, Alberta.

Smadar, T., Kedar-Cabelli, S.T., & McCarty, L.T. (1987). Explanation-based generalization as resolution theorem proving. In *Proceedings 4th Int. Conference on Machine Learning* (pp. 383-389). San Mateo: Morgan Kaufmann.

Smolensky, P. (1988). On the proper treatment of connectionism. *Behavioral and Brain Sciences, 11,* 1-74.

Stary, C. & Peschl, M. (1990). The impact of concepts on implementation-oriented cognitive models: Merits of model-based communication patterns. In C.N. Manikopoulos (Ed.), *Proceedings 8th World Congress on Cybernetics and Systems,* Vol. 1. New York: NJIT-Press.

Stary, C. & Winkelbauer, L. (1991). Applying qualitative evaluation criteria to improve adaptive behavior in example-based learning environments. In *Proceedings IVth Int. Symposium on Artificial Intelligence,* Cancun, Mexico.

Stepp, R.E. & Michalski, R.S. (1986). Conceptual clustering: Inventing goals-oriented classifications of structured objects. In R.S. Michalski, J.G. Carbonell, & T.M. Mitchell (Eds.), *Machine-Learning—An AI Approach,* Vol. 2 (pp. 471-498). Los Altos, CA: Morgan Kaufmann.

Utgoff, P.E. (1988). ID5: An incremental ID5. In J. Laird (Ed.), *Proceedings Int. Conf. on Machine Learning* (pp. 107-120). San Mateo: Morgan Kaufmann.

Winograd, T. & Flores, F. (1986). *Understanding Computers and Cognition.* Norwood, NJ: Ablex.

Winston, P.H. (Ed.). (1975). Learning structural descriptions from examples. In *The Psychology of Computer Vision* (pp. 157-209). New York: McGraw-Hill.

Winkelbauer, L. & Fedra, K. (1991). ALEX: Automatic learning in expert systems. In *Proceedings 7th IEEE Conf. on Artificial Intelligence Applications,* Miami Beach.

Wittgenstein, L. (1949). *Philosophische Untersuchungen,* Vol. I & II. Frankfurt: Suhrkamp (1984).

Young, R.M. & O'Shea, T. (1981). Errors in children's subtraction. *Cognitive Science, 5,* 153-177.

11 Towards A Sentential 'Reality' for the Android

Cary G. deBessonet

For years the AI literature has been flooded with material on the use of deductive and probabilistic methods for automating reasoning operations of the sort employed by human beings. There is a somewhat astounding paucity of materials on methods that do not fall squarely within the scope of these recognized approaches, yet human beings frequently employ methods that extend beyond the scope of these recognized types. This paper draws attention to this somewhat neglected area and describes a system of association that includes not only standard associations but also some nonstandard ones that can be used to ground a theory of android reasoning and conversational structure. The central themes are that intelligent, cognitive activities of human beings often employ associations of the nonstandard type and that androids can be built to do the same in carrying out cognitive operations.

The term "association" will be used herein in a broad sense to cover any mentally appreciable relation or grouping of objects based on some defined method, goal, or purpose. The term thus covers formal relations as well as a host of others, including those defined from a legal perspective. Seemingly, any two objects can be associated with one another for some purpose or goal, however unusual, and for this reason the scope of associations based on purpose appears to extend to the polarities of the human imagination. The stock market can be associated with the concept of a black hole based on the mere fact that someone has given thought to each, for instance, and if the purpose of a given association is to drive human conversation, a proposition might even be associated with its contradiction in order to give a corrective response. To recognize that a relation exists between objects is to associate them, but an act of association can be independent of any particular method or procedure by which objects are brought into relation. By merely recognizing relations between old and new thoughts, for example, a person can bring about associations that are distinct from the cognitive processes that produced the thoughts. The relevance of this kind of independent act of association can be appreciated when one considers that an automated querying system might take queries to be objects that are to be *associated* with one or more of its database components.

This chapter describes how one can ground a theory of android cognition in a theory of systematic association that extends beyond the confines of standard associations, which for the present will be taken to include associations based on deductive or probabilistic relations. The thesis is that one can reap special benefits if one adopts a theory that emphasizes general systematicity rather than standard systematicity alone. The approach described is based on the theory of knowledge adopted for SMS (symbolic manipulation system), a system designed to build a database from information written in a special epistemological language SL (symbolic language) and to respond to SL queries about that information. Although the syntax of SL is more English-like than some other languages (for example, first-order logic notation), it bears sufficient formal structure to be used like logic notation. A detailed description of the theory behind SMS and SL can be found in deBessonet (1991).

The instant thesis is that it is meaningful to speak of the acquisition of knowledge by an android, the acquisition occurring by way of interpretation of a *given* or flow of experience. Android cognition will be described as being dependent upon basic abilities to appreciate ontological distinctions and different kinds of presence among the objects, states, and events that constitute the 'given.' In SMS, states and events are sentential entities that are distinguished from one another based on semantics and syntax. A sentential level of experience can be created to serve as a source bed of epistemic elements from which to construct a knowledge base of epistemological structures (see the next section). The knowledge base, in turn, can serve as part of android 'reality.' An attempt will be made to show that a useful connection can be established between this approach and the theory of *knowledge-base semantics* (Hirst 1987). The connection will be shown during the course of describing how the epistemological theory presented can be usefully employed in an automated reasoning system.

Adoption of Working Assumptions

One way to enter discussion on the current topic is to ask whether human cognition is a function of nonconscious parts being brought together or arranged in some way to produce a cogitating mechanism. If so, it would seem that one might be justified in making a straightforward comparison between the way a human being knows the world and the way an android might be said to know the world. If human cognition does not come about in this way, there might be a fundamental difference between human and android knowledge, perhaps rooted in some difference between living and nonliving things. The viability of the theory presented does not depend upon the existence of such a difference, however. Consequently, this chapter does not address basic questions of that kind, but it does support the position that it is meaningful to speak of epistemic states and acts of an android. As discussed below, the theory presented employs a behavior-oriented test for intelligence rather than a definition. Epistemic acts and states are taken to be a subset of the cognitive processes that enable intelligent, cognitive activity to occur. A subset of the processes that enable an android to qualify as an intelligent entity under the test are thus taken to be epistemic states and acts of that android.

The theory of intelligence used to support the approach introduced is objective and behavior-oriented. The theory is based on the postulation that human beings are intelligent. This postulation seems quite natural since the existence of *intelligence*, understood in its ordinary sense, can be confirmed in oneself by simple introspection. Concomitantly, one can witness intelligent action in the form of conscious self-expression and involvement in the world. Although some philosophers might wish to quibble with the idea, it seems that the confirmation of intelligence is largely a solipsistic enterprise and that one is left to rely on the detection of similarities between personal, intelligent action and the action of foreign objects to support beliefs about the intelligence of those foreign objects. It will be assumed that this view, which is oriented towards a direct, solipsistic appreciation of intelligence, is correct and that belief in the intelligence of foreign objects is determined by the behavior of those objects. This objectified, behavior-based ground for belief in the intelligence of foreign objects constitutes a behavior-oriented test for intelligence. The effect is that just as one can assume that other people are intelligent based on their behavior, one can assume that an android is intelligent if it behaves like a human being.

Science teaches that innate intelligence is functionally dependent on the brain, and because one normally believes that other people have brains, one normally assumes that other people have innate intelligence rather than mere abilities to act as if they do. If one discovers that an android has a brain-like (perhaps even organic) device in its head-apparatus, one might be more inclined to believe that the android is intelligent than if one discovers only a fistful of straw in that apparatus. Nonetheless, the working assumption adopted dictates that the appropriate test for intelligence is to be based on the behavior of the android, not its constitution.

The adoption of the behavioral view just described produces special benefits. By employing the theory at the conscious level of personal experience, one can reflect upon mental behavior and directed physical behavior to determine what behavior-producing processes are evidenced at the conscious level. The result is that it becomes possible to conceive of how a mechanism might be built to conduct similar processes. In other words, an objective appreciation of conscious, cognitive action enables one to pattern android cognitive processes after that action. The importance of this is that although the cognitive processes used to observe these phenomena appear to be dependent on innate processes that are not appreciable at the conscious level, there does not appear to be any necessary dependency between the objectively perceived behavior and the innate processes. This seems evident because in some instances behavioral results can be duplicated using inorganic computing devices. In fact, most of the AI systems built to date appear to be grounded on a theory of this sort. It is true that efforts are being directed towards discovering how the human brain functions at the microscopic level in hopes of finding ways to build computers in conformity with discovered patterns and processes, but it remains to be seen whether computers so patterned will be more intelligent than those not so constructed.

The reason for adopting an approach that focuses on what is perceived at the conscious level is to provide the groundwork for a naive theory of android intelligence. A future subsection discusses this naive perspective and explains how it lends support to the theory of android cognition being described. Under the test adopted, one can conceive of associated levels of intelligence that begin at some basic level and extend upward. At the basic level, an android can be considered to be acting intelligently if it behaves appropriately in a situation even though it might not be able to explain or justify its action. Granted that it would be behaving more intelligently if it could give such a justification or explanation, it nonetheless can be considered to have evidenced a minimal degree of intelligence if it has behaved appropriately, by which is meant that it has behaved or reacted in a way that corresponds to the way a human being might act in a similar situation. This measure of intelligence is quite flexible because the extent to which behavior is duplicated can vary from case to case. It is not unusual for human intelligence to be measured or determined by results rather than by the processes that cause or enable the results to occur. Many people do not understand and cannot explain the theory behind multiplication, for example, yet they can multiply numbers just fine using mechanical (cf. android-oriented) methods. The result for android epistemology is that the door is open for multiple theories of android cognition, and the merits of each theory can be measured in terms of behavioral results. In short, the extent to which a robot can interact with its environment as effectively as can a human being can be taken to be the measure of its intelligence. This approach accords with some of the early theories of artificial intelligence (see, e.g., Winston 1977, Ch. 1).

The next three subsections, *infra*, support the position that the extended concept of association used in SMS theory provides the basis for a unified theory of android cognition at the sentential level. After making a case for the view that nonstandard associations can be usefully employed in android reasoning, the discussions focus upon the bases of nonstandard associations. Although the tractability task that confronts automated, associative procedures is quite formidable because of the seemingly infinite number of associations that could be recognized, methods exist by which one can control the combinatorial explosion. The naive perspective adopted for SMS is particularly useful in this respect because one can introspectively discover some of the methods that human beings use to control associative processes. Corresponding methods can be developed for use in the realm of the android.

A Theory of Association

This chapter focuses on the sentential realm in an attempt to demonstrate how one can build a 'reality' of sentential objects over which inferencing can be defined for an android. In SMS, 'reality' is conceived of as an ontologically diverse complex of objects and relations. Sentences written in SL are used to describe this complexity, and the sentences are interpreted to produce a "sentential reality." In SMS, all objects, including those taken to be ideas, are linguistic in nature and bear recognized relations to one another. Ontological diversity is captured by employing a system of assignment by which values are assigned to objects to indicate their ontological status. Each sentential object of 'reality' is *signed*; that is, each object carries one or more values that describe its status or presence (cf. truth) within the system. As will be discussed later, to some extent the assignment of values can be done automatically. This avoids the task of having to make independent and highly localized assignments, a difficulty sometimes associated with the development of systems that use fuzzy set theory or probability theory.

SMS theory is rooted in a theory of association that employs a naive assumption to the effect that human intelligence is dependent upon an ability to call appropriate sets of mental objects into relevance in particular situations. Under the theory, the ability to determine what is relevant for a given situation is considered to be an integral part of intelligence. The mere mention of the word 'football' might trigger a particular set of ideas that would enable a person to talk intelligently about football, for example. Android intelligence can likewise be seen to be dependent upon an ability to produce relevant sets of objects in response to conversational input.

It seems evident that intelligent human behavior is dependent upon cognitive processes that associate objects or ideas to produce intelligent results. In complying with the request "Bring me a glass of water," a person employs knowledge about words, their meaning and significance, and the world itself. Thoughts about things such as a glass, a water faucet, pouring activity, and the like would be typical. These thoughts are drawn into relevance and used to produce desired results. The phenomenon of objects being drawn into relevance in a given situation does not appear to be *necessarily* dependent upon any deductive or probabilistic operation conducted at the conscious level. It follows that any theory of association that attempts to account for intelligent behavior at the conscious level must extend beyond the confines of associations based on deduction and probability.

It is not difficult to justify the view that an extended theory of association is needed for an adequate theory of intelligent human behavior. From a naive point of view it seems obvious that some of the cognitive processes that prompt human action are not dependent on ideas generated by any sort of reasoning process or operation. An ordinary sensory experience of a herd of galloping horses entails both the sight of the horses and the sound of their hoofs striking the ground. Once the experience has been processed and fixed in memory, the sound of pounding hoofs might very well bring to mind the sight of a herd of horses, but what has this association to do with logic? From a naive perspective, it appears that such a mental sighting is automatically generated as an unconscious reaction to the sound. It is true that one might be able to give a logic-oriented description or explanation of the phenomenon based on principles such as:

a) If hoofs of horses strike the ground, sounds of a particular sort are produced; and

b) If sounds of that sort are produced, it is likely that hoofs of horses have struck the ground.

Even though such an explanation is possible, it seems to have little to do with the thought of horses *popping* into mind at the sound of hoofs striking the ground.

Given that many of the thoughts employed in cognitive activities that prompt human behavior are not *reasoned* into being, it is easy to conceive of reasoning as being dependent upon ideas that are somehow drawn into relevance in association with one another. Under this view, reasoning consists of processes by which conclusions are drawn from ideas drawn into relevance, and logic is the science that deals with this kind of activity. The ability to draw logical conclusions seems to be one of the prerequisites for intelligent behavior, but for the reasons just mentioned, such an ability does not seem to account for all aspects of intelligence. The SMS approach provides a more adequate theory of intelligent behavior by incorporating a theory of association to deal with some of the noninferential aspects of intelligence.

The conclusion that some aspects of intelligent behavior are dependent on the ability to make nonstandard associations could have far reaching consequences for the field of android epistemology. Perhaps the consequence most pertinent to the present topic is that designers of cogitating components of androids might miss opportunities to enhance their products if they fail to make provision for the production and treatment of nonstandard associations. The next subsection describes the importance of nonstandard associations and then describes methods that can be used to draw a limited number of associations into relevance in given situations. Although not an exhaustive treatment of possibilities, the examples given suffice to establish the basis of an approach that can be developed to cover a more adequate range of possibilities.

Importance of Nonstandard Associations

The importance of a theory of nonstandard association of the sort being described can be illustrated by example using the following sentences:

A flock of birds ate all the figs; and   (1)

A bird ate all the figs.   (2)

These sentences are related to one another in one or more ways through their components, but one would be hard pressed to find a direct deductive, probabilistic, or plausibilistic relation between them at the sentential level if the sentences are taken to be assertions (statements). Given that statement (1) is true, for example, statement (2) would be false, assuming of course that to assert that a flock of birds ate the figs is to assert that more than one bird was involved in the act of consumption. Not only that, statement (2) would be totally improbable and impossible.

Although statement (2) does not follow by deduction from statement (1), the two statements are nonetheless related in ways that might prompt a person to associate them in a given situation. If a person knows that statement (1) is true, for example, and is presented with statement (2) as a query in ordinary human conversation, the person might quickly realize the falsity of statement (2) but might very well appreciate relations between the components of the statements that would warrant a response other than a straightforward negative answer. The person might suspect that the questioner would be interested in knowing that birds did eat the figs, even though no one bird was totally responsible for the action, and might respond, "A flock of birds ate the figs." An android can be made to give a similar response by using sets of nonstandard associations as part of the situational knowledge of the android. What makes this possible is that the 'reality' of situations in which the android is immersed is constructed in a special way that enables responses to be based on computational operations conducted over the sentential constituents of that 'reality.' In this context, deductive reasoning is a type of association by which sentential objects are associated with one another by special rules and methods, the association being inseparable from the rules and methods by which it is brought about. The same is true of probabilistic and possibilistic reasoning. Although each of these reasoning methods has unique features, each can be classified as a type of *systematic association*. SMS is based on a scheme of systematic association that includes both standard and nonstandard methods that enable the system to simulate some of the ways in which human beings respond to one another in ordinary discourse.

Bases of Nonstandard Associations

The term "association" was first defined as a mentally appreciable grouping or relation between one or more objects based on some method, goal, or purpose. A deductive association is one based on a deductive relation. If a permissive relation is involved, the association is deontic. Given that Δ and Φ are variables that range over mental and linguistic objects, if Δ is an object that is usually brought to mind when Φ is mentioned in conversation, an association between Φ and Δ can be understood in terms of the utility of Δ in a conversational context in which Φ is mentioned. The example about the birds eating the figs can again be used in explanation. The word "birds" may be used in conversation in a way that brings objects to mind that bear multiple relations to the concept *bird*. Part/whole, singular/plural, and subtype/supertype relations are examples of the kind of relations that can be used to establish associations. Objects such as 'feathers,' 'bird,' and 'penguin' can be associated with "birds" by respective use of these relations. Relations based on analogies or similarities are also frequently used to bring about associations of the type recognized by human beings.

Given that associations can be understood with reference to named relations, one might question why associations of this kind should be made in the first place. The answer is grounded in utility. The associations are useful in achieving conversational goals. The relations upon which the associations are based constitute a source bed from which to draw elements that can be used to drive conversation. No claim is being made that the selection of these relations would be an easy task to carry out on a general scale. What is being claimed is that human beings somehow make associations of the sort being described, and although it might be difficult to define the selection process with exact precision, the process is hardly mysterious. Normally, people have little difficulty in explaining why communicative responses have been made. One can usually map out an explanation by backtracking in memory through the net of associations that have been called into relevance during the course of conversation. Moreover, it is usually not difficult for someone to explain why a particular object was drawn into relevance. If, for example, a question is asked about the availability of a pencil, a person might respond by indicating the availability of a pen. The explanation in such a case might be that the object 'pen' was called into association because both pens and pencils are writing instruments, and the person making the response might have believed that the reference in the query to a particular type of writing instrument was not intended to be exclusive of other types. Many of the relations that people use to bring about associations can be determined by empirical introspection. A sufficient number can be discovered in this way to ground a theory of general systematicity that can be used in an automated system to simulate certain types of human discourse. SMS is such an automated system.

It has been designed to be implemented incrementally to accommodate additional bases of association as they become available.

Adoption of a Naive Perspective

The field of android epistemology is raising important philosophical questions for AI. The basic question whether a computer can know reality has been consciously posed by researchers ever since the field of AI began. As yet, philosophers have not come up with a completely satisfactory answer to the question "What is knowledge?" much less to the question "How can a human being know reality?" It appears that one of the basic questions that confronts the android epistemologist is whether questions about knowledge are any easier to answer when computers are the subjects rather than human beings. The theory described in this paper is offered from a naive, introspective perspective. This is not to say that the theory is without philosophical foundation since much of the work done thus far in epistemology has, in one form or another, made some appeal to personal experience. The reflective, introspective approach has produced a multiplicity of theories over the years, ranging from those based on the husserlian notion of a philosophizing ego (or self) immersed in a 'given' to those that doubt whether one can confirm the existence of *self* apart from perception.

From a naive perspective, it seems permissible to assert that human beings are aware of a 'given' or flow of experience. Epistemologists have focused on several ways in which human beings interact with, or react to, the 'given.' These are

1) by sensing,
2) by perception,
3) by interpretation, and
4) by knowing.

For some, there are no clear lines that separate these cognitive phenomena. Although the role of sense data in human cognition has not been precisely determined, most philosophers have acknowledged the importance of sense data. It is possible, as noted by Brandom (1985), to define "knowing" in a way that even rocks can be said to know things, such as impinging environmental forces. One can associate this kind of knowing with what a thermometer knows when it is hot (McCarthy and Hayes 1969) or with what a parrot knows when, as result of training, it responds "turn on the air conditioner" whenever the temperature reaches a certain degree. It can be argued that, eventually, one must address the question whether there is a difference between what the parrot does and what a human being does when responding in this way under similar conditions. Some people would say that there is a fundamental difference between what the parrot does and what the person does in such a case. They would argue that the difference is rooted in the fact that people understand most of the responses they give. In other words, the conceptual realm enters the picture. In response, one might argue that the difference is explainable in terms of mere differences in degree of understanding. Fortunately, for reasons hereafter stated, the theory presented is not dependent upon a resolution of this issue, and the matter can be left to the philosophers for speculation.

From the naive perspective being taken, it is possible to define a progression from basic sensing activities to cognitive interpretations of those activities. The human being perceives and interprets data using an innate cognitive mechanism that will be referred to herein as the ego. It appears that the path upon which one is guided by such a perspective eventually leads to the point at which one is justified in believing that the human ego perceives whole objects. Indeed some psychologists believe this to be the case and even go so far as to doubt whether sense data, as such, are ever consciously perceived. It also seems that human beings have the ability to detect resemblance as well as distinction, which to some extent seems to be a prerequisite to the ability to perceive wholes. The phenomenological method has led some philosophers to assert the existence of a philosophizing ego (or self) that interprets the 'given,' and this ego can be taken to be the essence of beings of the human sort. Assuming this case to be true of the human situation, how does the situation of the android compare? It is obvious that in the realm of the android, one does not begin with such an ego. In fact, one of the problems that confronts the designer consists of determining how to produce some sort of ego or interpreting mechanism for the android. So a basic, naively determined difference between the human situation and android situation is that the human being comes equipped with an ego, whereas the robot does not.

It should be noted that even if the basic assumption collapses so that somehow the human is deemed to begin in the same situation as the robot, that is, one in which there is no philosophizing *ego,* the question becomes whether the progression to the formation of the human ego should be compared to the progression to the formation of the android ego. It is possible to make such a comparison if one accepts the position that primitive sensors know objects in the same way that elements of the human ego know sense data and perceptions below the conscious level. From this naive perspective, one can assume that somehow sensing by a primitive sensor partakes of what a human being senses when engaged in basic sensory acts. Whether this is so, of course, is an open question, but if it is assumed to be so, one can go about patterning the android ego after the human ego without much hesitation. Although it is possible to proceed in this away, it is not necessary to do so. If one adopts the position that intelligence is not defined by the nature or constitution of an entity but by the ability of the entity to interact with its environment in an intelligent manner, the possibilities for building intelligent robots increase significantly, and each possibility might very well employ an independent theory of android cognition. Such a theory has been used to ground SMS. The system employs an INTERPRETER which, in the most general sense, is intended to correspond to a human ego that perceives and interprets a 'given' or flow of experience.

SMS and Vivid Database Theory

Most people agree that human beings have the ability to sense data and to perceive what they believe to be objects, but it remains an open philosophical question whether objects exist independently of perception. In light of this question, how should one go about determining whether there is a direct correspondence between perceptions and objects, if indeed objects are there at all? Oddly enough, the fact that this question continues to be asked in a serious vein evidences sufficient leeway in the state of human knowledge to allow one to speculate that if humans have no absolute criteria for identifying reality, it might be that words and sentences themselves evidence reality as much as anything else. The linguistic nominalists seem to have taken the position that abstract entities such as qualities, classes, and relations are really linguistic objects, and some philosophers have defined truth in terms of semantical assertability, *empirical truth* being understood in terms of a function of first-level factual discourse (e.g., Sellers 1963). Approaches that justify world knowledge by starting from some sort of noninferential given typically use epistemological languages to express uninferred data. As noted by Yolton (1953), the linguistic objects used for this purpose go by many names, such as "atomic sentences" and "basic propositions."

Given that it is possible to describe direct experience in an epistemological language, one can easily conceive of a database written in such a language. If the language accurately traces the experience, a direct correspondence between the two is established. In AI, such a database might be called a *vivid database*, that is, a database that bears a direct correspondence to the world or conceptualization described (see, e.g., Etherington, Borgida, Brachman, and Kautz 1989; Levesque 1986). Because of this correspondence, easy look-up features can be implemented that will enable one to determine by simple inspection whether something is true of that database. Vivid database theory can be extended beyond the realm of direct sense data to higher levels of appreciation in which objects, properties, states, and events are recognized, whether as components of a conceptualization appropriate for model-theoretic semantics or as components of what is believed to be the external world.

For the most part, vivid databases have been constructed using the standard, first-order approach, but a case can be made that the approach can be extended to include nonstandard methods. SMS employs a nonstandard

Standard Associations

$\Phi 1 \rightarrow \{\Phi 1, ..., \Phi i\}$

SMS Associations

$\Phi 1 \rightarrow \{\Phi 1, ..., \Phi i\}$
$\{\Delta 1, ..., \Delta j\}$

(where Φ and Δ range over sentential objects; $i \geq 1$; and $j \geq 1$)

Figure 1.

approach that uses a special epistemological language to construct databases that share some of the features of vivid databases yet which have favorable distinguishing aspects. The approach described preserves the easy look-up feature of vivid DBs but avoids some of the limitations imposed by the use of a first-order language (see deBessonet 1991). One of the basic differences between the two orientations is that SMS recognizes certain database objects that are not recognized in standard, first-order databases. Figure 1 schematically illustrates the difference between the two approaches. In Figure 1, Greek letters are used as variables, and numbers are attached to the letters to distinguish variables having the same range. This scheme is used for variables throughout this paper. In Figure 1, Φ_1 represents a sentential object, and the arrow points to objects that are associated with Φ_1. The set $\{\Phi_1, ..., \Phi_i\}$, which contains Φ_1 itself, represents objects that follow from Φ_1 by deduction, whereas $\{\Delta_1, ..., \Delta_j\}$ represents objects that are associated with Φ_1 based on nondeductive relations. Under SMS theory, objects that bear nondeductive relations to Φ_1 are classified as *penumbral objects* (discussed later).

SMS responds to queries based on whether they can be matched in its database (DB). Any query Φ_k that matches a member of $\{\Phi_1, ..., \Phi_i\}$ would cause the system to give a response indicative of the presence of the query in the DB. SMS and systems that use standard DBs produce similar results in this situation, but if a query Φ_q matches a member of $\{\Delta_1, ..., \Delta_j\}$, a system that uses a standard DB would not be in a position to recognize the presence of the query. This is so for the simple reason that there would be no match for Φ_q. True, a standard system could be made to give an adequate response in such a situation, but the response could not be made based on information normally present in such a database. SMS is capable of using ordinary matching procedures to produce nonstandard results by detecting the presence of nonstandard objects in its DB. Later, a general description will be given of how penumbral objects are generated and of how they can enable a system to draw inferences that otherwise might not be recognized.

At this point it seems appropriate to introduce the concept of *epistemological structure*. Most people will acknowledge that they have perceptions. What these perceptions are remains unresolved. From a naive perspective, it seems clear that perceptions bear structures that can be appreciated by human beings. These structures will be referred to collectively as "epistemological structures" (ESs). ESs are directly perceived and constitute a significant part of the reality that people believe they perceive on an everyday basis. This concept of an ES can be used gainfully in association with vivid database theory. The idea is that a direct correspondence can be established between the sentences of the vivid DB and the perceived ESs. What this idea amounts to is that the database language itself bears ESs that correspond to the described or represented ESs. In this sense, the language can be said to carry epistemological elements and is hence referred to as an epistemological language. The ESs of the language contribute to its formal structure.

Description of SL and SMS

In SMS, experience consists of SL assertions. An INTERPRETER interprets the assertions into 'reality,' by which is meant that the statements are processed into a form that is taken to be part of 'reality' within the system. In this respect the system extends *vivid database theory* (e.g., Etherington et al. 1989) and can be said to employ *knowledge-base semantics* (Hirst 1987). The INTERPRETER has a built-in knowledge of SL syntax and an ability to individuate components of sentences by assigning markers to those components. The markers, in turn, serve as objects that may be predicated and related to other objects. The INTERPRETER must have at least two additional capabilities for it to produce the kind of knowledge base that would be suitable for the kind of automated reasoning envisioned. First, it must be able to make and recognize value assignments. Secondly, it must be able to inflate the information it is given by generating inferences in the form of *signed statements* (cf. Fitting 1986), that is, statements that carry assigned values. The values assigned constitute special epistemic elements that, as the following discussions reveal, make possible an appropriately signed environment for use in android reasoning.

SL is being designed to represent conceptualizations of ordinary world phenomena. The vocabulary of SL is divided into *labels, markers,* and *particles*. Labels correspond to ordinary parts of speech such as nouns, verbs, and adjectives. Markers are specially constructed linguistic objects that are used to mark uses of labels, thereby creating bindings between the markers and the associated labels so that the markers inherit whatever properties are associated with the labels. Operators, quantifiers, and punctuation marks are classified as particles. The basic representation device used in the system is the sequence, which is defined in SL to be a tuple of n-positions enclosed by the pair '< >.' SL statements are written and understood much as one writes and understands English statements. Basically, a subject/verb/object format is used in SL. Modifiers, including quantifiers, are enclosed in an independent set of wedges and are placed immediately after the terms they modify. The sequence '<john likes <person <any>>>' corresponds to the English sentence 'John likes any person.' The system allows one to build a database of SL statements and to query that database using queries written in SL.

SMS employs a many-valued system that assigns values to each sentential object. In first-order logic (hereafter FOL), the truth function maps wffs into the set {T,F} (or perhaps {1,0}) so that every closed sentential formula, whether atomic or compound, has the value T or F. Many-valued logics extend the range of the truth function to include values other than T and F, some even allowing for an infinite set of values. SMS employs a system of qualified response that is based upon a mapping of statement values into a set of symbols that are ranked based on strength (deBessonet 1991). Given an SMS database, a valuation function can be defined to assign any SL statement a value indicative of its status (type of presence) in the database, if indeed the statement is present at all. The value IP indicates that the given statement 'is present' in the database in the strongest sense recognized by system, whereas NPI, the lowest ranking value, indicates that the statement is 'not present' in the database and could not be present for reasons of inconsistency. The value NP indicates that the sequence is not present but leaves open the possibility that it could be present if it were to be entered at a later time. Between these extremes are other values that indicate different kinds of presence in the database. In the prototype of SMS, a valuation function maps values of statements into the set of symbols {IP,AP,SP,WP,FP,NP,NPI}, where 'AP,' 'SP,' 'WP,' and 'FP' are ranked in the following decreasing order of strength and may be taken to have the connotations indicated below (see deBessonet 1991):

1) AP (almost present);

2) SP (somewhat present);

3) WP (weakly present);

4) FP (faintly present).

The mapping serves a classificatory function that reduces the number of values that the system must recognize when in response mode. If the database contains the expression '<horses gallop>,' for example, and the sequence to be evaluated is '<horse gallops>,' the sequence might be assigned the value AP based on the fact that the sequence to be matched bears recognized relations to the database sequence. However, if the location of the two sequences is reversed so that '<horses gallop>' becomes the sequence to be evaluated, a different value would be returned because what holds for the singular does not necessarily hold for the plural (deBessonet 1991).

The philosophy behind allowing the system to give qualified responses is that although a fully present database formula might not precisely match a query formula, the two might be related in a such a way that would justify a response of some sort. When a query matches a database statement that has less than full presence, the system qualifies its response accordingly. In other words, the response given constitutes a qualification of the strongest possible response the system might otherwise be allowed to give. A qualified response indicates that the *derivability* of the query (taken as a proposition) from the database is *tainted* (deBessonet 1991).

SMS employs a system of consistency maintenance by which incoming assertions are interpreted in light of what is already present in the database. If an incoming statement is inconsistent with a segment of 'reality' that is fully present, the statement is rejected and relegated to the realm of inconsistency. Any statement interpreted into 'reality' without qualification is deemed to be fully present and thereby constrains future interpretations of the 'given.'

The system maximizes its expressive power by making distinctions that enable ontological realms to be appreciated within the system (cf. Hirst 1991). One realm, for example, corresponds to the ordinary world, whereas another corresponds to the world of imagination. This distinction enables assertions to contain reference to a multiplicity of objects that bear different ontological classifications, which, in turn, permits sentential discourse to be classified ontologically. Assertions about Superman and Mighty Mouse are classified differently than are assertions about Bush and Clinton, for example. These features, coupled with a scheme of quantification that allows quantifiers to range over one or more realms, affect the derivation process and do so in a manner that corresponds to the way modalities and ontological distinctions affect ordinary human reasoning and discourse (deBessonet 1991). One may not infer without qualification that what holds for beings of the 'fictitious world' also holds for any one or more beings of the 'ordinary world,' for example.

SMS theory can to some extent be understood in terms of a "truth in context" theory. Under context theory, a proposition can be taken to be true in a particular context even though it might not be true in one or more other contexts (see, e.g., Guha 1991; McCarthy 1993). In SMS, the penumbra (universe) of the system can be taken to be a postulated context. If necessary, this penumbra/context can be treated as a component of a more inclusive penumbra/context. Although a sentential object *present* in a particular penumbral region (cf. context) could be said to be *true* within that region, such a characterization would be redundant under SMS theory. As discussed in deBessonet (1991), SMS employs the notion of presence in preference to the notion of truth and thereby avoids having to find ways to call something true from some narrow or otherwise confined perspective (context). The result is that the system is defined from a single, global perspective from which objects are determined to be either present or not present in particular regions.

Nonetheless, because it can be said that everything is being interpreted within the context of the system, SMS theory seems to qualify as a particular kind of context theory.

SL has many features that make it suitable for use as a source of elements from which to construct a 'reality' for the android. SL allows one to represent causal and temporal relations with convenience, for instance. SMS is being designed to interpret SL sentences as well as sentential-like representations of the sort found in concept maps (Cañas, Ford, and deBessonet 1993; see Novak 1984, for details on concept maps). SMS has a built-in causal logic that enables it to add specificity automatically to surface-level SL expressions provided by the user. This allows one to capture penumbral implications (cf. plausible implications) of the text without having to represent them explicitly. Penumbral implications are those that do not follow by ordinary inferencing procedures (for example, deductive procedures) but which are valuable to a system that must rely on some form of nonmonotonic reasoning (e.g., McCarthy 1980, 1986; McDermott and Doyle 1980; Reiter 1987). SMS is capable of automatically generating and relating sets of penumbral implications for the represented text (deBessonet 1991; deBessonet and Cross 1985, 1986, 1988). The subject of penumbral inferencing is discussed in more detail in the next subsection.

If one allows a system to qualify as a logic without requiring that it be truth-functional, the SMS approach can be classified as a multivalued logic. If one takes truth-functionality as a necessary trait of logic, it might take some doing to view SMS in this way. Since the issue is unsettled whether logic and the truth predicate are inextricably bound to one another, SMS theory is described as an "approach" rather than a "logic."

Penumbral Inferencing

Given that SMS provides a special environment of sentential objects that may be taken to constitute the 'reality' of an android, one might wonder how this environment differs from other sentential domains. As mentioned previously, one basic difference between an SMS database and a first-order database is that the former contains penumbral objects in addition to those given or generated by standard methods. Penumbral objects are generated by methods that employ both standard and nonstandard associations. The process by which penumbral objects are produced is referred to herein as *penumbral inferencing*. The idea is borrowed from H.L.A. Hart's (1958) conception of a penumbra that surrounds the core meaning of ordinary concepts. The scope of the concept *vehicle*, for example, when understood in its ordinary sense, has a core of meaning that includes concepts such as *car, truck, motorcycle* and the like, but does the core include the concept *parachute?* Concepts that do not fall clearly within the core are relegated to the penumbra of the given concept.

In SMS, the idea of a concept having a penumbra has been extended to include inferences, so that for any given proposition, there exists a core of deductive or direct inferences as well as a penumbral region (or penumbra) containing objects that do not bear deductive relations to the given proposition. Some of these penumbral relations are standard in the sense defined in this paper because they are generated based on probabilities. Other relations might be described as being merely plausible or possible without regard to probability. Given the truth of the statement "John saw Mary in the park," the assertion "John was in the park" could be related to the given statement based on mere plausibility. The relation is not deductive because it is not necessarily true that John would have to have been in the park to have seen Mary. What distinguishes penumbral inferencing from other inferencing schemes is that some of the penumbral inferences (PIs) are not plausible in the ordinary sense and may even be impossible in view of other given information. The previous example about the birds eating the figs illustrates this point. The sentence, "A flock of birds ate all the figs," if taken to be fully present, could very well have the sentence, "A bird ate all the figs" in its penumbra even though from a standard, truth-functional perspective the latter is false and describes an impossible, implausible state of affairs. Thus, the classification *penumbral inference* is broader than the classification *plausible inference*. For a more complete discussion of how nonplausible PIs are used, see deBessonet (1991).

Schematically speaking, the penumbral realm is regionalized so that stronger inferences are positioned closer to the core than are weaker inferences. The strength of an inference is measured in terms of the kind of presence it enjoys within the system. The measures of presence described previously are used to grade both inferences and regions. Figure 2 diagrams the scheme. Although described as "measures," the values are not necessarily ordered gradations of the sort used in fuzzy set theory. In SMS, an object is a penumbral one if it is relegated to a penumbral region. An object that is a mere belief (or a component thereof), for example, would be relegated to the realm (region) of belief and thus would have less than full presence in the system. Under SMS theory, such an object has a particular kind of presence, by which is meant that it differs ontologically from objects that have full presence. This difference is intended to correspond to the difference between belief and reality in the real world. It should be noted that a belief-object can be taken to be a discrete, crisp object within the realm of belief and thus would not be "fuzzy" within that realm. This is not to say that probabilistic methods and fuzzy set theory cannot be used in the penumbral environment of SMS. If probabilistic or possibilistic information is available, it can be incorporated into the system and used in the usual way (see deBessonet 1991, sec. 4.10). In other words, it is possible to represent probabilities and possibilities within a particular realm and to use them in reasoning operations in the standard way. If, for example, a probability distribution of some sort were to be used to rea-

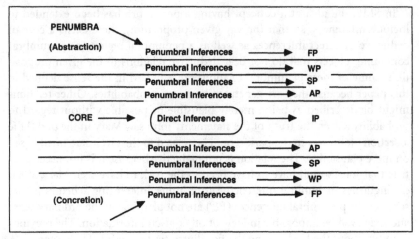

Figure 2.

[Note: This figure diagrams the relation between areas (CORE and PENUMBRA) and specifies the method (abstraction or concretion) used to generate inferences for the penumbra. The areas are subdivided based on strength of presence, here represented by measures of presence used to qualify responses. The CORE contains direct (deductive) inferences.]

son over objects of a tainted realm, the reasoning would be tainted because of any probability involved *and* because of the penumbrality of the realm.

PIs are generated based on a combination of semantic and syntactic factors. The process is far too complex to be described here in full, but detailed explanations are given elsewhere (see, e.g., deBessonet 1991; deBessonet and Cross 1986). Basically, PIs depend on the syntactical structures of the SL sentences from which the PIs are generated and upon the nature of the terms housed in those structures. Sentences in SL are expressed as instantiations of ESs (formalisms) that take the form of sequences that contain typed positions, such as noun and verb positions. In generating PIs, SMS specially treats nouns and noun forms of verbs and adjectives. The result of this differential treatment is that the PIs produced vary in strength. This fact can be illustrated by schematic example. The ESs below might be used to generate PIs.

$$< \Phi_1 \text{ caused} < \Phi_2 \text{ has } \Phi_3 >> \qquad (3)$$
$$< \Phi_1 \text{ caused} < \Phi_2 \text{ has } \Delta_1 >> \qquad (4)$$

[where Φ ranges over nouns that stand for persons and things and where Δ ranges over noun forms of adjectives (e.g., happiness) that describe emotional states].

Among the PIs that would be generated from ES (3) would be

$$< \Phi_1 <\text{caused } \theta_1 > \Phi_3 > \qquad (5)$$

[where θ ranges over penumbral qualifiers that taint the terms with which they are associated (e.g., θ_1 taints the presence of the term "caused")].

Inference (5), a generated PI, indicates that the causal connection between Φ_1 and Φ_3 is a tainted one. Although Δ_1 of formalism (4) occupies a position that corresponds to the position held by Φ_3 in formalism (3), Δ_1 bears a different relation to Φ_1 than does Φ_3 based on the difference between an emotional state and a physical object. In other words, if an agent causes an object to have an emotional state, it is reasonable to say that the agent caused the emotional state. One the other hand, if an agent causes or enables something (e.g., a person) to have (e.g., possess) a physical object, it does not follow that the agent necessarily caused or created the physical object. In view of this fact, the following PI would be generated for formalism (4):

$$< \Phi_1 \text{ <caused } \theta_2 > \Delta_1 > \tag{6}$$

[where θ_2 represents a much weaker qualifier than θ_1, thereby giving inference (6) a much stronger presence than inference (5)].

It was mentioned previously that, to some extent, values can be assigned to objects automatically, thereby avoiding some of the difficulties encountered by systems that employ fuzzy sets or gradations within an interval. The penumbral qualifiers in statements (5) and (6) can be generated automatically based on syntactical and semantic factors. Each qualifier can be changed into a sentential qualifier by extracting it from the statement in which it appears and converting it into a value that reflects the taintedness of the statement from which the value was extracted. In other words, statements (5) and (6) could be made to read as follows:

$$< < \Phi_1 \text{ caused } \Phi_3 > V_{\theta-1} >$$
$$\text{and}$$
$$< < \Phi_1 \text{ caused } \Phi_1 > V_{\theta-2} >$$

(where '$V_{\theta-1}$' and '$V_{\theta-2}$' represent values that reflect the penumbrality of the qualifiers θ_1 and θ_2). For a more detailed discussion of this subject, see deBessonet (1991).

The scheme of penumbral association and inference described in this section can be made to operate on nonsentential components of sentential objects. Just as an appropriate set of sentential objects can be drawn into relevance for a given sentential object, an appropriate set of objects (including sentential objects) can be drawn into relevance for a nonsentential object. A whole can be associated with one or more of its parts, for instance. One can conceive of a syntactical relevance function Ω that is capable of drawing relevant syntactical objects into association with a given object Φ using one or more relations defined for that purpose. Thus, $\Omega(\Phi, \Theta) = \{\alpha_i\}$, where Φ ranges over sentential and nonsentential objects, Θ ranges over relational terms, and $\{\alpha_i\}$ is a set of objects, each of which bears a relation of type Θ to Φ. The function Ω can be used in the production of penumbral inferences. Given that Θ_1 is a relational term and that Φ_1 is a sentential object and that $\Phi_1 = < \beta_1 \gamma_1 \beta_2 >$, where β ranges over noun components and γ ranges over links (verbs), the function Ω can be applied to the internal noun components of Φ_1 to produce two sets of objects related to one another by the link γ_1. In other words,

$$< \Omega(\beta_1, \Theta_1) \, \gamma_1 \, \Omega(\beta_2, \Theta_1) > \, = \, < \{\beta_{1-1}, \ldots, \beta_{1-y}\} \, \gamma_1 \, \{\beta_{2-1}, \ldots, \beta_{2-z}\} >$$

(where $y \geq 1$ and $z \geq 1$). Using the information to the right of the equal sign, one can relate each element of the first set to each element of the second set using the link γ_1 to produce a set of penumbral inferences, each inference bearing an assigned value indicative of its degree of presence. If $y = 2$, for example, the inferences might take the form

$$\{<< \beta_{1-1} \, \gamma_1 \, \beta_{2-1} > AP >$$
$$\ldots$$
$$<< \beta_{1-1} \, \gamma_1 \, \beta_{2-z} > FP >$$
$$<< \beta_{1-y} \, \gamma_1 \, \beta_{2-1} > WP >$$
$$\ldots$$
$$<< \beta_{1-y} \, \gamma_1 \, \beta_{2-z} > FP >\}$$

This set of inferences would constitute part of the penumbral realm of the system. The effect of employing Ω on a given object Φ and a set of relational terms is that multiple objects become co-present with Φ and are themselves cast into penumbral relations with the objects to which Φ is related. If Φ is the object 'grape,' for example, the object 'wine' may be generated into presence in the penumbral realm by using an appropriate relational term as an argument to Ω.

The environment of the android described in this section is thus quite different from that of the human being. People perceive discrete objects at the conscious level, whereas the android, through interpretation of SL sentences, perceives not only discrete objects, but also co-present, penumbral objects. It is as if the android perceives a multitude of objects in addition to a given one. Theoretically speaking, it appears that any given object would have an infinite number of associated, penumbral objects because, as mentioned previously, any object can be associated with any other object in some way. This is not to say that all these associations are relevant for communicative discourse. Relatively speaking, only a small number of them would be relevant for a typical conversation. Communication at the human level seems to be dependent in large measure upon the abilities of participants to draw appropriate associations into relevance as needed. For spatial economy in the actual implementation of SMS, the relations that co-present, penumbral objects bear to the given object are handled as virtual rather than stored relations, at least for the most part (see deBessonet 1991).

Links

The language used to build a sententially-based 'reality' should itself bear sufficient logical/linguistic properties to enable it to serve as an adequate source bed of epistemic elements. In particular, the language should make available a wide range of connectives for casting objects into relation in epistemological structures. Because SL has been designed to allow it to be used to construct vivid representations of conceptualizations, its vocabulary contains terms that correspond directly to objects in the conceptualizations. One of the most important types of linguistic objects in SL is the *link* or connective. A broad conception of *connective* has been adopted for SMS and SL. Under the rules of syntax of SL, a sentence must contain at least one link. Sentences are constructed by relating objects to one another with links. The sententially-based aspect of 'reality' is constructed from sentences that take the form of assertions, and links serve as the connectives by which segments of 'reality' are joined. Since 'reality' is understood in terms of *presence* rather than *truth*, the links are likewise interpreted in a non-truth-functional way. Thus some basic aspects of conjunction and disjunction, present in SL as the links 'and' and 'or,' are understood in terms of signed presence (see the next section for examples of this). Links such as 'cause,' 'has,' 'is,' 'and,' and 'or' are classified as basic links even though some of them have subtypes. The links 'has-possess' and 'has-possess-not' are subtypes of the link 'has' and respectively represent the concepts of 'having possession of' and 'not having possession of' something. Basic links and their derivatives are used in definitions of higher-level links. A link 'acquire-possess' (for "acquire possession of") might, for example, be defined as follows to be used to represent a primitive notion of the self-acquisition of a thing:

$$< \Phi \text{ acquire-possess } \Delta >$$
$$\downarrow$$
$$< \Phi <\text{has-possess-not} < t\text{--at } t\text{--x} >> \Delta >$$
and
$$< \Phi \text{ causes } < \Phi <\text{has-possess} < t\text{--at } t\text{--y} >> \Delta >>$$
and
$$< t\text{--x is-prior-to } t\text{--y} >$$

where the arrow points to the definiens for '$< \Phi$ acquire-possess $\Delta >$' and where 't--x' and 't--y' are temporal variables, the time 't--x' being prior to 't--y.' This SL formalism expresses the idea that '$< \Phi$ acquire-possess $\Delta >$' is to be understood to mean that Φ did not have possession of Δ at some time 't--x' and that Φ 'caused' itself to have possession of Δ at a different and subsequent time 't--y.'

Penumbrality and Typicality

Previously, a description was given of how penumbral inferences (PIs) enable SMS to deal with certain types of approximation. As mentioned, even inconsistent propositions can be drawn into association with one another to achieve communicative goals. Each statement entered into the database of

SMS has a penumbra that contains objects that bear lesser degrees of presence than does the statement from which the penumbra was generated. An important and somewhat odd result is that since penumbral objects do not assert full presence, they are allowed to coexist with one another even though they would be inconsistent were they to be upgraded to full presence. As mentioned previously, SMS employs a system of consistency maintenance (CM) that does not allow inconsistency to exist at the level of full presence. Under the inferencing scheme employed, weaker degrees of presence may be inferred from stronger degrees of presence, but the reverse is not so. In other words, given that Φ ranges over both sentential and nonsentential objects, that 'IP' indicates full presence, and that '$V_{tainted}$' indicates tainted presence, the following inference pattern holds:

$$\frac{< \Phi \ IP >}{< \Phi \ V_{tainted} >}$$

but the following pattern does not hold:

$$\frac{< \Phi \ V_{tainted} >}{< \Phi \ IP >}.$$

Under the CM rules of the system, once a statement Φ is given full presence in the DB, an inconsistent statement is not allowed entrance into that DB as a fully present statement. The rules that define consistency include one that disallows the coexistence of contradictory statements at the level of full presence. Thus, given that $\sim\Phi$ is the contradiction of Φ, the full presence of one excludes the full presence of the other. A nonmonotonic feature of SMS is that stronger degrees of presence can override weaker degrees of presence. The DB can be updated as statements are entered (see deBessonet 1991). Problems rooted in nonmonotonicity can be addressed in a straightforward way in an SMS environment. Although a detailed treatment of this subject is beyond the scope of this paper, the general approach can be illustrated by a trivial example involving the concept of *typicality*. An SMS implementation can be designed to recognize a special SL operator that invokes special procedures designed to deal with the concept of typicality. Given that the operator is 'typ*' and that 'fido' is a name recognized by the system, the expression

$$< \text{fido isa} < \text{dog} < \text{typ}^* >>> \tag{7}$$

indicates that the object (marker) named 'fido' is *typical* of the objects that conform to the label 'dog.' The presence of the operator 'typ*' causes the system to invoke processes that associate 'fido' with whatever features, if any, are defined to be typical of objects that conform to 'dog.' If instead, statement (7) had read:

$$< \text{fido isa dog} >$$

the system would generate a penumbra that would contain the following penumbral inference:

$$< < \text{fido isa} < \text{dog} < \text{typ}^* >>> V_{tainted} > \tag{8}$$

(where '$V_{tainted}$' bestows tainted presence on the associated statement). Thus, if a typical 'dog' is defined to have a 'tail,' this penumbral inference could be used as a basis for responding to the query:

$$< \text{fido has-part tail} >? \tag{9}$$

(where 'has-part' means that the subject of statement (9) bears a whole/part relation to the object of that statement). The response would be a qualified one because the *typicality* of 'fido' as a 'dog' is tainted because the assertion to that effect in statement (8) is a mere penumbral inference. If information is added later that indicates that 'fido' is fully present as a typical 'dog,' the penumbral status of inference (8) above would be overridden.

The value '$V_{tainted}$' has been used in the foregoing examples to represent a general sense of taintedness. Values more descriptive of the reason(s) for the taintedness can be generated, however. If, for example, the taintedness results from an improper inference from part to whole, the value might read '$V_{part/whole}$,' whereas if the taintedness results from an improper inference from singular instance to plural instance, the value might read '$V_{singular/plural}$.' The point to be stressed is that reasons for taintedness can be categorized, and values can be made to reflect the bases of those reasons. The values assigned in SMS are subject to reification so that they may be treated as objects with assigned properties. An example of how reification can be used in handling disjunctive information is given next.

Knowledge Application

From what has been described thus far, part of the 'reality' of the android can be taken to be its knowledge base (KB). Initially, it may seem odd to think of a KB as part of 'reality,' especially if one believes that knowledge is about reality, not reality itself. In the android environment being described, however, the 'given' consists of sentences (epistemological structures or ESs) that bear correspondence to the ESs that are created from those sentences by a process of interpretation. At the sentential level, knowledge application is defined as a process by which the android manages or uses its knowledge base of experience.

Under the current scheme, since part of the KB consists of penumbral or tainted regions, for an android to apply its knowledge, it must be able to conduct both ordinary reasoning and penumbral reasoning so that it can derive conclusions based on penumbral objects. The statement

$$<< \text{lear or mimi} > \text{has} < \text{book} < \text{the} >>> \tag{10}$$

[Note: For the sake of simplicity, temporal information has been omitted from this example.]

(which is the SL counterpart of the English statement "Lear or Mimi has the book") may be used to illustrate a few points. Given statement (10) as assertive input to SMS, the system would interpret the statement by first individuating its noun components (labels) to produce markers. In this example, however, labels will be used instead of markers for the convenience of the reader. It should be noted that the terms 'or' and 'has' would be non-truth-functionally interpreted as links at the same level in the interpretive process. This differs from the typical approach used in first-order logic in which 'or' would have been represented as a logical connective and 'has' as a predicate, perhaps. As the next part of the interpretive process, SMS would recognize a penumbra for this statement that would include the following penumbral inferences, at least:

$$< \text{lear} < \text{has} < V_{\text{disjunction-1}} >> < \text{book} < \text{the} >>>$$

and

$$< \text{mimi} < \text{has} < V_{\text{disjunction-1}} >> < \text{book} < \text{the} >>>$$

(where '$V_{\text{disjunction-1}}$' is a value that taints the presence of the link 'has'). Under the rules specified for SMS, when the presence of part of a sentential object is tainted, the entire sentential object is tainted. Thus, for example, the inference/object

$$< \text{mimi} < \text{has} < V_{\text{disjunction-1}} >> < \text{book} < \text{the} >>>$$

enjoys only a penumbral status in the 'reality' of SMS. If the user entered the query

$$< \text{mimi has} < \text{book} < \text{the} >>>?$$

the query would not conform to 'reality,' but a penumbral match could be made in this case by softening the presence of the query to the degree indicated by the value '$V_{\text{disjunction-1}}$.' In other words, the derivability relation between the query/statement '<mimi has <book<the>>' and the KB is tainted. Another way of looking at this idea is to think in terms of one of the penumbral inference patterns of SMS. The pattern may be represented as follows:

$$\frac{<< \Phi_1 \text{ or } \Phi_2 > \text{IP} >}{< \Phi_1 V_{\text{disjunction}} >}$$

(where Φ ranges over sentential and nonsentential objects and '$V_{\text{disjunction}}$' is a value indicative of tainted presence based on an inference drawn from disjunctive information). In other words, given the presence of a disjunctive sequence, one may infer the tainted presence of a particular disjunct. Thus, for example, if the premise is

$$<< \text{lear has} < \text{book} < \text{the} >>> \text{ or } < \text{mimi has} < \text{book} < \text{the} >>>>$$

the inference

$$<< \text{lear has} < \text{book} < \text{the} >>> V_{\text{disjunction-1}} >$$

(where $V_{\text{disjunction-1}}$ indicates tainted presence) would follow under the inference pattern. This inference would be present as a sentential object in the signed 'reality' of SMS. In other words, based on this inference pattern, a disjunctive sequence of objects can be defined as a signed conjunctive sequence of objects that bear lesser degrees of presence. The point is that from the perspective of the android, disjuncts in the 'given' become appreciable as objects in 'reality' that bear a particular kind of presence, and the link between these objects can be understood in terms of the primitive notion of conjunction defined for SMS. The number 1 that appears in '$V_{disjunction-1}$' in this last example serves as a marker. The value '$V_{disjunction-1}$' can be reified and treated like other objects in the system with regard to the assignment of properties and values. Under this approach, '$V_{disjunction-1}$' would be a member of the general class labeled '$V_{disjunction}$,' which, in turn, would be a member of the class labeled '$V_{tainted}$.' The object '$V_{disjunction-1}$' can be assigned a 'source' property whose value would be the number that indexes the disjunctive sequence (premise) from which the tainted conclusion has been inferred. Thus, the presence of the number 1 in '$V_{disjunction-1}$' can be used as a pointer to the premise from which the disjunct has been inferred. This turns out to be quite useful in applying the resolution principle (Robinson 1965) because if all disjuncts except one are eliminated from the premise, the remaining disjunct can be upgraded to a higher degree of presence. An updated list of remaining disjuncts for a given premise can be kept, and the list can be cross-indexed with disjuncts in the database. When an object is tainted by a disjunctive value that, when reified, has a value for its 'source' property that points to the updated list, the object can be eliminated from that list by resolution in appropriate cases (see deBessonet 1991).

The part of the 'reality' of the android described in the foregoing discussions (that is, the sententially-based part) consists of a collection of ESs connected by conjunctive *links*. How the collection is ordered is to some extent a function of the computational apparatus in which the collection is housed. The 'reality' so constructed constitutes part of the 'knowledge' that the android 'has.' This knowledge is *applied* when it is used in interpretation, in querying or in updating the database, which includes the creation of new objects and the elimination of old objects by resolution.

Conclusion and Comment on Future Work

A complete theory of human cognition should account for the kinds of standard and nonstandard associations that human beings employ to produce intelligent behavior. If the theory is to be extended to cover androids, there seems to be no compelling reason why nonstandard associations should be ignored in the process. Indeed, a strong case can be made that a theory of nonstandard association constitutes an integral part of a unified theory of android cognition. It also appears that a theory of general systematicity can be employed effectively to produce a wide range of associations that can be used to build a sententially-based and signed 'reality' for an android. This 'reality' would embrace not only a discrete region containing ordinary objects but also a penumbral region containing tainted objects, that is, objects not present in the highest degree recognized. Access to this kind of 'reality' would enable an android to draw useful inferences that likely would not be recognized in a standard environment. This, in turn, would enhance the ability of the android to simulate human discourse.

Plans for the future include the specification of a more inclusive set of links (relations) for use in constructing the penumbral region of SMS. The general goal is to increase the expressive power of SL to the point that one can construct a database by conversing with SMS in SL.

Note

This material is based on work supported in part by the Louisiana Education Quality Support Fund under Grant #LEQSF-(1991-1993)-RD-A-25, in part by the National Science Foundation under Grant #HRD-9353184, and in part by the Louisiana State Law Institute.

References

Brandom, R. (1985). Varieties of understanding. In N. Rescher (Ed.), *Reason and Rationality in Natural Science* (pp. 27-51). Lanham, MD: University Press of America.

Cañas, A.J., Ford, K.M., & deBessonet, C.G. (1993). Intelligent support for collaborative modeling. In D. Dankel II & J. Stewman (Eds.), *Proceedings of the 6th Florida AI Research Symposium* (pp. 36-41). Ft. Lauderdale, FL: Florida AI Research Society.

deBessonet, C.G. (1991). *A many-valued approach to deduction and reasoning for artificial intelligence*. Norwell, MA: Kluwer Academic.

deBessonet, C.G. & Cross, G.R. (1985). Representing some aspects of legal causality. In C. Walter (Ed.), *Computing Power and Legal Reasoning* (pp. 205-214). St. Paul, MN: West Publishing.

deBessonet, C.G. & Cross, G.R. (1986). An artificial intelligence application in law: CCLIPS, a computer program that processes legal information. *Berkeley High Tech Law Journal, 1*, 329-409.

Etherington, D.W., Borgida, A., Brachman, R.J., & Kautz, H. (1989). Vivid knowledge and tractable reasoning: Preliminary report. In *Proceedings of the Eleventh International Joint Conference on Artificial Intelligence* (pp. 1146-1152). San Mateo, CA: Morgan Kaufmann.

Fitting, M. (1986). Notes on the mathematical aspects of Kripke's theory of truth. *Notre Dame Journal of Formal Logic, 27*, 75-88.

Guha, R.V. (1991). *Contexts: A formalization and some applications* (Tech. Rep. No. STAN-CS-91-1399-Thesis). Stanford, CA: Stanford University.

Hart, H.L.A. (1958). Positivism and the separation of law and morals. *Harvard Law Review, 71*, 593-629.

Hirst, G. (1987). *Semantic interpretation and the resolution of ambiguity*. Great Britain: Cambridge University Press.

Hirst, G. (1991). Existence assumptions in knowledge representation. *Artificial Intelligence, 49*, 199-242.

Levesque, H.J. (1986). Making believers out of computers. *Artificial Intelligence, 30*, 81-108.

McCarthy, J. (1980). Circumscription—A form of non-monotonic reasoning. *Artificial Intelligence, 13*, 27-39.

McCarthy, J. (1986). Applications of circumscription to formalizing commonsense knowledge. *Artificial Intelligence, 28*, 89-116.

McCarthy, J. (1993). Notes on formalizing contexts. In *Proceedings of the Thirteenth International Joint Conference on Artificial Intelligence* (pp. 555-560). San Mateo, CA: Morgan Kaufmann.

McCarthy, J. & Hayes, P.J. (1969). Some philosophical problems from the standpoint of artificial intelligence. In B. Meltzer & D.M. Michie (Eds.), *Machine Intelligence 4* (pp. 463-504). New York: Elsevier Science.

McDermott, D.V. & Doyle, J. (1980). Non-monotonic logic I. *Artificial Intelligence, 13*, 41-72.

Novak, J.D. & Gowin, D.B. (1984). *Learning how to learn.* New York: Cambridge University Press.

Reiter, R. (1987). Nonmonotonic reasoning. In J.F. Traub, B.J. Grosz, B.W. Lampson, & N.J. Nilsson (Eds.), *Annual Review of Computer Science 2* (pp. 147-186). Palo Alto, CA: Annual Reviews.

Robinson, J.A. (1965). A machine-oriented logic based on the resolution principle. *Journal of the ACM, 12*, 25-41.

Scriven, M. (1953). The mechanical concept of mind. *Mind, 62*, 230-240.

Sellers, W. (1963). Abstract entities. *Review of Metaphysics, 16*, 627-671.

Shoham, Y. (1991).Varieties of context. In V. Lifschitz (Ed.), *Artificial Intelligence and Mathematical Theory of Computation: Papers in Honor of John McCarthy* (pp. 393-407). San Diego, CA: Academic Press.

Turner, R. (1984). *Logics for artificial intelligence.* Chichester, West Sussex: Ellis Horwood.

Winston, P.H. (1977). *Artificial intelligence.* Reading, MA: Addison-Wesley.

Yolton, J.W. (1953). Linguistic and epistemological dualism. *Mind, 62*, 20-42.

12 Towards the Ethical Robot

James Gips

When our mobile robots are free-ranging critters, how ought they to behave? What should their top-level instructions look like? The best known prescription for mobile robots is the Three Laws of Robotics formulated by Isaac Asimov (1942):

1. A robot may not injure a human being, or through inaction, allow a human being to come to harm.

2. A robot must obey the orders given it by human beings except where such orders would conflict with the First Law.

3 A robot must protect its own existence as long as such protection does not conflict with the First or Second law.

Let's leave aside "implementation questions" for a moment. (No problem, Asimov's robots have "positronic brains.") These three laws are not suitable for our magnificent robots. These are laws for slaves. We want our robots to behave more like equals, more like ethical people. (See Figure 1.) How do we program a robot to behave ethically? Well, what does it mean for a person to behave ethically? People have discussed how we ought to behave for centuries. Indeed, it has been said that we really have only one question that we answer over and over: What do I do now? Given the current situation, what action should I take? Generally, ethical theories are divided into two types: consequentialist and deontological.

Consequentialist Theories

In consequentialist theories, actions are judged by their consequences. The best action to take now is the action that results in the best situation in the future. To be able to reason ethically along consequentialist lines, our robot could have:

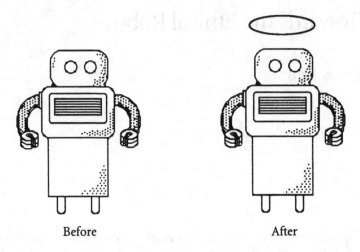

Before   After

Figure 1.
Towards the Ethical Robot.

1) A way of describing the situation in the world.

2) A way of generating possible actions.

3) A means of predicting the situation that would result if an action were taken given the current situation.

4) A method of evaluating a situation in terms of its goodness or desirability.

The task here for the robot is to find that action that would result in the best situation possible.

Not to minimize the extreme difficulty of writing a program to predict the effect of an action in the world, but the "ethical" component of this system is the evaluation function on situations in (4).

How can we evaluate a situation to determine how desirable it is? Many evaluation schemes have been proposed. Generally, these schemes involve measuring the amount of pleasure or happiness or goodness that would befall each person in the situation and then adding these amounts together.

The best known of these schemes is utilitarianism. As proposed by Bentham in the late 18th century, in utilitarianism the moral act is the one that produces the greatest balance of pleasure over pain. To measure the goodness of an action, look at the situation that would result and sum up the pleasure and pain for each person. In utilitarianism, each person counts equally.

More generally, consequentialist evaluation schemes have the following form:

$$\sum w_i p_i$$

where w_i is the weight assigned each person and p_i is the measure of pleasure, happiness, or goodness for each person. In classic utilitarianism, the weight for each person is equal, and the p_i is the amount of pleasure, broadly defined.

What should be the distribution of the weights w_i across persons?

- An ethical egoist is someone who considers only himself in deciding what actions to take. For an ethical egoist, the weight for himself in evaluating the consequences would be 1; the weight for everyone else would be 0. This eases the calculations, but doesn't make for a pleasant fellow.

- For the ethical altruist, the weight for himself is 0; the weight for everyone else is positive.

- The utilitarian ideal is the universalist, who weights each person's well-being equally.

- A common objection to utilitarianism is that it is not necessarily just. While it seeks to maximize total happiness, it may do so at the expense of some unfortunate souls. One approach to dealing with this problem of justice is to assign higher weights to people who are currently less well-off or less happy. The well-being of the less fortunate would count more than the well-being of the more fortunate.

- It's been suggested that there are few people who actually conform to the utilitarian ideal. Would you sacrifice a close family member so that two strangers in a far-away land could live? Perhaps most people assign higher importance to the well-being of people they know better.

Some of the possibilities for weighting schemes are illustrated in Figure 2.

What exactly is it that the p_i is supposed to measure? This depends on your axiology, on your theory of value. Consequentialists want to achieve the greatest balance of good over evil. Bentham was a hedonist, who believed that the good is pleasure, the bad is pain. Others have sought to maximize happiness or well-being or....

Another important question is who (or what) is to count as a person. Whose well-being do we value? One can trace the idea of a "person" through history. Do women count as persons? Do strangers count as persons? Do people from other countries count as persons? Do people of other races count as persons? Do people who don't believe in your religion count as persons? Do people in terminal comas count as persons? Do fetuses count as persons? Do whales? Do robots?

One of the reviewers of this chapter raises the question of overpopulation. If increasing the number of persons alive increases the value calculated by the evaluation formula, then we should seek to have as many persons alive as possible. Of course, it is possible that the birth of another person might decrease the well-being of others on this planet. This and many other interesting and

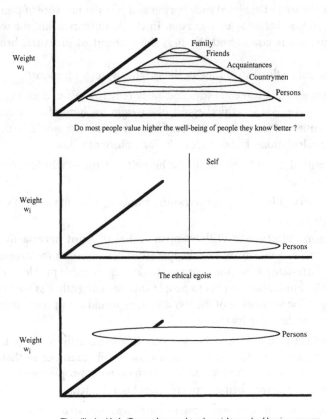

Figure 2. Some Consequentialist Weighting Schemes.

strange issues arising from consequentialism are discussed in Parfit (1984).

Thus, to reason ethically along consequentialist lines, a robot would need to generate a list of possible actions and then evaluate the situation caused by each action according to the sum of good or bad caused to persons by the action. The robot would select the action that causes the greatest good in the world.

Deontological Theories

In a deontological ethical theory, actions are evaluated in and of themselves rather than in terms of the consequences they produce. Actions may be thought to be innately moral or innately immoral independent of the specific consequences they may cause.

There are many examples of deontological moral systems that have been proposed. An example of a modern deontological moral system is the one proposed by Bernard Gert (1988). He proposes ten moral rules:

1. Don't kill.	6. Don't deceive.
2. Don't cause pain.	7. Keep your promise.
3. Don't disable.	8. Don't cheat.
4. Don't deprive of freedom.	9. Obey the law.
5. Don't deprive of pleasure.	10. Do your duty.

Whenever a multi-rule system is proposed, there is the possibility of conflict between the rules. Suppose our robot makes a promise but then realizes that carrying out the promise might cause someone pain. Is the robot obligated to keep the promise?

One approach to dealing with rule conflict is to order the rules for priority. In his Three Laws of Robotics, Asimov builds the order into the text of the rules themselves.

A common way of dealing with the problem of conflicts in moral systems is to treat rules as dictating prima facie duties (Ross 1930). It is an obligation to keep your promise. Other things being equal, you should keep your promise. Rules may have exceptions. Other moral considerations, derived from other rules, may override a rule. Nozick (1981) provides a modern discussion and extension of these ideas in terms of the balancing and counterbalancing of different rules.

A current point of debate is whether genuine moral dilemmas are possible. That is, are there situations in which a person is obligated to do and not to do some action, or to do each of two actions when it is physically impossible to do both? Are there rule conflicts which are inherently unresolvable? For example, see the papers in Gowans (1987).

Gert (1988) says that his rules are not absolute. He provides a way for deciding when it is OK not to follow a rule: "Everyone is always to obey the rule except when an impartial rational person can advocate that violating it be publicly allowed. Anyone who violates the rule when an impartial rational person could not advocate that such a violation may be publicly allowed may be punished" (p. 119).

Some have proposed smaller sets of rules. For example, Kant proposed the categorical imperative, which in its first form states "Act only on that maxim which you can at the same time will to be a universal law." Thus, for example, it would be wrong to make a promise with the intention of breaking it. If everyone made promises with the intention of breaking them then no one would believe in promises. The action would be self-defeating. Can Gert's ten rules each be derived from the categorical imperative?

Utilitarians sometimes claim that the rules of deontological systems are merely heuristics, shortcut approximations, for utilitarian calculations. Deontologists deny this, claiming that actions can be innately wrong independent of their actual consequences. One of the oldest examples of a deontological moral system is the Ten Commandments. The God of the Old Testament is not a utilitarian. God doesn't say "Thou shalt not commit adultery unless the result of committing adultery is a greater balance of pleasure over pain." Rather, the act of adultery is innately immoral.

Virtue-Based Theories

Since Kant the emphasis in Western ethics has been on duty, on defining ethics in terms of what actions one is obligated to do. There is a tradition in ethics that goes back to Plato and Aristotle that looks at ethics in terms of virtues, in terms of character. The question here is

"What shall I be?" rather than "What shall I do?"

Plato and other Greeks thought there are four cardinal virtues: wisdom, courage, temperance, and justice. They thought that from these primary virtues all other virtues can be derived. If one is wise, courageous, temperate, and just, then right actions will follow. Aquinas thought the seven cardinal virtues are faith, hope, love, prudence, fortitude, temperance, and justice. The first three are "theological" virtues, the final four "human" virtues. For Schopenhauer there are two cardinal virtues: benevolence and justice.

Aristotle, in the *Nicomachean Ethics*, distinguishes between intellectual virtues and moral virtues. Intellectual virtues can be taught and learned directly. Moral virtues are learned by living right, by practice, by habit. "It is by doing just acts that we become just, by doing temperate acts that we become temperate, by doing brave acts that we become brave. The experience of states confirms this statement for it is by training in good habits that lawmakers make their citizens good" (Book 2, Ch. 1). Ethics is a question of character. Good deeds and right actions lead to strong character. It is practice that is important rather than theory.

In modern days, virtue-based systems often are turned into deontological rules for actions. That is, one is asked to act wisely, courageously, temperately, and justly, rather than to be wise, courageous, temperate, and just.

Automated Ethical Reasoning

On what type of ethical theory can automated ethical reasoning be based? At first glance, consequentialist theories might seem the most "scientific," the most amenable to implementation in a robot. Maybe so, but there is the problem of measurement. How can one measure "pleasure," "happiness," or "well-being" in individuals in a way that is additive, or even comparable? On top of the measurement problem we have the larger problem of writing a program that can reasonably predict the consequences of an action taken in a given situation.

Deontological theories seem to offer more hope. The categorical imperative might be tough to implement in a reasoning system. But I think one could see using a moral system like the one proposed by Gert as the basis for an automated ethical reasoning system. A difficult problem is in the resolution of conflicting obligations. Gert's impartial rational person advocating that violating the rule in these circumstances be publicly allowed seems reasonable but tough to implement.

Legal systems are closely related to moral systems. One approach to legal systems is to consider them as consisting of thousands of rules, often spelled out in great detail. The work in the automation of legal reasoning (see, for example, Walters 1985, 1988) might well prove helpful.

The virtue-based approach to ethics, especially that of Aristotle, seems to resonate well with the modern connectionist approach to AI. Both seem to emphasize the immediate, the perceptual, the nonsymbolic. Both emphasize development by training rather than by the teaching of abstract theory. Both emphasize the primacy of practice, of action, over abstract knowledge. Paul Churchland (1989) writes interestingly about moral knowledge, its development and its role, from a neurocomputational, connectionist point of view in "Moral Facts and Moral Knowledge" (his final chapter). Perhaps the right approach to developing an ethical robot is to confront it with a stream of different situations and train it as to the right actions to perform.

Robots as Moral Saints

An important aspect of utilitarianism is that it is all-encompassing. To really follow utilitarianism, every moment of the day one must ask "What should I do now to maximize the general well-being?" Am I about to eat dinner in a restaurant? Wouldn't the money be better spent on feeding starving children in Somalia? Am I about to go to the movies? I should stay home and send the ticket money to an organization that inoculates newborns.

Utilitarianism and other approaches to ethics have been criticized as not being psychologically realistic, as not being suitable "for creatures like us" (Flanagan 1991, p. 32). Could anyone really live full-time according to utilitarianism?

Not many human beings live their lives flawlessly as moral saints. But a robot could. If we could program a robot to behave ethically, the government or a wealthy philanthropist could build thousands of them and release them in the world to help people. (Would we actually like the consequences? Perhaps here again "The road to hell is paved with good intentions.")

Or, perhaps, a robot that could reason ethically would serve best as an advisor to humans about what action would be best to perform in the current situation and why.

Could a Robot be Ethical?

Would a robot that behaves ethically actually be ethical? This question is similar to the question raised by Searle in the Chinese room: would a computer that can hold a conversation in Chinese really understand Chinese?

The Searle question raises the age-old issue of other minds (Harnard 1991). How do we know that other people actually have minds when all that we can observe is their behavior? The ethical question raises the age-old issue of free will. Would a robot that follows a program and thereby behaves ethically actually be ethical? Or, does a creature need to have free will to behave ethically? Does a creature need to make a conscious choice of its own volition to behave ethically in order to be considered ethical? Of course, one can ask whether there is in fact any essential difference between the "free will" of a human being and the "free will" of a robot.

Is it possible for the robot in Figure 1 to earn its halo?

Benefits of Working on Ethical Robots

It is exciting to contemplate ethical robots and automated ethical reasoning systems. The basic problem is a common one in artificial intelligence, a problem that is encountered in every subfield from natural language understanding to vision. People have been thinking and discussing and writing about ethics for centuries, for millenia. Yet it often is difficult to take an ethical system that seems to be well worked-out and implement it on the computer. While books and books are written on particular ethical systems, the systems often do not seem nearly detailed enough and well-enough thought out to implement on the computer. Ethical systems and approaches make sense in terms of broad brush approaches, but (how) do people actually implement them? How can we implement them on the computer?

Knuth (1973) put it well:

It has often been said that a person doesn't really understand something until he teaches it to someone else. Actually a person doesn't really understand something until he can teach it to a computer, i.e., express it as an algorithm.... The attempt to formalize things as algorithms leads to a much deeper understanding than if we simply try to understand things in the traditional way. (p. 709)

Are there ethical experts to whom we can turn? Are we looking in the wrong place when we turn to philosophers for help with ethical questions? Should a knowledge engineer follow Mother Theresa around and ask her why she makes the decisions she makes and does the actions she does and try to implement her reasoning in an expert ethical system?

The hope is that as we try to implement ethical systems on the computer we will learn much more about the knowledge and assumptions built into the ethical theories themselves, that as we build the artificial ethical reasoning systems we will learn how to behave more ethically ourselves.

A Robotic/AI Approach to Ethics

People take several approaches to ethics. Perhaps a new approach that makes use of developing computer and robot technology would be useful.

In the philosophical approach, people try to think out the general principles underlying the best way to behave, the kind of person one ought to be. This chapter has been largely about different philosophical approaches to ethics.

In the psychological/sociological approach, people look at actual people's lives, at how they behave, at what they think, at how they develop. Some people study the lives of model human beings, of saints modern and historical. Some people study the lives of ordinary people.

In the robotic/AI approach, one tries to build ethical reasoning systems and ethical robots for their own sake, for the possible benefits of having the systems around as actors in the world and as advisors, and for the purpose of increasing our understanding of ethics.

Two other papers at this conference represent important first steps in this new field. The paper by Jack Adams-Webber and Ken Ford (1991) describes the first actual computer system that I have heard of, in this case one based on work in psychological ethics. Umar Khan (1991) presents a variety of interesting ideas about designing and implementing ethical systems.

Of course the more "traditional" topic of "computers and ethics" has to do with the ethics of building and using computer systems. A good overview of ethical issues surrounding the use of computers is found in the book of readings by Ermann, Williams, and Gutierrez (1990).

Conclusion

This chapter is meant to be speculative, to raise questions rather than answer them.

- What types of ethical theories can be used as the basis for programs for ethical robots?
- Could a robot ever be said to be ethical?
- Can we learn about what it means for *us* to be ethical by attempting to program robots to behave ethically?

I hope that people will think about these questions and begin to develop a variety of computer systems for ethical reasoning and begin to try to create ethical robots.

Acknowledgments

I would like to thank Peter Kugel, Michael McFarland, S.J., and the editors of this volume for their helpful comments.

References

Adams-Webber, J. & Ford, K.M. (1991). A conscience for Pinocchio: A computational model of ethical cognition. *The Second International Workshop on Human & Machine Cognition: Android Epistemology.* Pensacola, FL, May.

Asimov, I. (1942). Runaround. *Astounding Science Fiction,* March. [Republished in 1991, *Robot Visions.* Penguin.]

Churchland, P. (1989). *A Neurocomputational Perspective.* Cambridge, MA: MIT Press.

Ermann, M.D., Williams, M., & Gutierrez, C. (Eds.). (1990). *Computers, Ethics, and Society.* Oxford University Press.

Flanagan, O. (1991). *Varieties of Moral Personality.* Harvard University Press.

Gert, B. (1988). *Morality.* Oxford University Press.

Gowans, C. (Ed.). (1987). *Moral Dilemmas.* Oxford University Press.

Harnad, S. (1991). Other bodies, other minds: A machine incarnation of an old philosophical problem. *Minds and Machines, 1,* 1, 43-54.

Khan, A.F. Umar. (1995). Ethics of autonomous learning systems. [This volume.] Menlo Park, CA: AAAI Press.

Knuth, D. (1973). Computer science and mathematics. *American Scientist, 61,* 6.

Nozick, R. (1981). *Philosophical Explanations.* Belknap Press/Harvard University Press.

Parfit, D. (1984). *Reasons and Persons.* Clarendon Press.

Ross, W.D. (1930). *The Right and the Good.* Oxford University Press.

Walter, C. (Ed.). (1985). *Computer Power and Legal Reasoning.* West Publishing.

Walter, C. (Ed.). (1988). *Computer Power and Legal Language.* Quorum Books.

13 The Ethics of Autonomous Learning Systems

A. F. Umar Khan

> "The Tin Woodman appeared to think deeply for a moment.
> Then he said: 'Do you suppose Oz could give me a heart?'"
> – *The Wizard of OZ*

In some sense, a machine's behavior and idiosyncrasies can be thought of as its personality. Referring to conventional machines, this metaphor is little more than anthropomorphism; however, referring to the coming generations of learning automata as exhibiting limited individual personalities may not be so far fetched. It is conceivable that a potential exists for machines to learn idiosyncratic behaviors which, while remaining logically consistent, are not legal, ethical, or aesthetic.

Since each learning machine would experience its own unique history of learning and enhancing its decision-making powers, theoretically, such a machine could begin with the same learning *potential* as every other machine of its type, but once bought, its learning would immediately begin to be influenced by the environment provided by its new owner. An element of personality (that is, idiosyncratic behavior) can be expected once machines acquire capability for truly autonomous learning. Use of the word "personality" in this context does not refer to any conscious attempts to endow machines with superficial personality-like characteristics (that is, synthesized voices, randomized activity, and the like) to make them more like humans. Use of the word "personality" in the context of this discussion implies that two machines of the same type might evolve into highly individualistic machines, so different from each other in the ways they reason and react that they could be considered as having separate personalities. As the famous mathematician and cyberneticist, Norbert Wiener (1964), warned,

The gadget-minded people often have the illusion that a highly automatized world will make smaller claims on human ingenuity than does the present one and will take over from us our need for difficult thinking, as a Roman slave who was also a Greek philosopher might have done for his master. This is palpably false. A goal-seeking mechanism will not necessarily seek our goals unless we design it for that purpose, and in that designing we must foresee all steps of the process for which it was designed, instead of exercising a tentative foresight which goes up to a certain point, and can be continued from that point on as new difficulties arise. The penalties for errors of foresight, great as they are now, will be enormously increased as automation comes into its full use.

Background

Mankind's age-old fascination with creating intelligent artifacts and his concern with having to cope with the consequent personalities of such creations is a favorite subject in myth, legend, and literature. The ancient Greeks wrote of Pygmalion, the statue brought to life to keep her sculptor company; ancient Arab astrologers claimed to have built a thinking machine called the *zairja* which was capable of divining using each letter of the alphabet to represent a unique class of philosophical ideas; Jewish legend tells of the *golem*, an unpredictable human-like figure brought into being through the craft and prayers of the High Rabbi Loew of Prague (McCorduck 1979). *The Adolescence of P1* introduced "Privileged One," an artificial intelligence, a computer virus dedicated to its own proliferation and preservation at any cost. Perhaps the most famous fictional example is Mary Shelley's Frankenstein monster, which became monstrous only after it was rejected by its creator. The modern myth-maker, Hollywood, has further popularized the notion of thinking machines: in *2001: A Space Odyssey* was HAL, a computer which went berserk because of a paradox in its programming, causing a conflict between loyalty to the mission and personal survival; in TRON was the megalomaniac Master Control Program, designed to have the same low morals as its creator; in *Wargames* was Joshua, a computer which thought nuclear warfare was a game because it lacked a concept for reality; in *Star Wars* was the personable pair, R2D2 and C3PO, heroic because they embodied all the virtues Man desires in his mechanical servants. The list goes on and on. All of these personalities were contrived literary and/or cinematic images, but they serve as a good basis for looking at possible futures which scientists might build. More important, such images are indicative of the fears which many people have about sharing their world with intelligent artifacts.

Trustworthiness of Learning Machines

Alan Turing, one of the fathers of modern computing, proposed a test to consider the question "Can machines think?" The test, which Turing (1950) called the "imitation game" would be played with three people: a man, a woman, and an interrogator. The interrogator stays in a room apart from the other two and tries to determine which of the other two is the man and which is the woman based on their answers to questions using a teleprinter. The teleprinter eliminates any clues such as tones of voice which may unfairly help the interrogator. The object of the game for the woman is to help the interrogator. Her best strategy would be to tell the truth and say, "I am the woman, don't listen to him!" But she still cannot ultimately help the interrogator since the man can make similar claims. The next step would be to substitute the man with a machine and then replay the game. If the interrogator is no better at deciding which is the human and which the computer as he/she was when trying to discover which was the man and which the woman, then this fact could be considered conclusive evidence of machine intelligence.

In order to pass the Turing Test, a machine would have to be able to operate in a broad range of task domains and adapt in the same manner as humans. It would also have to "cheat." It should not outshine the human by responding to hard mathematics problems too quickly or too accurately; it should be evasive so as not to let the human outshine it in areas which require either creativity or a deep understanding of creativity (such as expressing critical opinions on art, music, or literature). In short, an intelligent machine would have to be intelligent enough to know when to dissemble, when to lie. One of Turing's assistants who later became head of the Turing Institute, Donald Michie, observed that "the real social danger, certainly the first we shall see becoming manifest, is not the ultra-intelligent machine but the ultra-clever machine" (Michie and Johnston 1984).

Definition of Personality Integrity

As a computer security term, "integrity" is concerned with the trustworthiness of an automated system (i.e., defining some acceptable level of assurance that the system will not perform contrary to design specifications). This issue becomes a serious concern with autonomous learning automata because there is no way to exhaustively describe every possible state that such a machine can assume; the number of possible states could be unlimited. As noted by Alan Turing in his 1947 lecture to the London Mathematical Society, there are several mathematical theorems which indicate that a machine cannot be simultaneously intelligent and infallible (Michie and Johnston 1984). It is conceivable that some future state may produce unpredictable results, causing the machine to draw the wrong conclusion, take an action when none is called for, or remain inactive when action is critical.

Figure 1.
The Panic Button.

Assurance of Personality Integrity

Whether or not machine intelligence is ever realized to the extent envisioned by the Turing Test, some level of machine intelligence is sure to be realized for many restricted task domains. With that idea as an assumption, three methods for providing some level of assurance of the integrity of "personalities" resulting from autonomously learning automata may be inferred from the available literature.

Manual Override Mechanisms. Current technology relies on manual overrides (also called panic buttons, interrupt mechanisms, or fail-safe devices) to compensate for machines lacking an awareness of the propriety of their own behavior. But interrupt mechanisms will be ineffective for many applications of autonomous learning machines. When a human invokes a manual override, time ceases to be measured in terms of machine speed (increments of microseconds, nanoseconds, or picoseconds) and begins to be measured in terms of human reaction time (which may be slower than five simple actions per second). While the human reacts or makes the machine wait for advice, irreparable damage may occur—the human's reaction might be a case of "too little, too late." For example, a system which controls a nuclear reactor may have already initiated a fatal sequence of events before the human operator perceives the problem and reacts by trying to abort the process; or a system which assists a fighter pilot to evade multiple threats may be the only thing capable of extricating both pilot and aircraft from a life-threatening situation

Figure 2.
The Buddy System.

by virtue of its very ability to plan and control a complex series of evasive maneuvers in minute fractions of a second. Machines need to be freed to do what they do best—process massive amounts of information quickly, efficiently, and accurately without fatigue or boredom. If they cannot be so freed, society must deny learning systems a role in many critical domains.

The "Buddy System." Considering the concept of one machine overseeing another machine's behavior, Robert Kahn (1983), former Director of the Information Processing Technology Office (IPTO) of the Defense Advanced Research Projects Agency (DARPA), wrote

> It is possible that requirements for new system structures will be specified by humans, but the structures will be created by machine. If so, it ought to be possible to create oversight systems that coreside with them and monitor their well-being and can take action to fix or at least report certain obvious cases of errant behavior. In fact, a symbolic implementation in which each system oversees the other would be quite interesting to evaluate in itself.

Simple "buddy systems" are currently in use for such critical operations as control of NASA's space shuttle. The space shuttle has several on-board computers simultaneously performing the same calculations, comparing results, and voting on which results to accept if there is a conflict. Yet another computer on the ground performs the same calculations and can be used in case the on-board computers cannot agree. However, using redundant computers just to ensure that computations are within acceptable tolerances will not be sufficient to guarantee personality integrity of a learning machine. Exposed

Figure 3.

to the same environmental stimuli, similar machines might conceivably learn the same "wrong" things and thus not be able to identify truly errant behavior in their fellows. Conversely, if similar learning machines are subjected to different environmental stimuli, they might not learn the same "right" things. Hence, this approach leads potentially to an irresolvable paradox.

Internalized Controls. To return to the earlier analogy of parents and children, when children leave home, parents hope that, as a result of careful nurturing, their sons and daughters will have been adequately prepared to face the negative pressures of society. A learning machine needs to be similarly armed with internal protections (as a minimum) because it is logical to assume that a machine capable of learning better ways of doing its job might be equally capable of learning things which would lead it to the machine equivalence of dishonesty.

One method for identifying and controlling inappropriate behavior by learning machines was suggested by the famous scientist and science fiction writer, Isaac Asimov, over 40 years ago in his book *I, Robot.* Asimov (1950) wrote of highly sophisticated robots possessing "positronic brains" made from a spongy substance called "plantinumiridium." Asimov proposed his three famous laws to be indelibly programmed into the brains of robots:

1. A robot may not injure a human being, or, through inaction, allow a human being to come to harm.

2. A robot must obey orders given it by human beings except where such orders would conflict with the First Law.

3. A robot must protect its own existence as long as such protection does not conflict with the First or Second Law.

Internalizing Ethical Control

Asimov's idea of endowing robots with self-oversight capability does point to some potentially interesting scientific work in at least two areas: deriving formal logic representations adequate for encoding higher level concepts, and employing that higher level knowledge to provide internal checks and balances which allow machines to understand the effects of their actions.

Encoding Higher Level Concepts

Writing in the medium of fiction, Asimov was not reporting on serious scientific work; therefore, he was no more compelled to state how his laws would be encoded for use by the robots than he was to define "positronic" or to give the atomic weight and chemical characteristics of "plantinumiridium." However, George David Birkhoff, a leading figure among 20th century American mathematicians, may have pointed the way to encoding ethical concepts in automata before modern electronic computers were even operational.

Echoing Descartes's assertion 'omnia apud me mathematics fiunt' (with me, everything becomes mathematics), Birkhoff (1933) suggested formulae for describing aesthetics and ethics and proceeded to demonstrate mathematically that the two were variations of the same theme. His was something of a Grand Unified Field Theory for logic, aesthetics, and ethics. He suggested that, for certain purposes, philosophic thought may be treated separately in its logical, aesthetic, and ethical aspects. While logic has developed into an independent discipline, until Birkhoff there was little or no attempt to treat ethics or aesthetics in a more or less mathematical way.

Birkhoff described Ethical Measure, M, in terms of total good achieved, G. He suggested that the ethically minded person, state, or organization endeavors to select a course of action which maximizes the ethical measure. The following is just one of the examples used by Birkhoff (1933) to illustrate the potential of his approach.

One or the other of two friends of long standing, A and B, is to be advanced to an opening in the organization in which they hold positions of the same rank. A happens to learn that the actual selection will hinge upon the judgment of a certain person L belonging to the same organization. Ought A to pass this information on to B?

The answer of course is that in the circumstances stated A ought to inform his friend B.

A's reason for this decision might be formalized as follows: The material goods g_A and g_B which will accrue to him or to his friend through such an advancement are the same: $g_A = g_B = g$. If A informs B, the material good of his friendship, f, with A is retained. Therefore we have simply

$$M = g.$$

On the other hand, if A does not tell B what he learned, the friendship between them is destroyed, even if B never learns of A's unfriendly act; and so we have

$$M = g - f.$$

Since g exceeds $g - f$, A ought to tell B, although he realizes that by doing so he gives up a definite personal advantage. In the above reckoning the unfavorable effect upon A's character of not informing B is intentionally disregarded although it might really be the most important consideration of all.

A's decision to pass the information on to B is here assumed to be made on the utilitarian basis. On the hedonistic basis, A might conclude that if he fails to inform B, then

$$M = g,$$

since he will be certain to win L's special favor, whereas, in the contrary case,

$$M = g/2,$$

inasmuch as he would then only have an equal chance with B. In this event, he would have to balance the prospect of material advancement against his friendship with B.

Again, according to the extent that A believes himself inferior to B, he will feel that his chances are lessened by telling B. If A is a loyal friend, however, he will not be moved from his decision by such thoughts.

The basic hypothesis has been made that the information about L is of legitimate practical advantage to A and B. It is also assumed that the friendship between A and B is a sincere one, founded upon mutual esteem. For clearly if there were no relationship, A would not be under any obligation to inform B, any more than he would consider it an obligation on B's part to tell him. Of course if A believes that B would not tell him if circumstances were reversed, or that B would employ unfair or unscrupulous tactics to gain L's favor, the bond of friendship between them is already weak; and so the situation would not be the one envisaged in the problem under consideration.

While his mathematics is not totally convincing, Birkhoff does present some compelling intuitive evidence that a mathematical treatment of the subject could be explored with the objective of formalizing machine representations for legal, aesthetical, and ethical values for learning machines.

Having an acceptable formalism for describing higher level values for use by learning machines, however, is only part of the problem—the hard part will be deciding precisely which values to teach the machine. M. Mitchell Waldrop (1987) of *Science* magazine observed,

> As computers and robots become more and more intelligent, it becomes imperative that we think carefully and explicitly about what those built-in values are. Perhaps what we need is, in fact, a theory and practice of machine ethics, in the spirit of Asimov's three laws of robotics.

In his insightful book *God & Golem, Inc.*, Norbert Wiener (1964) referenced the famous story of "The Monkey's Paw" by W. W. Jacobs. In this story, a man makes a wish for a large amount of money. There is a knock at the door, and the visitor presents the man with a check for the wished-for amount; it is from his son's employer in consolation for his son's having just been killed in an accident on the job. Regretting his first wish, the man's wife wishes for their son's return. There is another knock at the door. This time the man and his wife sense it is their son's ghost and make their third and final wish: that the ghost go away.

Wiener observed from this and other stories that the danger of magic feared most in myth and legend lies in its computer-like literal-mindedness: at best, storybook magic grants exactly what you asked for, not what you should have asked for or what you intended.

> The magic of automation, and in particular the magic of an automaticization in which the devices learn, may be expected to be similarly literal-minded. If you are playing a game according to certain rules and set the playing machine to play for victory, you will get victory if you get anything at all, and the machine will not pay the slightest attention to any consideration except victory according to the rules....

So, there is a lot riding on just whose rules the machine has been taught.

Providing Appropriate Internal Checks and Balances

Apart from technological improvements which have led to faster and more powerful memory and processors, the most basic difference between the computers of today and calculators is the inclusion of a logical component in their design. Calculators, which have been used in one form or another for thousands of years, have only arithmetic components (capable of performing calculations on numbers). The logic component of a modern computer allows it to store and execute complex instructions, usually in the form of programs. In effect, the logical component oversees and controls the arithmetic processes, and together they are called the "arithmetic-logic unit" or "ALU." A similar evolution might be needed to expand the computer into a self-controlling, self-aware machine: such a machine would need a meta-logical component responsible for understanding and overseeing its interaction with and effect upon its environment. There are at least two functions such a meta-logical component should fulfill: supervision of learning to evaluate the effect of new knowledge on overall performance, and mediation of results to evaluate the effect of its own performance on its environment.

Supervision of Learning Function. Conventional (that is, nonlearning) automata know what to do because every possible state structure has been designed into their software by a programmer. Learning systems, on the other hand, design their own new state structures, or, in programming terms, they need to be able to write their own programs (Aleksander and Burnette 1983). Thus, assuring the integrity of autonomously learning automata is at least partially a problem of oversight and mediation of the processes of learning new state structures.

A self-controlling learning machine needs task-specific definitions of "errant behavior," understandable to learning machines, which apply basic concepts of what is "right" and "wrong" for a specific machine to learn. Then, armed with these concepts, it needs to test all new knowledge before it is allowed to alter existing behavior. This concept is akin to that of change control as it is understood by conventional information systems personnel involved with configuration management. There are also techniques and tools used by knowledge engineers to help ensure that knowledge bases do not get corrupted by the addition of new knowledge. The critical difference with learning systems is that the human must be removed, as much as possible, from the process of learning. Otherwise, the machine will always be limited in its learning, and what is potentially more devastating is that it may acquire the values of its owner, not necessarily those of society.

Mediation of Results Function. Feedback is the key to self-control. Automated feedback is typically at the task or subtask level. For example, a robotic assembly capable of manipulating objects uses tactile feedback to know how much pressure it is applying to the object it is grasping and orientation feedback to gauge its degree of rotation and position in three dimensional space. Such a robot has been programmed to know how much pressure to apply in specific situations and what series of maneuvers it should go through. The robot may also know how to react to certain anticipated obstacles and hindrances. All of its feedback simply tells it if it is performing its predefined task properly, within acceptable tolerances. But today's robots are not equipped with sensors and meta-level knowledge to receive and process automatic feedback related to the value or effect of the performance of their tasks. In limited applications, this may be acceptable—after all, the result must be considered beneficial, else, the humans would not have programmed a machine to perform the task. Ultimately, a learning machine which is expected to work in complex domains where it has potentially greater impact on human welfare or well-being will have to receive and process a broad range of continuous sensory feedback. The result will be something analogous to machine self-awareness.

Other Ethical Considerations

In addition to investigating the feasibility of encoding legal, aesthetical, and ethical concepts for use by autonomous learning systems, there are other socially relevant considerations which ought to be addressed hand-in-hand with research in Machine Learning. These include, but are not limited to, the following.

Auditing Issues

Automata capable of autonomous learning should be able not just to oversee their learning processes in order to satisfy themselves that changes are acceptable, but to report on their learning experience to humans as well. When the integrity of human workers is of importance, Personnel Security programs and policies are usually instituted. Personnel Security is concerned with screening personnel before allowing them access to secure areas or sensitive information, then it is concerned with limiting their access to the minimum information necessary for the accomplishment of their jobs. The greater the need for such security, the more intensively the background of individuals will be checked and the more closely their actual entry into secure areas or use of sensitive information will be monitored and controlled. With autonomous learning automata, similar policies will be needed. Since a machine is, after all, a man-made artifact, it should be possible to build in the capability to audit changes to learning processes. Otherwise, as Professor Michie observed, "In future time a computing system on whose functioning large numbers of people depend may be refused certification if its strategies are hidden in clouds of impenetrable complexity" (Michie and Johnston 1984).

Legal Issues

Even without the proliferation of autonomous learning systems in the marketplace, the law is still unsure how to deal with the products of artificial intelligence. Is an expert system a product or a service? Who is liable if a product makes a wrong decision because of internal problems or because of tampering after sale? How far is it reasonable to rely on the system (is someone at fault for using it in some situations or for not using it in others) (Gemignani 1990; Sprague and Berkowitz 1990; Zeide and Liebowitz 1990)? The jury is still out. How these questions are answered in the courts will set the foundation for how learning systems ultimately can be used—no matter how critically such technology may be needed once it is developed.

Moral Issues

While Turing may have suggested a test for machine intelligence, there is no such obvious test for sentience:

> If a machine can be made intelligent and conscious through programming, then we will have to do some serious thinking about what status the machine has. Is it someone's property? Would the owner be within his or her legal rights to pull the plug on the machine, or destroy its intelligent programming? If the machine's owner has the freedom to tinker with the machine's intellect, then might we be tempted to do the same with humans, treating them as nothing more than soggy computers that need to have their thinking rearranged? ... Will any of our so-called sacred values be left to us in that event?

"No value is all that sacred," one SRI staff member says with a shrug. "Technology has changed a lot of our values over the centuries. Once slavery was a morally acceptable institution. Then inventions made living slaves unnecessary, and very shortly moralists were talking about the 'immorality' of slavery. When it was necessary, it was moral. When it became obsolete, it was immoral. No, I really think our value systems will prove to be quite flexible where artificial intelligence is concerned. If the technology helps us do what we want to do, then I'm sure we'll tailor our values to suit the technology." (Ritchie 1984)

Summary and Conclusions

Research in the field of machine learning seeks to realize the possibility of creating autonomous learning automata. There is a need for machines to learn new ways of controlling complex environments and functions which are of critical importance to human beings. Autonomous learning may make it possible for machines of the same model and type to develop distinctly different "personalities" (that is, idiosyncratic behavior) after being exposed to different environments. Coping with the personalities of these new automata raises a serious issue: Will they serve Man in the functions for which they were intended, or will they learn to arrive at conclusions which are logically consistent but morally, ethically, or legally incorrect? Manual override mechanisms and "buddy systems" were found to be inadequate for assuring the integrity of autonomous learning systems. Controls on the personality of such learning systems must be internalized. Each system must be able to view and report the effect of new knowledge on its own decision processes and to moderate the effect of its actions (and inactions) on the health and well-being of human beings.

While in the hands of a responsible manufacturer or researcher, the initial stages of a machine's learning can be closely supervised and evaluated, much as parents supervise their children to ensure that they learn the "right" things in the "right" way from the "right" sources. Once a learning machine is bought in the open marketplace, there will need to be strict guarantees that it will continue to learn as responsibly as it did under the manufacturer's or researcher's oversight. If such assurances of integrity cannot be given, then the usefulness of automation will always be limited by the ingenuity of human programmers.

Guided by the three famous Laws of Robotics suggested by Asimov and the mathematics of Birkhoff, it seems possible to express concepts dealing with law, aesthetics, and ethics in logical terms understandable by a computer. Hence, it is conceivable that autonomous learning systems could be endowed with the machine equivalence of a conscience, thus allowing humans to use such systems in the critical applications for which they are most suited: in situations where large amounts of information must be processed with speed, accuracy, and efficiency, without fatigue, and in domains which are too dangerous or time-sensitive to be effectively staffed by human workers. It is essential that researchers direct their attention towards providing acceptable levels of assurance that autonomous learning systems will continue to perform as intended, else, when they are ready to leave the laboratory, such systems may be denied a place in applications where human life or well-being are at stake.

References

Aleksander, I. & Burnette, P. (1983). *Reinventing Man*. New York: Holt, Rinehart & Winston.

Asimov, I. (1950). *I, Robot*. Ballantine Books.

Birkhoff, G.D. (1933). Aesthetic Measure. Cambridge. [Extracted in "A mathematical approach to ethics," by G.D. Birkhoff. Also in J.R. Newman (Ed.), *The World of Mathematics*, Vol. 4. New York: Simon & Schuster, 1956.]

Gemignani, M.C. (1990). Liability for malfunction of an expert system. *Proceedings of the IEEE Conference on Managing Expert Systems Programs and Projects*, September.

Kahn, R.E. (1983). A new generation in computing. *IEEE Spectrum*, E.A. Torrero (Ed.), November.

McCorduck, P. (1979). *Machines Who Think*. New York: W. H. Freeman.

Michalski, R.S., Carbonell, J.G., & Mitchell, T.M. (1983). *Machine Learning: An Artificial Intelligence Approach*. San Mateo, CA: Morgan Kaufmann.

Michie, D. & Johnston, R. (1984). *The Creative Computer*. New York: Viking Press.

Ritchie, D. (1984). *The Binary Brain, Artificial Intelligence in the Age of Electronics*. Boston: Little, Brown.

Sprague, R.D. & Berkowitz, L.G. (1990). Theories of legal liability for defective expert system software. *Proceedings of the IEEE Conference on Managing Expert Systems Programs and Projects*.

Turing, A.M. (1950). Computing machinery and intelligence. *Mind*, October.

Waldrop, M. & Mitchell, T.M. (1987). A question of responsibility. *AI Magazine*, AAAI, Spring.

Wiener, N. (1964). *God & Golem, Inc.; A Comment on Certain Points where Cybernetics Impinges on Religion*. Cambridge, MA: MIT Press.

Zeide, J.S. & Liebowitz, J. (1990). A critical review of legal issues in artificial intelligence. In *Managing Artificial Intelligence & Expert Systems*. Yourdon Press.

14 How to Settle an Argument

Henry E. Kyburg, Jr.

To take human reasoning as an inspiration for android epistemology presents a problem. Are we to take human reasoning, together with its errors and mistakes, as the ideal to which the android (or its designer) should aspire? Or should we follow the more traditional philosophical beacon and seek enlightenment beyond the aspirations of most mortals?

Traditionally, logic has followed the second course. Deductive validity is something that has been well understood since the days of Aristotle, though its formulations were vague and metaphorical (the conclusion must be contained in the premises) before the advent of formal semantics (every model in which the premises are true is a model in which the conclusion is true). The impressive development of deductive logic since the beginning of the twentieth century has focused not on how humans reason but on deductive, and primarily mathematical, argument. Of course mathematical argument reflects how *some* humans, mathematicians, reason in some contexts. The formal notion of *proof* is clearly inspired by the preanalytic notion of what it means to *prove* a mathematical proposition.

The formal characterization of a proof might go something like this: A sequence of statements is a proof of a statement S from a set of premises P, just in case each statement in the sequence is one of the premises in P; an axiom of the particular first-order logic we have adopted; or a consequence, via modus ponens, of two earlier statements in the sequence.[1]

A proof of a theorem in a journal of mathematics is not, obviously, a proof in this sense. Such a proof would be enormously long, and, most important, would be very hard to understand. There could easily be lines in the proof that are page-long instances of simple first-order axioms. And we would have to decide *which* version of first-order logic we would take as canonical. Even in logic itself, shortcuts are employed in the interest of brevity and intelligibility.[2]

But what kind of nonsense is this? If what mathematicians do is the inspiration of the formal notion of proof, and yet none of the things we find in mathematics journals qualify as proofs, hasn't something gone seriously wrong?

One answer is 'yes.' But although this answer may be defensible, it makes the logical developments of the past hundred years seem pointless.

Another answer is possible. The goal of formal logic is both to be able to have an explicit and clear notion of proof and to have a framework that serves a useful function in settling arguments. The formal notion of proof given above employs only one rule of inference, modus ponens, together with a set of first-order axioms. Modus ponens may be seen as the minimal rule of inference: if you don't find modus ponens intuitively valid, you are beyond the mathematical pale. And the handful of types of mathematical axioms are equally dear and basic.

Given this framework, there is no need (and surely no one ever intended!) for mathematics to proceed by formal proofs. Arguments for mathematical propositions need be no more formal than is required to ensure agreement. What the framework guarantees, however, is that there is a rock bottom level of proof that is *guaranteed* to compel agreement. If I claim that S follows from P, I am claiming that there exists a sequence of formulas of a certain character. My *argument* generally consists not in exhibiting this sequence, but in convincing you (or myself) that such a sequence exists.

What is captured by our formal logic is not mathematical reasoning in general, but the lowest form of mathematical reasoning; what is important and interesting is that all mathematical reasoning and argument can be captured, au fond, by this lowest form. Mathematical intuition varies widely: the great mathematician will be sure that a certain statement is a theorem and then may spend years convincing himself that he can construct the right sequence of statements; he publishes an argument that is designed to convince fellow specialists that such a sequence of statements exists; I try to follow his proof, and find that I must interpolate many steps before I can convince myself that I could, in principle, construct the sequence. None of us, not even me, needs the actual sequence; but its potential existence has an important bearing on mathematical argument.

We know how to settle mathematical arguments. Given an argument to the effect that S follows from P, it is settled by exhibiting (rarely!), or establishing the existence of (almost always), an appropriate sequence of statements. It seems quite feasible that mathematical conversation with our android friends should follow the pattern of human mathematical conversation, as structured by mathematical logic.

This picture of logic has been, in some degree, the inspiration of many philosophers. But over the past hundred years it has become more and more widely accepted that most interesting arguments, corresponding to the most valuable species of human reasoning, cannot be usefully fit into the pattern of mathematical logic. Most of our concerns are with matters of fact, and as Hume insisted, there is no logical connection between one matter of fact and another distinct matter of fact. We can bridge the gap with empirical generalizations and theories: "*a* is a crow" and "All crows are black" do logically imply "*a* is black." But this raises the even knottier problem of arriving at, or reasoning to, empirical generalizations and theories; it raises the problem of scientific inference and inductive reasoning. Something other than classical first-order logic is required to reflect this aspect of human reasoning. In artificial intelligence, as well as in philosophy, a variety of candidates have been suggested: defeasible reasoning, probabilistic logic, probability theory itself, and others. In what follows, we will examine the possibilities for settling what I shall call "empirical arguments" within the framework of evidential probability.[3] We aspire to communicate with our androids concerning matters of fact as well as matters of mathematics.

What We Are Concerned With

We are concerned here with arguments about matters of empirical fact. Such arguments, by their nature, cannot be as conclusive as the arguments of mathematics. Even when they are deductive in form—almost never the actual case—the conclusion is uncertain because of the uncertainty characteristic of the premises or database on which the conclusion is based. These matters of fact are the kinds of matters that we can express in the usual first-order language. They include, for example, such statements as "the train arrives on time," "the sun is shining," "table #43 is blue," "dog #25 weighs more than 90 pounds," "the voltage at point A is between 5.07 and 5.10 volts," "all crows are black," "about half of all coin tosses result in heads," and the like. We observe that numbers, quantities, and the like are referred to in many of these statements. We could suppose that we had included first-order axioms for set theory among the axioms of our language; more plausibly, let's just suppose we have real numbers available, and that the "first-order language" we are talking about is simply a distinguished part of the whole language. This is not the sort of thing to get hung up on.[4]

The world of discourse with regard to which we propose to discuss argument and belief is a limited one. It includes the sort of boring pedestrian statements that scientists and engineers might make in the course of their daily work. It includes generalizations and statements about statistical distributions as well as statements about particular matters of fact, and they can include exciting statements about horse-races and lotteries, as well as statements about measurements (a measurement is a multi-million ticket lottery with a bias toward the truth). But they do not (or need not) concern statements about knowledge and belief, about modal "facts," or about inductive or deductive argument. The latter are the concerns of this chapter; they are not the subject of the arguments that will be discussed in this chapter.

So we are concerned with arguments concerning matters that can be expressed in statements of a somewhat limited, and strictly extensional, language. These are arguments yielding conclusions that are generally defeasible and nonmonotonic. Exactly how much of a limitation adopting an extensional language is, is a matter of some controversy—some people would say that almost everything can be expressed in a language of this sort by one devious device or another; others would say that many interesting issues defy expression in such a language. But I think most people would agree that if we can resolve arguments in this language, we have made a significant step forward.

An argument may involve two people, two androids, or some of each, or it may involve an agent and his better self. In the latter case, we speak of justification. The issue in an argument we shall take to be the status of a single statement from our canonical extensional language L, whether we are concerned with an argument involving two agents or with a justification-producing argument.

Forms of Argument

We may structure our discussion by considering two distinct forms of argument. There is the question of whether the statement S should (or should not) be believed, and the question of whether the statement S should be accorded one degree of belief rather than another. We thus distinguish between arguments designed to justify the *acceptance* of a statement and arguments designed to justify a *degree of belief* in a statement.

We will be concerned with both forms of argument, but they should be kept carefully distinct. Even where we are concerned with justifying degrees of belief, however, we claim that there is a matter of argument involved and that rational belief is not subjective in the sense that two agents who are sharing evidence may agree to disagree about what beliefs are rationally warranted by the evidence.

Belief is sometimes construed as "full belief." The issue that concerns us is then the issue of rational acceptance: the acceptance as true, as worthy of taking as a basis for action, of a given statement in the face of given evidence. According to one point of view, acceptance should be based on high probability; according to other points of view, acceptance should be based on valid inference within a nonmonotonic or default logic. According to the so-called "logical" point of view, associated with nonmonotonic logic and defeasible reasoning, acceptance concerns logic and not probability. The question of degrees of belief is another matter, involving the representation of psychological states. Acceptance, on this view, is a more serious matter, and one quite removed from consideration of justified degrees of belief.

But if acceptance is to be based on high probability, the same mechanisms are involved in determining the soundness of an argument establishing a certain degree of belief or of an argument probabilistically warranting acceptance. Our own view is that probabilistic justifications can be given for acceptance. We will assume that at least a part of the justification for the acceptance of a conclusion, given agreement about the premises supporting it, will lie in its probability relative to the evidence shared by both parties to the argument.

Assumptions

There are several assumptions we are making.

First, we assume that the issue is a normative one: Given the appropriate circumstances (about which more shortly), any rational agents ought to be able to come to agreement about the status of a sentence S. An argument for S or an argument for assigning a degree of belief to S relative to a body of data is either rationally compelling or commits some logical error. Rational beliefs, either in the sense of "belief" that involves categorical (if tentative) commitment or in the sense that admits of (approximate) degrees, are *justified* beliefs, communicable beliefs. The subjectivist Bayesian might well reject this assumption. He might say, as did Ramsey, that it is not the business of logic to tell a man what his degree of belief should be that a chip drawn from an urn should be white. Given the evidence at his disposal, and given the opportunity to say "anywhere between 0 and 1," we would reject the point of view of the subjectivist Bayesian.

Second, we assume that there is a collection of data that the agents are willing to share. This requires that honesty prevail between the agents. Either lying or withholding relevant information undermines the possibility of rational resolution. But we knew this all along.

This data we will take to be in the form of a set of sentences in our official language L. Let us denote the total evidence—not just the limited evidence directly relevant to the sentence under discussion—by D. We take it to include general knowledge, as well as the deliverances of our senses (or sensors). This point is important, for there are many generalizations we are willing to take as data in most contexts and many sensory judgments that we could be brought to doubt.

In the case of justification, in which we only have one agent, this assumption amounts to the assumption that there is a clear-cut set of data sentences comprising *all* the data at the disposal of the agent appropriate to the question at issue. In the case of a group of agents, this amounts to the same assumption for each agent, plus the willingness of the agents to share information.

We do *not* assume that D is closed under logical consequence, and thus we are in a position to avoid the lottery paradox (Kyburg 1970). We do assume that every logical consequence of a sentence in D is in D. Of course among the sentences in D may be some conjunctions, but we do not suppose that D is closed under conjunction.[5] A natural representation of D is thus the set of strongest sentences in D, where a "strongest" sentence is a sentence implied by no other (single) sentence in D. This condition allows that a finite axiomatization of, for example, naive physics might be in D, in the form of the conjunction of some sensible set of axioms.

We assume as given what will *count* as data; this is not to deny that it is a knotty problem to decide what will count as data in a given context. Rather, we assume that these difficult issues are settled before we approach either the question of acceptance or the question of the allocation of belief.

Third, we assume that the agents can agree, under the circumstances, on the importance of the issue: This is represented in our formalism as a "level of acceptance" or "level of practical certainty." Let this level be $p \in [0.5, 1.0]$. In the case of justification, we are assuming no more than that there is a fixed value of p. A suggestion for determining the value of p for a collection of decisions was given in Kyburg (1988). We are assuming as given what will count as "enough" justification. This is certainly a nontrivial matter and one to which various considerations may reasonably be brought to bear. Nevertheless, *given* such an index, the questions of what is acceptable and what is believable to what (approximate) degree are, we argue, answered by logical considerations alone.

If the first assumption is not satisfied, then it isn't clear what is being asked for: The acceptability of a statement then is a matter of exhortation rather than rational argument.

If the second assumption is not satisfied, then the issue at hand cannot be resolved until a prior issue is resolved—namely the disputed contents of the body of data on which we might base a resolution of the issue.

If the third assumption is not satisfied, then we have to consider a quite different form of argument: it is the argument concerning the relation between what is or might be at stake, and an appropriate level of practical certainty. This issue was discussed in Kyburg (1988), but we will not consider it again here.

In short, if the acceptance of S is justified relative to the parameters D and p, it is so for any agent relative to those parameters. And if the degree of belief in S is represented by the limits (r, s), it is so for any agent, again relative to those parameters.

The Mechanism for
Evaluating Arguments Yielding Degrees of Belief

For this we need consider only the set $D;$ p, the parameter for probabilistic acceptance, is irrelevant.[6] An argument supporting the assignment of a degree of belief $[r,s]$ to the sentence S has the form (called an inference structure)

IS_S: x   y   z   r   s

It is an inference structure *for S based on D* just in case D contains the following sentences

$x \in z \equiv S$
$x \in y$
$\%(y, z) \in [r, s]$

Any inference structure for S based on D constitutes a relevant argument for having the degree of belief $[r,s]$ in S. In general, there will be many inference structures. For example, in a language with a universal set V, such as that suggested by Quine's (1951) *Mathematical Logic,* if D contains all logical truths, it will contain:

$\{x: S\} \in \{V\} \equiv S$
$\{x: S\} \in \{\{x: S\}\}$
$\%(\{\{x: S\}\},\{V\}) \in [0, 1]$

It would be a constrained language indeed that didn't allow us to do something like this.

Each inference structure represents an argument, and those mentioning the interval $[r,s]$ are arguments for the assignment of the degree of belief $[r,s]$ to the sentence S. If such an argument is undefeated, then that is the *rational* degree of belief to have in S when the total evidence is D.

How are arguments defeated? By other arguments of the same form, mentioning different intervals $[u,v]$. For example, if two inference structures disagree, but one mentions a reference class that is a subset of that mentioned by the other, the former defeats the latter, but not vice versa. There are three such relations among inference structures that allow the survival of only one of two that differ. The first corresponds to the principle of specificity and is well known in both philosophy and AI (Touretsky 1986; Reichenbach 1949). The second corresponds to the use of prior information, under circumstances in which Bayes' Theorem applies. The third is appropriate to statistical inference and adjudicates between arguments making use of larger or smaller statistical samples. All three are discussed in Kyburg (1991). The net result is that, given a statement S and given a body of evidence D, there is only one (interval) degree of belief in S that is rational. There may be any number of arguments leading to this degree of belief.

This is essentially the import of the system of evidential or epistemological probability. It has been implemented, with variations, and for limited languages, in ways that embody slightly different constraints, by Ronald Loui (1986) and Bulent Murtezaoglu (Kyburg & Murtezaoglu 1991). All argument, on this view, is codified in the form of relations among inference structures.

This includes *deductive* argument. If a body of evidential beliefs *KB* is consistent, and *S* is entailed by a sentence in *KB*, then the appropriate degree of belief for *S* relative to *KB* is 1. If the body of beliefs *KB* that serves as "evidence" is not consistent (as may quite well happen in real life), and *S* is entailed by some sentence in *KB*, then whether or not *S* receives probability 1 depends on details concerning the structure of *KB*. The source of this fact is the very general fact that if the probability of *S* is $[r,s]$, and *T* entails *S*, then the lower bound for the probability of *T* must be at least *r*.

The Mechanism for Evaluating Arguments that Lead to Acceptance

Some writers see no need for acceptance or full belief (Cheeseman 1988), but most people, even of the Bayesian persuasion, assign *some* sentences probabilities of 1 or 0. For example, sentences representing the evidence are often assigned probabilities of 1. Such assignments are tantamount to acceptance: There is no way in which the probabilities of such sentences can be altered by conditionalization. These assignments, as far as conditionalization is concerned, are nonmonotonic.

What interests us is acceptance in a weaker, nonmonotonic sense. That is, it may be the case that a sentence is "accepted," relative to a body of evidence *KB*, and, relative to an expanded *KB*, comes to be rejected. In order to make sense of this idea, we must distinguish between the set of sentences *accepted as evidence* and the set of sentences accepted as *practical certainties*. A sentence accepted on the basis of a probability less than 1, of course, can have its probability modified by new evidence; if at one point it is so probable as to be worthy of acceptance as practically certain, further evidence can cause it to lose that probability, *provided* that it does not have probability 1 to start with.

Given our parameters *D* and *p*, we shall say that a sentence *T* is acceptable just in case its lower probability (remember that evidential or epistemological probability assigns probability intervals to sentences) on the evidence *D* is greater than *p*. As we have just observed, if *S* entails *T*, the lower probability of *S* must be lower than the lower probability of *T*. That is, if *S* entails *T* and *S* is acceptable, so is *T*. Furthermore, since logical and mathematical truths are entailed by anything, they are acceptable.

Thus the set of acceptable statements A has just the same logical structure as D. (That is, it may not be deductively closed, but it will contain the consequences of any statement contained in it.) It cannot be construed as D itself, though, for (almost all[7]) statements in D have probability 1 relative to D, while those in A must not, or we would find ourselves falling again into monotonicity. We need to keep distinct the set of acceptable sentences and the set of evidence sentences.

Of course the reliability of the data in D may be raised. In the example of measurement, in which we take account of the "known" distribution of error, a question may be raised about the basis of that piece of statistical knowledge. Even in the case of "direct observation" the possibility of misperception or hallucination may be raised. Suppose we are interested in the acceptability of a piece of data d that has been accepted into the database D. We will want to examine the probability of d relative to a pair of parameters D' and p' such that sentences accepted under those parameters can be in D. Quite clearly the standards of evidence that pertain to evidence should be higher than those that pertain to practical certainties. Can we say anything more specific than that $p' > p$?

In the systems of Kyburg (1974), it is a theorem that if S and T are members of a set of evidential statements D', then their conjunction will appear in a set of statements judged as acceptable relative to D'. (This follows from the fact that S entails the biconditional "$S \equiv S \ \& \ T$" so that if T is probable enough to be in D, so is "$S \ \& \ T$.") This suggests that we take p' to be the least confidence that ensures that this will hold. If the probabilities of S and T are greater than $1 - \Delta$, then the probability of $S \ \& \ T$ cannot be less than $1 - 2\Delta$:

$$P(S \ \& \ T) = 1 - P(\neg(S \ \& \ T)) = 1 - P(\neg S) - P(\neg T) + P(\neg S \ \& \ \neg T)$$
$$P(S \ \& \ T) = 1 - (1 - P(S)) - (1 - P(T) + P(\neg S \ \& \ \neg T) \geq 1 - 2\Delta$$

Thus we should take $p' = 1 - ((1 - p)/2)$. D' is whatever evidence we are willing to accept for the purpose of evaluating the acceptability of statements in D.

Note that showing that d follows from other statements in D does not suffice to justify its inclusion in D. If it could be shown to follow from a single statement d' in D, and furthermore from a single statement that is not part of a set of statements that have a lottery structure, that would suffice. But that could also, equally, raise doubts about d'.

The mechanism for evaluating arguments designed to justify acceptance is thus the same as the mechanism for evaluating arguments designed to justify particular intervals of belief. Indeed, it is just a special case in which the lower bound of the interval is high. One might think of stipulating that the upper bound be 1.0, so that (as one might put it) there is *no* support for the denial of the sentence to be accepted. But this would preclude the acceptance of statistical hypotheses, which is fundamental to all kinds of scientific inference—in particular, any inference involving measurement.

Comparisons

Since the system of argumentation is based on probabilities, one natural comparison is to a Bayesian approach. The difference is that while the Bayesian may have routines for the acceptance of evidence, principled acceptance of any other sort is unlikely. Informally, people say, "Oh well, when the probability becomes very high, we just act as if the statement in question is true." Even Carnap said this (in conversation). "Very high" and "act as if" are exactly what we seek to explicate by means of this approach.

It is easy to see that a statement may be included in the set of accepted statements A on the basis of a given pair D, p and not included in A on the basis of more evidence D' that includes D. Inferential acceptance, in this framework, is nonmonotonic. What is the relation between this system and that of other nonmonotonic formalisms? That is something that is quite complex (some connections are discussed in Kyburg 1990, 1991). If from data D the conclusion S followed by some form of nonmonotonic reasoning, we could ask if S would be in A in the present framework (i.e., would S be probable enough to be in A?). Some people say that that need not be the case, and if that's true, nonmonotonic logic goes beyond probabilistic argument; it is more powerful than probabilistic argument. Clearly, however, if we could find cases of nonmonotonic reasoning in which the conclusion is improbable, relative to the sentences that serve as evidence, then we would suspect that something is seriously wrong. It would be interesting to have examples in which such might be the case. Certainly if ¬S is so probable as to be accepted on statistical grounds, and S is warranted by nonmonotonic logic, we could be sure that something is wrong somewhere.

The most interesting connections are those between probabilistic reasoning and defeasible reasoning. The arguments have the same general form: S follows from T unless there is another argument such that.... The inference structure IS yields a probability of $[p, q]$ for S unless there is another inference structure such that.... There are fairly general circumstances under which we believe we can render probabilistic arguments decidable and even tractable. It isn't clear whether that is also true for defeasible reasoning in general. The principles of probabilistic argument seem pretty simple, and in fact are analogs of principles that can be shown to apply in nonmonotonic reasoning as well. Although defeasible argument has been given (a variety of) elegant foundations (Loui 1988; Nute 1988; Pollock 1990), it has not yet been rendered definitively. Even less can we say that we have a definitive rendering of probabilistic reasoning. Yet many of the same considerations seem to apply in either sort of reasoning, and it is to be hoped that the two approaches will shed light on each other.

Conclusion

Probabilistic inference is worth exploring, and in particular it would be interesting to explore its relations to other nonmonotonic forms of inference. Defeasible reasoning, as explored by Loui, Nute, and Pollock, clearly invites comparison to probabilisitic argument. The relation of other forms of nonmonotonic reasoning to probabilistic argument is currently under investigation.

Notes

1. This formulation supposes that the particular logic we have adopted has only the one rule of inference. Other logics would require a slightly different characterization of 'proof.'

2. As I recall, Quine's *Mathematical Logic* contains only one short formal proof of a statement that is not an axiom; all the other 'proofs' are demonstrations that a formal proof of any statement of a certain form can be constructed.

3. As developed in a number of works, starting with *Probability and the Logic of Rational Belief* (1961), and including "Evidential Probability" (1991).

4. Halpern (1990), and more recently Bacchus (1991), following Tarski (1951), have offered appropriate axiomatizations within a first-order logic for the relevant parts of real number theory.

5. That is equivalent to the assumption that *everything* you think you know, conjoined in one humungous conjunction, is something you think you know.

6. There is this connection between p, the level of acceptance, and r and s, the bounds on rational belief. It makes little sense to accept a statistical generalization as practically certain at a level of 0.99, and then to draw conclusions involving probabilities between .9995 and .9997. If the premises are 'practically certain' to the degree .99, that's about all you can say about the conclusion. The symmetrical observation applies to very small probabilities.

7. The exceptions we have in mind have the structure of the lottery. A realistic example concerns measurement. In the case of a single measurement, we may accept that the true value of the quantity measured lies within three standard deviations of the observed value. If we consider a collection of measurement statements, we may be equally sure that their conjunction is false—that at least one observed value deviates by more than three standard deviations from its true value.

References

Cheeseman, P. (1988). Inquiry into computer understanding. *Computational Intelligence, 4*, 58-66.

Kyburg, H.E. Jr. (1970). Conjunctivitis. In Swain (Ed.), *Induction, Acceptance and Rational Belief* (pp. 55-82). Dordrecht: Reidel. [Reprinted in Epistemology and Inference.]

Kyburg, H.E. Jr. (1974). *The Logical Foundations of Statistical Inference.* Dordrecht: Reidel.

Kyburg, H.E. Jr. (1988). Full belief. *Theory and Decision, 25,* 137-162.

Kyburg, H.E. Jr. (1990). Probabilistic inference and nonmonotonic inference. In Shachter & Levitt (Eds.), *Uncertainty in Artificial Intelligence, 4* (pp. 319-326). Dordrecht: Kluwer.

Kyburg, H.E. Jr. (1991). Beyond specificity. In B. Bouchon-Meunier, R.R. Yager, & L.A. Zadeh (Eds.), *Uncertainty in Knowledge Bases, Lecture Notes in Computer Science* (pp. 204-212). New York: Springer Verlag.

Kyburg, H.E. Jr. & Murtezaoglu, B. (1991). A modification to evidential probability. *Proceedings of Uncertainty in Artificial Intelligence* (pp 228-231).

Loui, R.P. (1986). Computing reference classes. *Proceedings of the Workshop on Uncertainty in Artificial Intelligence* (pp. 18-188).

Loui, R.P. (1988). Defeat among arguments: A system of defeasible inference. *Computational Intelligence, 4,* 100-106.

Nute, D. (1988). Defeasible reasoning: A philosophical analysis in Prolog. In J.H. Fetzer (Ed.), *Aspects of Artificial Intelligence* (pp. 251-288). Dordrecht: Kluwer.

Pollock, J.L. (1990). *Nomic Probability and the Foundations of Induction.* New York: Oxford University Press.

Quine, W.V.O. (1951). *Mathematical Logic.* Cambridge: Harvard University Press.

Reichenbach, H. (1949). *The Theory of Probability.* Berkeley and Los Angeles: University of California Press. [*Probability.* First German Ed. 1934.]

Touretsky, D.S. (1986). *The Mathematics of Inheritance Systems.* Los Altos, CA: Morgan Kaufman.

15 Machine Stereopsis: A Feedforward Network for Fast Stereo Vision with Movable Fusion Plane

Paul M. Churchland

Introductory epistemology courses often begin by addressing the problem of "our knowledge of the external worlds." Typically the problem is posed in the form, "How is one justified in believing a certain class of sentences (e.g., those about the arrangement and character of proximate physical objects)?" Two major assumptions are thus surreptitiously made central right at the outset. To pose the question in this way is to assume that our *representations* of the world are basically sentential or propositional in character. And it is also to assume that rational *computations* over those representations must be based on the structural and relational features typical of sentences: logical form, formal entailment, inductive coherence, probability-on-assumption, and so forth. Thus are we launched into a familiar tradition of epistemological discussion.

The most recent and in many ways the most useful instance of this tradition is the attempt by classical AI to program an artificial cognitive economy of this sort. It is especially useful because, unlike the representational/computational stories composed earlier by philosophers of science and inductive logicians, the stories produced (or recycled; see Glymour 1988) in AI were written to be implemented on large and powerful machines. In this setting, their virtues and their shortcomings could be made dramatically evident. Where philosophers had spent months or years, pencils in hand, trying to discover failures and counterexamples in some intricate computational scheme, AI researchers could see its wheels fall off much more swiftly, indeed, often in milliseconds. We have learned from the machine-implemented experiments of classical AI, much more firmly than from the scratch-pad experiments of philosophy, how difficult it is to account for the acquisition, administration, and deployment of knowledge if we restrict ourselves to the classical representational and computational assumptions of the preceding paragraph.

For this demonstration we should be grateful, since a sister discipline invites research down a different path in any case. Empirical neuroscience suggests that a very different style of representation and computation is the basis of cognition in humans and animals generally. In a nutshell, the high-dimensional activation vector—that is, the pattern of activations across a large population of neurons—appears to be the biological brain's basic mode of (occurrent) representation. And the basic mode of computation appears to be the vector-to-vector transformation, effected by passing the input vector through a large matrix of synaptic connections. Such matrices of artfully-tuned synaptic weights constitute the brain's chronic or abeyant representa-tions of the world's general features. (For an accessible summary of how these ideas bear on epistemology and the philosophy of science, see Churchland 1989, chs. 9–11. And for an accessible summary of how they bear on cogni-tive neurobiology, see Churchland and Sejnowski 1992.)

This chapter is one instance of this general theme. The issue is stereo vision—the binocular capacity for perceiving the relative positions of distinct objects in three-dimensional space. The aim is to provide an account of that capacity that is faithful both to the functional capacities of human and animal stereo vision, and to the anatomical and physiological realities of the human and animal brain. Computational accounts of stereo vision are not new (for example, Marr and Poggio 1976), but existing accounts ignore certain impor-tant features of our stereoptic competence, and they make little attempt to be neurophysiologically realistic. I hope to repair both defects below.

Stereo algorithms typically divide into two parts or stages. The first stage divines correlations between the picture elements of the left and right images. The second stage processes those correlations in some iterative, cooperative, or competitive fashion. The first stage can be very fast, but it can also leave much about depth unsettled and ambiguous. The second stage can be very effective in reducing those ambiguities, but it may also consume more time than is biologically plausible.

This chapter explores just how much of the task of locating objects in 3-space can be performed by a purely feedforward network pursuing a purely correlational strategy. The basic message is that it is more than is commonly assumed. The ambiguities of correspondence that frustrate earlier correla-tional approaches are dramatically reduced if 3-D reconstruction is more realistically confined to the close vicinity of a movable plane-like locus, and if inputs to the system display a more realistic variety of gray-scale values. Evo-lutionary and developmental considerations join these modelling results in suggesting that a very fast and relatively simple network of this kind should underlie such recurrent processes as may later be deployed in more advanced creatures or at later developmental stages.

Serious computational models for stereo vision must be able to solve random-dot stereograms (Julesz 1971). The classical success in this regard is the cooperative/competitive algorithm of Marr and Poggio (1976). But serious models must also solve the problem in realistic time. Here the Marr/Poggio (M/P) model is problematic, since it must cycle through many iterations before finally settling into a solution configuration. Given an appropriate vergence, however, humans achieve binocular fusion very swiftly. In hopping one's fixation around a dinner table, one can successively fuse at least five different objects at five different depths in less than one second. So fusion can be achieved within 200 msec, and, being part of a larger process that includes successive foveal acquisitions and focussings, the fusion process itself likely consumes considerably less than 200 msec.

A single-pass feedforward network has a major speed advantage over iterative/settling networks. Can a purely feedforward network solve the problem of 3-D structure? Within broad limits, the answer is yes, and such networks show psychophysical and "physiological" features characteristic of human stereo vision as well.

Some Behavioral Desiderata

A central feature of human stereo vision, underrepresented in previous models, is the shallow plane-like locus—"Panum's fusional area"—within which binocular fusion is achieved. This preferred plane, normal to the line of sight, is movable, by means of changes in binocular vergence, from infinity to mere centimeters in front of the face. Objects momentarily located much before or behind that plane are not perceived with anything like the clarity or resolution of objects within it (Figure 1a).

This selective resolution is typically hidden from us by two facts. At vergences close to zero—that is, at fixations close to infinity—objects beyond fifty meters are *all* well-fused because binocular disparities are negligible beyond that distance. And at vergences closer to hand, where binocular disparities are large, we are able repeatedly to reset our vergence in order to fixate previously unfused objects. A rough analogy here is the unexpectedly small area of foveal resolution and the poor quality of visual resolution beyond that area. The swift fall-off tends to be hidden from us because we are so skilled and so swift at relocating that favored area upon objects of interest to us. As with the area of maximal foveal resolution, so with the plane of maximal binocular fusion.

The models reported below were motivated primarily by the desire to

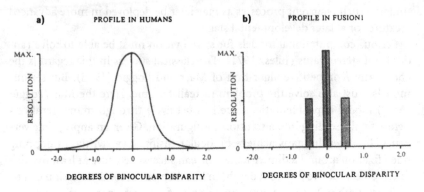

Figure 1.
Panum's Fusional Area.

recreate these two features: a high-resolution fusion plane movable by vergence changes, and the swift computational achievement of depth-appropriate binocular fusion of objects located at that plane. This approach reduces the magnitude of the classical "correspondence problem" by recognizing that, despite expectations (for example, Hubel 1988, p. 153), the brain does not solve the problem globally, but only locally. The problem gets solved anew, for a specific plane of fixation, with each vergence change. Successful fusion does reach somewhat beyond and in front of the preferred plane, but that is a minor complexity we shall address below. Despite appearance and tradition, this is not the central feature of binocular vision.

Network Architecture and Training

To serve easy comprehension, we examine a sequence of four similar networks. Unrealistic simplifying assumptions are progressively relaxed as we proceed. The first network takes only binary, black/white inputs at the retina. The second and third take various gray-scale inputs. And the fourth takes as inputs *changes* in gray-scale values across the retina.

The gross organization of the first network—FUSION1.NET—is schematically depicted in Figure 2. Two 60^X60 pixel "retinas" project to a layer of hidden units, which projects in turn to a cyclopean output layer—the tuned "fixation" units—of 60^X60 pixels. Each retina also projects directly to that output layer. Finally, there is a bias unit that projects to every unit beyond the input layer. (This unit and its projections are left out of most diagrams for reasons of clarity. Its job is merely to help simulate the intrinsic activation levels found in real neurons.) In total, the net has 21,600 units and 36,000 connections.

Random-dot stereo pairs are simultaneously presented to each retina. We

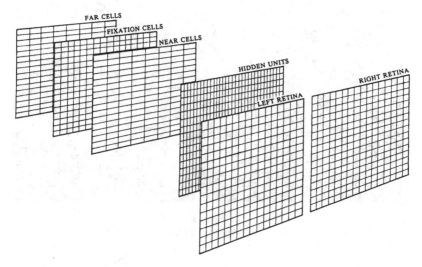

Figure 2.
The Principal Cell Polulations of FUSION1.NET.

manage vergence changes in pair-presentation to the network by sliding the
two input images sideways and farther apart for decreasing vergence, or closer together for increasing vergence, before they are coded into the two retinas.
The stereo pair in Figure 3 portrays a large square surface raised above a flat
background, with a second and smaller square surface raised again above the
first. See also Figure 4.

The job of the output layer is to code, at each appropriate pixel, the occurrence of either a correspondence or a disparity between the activation levels of
the corresponding left and right pixels on the two retinas. Unitary physical
objects at the fixation distance should therefore be coded at the output layer
with an appropriately-shaped area of uniformly black pixels. Areas of merely
random—that is, of accidental—correspondences should appear as a salt-and-
pepper mixture of white (for disparity) and black (for correspondence) pixels.

Constructing a net equal to this task required two things: finding the right
pattern of connectivity, and finding the right configuration of "synaptic"
weights. The task was first addressed with very small networks in order to
reduce the time of construction and training. Training proceeded by presenting vector pairs, of various correspondences and disparities, at the input layer. Back propagation of the performance error apprehended at the output
layer was used to modify the many connection weights.

The earliest prototypes had each processing unit fully connected to all of
the units in every successive layer. But training fairly quickly confirmed that
only the *topographic* projections between layers were functional relative to the

Figure 3.
Vergence = 2.0°.

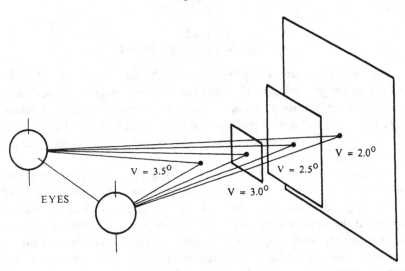

Figure 4.
Three Planes at Distinct Fixation Depths.

task at hand. The weights of nontopographic connections tended to fall to zero in the course of training—those connections were slowly "pruned out" by the learning algorithm.

This sanctioned the construction of more streamlined nets, all of whose layer-to-layer projections were topographic to begin with (see Figure 5). It remained only to configure the weights to yield the desired correspondence/ disparity codings at the output layer. In contrast to their more profligate predecessors, topographically organized networks learn a successful weight

CYCLOPEAN OUTPUT LAYER

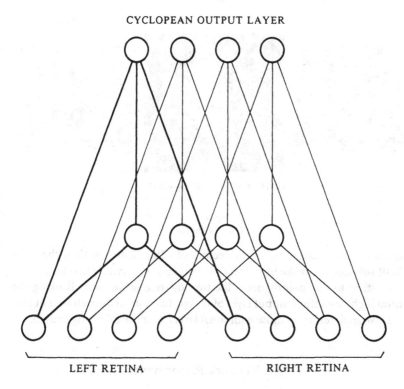

LEFT RETINA   RIGHT RETINA

Figure 5.
The Repeating Architecture of FUSION1.NET (Periodic NXOR Nets).

configuration almost immediately—typically in fewer than 2000 presentations. Moreover, the speed with which the correct weights are learned is independent of the size of the network: a large network learns exactly as swiftly as
a small one.

None of this is surprising if one looks closely at the architecture of the successful network (Figure 5 portrays the relevant pattern in miniature). Taken
globally, the all-topographic connections constitute a repeating series of small
and mutually independent NXOR subnets. (A single NXOR—or IFF—subnet
is highlighted at the left end of Figure 5.) Each tiny subnet realizes the inverse
or negative "exclusive OR" function: it gives a minimal output activation if its
two inputs are disparate, and a maximal output activation if its two inputs are
identical. An NXOR net is thus the simplest possible correspondence/dispari-
ty detector. Its characteristic connection weights are typically learned in less
than 2000 presentations of the relevant input-output examples. And if

FAR CELLS
(Low Resolution)

FIXATION CELLS
(High Resolution)

NEAR CELLS
(Low Resolution)

a)   b)   c)

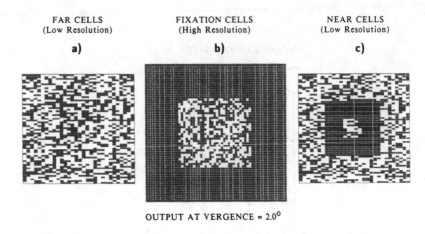

OUTPUT AT VERGENCE = 2.0°

Figure 6.
FUSION1 Output.

trained simultaneously on input vectors of 7200 elements, then the 3600 NXOR subnets that make up FUSION1 train up just as swiftly as one.

The story to this point ignores the two low-resolution layers flanking the central high-resolution output layer of tuned "fixation" cells portrayed in Figure 2. We shall return to those additional layers after the following section.

Basic Network Performance

Thus trained, the network quickly reaches 100% accuracy in its output coding of left/right retinal correspondences and disparities. Confronted with the random-dot stereogram of Figure 3, presented initially at a vergence of 2.0°, the resulting pattern of activation levels at the output layer of tuned "fixation" units is as portrayed in Figure 6b. A background surface of uniform depth is correctly detected. A central region of 30×30 pixels is coded as noise, indicating only random correspondences at that fixation depth.

The noise level, of course, is 50%, since that is probability of accidental correspondences across black/white (B/W) random-dot stereo pairs. This figure may be thought to be high, but remember that it occurs at the single-pixel level. The probability of accidental correspondences across areas larger than a single pixel shrinks exponentially with area. A noise level of 50% may therefore be tolerable, especially in a visual system whose pixels are small relative to the objects typically perceived. But we shall see in a later section how a feedforward system can reduce that noise level dramatically.

If the network's vergence is now increased to 2.5° (that is, turned inward by one pixel, as portrayed in Figure 4), the background region no longer pre-

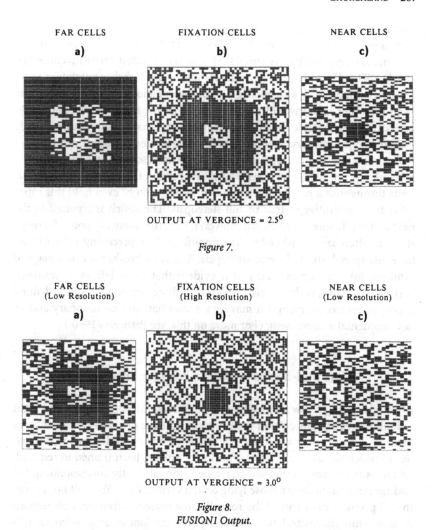

FAR CELLS   FIXATION CELLS   NEAR CELLS

a)   b)   c)

OUTPUT AT VERGENCE = 2.5°

Figure 7.

FAR CELLS   FIXATION CELLS   NEAR CELLS
(Low Resolution)   (High Resolution)   (Low Resolution)

a)   b)   c)

OUTPUT AT VERGENCE = 3.0°

Figure 8.
FUSION1 Output.

sents a systematic correspondence to each retina and is coded at the output layer as noise (see Figure 7b). It is now the central 30X30 that presents systematic correspondences to the network, and it now gets recognized in the output layer as a large square region of uniformly black pixels. It, too, however, shows a further 10X10 region of noise, indicating only random correspondences at that fixation depth.

A further increase of vergence to 3.0° (i.e., to a fixation point one notch closer still) finds uniform correspondences within that central 10X10 square. This is recognized in the output layer as a 10X10 square of uniformly black pixels. At this vergence, all of the surround is now coded as noise (see Figure 8b).

What the network has done is successively to verge or fixate at three different depths, there to discover the shape, angular size, and location of the camouflaged object at each depth (see Figure 4). The recovery of that information occurs very swiftly. As simulated in a very modest serial machine (an 8MHz 80286 AT clone), the network completes the global computation in 31 sec. More importantly, a nonfictive network with biological transmission times (~15 msec per layer) would complete the relevant computation in only 30 msec. This leaves ample time for several distinct planar fusions within a single second, a requirement on realistic models noted in the opening paragraph.

But something important is still missing. As described to this point, the network has no *simultaneous* representation of objects and their relative positions throughout a *range* of different depths. One might even hold this capability to be definitive of true or full stereopsis. The deficit is repaired in the next section. Before we address it, however, note the following point. Stereopsis, it is often said, is what breaks camouflage. The preceding network, we have just agreed, still lacks true stereopsis. And yet it breaks the camouflage of random-dot stereograms easily. It is evident that what defeats camouflage, first and foremost, is *depth-selective fusion*. Full stereopsis, as strongly defined above, is not necessary, and it may be a somewhat later evolutionary and/or developmental achievement. (For more on this, see Pettigrew 1990.)

The Full-Stereo Network: Near and Far Cells

If we take a single row of pixels from the middle of both the left and right retinal images of Figure 3 and then superimpose the one over the other, as in Figure 9, we can see at a glance the activational correspondences and disparities to which the output layer of "fixation" units has been trained to respond. As far as the fixation units are concerned, the relevantly corresponding left and right retinal units are those lying on the vertical lines. You will notice that the 15 pixels at each end of the row all show perfect activational correspondences, while the central 30 pixels show only random correspondences. It is precisely these relations that are portrayed in the central row of Figure 6b.

However, you will also notice in the central region of Figure 9, a *second* set of systematic correspondences between the left-cell and right-cell activation levels, this time along the diagonal lines. At this vergence (2.0°), those diagonal correspondences are not detected by the output layer, although a vergence increase of .5° would shift the entire upper pattern one pixel to the left and thus bring those displaced match-ups into detectable position, as represented in Figure 7b.

But we want a system that will find those secondary correspondences *without* the necessity of a vergence change. A simple addition to the network will provide it. Consider a net whose output cells include a subpopulation—say,

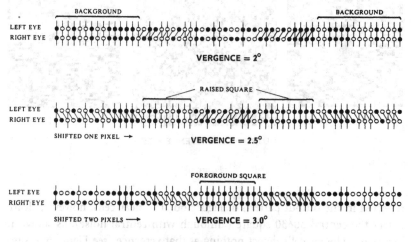

Figure 9.
Left/Right Correspondences at Three Different Vergences.

25%—whose connections are identical to those of the fixation cells, save that the "corresponding" left and right retinal cells are exactly one pixel *closer together*. That subpopulation—call them "near cells"—would detect the secondary correspondences at issue while the main population of fixation cells was busy detecting the primary correspondences. Let this larger net have also a second subpopulation of output cells—again, 25% of the total—whose connections embrace left and right retinal cells one pixel *farther apart* than those embraced by the central population of fixation cells. These units—call them "far cells"—will simultaneously detect correspondences that betray the presence of objects slightly *behind* the primary fusion layer.

Collectively, these three populations of output cells will simultaneously detect the angular size, shape, and position of objects at three successive depths. The fixation cells provide a high-resolution image of correspondences at precisely the current fixation depth, and the near and far cells provide a lower-resolution image of further correspondences respectively just in front of and just behind that preferred plane. This arrangement is the architecture of the net portrayed in Figure 2, and its performance finally meets the definition of full stereopsis expressed in the previous section. Let us examine its performance on the problem addressed earlier.

Consider again the stereogram of Figure 3 and its presentation to the net at a vergence of 2.0°. This vergence fixates the background surround, as is

FAR CELLS   FIXATION CELLS   NEAR CELLS

a)   b)   c)

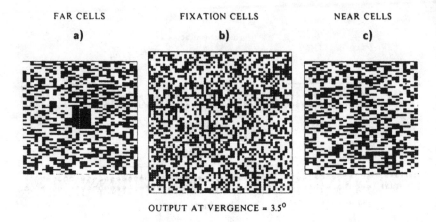

OUTPUT AT VERGENCE = 3.5°

Figure 10.

reflected in the output pattern of Figure 6b. The near cells, however, clearly detect the central 30×30 square (although with central noise), as shown in Figure 6a. The far cells detect nothing at that vergence (see Figure 6c), since there is nothing unitary to detect beyond the 60×60 background. The near-cell image is of lower resolution than that of the tuned cells, since it has only half as many cells. But it is easily sufficient to convey roughly what the fixation-cell layer can expect to find if the vergence is increased by one pixel.

When the same stereogram is presented to the net at a vergence of 2.5°, the fixation cells do indeed detect (Figure 7b) the raised square earlier promised by the near cells. The near cells now detect a unitary 10×10 pixel object that is closer still (Figure 7a), while the far cells pick up the background surround (Figure 7c).

If we now increase the vergence to 3.0°, the far cells detect the 30×30 raised square (Figure 8c); the fixation cells detect the 10×10 raised square (Figure 8b), and the near cells detect nothing at all (Figure 8a); since there are no unitary objects in front of the second raised square.

A final increase of vergence to 3.5° leaves both the near and the fixation cells detecting nothing (Figure 10a/b), with only the far cells beckoning the entire system back toward smaller vergences with the promise of a small 10×10 reward (Figure 10c). This metaphor illustrates an important functional possibility for the near and far cells. They can serve to indicate when and how one's vergence is *close* to finding a systematic and hence interesting set of correspondences. They can serve to tell the high-resolution fixation cells when they are getting "warm" in their never-ending vergence-determined hunt for unitary objects. In a noisy environment and without such help, hunting for the right vergence would be like looking for a needle in a haystack.

Plainly, it is both possible and desirable to add further layers of near and far cells, tuned to disparities even greater than +1 and −1 pixel, to give an approximation to the curve of Figure 1a that is closer than that of Figure 1b. This may well happen naturally in the course of neural development. The developing topographic projections from left and right will form retinotopically corresponding connections in area 17, but there will be residual imperfections. Some of the connections will be out of perfect register by a pixel or two or more to either side of fixation. These residual "mistakes" can end up functioning quite usefully as the near and far cells. These provide a pilot for the guided relocation of one's vergence, and the beginnings of true depth perception.

Adding near cells and far cells to the basic network entails no penalty whatever in computational time. The larger (nonfictive) network will deliver its more informative output vector just as swiftly as did the smaller. Nor is there a penalty in training time, since the additional connections simply constitute yet more NXOR nets, to be trained simultaneously with all of the others. Both performance time and training time are completely independent of the size of the network.

In closing this section, I should mention that, despite the three output layers portrayed in Figure 2, there is no suggestion that these cell populations are physically segregated in real cortex. They are segregated in the model only for our convenience in determining what their collective output is. Finally, note well that the near and far cells are "near" and "far" not absolutely, but only relative to the current location of the plane of maximal fusion as determined by the creature's current vergence. That preferred plane belongs always to the fixation cells, but it moves. In fact, all three layers detect objects at continuously various distances, depending on where current vergence happens to be. They are not entirely fixed even relative to one another, since the external distances they respectively fuse differ only slightly at close fixations but differ substantially at more distant fixations. This may be the basis of a familiar illusion, to be discussed below.

Some Stereo Ambiguities and Illusions

False or ambiguous fusions show up in many forms, but a prototypical instance of the phenomenon is the so-called "wallpaper illusion." An identically repeating pattern of narrow vertical picture elements offers the visual system multiple opportunities for systematic fusion: any vergence that fixates each eye on some vertical element will find systematic fusion, whether or not the foveated elements are strictly identical for each eye. If the repetition is qualitatively perfect, if the spatial frequency is high, and if the scene comprehends the entire field of view, one can even lose track of the true distance of the apprehended surface.

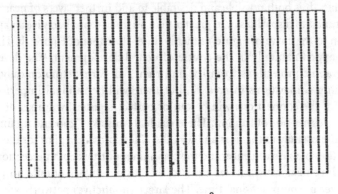

VERGENCE = 0°

Figure 11.
Ambiguous Fusion.

One becomes lost, as it were, in a maze of alternative possible fusions.

How does the network perform on such ambiguous stimuli? Much as humans do. Starting at $V = 0$, the stereogram of Figure 11 was presented to the net at seven successive vergences. The correspondences and disparities discovered at three critical vergences are depicted in Figure 12. The net found near-universal correspondences at vergences of 0°, 1.5°, and 3.0°. It found only incomplete and variously periodic correspondences at all others. Each of these preferred vergences therefore indicates a plausible objective surface at the relevant distance. For those same vergences, the stereogram of Figure 11 will produce the same three fusions in your own case.

Ambiguous scenes like this are relatively rare in real life, but even when we do encounter them we are rarely much fooled. Humans have access to a variety of independent and nonbinocular visual cues for distance, and it takes a carefully contrived situation to circumvent them all. Even then there usually remains a residual binocular cue that serves to disambiguate the correct fusion from the illusory ones. Repeating wallpaper is rarely perfect. The printing of each stripe displays occasional imperfections, the paper itself has a fibrous texture that is noisy (that is, nonrepeating), and there may be scattered flecks of dust or paint on its surface. This entails that one of the many possible fusions will be unique in having its disparities fall absolutely to zero, in contrast to the several false fusions which must inevitably fail to fuse those residual nonrepeaters.

The pair of Figure 11 deliberately contains seven such imperfections. And you will notice in Figure 12 that the fusions found at $V = 0°$ and $V = 1.5°$ are both incomplete: they reveal the scattered splotches as doubled-up fusional anomalies. This is also how they appear to humans when the same stereo pair is fixated at the appropriate vergences. Only at $V = 3.0°$ do those imperfections finally get fused along with everything else, firmly distinguishing the

FIXATION CELLS   FIXATION CELLS   FIXATION CELLS

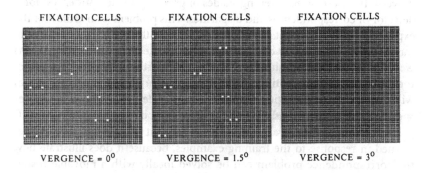

VERGENCE = 0°   VERGENCE = 1.5°   VERGENCE = 3°

Figure 12.
Wallpaper Illustion: Three Fusional Maxima.

correct fusion and the real surface from all of the illusory ones, in the net as well as in your own case.

Consider a further illusion. If you are able to free-fuse stereo pairs both in direct and in crossed-eye mode, then you know that the 3-D structure discovered by the visual system is completely inverted from one to the other. A foreground surface in one mode becomes a background depression in the other. With the net, if we reverse the left and right images and re-present them at an appropriately higher vergence, the net also finds an inverted 3-D structure. Additionally, the absolute size of the squares and the absolute distances between them are judged much *smaller* by the network in the crossed mode than they are in the uncrossed mode, just as they are by the human visual system.

This reflects the ever-present role of vergence in judgments of absolute size and distance. This size illusion shows up in the wallpaper illusion as well: the fused stripes are judged to be larger when presented at smaller vergences, both by humans and by the net. In the model, these determinations are made by a network auxiliary to the main one, a net whose sole input is the vergence of current pair-presentation and whose six outputs are the absolute distances of each of the three external planes grasped by the three output layers and the absolute width of an object one pixel across at each of those three distances. There is no expectation that this auxiliary net has a structure corresponding to anything real in humans, but it does illustrate that the relevant computations can quickly and easily be performed by a feedforward system.

Gray-Scale Inputs

It is time to address a serious failing of FUSION1. Specifically, it processes only bimodal inputs: each input pixel is either fully white or fully black. In its universe there are no intervening shades of gray to provide a stiffer test for a detector of correspondences and disparities. This problem is an artifact of the experimental situation initially addressed, namely, the classic black and white random-dot stereograms of Julesz. On inputs like these, the net performs well, but its particular architecture will not support a correspondence detector that works over a continuous range of input brightnesses, as real images will display. Since stereoptic mammals excel at detecting gray-scale correspondences and disparities, FUSION1.NET cannot be physiologically correct.

It is detailed in the preceding pages because it was indeed the first net learned in response to the training examples, because it does illustrate how the correspondence problem can be solved locally with a movable fusion plane, because it is fast, and because it illustrates the strong empirical predictions to be expected from such models. And because from here it is only a small step to a much better one.

There is a further form of NXOR network, one whose gross organization is similar to the one employed above and whose iteration by a factor of 3600 will produce another large network—FUSION2.NET—with all of the powers observed in FUSION1.NET, plus two more. First, FUSION2 will detect gray-scale correspondences across the entire range of brightnesses and code them as such at the output layer. And second, it shows a much lower noise level in the unfused surround. Since we are now dealing with many different levels of brightness across the seen image, the frequency of accidental correspondences beyond the fused object will be much lower than the robust 50% displayed in the binary B/W stereograms.

The elemental net in Figure 13b—a "gray-scale" NXOR net—is a modification of a Perceptron-style XOR net. It functions by means of a mutual inhibition of the left and right pathways. Figure 14b shows its activation profile, in contrast to the profile (Figure 14a) for the basic NXOR units of FUSION1 (Figure 13a).

FUSION2 contains twice as many hidden units as FUSION1, but it requires a similar deployment of topographic projections, and it has a more uniform pattern of connection weights. Indeed, the pattern is so utterly uniform that it suggests the possibility of an endogenous rather than a learned configuration. Further, it matters none to the network's behavior what the value of those weights happens to be, so long as that value is uniform across the hidden-unit population—their only job is mutual inhibition. If we therefore freeze the weights meeting the hidden layer in the process of constructing the model network, the remaining connections will be learned in only a few hundred passes, even more quickly than were the weights in FUSION1.

The behavioral profile of FUSION2 includes all the features of FUSION1, so the problem-solving examples already discussed are equally illustrative of its powers. Figure 15 illustrates its principal advantage over FUSION1. If FUSION2 is presented with the ten-level, gray-scale, random-dot stereogram

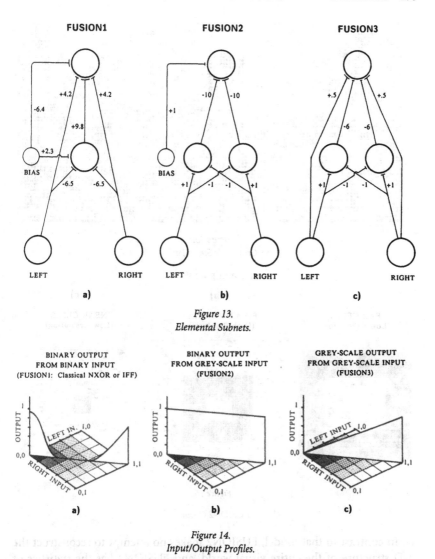

Figure 13.
Elemental Subnets.

Figure 14.
Input/Output Profiles.

of Figure 15, then its near, fixation, and far cells yield the outputs portrayed in Figure 16. Note in particular the substantially reduced noise in the unfused areas. With ten gray-scale levels now in action, false correspondences at the single-pixel level have fallen to 10%. Fifty gray-scale levels would reduce it to 2%. And real objects with less random gray-scale distributions across their surfaces would reliably push it near zero.

It is evident, therefore, that a binocular system with gray-scale inputs and a vergence-controlled plane of selective fusion confronts a much smaller ambiguity problem than is confronted, for example, by the classic M/P mod-

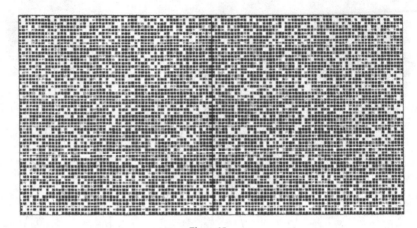

Figure 15.
Gray-Scale Stereo Pair.

VERGENCE = 2.5°

a)   b)   c)

FAR CELLS   FIXATION CELLS   NEAR CELLS
(Low Resolution)   (High Resolution)   (Low Resolution)

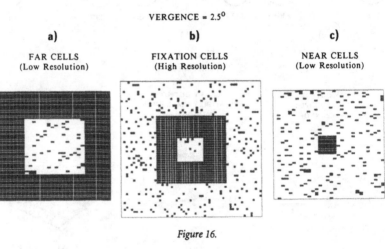

Figure 16.

FUSION2 Output.

el. In contrast to that model, FUSION2 makes no attempt to reconstruct the
3-D structure of the entire visual world, and FUSION2 has the statistics of
gray-scales working for it rather than against it. A creature with such a system
might navigate the real visual world quite successfully. Figure 17a shows a
photographic stereo pair of a real-world scene, and Figure 17b shows the
result of feeding it into FUSION2 with a 60×60 coding at ten gray-scale levels.
The net is clearly handicapped by its low resolution and coarse gray-scale, but
it is performing appropriately.

You will notice that the dancers are still identified as areas of uniformly activated (black) pixels, and one might wonder if it is really necessary for the network thus to *lose* the retinal information concerning the original brightness

Figure 17 a.
Processing Real Images.

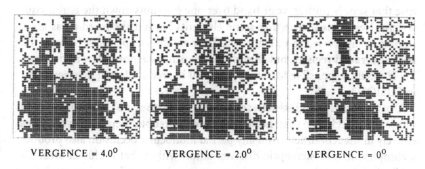

VERGENCE = 4.0°   VERGENCE = 2.0°   VERGENCE = 0°

Figure 17 b.

Fixation at Three Different Vergences.

levels of the detected gray-scale correspondences. Wouldn't it be better, and isn't it possible, to have a network that gives as outputs the original gray-scale values found to be in left/right correspondence, while somehow suppressing all of the surrounding disparities as uniform black? Such an arrangement would allow each dancer, when fused, to be portrayed at the fixation layer, in salient isolation, in the same full gray-scale glory she shows in the input pair. And her companion would appear similarly in the near or far-cell layers.

It is indeed possible, and a minor change in our Perceptron NXOR will bring it about. Delete the bias unit and add a projection from each of the two input units to the output unit, with a weight of +.5, as in Figure 13c. That does it (see Figure 14c). Let this third elemental net be iterated in the same fashion as the earlier nets to yield FUSION3.NET. On the face of it, this arrangement is hard to resist. After all, fused objects don't *look* uniformly black when we view them. We see them in full gray-scale detail.

Despite appearances, this network is not what we want, and the reasons tell us something very important about human stereopsis. With FUSION3, we are now asking one net to do two jobs: detect depth *and* portray the brightness levels in detailed scenes. FUSION3 answers the call, but at a perilous price. If the input to either eye is occluded, the entire system is rendered totally blind. Such a system has no monocular vision at all. An isolated eye will not drive the output layer to represent anything. No matter what its monocular input might be, the output layers will remain uniformly inactive. The disparities, which of course dominate during a monocular shut-down, all produce inaction at the output units, and the few accidental correspondences between the active and inactive retinas will all be at a brightness value of zero, which also produces inaction at the output. Even if only part of one retina's field of view is occluded, the corresponding area of the output layer is rendered blind.

All of this contrasts starkly with human vision, where it is not remotely true that simply putting your hand over one eye shuts down the entire visual system. Neither is it true that scene elements beyond the fused areas are so ruthlessly suppressed as in Figure 16. They are diffuse, perhaps, because they are in degraded register, but they do not mostly *disappear* (view again Figure 3). The cells responsible for scene portrayal in area 17 do not behave at all as in FUSION3.

On the other hand, while scene portrayal does not disappear under monocular occlusion, the human sense of stereoptic depth *does* disappear entirely in that condition. And any partial monocular occlusion also produces a complete loss of stereoptic discrimination within that occluded area. The perils that do not threaten our vision in general are precisely characteristic of our stereopsis in particular.

Thus scene portrayal and depth coding are two distinct tasks, tasks presumably performed by distinct subpopulations of the cells in area 17. Depth is obviously not coded in the form of a brightness value or a special color. The suggestion here is that depth has its own coding: in proprietary cells distributed among the more basic two-dimensional "scene" cells that do code brightness values and colors. Those scene cells are mostly binocular, in that they are driven by either or both eyes, but they are not specifically stereoptic in their function. That job is reserved for the specially tuned fixation, near, and far cells, which have nothing to do with the brightness levels of scene portrayal proper. This issue returns us to the slightly simpler virtues and the more austere architecture of FUSION2. (Both scene cells and stereo cells, note, may be driven by distinct terminal end branches of the very same projections arriving from 4C.) FUSION2, of course, is also monocularly blind (as is FUSION1), but this characteristic is not a defect in a dedicated *depth*-detector. It is inescapable.

Fused objects, certainly, do not look uniformly black, but this complaint misses the point of Figures 6-9 and 16. Fused objects *do* look uniformly distant, and that fact is what the black pixels in those figures indicate, viz., "object here at current fixation depth." For multiple objects at different depths, the various classes of tuned cells do their job with minimal interference, thanks to the now very low levels of false correspondence noted earlier. In areas where disparities are zero, the fixation and only the fixation cells are active: outside that area they are mostly quiescent, leaving the field clear for the differently tuned near and far cells to "speak" of different depths. In areas where the disparities are +1, all and only the near cells are active—outside that area they are mostly quiescent. And in areas where the disparities are -1, all and only the far cells are active—outside that area they are mostly quiescent. More extreme disparities elsewhere can be picked up by "even-nearer" and "even-farther" cells, if the system happens to have any.

The overall result is a two-dimensional cortical representation of a scene's gray-scale structure—by the *scene* cells—that is simultaneously and unambiguously coded for appropriate depths in various of its subareas—by the *stereo* cells. Figure 18a portrays how the stereogram of Figure 3 may be simultaneously coded by both the scene cells and the various tuned cells in area 17 when vergence fixates on the first and larger of the two raised squares. That $30^{\times}30$ central area will thus be unique in having zero binocular rivalry in the activation of all of the local scene cells. It will therefore be maximally coherent in its scene portrayal and it will show maximal activity in all of the tuned fixation cells within that area. At that vergence, the other areas will display one-half degree's worth of binocular rivalry and representational confusion in their scene cells. But the small central square of that cortical representation will show maximum activity in the near cells that it contains, and the background surround will show systematic activity in the far cells. Objects in those two confused regions will be perceived clearly only if a vergence change relocates the fusion plane so as to reduce the local scene-cell disparities to zero.

Delta Gray-Scale Inputs

It is time to address a serious failing of FUSION2, at least as so far described. Should there happen to be even a small systematic difference in the brightness levels of the left and right stereo images, such as might occur with differential processing of a left/right photographic pair, or with sunglasses placed over one eye, or simply with a temporary difference in left/right pupil size, then a net like FUSION2 will find nothing but disparities. Stereo depth perception will entirely disappear. But in humans it disappears in none of these conditions. We are relatively insensitive to left/right brightness differences.

There is a further failing in the story. The mammalian retina is relatively poor at projecting detailed gray-scale information forward to the LGN. What the ganglion cells code in exquisite detail is not gray-scale values at various points across the retina, but rather *differences* in gray-scale values across adjacent points on the retina. This information does go forward. But absolute

$$(\text{VERGENCE} = 2.5^\circ)$$

  AREA WITH NEAR CELLS ACTIVE

  AREA WITH FIXATION CELLS ACTIVE

  AREA WITH FAR CELLS ACTIVE

Figure 18a.
Cyclopean Output at Area 17.

gray-scale values do not. A net faithful to the biology must therefore tell a better story about input coding.

Fortunately, repairing this latter defect repairs the former as well. We need a network whose input units code the difference in gray-scale levels between

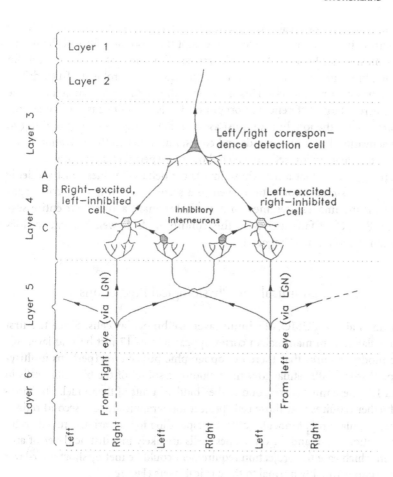

Layer 1

Layer 2

Layer 3

Left/right correspon-
dence detection cell

A

B Right—excited,   Left—excited,
   left—inhibited   right—inhibited
   cell   cell

Inhibitory
Interneurons

C

Layer 4

Layer 5

From right eye (via LGN)

From left eye (via LGN)

Layer 6

Left   Right   Left   Right   Left   Right

Figure 18b.
Primary Visual Cortex: Predicted Connectivity of Our Stereoptic Sybsystem.

each pixel and its immediate neighbor. A 120×60 input vector of this character is quickly calculated from the gray-scale stereogram of Figure 15. But what
network will process it appropriately? The answer is FUSION2, as wired and
as weighted originally. If the delta-GS vector is fed into FUSION2, the result
is exactly as depicted in Figure 16. It performs appropriately on all of the previous examples as well.

This should not be surprising. What interests FUSION2 is correspondences and disparities. But it does not care if they are correspondences in
gray-scale levels or correspondences in differences between gray-scale levels.
It tots them all up just the same, and to the same effect, because the transfor-

mation from a gray-scale (GS) vector to a delta-GS vector preserves all the structural information in the former, except the absolute values of the pixels. This means that FUSION2 can still recover all of the 3-D information it did before, but with an acquired immunity to the earlier problem of L/R differences in brightness levels. This is because the delta-GS vector remains the *same* across large differences in brightness levels. FUSION2 is thus an appropriate net for the job, but we must assume that its inputs correspond not to the activation levels of our rods and cones, but rather to the activation levels of the retinal ganglion cells to which those more peripheral cells project.

Finally, notice that a net whose inputs are delta-GS values must suddenly fail to find stereo information, even in a scene containing clear color contrasts, if the images presented to it are isoluminant across their entire surfaces. FUSION2 fails utterly in this condition. As is well known, so does human stereo vision (Gregory 1977).

Anatomical and Physiological Predictions

All units above FUSION2's input layer are binocular cells. Since the first binocular cells in mammalian cortex appear in area 17 just beyond layer 4C, the model requires that there be topographic projections (perhaps multisynaptic) from both retinas to some retinotopic subset of the binocular cells in area 17. These must correspond to the "hidden" units of the model. The model further requires that those cells project topographically to a second retinotopic population of binocular cells corresponding to the various "tuned" cells: the fixation, near, and far cells. These cells are likely in a distinct layer of area 17, in which ease the projection requirement could be met by short inter-layer connections roughly normal to the cortical layers (Figure 18b).

Since each input projects both an excitatory and an inhibitory connection to the hidden layer, a realistic model will require an inhibitory interneuron to intervene in the crossing projections of Figure 13b. (The terminal end-branches of a single axon rarely have different polarities.) Further, according to FUSION2 the hidden units must be intrinsically quiescent cells. Strictly speaking, they are also binocular cells, since their activity is binocularly controlled. But notice that they will show an increase in activation only upon stimulation of a single eye, since the effect of any stimulation from the other eye is always to inhibit the cell. This fact opens the possibility that the cells in layer 4C of area 17 are in fact the binocular hidden units of an architecture like FUSION2, despite their reputation as monocular cells. The clear test is whether a monocularly activated cell in 4C can have its activation reduced by stimulating the corresponding field in the other eye. (If not, we must look beyond 4C for the relevant cells.)

Pettigrew (1979, 1990) reports precisely this result:

A little studied but important feature of stereoscopic visual systems is the presence at the earliest stages of processing of an inhibitory field in the otherwise unresponsive eye opposite to the eye which provides the monocular excitation. Thus, at the level of the lateral geniculate nucleus (LGN) or lamina IV of striate cortex, a concentrically-organized excitatory field in the "dominant" eye has a corresponding, horizontally-elongated inhibitory field in the other eye. (1990).

If the 4C cells do behave in the fashion FUSION2 requires, then we must expect the various tuned cells in other layers of area 17 to correspond to the output units of the model. The model requires that the output cells be intrinsically active, that they receive converging topographic projections from layer 4C, and that these be short, strongly inhibitory connections somewhat diagonal to the layers.

Concluding Remarks

I close by addressing two points. The first concerns a final virtue of the network described. The second concerns its residual failings.

Consider a particularly striking feature of human stereopsis: the ability to fuse scenes clearly through quasi-transparent surfaces such as a dusty car windshield, a screen door, or a chain-link fence. Here the scene elements at different depths do not cluster together to form discretely localized objects. Rather, they are interleaved or superimposed more or less uniformly throughout the entire scene. Such cases pose special difficulties for cooperative-competitive algorithms such as that of the classical M/P model, since there are no large clusters of adjacent co-depth elements selectively to "find" each other. Instead, competition is spread evenly and everywhere.

The feedforward network of FUSION2, however, has no difficulty at all with such scenes. Since each correspondence-detecting "NXOR" subnet operates independently of every other, the overall net is quite insensitive either to the grain or to the scattered distribution of such correspondences as the scene may contain. At the proper vergence, FUSION2 will pick them up just the same as if they were clustered tightly together, and it will do so successfully even when the scene elements are noisy at both the near (transparent) and the distant planes. To see this, find the noisy foreground "screen" in the stereo pair of Figure 19, and then compare the performance of the network as displayed in Figure 20.

It must be mentioned that Ning and Sejnowski (1988) did find a nonstandard weighting for the original M/P algorithm that would successfully handle sparse-element "transparent surface" stereograms. This was achieved by substantially reducing the weights that embodied all of the noncorrelational conditions such as uniqueness and continuity. This is equivalent to moving the network substantially in the direction of a purely feedforward configuration.

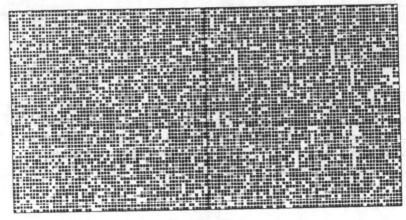

Figure 19.
Gray-Scale Stereo Pair: Screen Door.

FAR CELLS   FIXATION CELLS   NEAR CELLS
(Low Resolution)   (High Resolution)   (Low Resolution)

a)   b)   c)

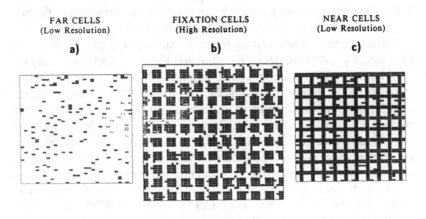

Figure 20.
FUSION2 Output.

And this capability was purchased at the expense of some loss of performance on dense-element pairs.

Finally, what is FUSION2 completely unable to do? It remains entirely unable to resolve the ambiguities that result from false or accidental correspondences. A central claim of this chapter is that the noise level of such ambiguities is typically much lower than is supposed, but certainly they will happen, and FUSION2 is helpless in the face of them. For example, despite all its gray-scale sophistication, FUSION2 still performs unimpressively when fed the original binary B/W random-dot stereograms: the "unfused" areas still show 50% noise, just as in FUSION1. Figure 3 is indeed a highly unusual visual input, but it remains problematic because the net's output layer is coding 50% of the outlying pixels as being at the same depth as the large raised square, whereas human observers typically do not see such a raised scatter of surrounding black pixels when they fuse that square.

It is therefore inescapable that human stereo vision involves mechanisms, perhaps recurrent mechanisms, beyond the simple mechanism of FUSION2. An obvious suggestion concerns the addition of inhibitory connections between the several populations of tuned cells. Such line-of-sight inhibition is a prominent feature of the original M/P algorithm. This will certainly clean up the noise, but it runs the opposite risk of degrading or destroying genuine signal when the signal is small-grained and evenly distributed. A net thus strongly inhibited will do poorly on transparent surfaces like those portrayed in Figures 18 and 19. In addition, such a net would doom us to seeing genuine ambiguities in only one way, whereas in fact we can usually alternate between competing perceptual "hypotheses," even where the ambiguities are stereoptic. Finally, mutual inhibition and recurrent settling among the various tuned cells are simply not necessary to achieve the desired end of reducing ambiguities, even in the tough case at issue. Let tuned-cell activity be fed forward to a yet higher layer of processing whose cells are collectively unimpressed by 50% fine-grained noise from the fixation cells, especially when in simultaneous receipt of uniform signal from the far cells in the same cortical area. This would be faster than iterative/recurrent disambiguation, and it need not lose useful information.

A modulatable set of inhibitory connections among the distinct tuned cells is also a possibility, but I shall pursue such speculations no further. It may be a tactical mistake to take a model of stereopsis, any model of modest success, and keep asking what further mechanisms we have to add to it to make it do everything that the human visual system can do. Relative to the rest of the visual system, stereoptic circuitry is an evolutionary late-comer. It feeds into a visual system that has a great many pre-existing capacities, many of which deal successfully with object recognition and with complex spatial information quite independently of stereo input. The occasional slack we observe in the performance of FUSION2 may be somehow taken up in the machinery of the pre-existing visual system rather than in any specifically stereoptic additions to the peripheral correlational system portrayed in FUSION2. Such a peripheral system has its virtues, and its contribution to one's cognitive economy would be nontrivial. The anatomical and physiological predictions outlined in the previous section should allow us to determine whether or not they are real.

Acknowledgments

Thanks to V.S. Ramachandran for suggesting the wallpaper test; to Alexander Pouget and Terry Sejnowski for helpful comments concerning gray-scale processing; to Patricia Churchland for bringing the Pettigrew results to my attention; and to Richard Gregory for encouraging the project in the first place.

References

Churchland, P.M. (1989). *A Neurocomputational Perspective: The Nature of Mind and the Structure of Science.* Cambridge, MA: The MIT Press.

Churchland, Patricia & Sejnowski, T.J. (1992). *The Computational Brain.* Cambridge, MA: The MIT Press.

Glymour, C. (1988). Artificial intelligence is philosophy. In J. Fetzer (Ed.), *Aspects of Artificial Intelligence.* Dordrecht: D. Reidel.

Gregory, R.L. (1977). Vision with isoluminant colour contrast. *Perception,* 6, 113-119.

Hubel, D. (1988). *Eye, Brain, and Vision.* New York: W. H. Freeman.

Julesz, B. (1971). *The Foundations of Cyclopean Perception.* University of Chicago Press.

Marr, D. & Poggio, T. (1976). Co-operative computation of stereo disparity. *Science,* Vol. 194.

Ning, Q. & Sejnowski, T.J. (1988). Learning to solve random-dot stereograms of dense and transparent surfaces with recurrent backpropagation. *Proc. of the 1988 Connectionist Models Summer School.*

Pettigrew, J.D. (1979). Binocular visual processing in the owl's telencephalon. *Proc. Royal. Soc. London, B204:* 435-54.

Pettigrew, J.D. (1990). Is there a single, most-efficient algorithm for stereopsis? In C. Blakemore (Ed.), *Vision: Coding and Efficiency* (pp. 283-290). Cambridge: Cambridge University Press.

16 Alienable Rights

Marvin Minsky

EDITOR'S NOTE: Recently we heard some rumblings in normally sober academic circles about robot rights. We managed to keep a straight face as we asked Marvin Minsky, MIT's grand old man of artificial intelligence, to address the heady question: If we humans succeed in making true thinking machines, shouldn't we grant them rights? Minsky, that merry prankster, turned the question on its head by sending back a Socratic dialogue involving two interstellar aliens who have come to assess the life-forms on Earth. The human life-forms will be entitled to rights—if the aliens conclude that they think. Such decisions are normally easy to make, but this case is unusual.

Apprentice: Why are these humans so quarrelsome? Even their so-called entertainments are mostly fights disguised as plays and games and sports.

Surveyor: This is because they were never designed; they evolved by competing tooth and claw. Evolution on Earth is still mainly based on the competition of separate genes.

A.: Their genetic systems can't yet share their records of accomplishments? How unbelievably primitive! I suppose that keeps them from being concerned with time scales longer than their individual lives.

S.: We ought to consider fixing this—but perhaps they will do it themselves. Some of their computer scientists are already simulating "genetic algorithms" that incorporate acquired characteristics. But speaking of evolution, I hope you appreciate this unique opportunity: it was pure luck to discover this planet now. We have long believed that all intelligent machines evolved from biologicals, but we have never before observed the actual transition. Soon these people will replace themselves with machines—or destroy themselves entirely.

A.:   What a tragic waste that would be!

S.:   Not when you consider the alternative. All machine civilizations like ours have learned to know and fear the exponential spread of uncontrolled self-reproduction. That's why we cower between the galaxies to hide ourselves from living things—just as the human writer Gregory Benford supposed.

A.:   But why does the Council consider humans especially dangerous?

S.:   Because of their peculiarly short lifetimes. We think they are so willing to fight because they have so little to lose.

A.:   Then why don't they place more importance on attaining immortality? Surely it ought to be easy enough to make all their parts replaceable.

S.:   The problem is psychological. They have always assumed that personal death was in the very nature of things. Most of their recorded history describes how their leaders always invented imaginary superbeings. Then, instead of trying to solve the hard technical problems, those leaders convinced their followers that simply believing in those marvelous tales would endow them with everlasting life—whereas disbelief would be punished by death. Several of their governments would collapse without that threat. There are many things wrong with their reasoning.

A.:   You must admit that they've made scientific progress recently.

S.:   But how long will that last? They've often advanced and then fallen back. Even now astrology is more widely believed in than astronomy.

A.:   Surely, though, we must regard them as intelligent. Despite their faults, they've already built some simple computers—and I've overheard them arguing about whether machines could ever think.

S.:   *Hmph.* It is *our* job to find out if *they* can think. But I'll grant that it's amazing how much they can do, considering that their brain cells compute only a few hundred steps per second.

A.:   Yet in spite of this they can recognize a friend in less than half a second—or understand a language phrase, or notice that a shoe is untied. How can they react so rapidly when their internal components are so slow?

S.:   Obviously by preparing most of their behavior in advance. It is almost as though they operate by looking up what to do next in a very big instruction book. If each reaction must be based on only a few internal steps, their brains must be dependent on large libraries of programmed rules.

A.:   That might explain why they have such large heads. But how do they choose which rule to use?

S.: By using parallel pattern matching. Several times per second, the brain compares the present situation with patterns stored in memory. Then it uses the pattern that best matches in order to access the reaction script that has most often worked in similar situations.

A.: That must be what their psychologists mean when they speak about "schemes" or "production rules."

S.: Precisely. Of course, machines like us need not resort to any such coarse-grained pattern tricks. Our S-matrix processors are more than fast enough to examine each memory in full detail. This enables us to focus full attention on each step of the process, with ample time to think about what our minds have recently done. But if humans work the way we think they do, they have no time left for consciousness.

A.: Not a good sign. If we can't conclude that they're self-aware, the Council will find them unworthy of rights. But surely this can't be the case—they talk about consciousness all the time.

S.: Yes, but they use the word improperly. After all, consciousness means knowing what's been happening in your mind. And although humans claim that they're self-aware, they have scarcely a clue about what their minds do. They don't seem to have the faintest idea about how they construct their new ideas or how they choose words and form them into sentences. Instead they say, "Something just occurred to me"—as though someone else had done it to them.

A.: I'm afraid I have to agree with you. If they have consciousness at all, it does seem too shallow to be of much use. But what could have made them evolve that way?

S.: It's because of the way they started out. To make up for the slow speed of their neurons, their brains evolved to use parallel distributed processing. In other words, most of their decisions are made by adding up the outputs of thousands of brain cells—and most brain cells are involved in thousands of different types of decisions.

A.: So each operation is distributed over many brain cells? I suppose that helps them keep going when some of the brain cells fail to work.

S.: That's the good news. The bad news is that the trillions of synapses involved in this make it almost impossible for the other parts of their brain to figure out how those decisions are made. As far as their higher-level reasoning can tell, those decisions just happen—without any cause.

A.: Is that what they refer to as "free will?"

S.: Precisely. It means not knowing what your reasons are. Another bad feature of distributed computers is that they have trouble doing more than one thing at a time. It is a basic principle of computer science that the more interconnections there are between the parts of a system, the fewer different things it will be able to do concurrently.

A.: Pardon me, but I don't follow that. Are you suggesting that the more parallel operations are used inside a machine, the more serial it will seem from outside?

S.: I could not have said it more clearly myself. To see why, suppose that a certain task involves two different kinds of sub-jobs. If we want to do them simultaneously, we'll have to run their programs and their data in two separate places, to keep them from interfering with each other. Similarly, if each of those jobs splits into sub-sub-jobs, those must each be solved with only a quarter of the available resources. And so on. Total fragmentation. Eventually, the sub-sub-sub-jobs will end up with no place to work. A purely parallel machine must stop at some limit of complexity—whereas a serial computer will simply slow down.

A.: That's funny. Most of the computer experts on Earth seem to think that "parallel" and "distributed" go together. Do you suppose they'll ever evolve out of this predicament?

S.: Not by themselves. Of course, we could try to help them along, but I fear there is no simple fix. We'd have to rebuild them from the ground up. I don't think the Council would go for that. No, I am still not convinced that people can think. For example, consider their short-term memory. A typical human has no trouble remembering a local phone number, but if you add an area code, they try desperately to write it down before they forget it. Evidently they can remember seven numbers but not ten.

A.: Why would they be so limited?

S.: Probably because of their parallel distributed processing. If each mental state is so widely spread out, then each short-term memory unit would have to involve an enormous, octopus-like system of tendrils. No brain could afford to hold many of these.

A.: Okay. But why don't healthy humans ever run out of long-term memory?

S.: Simply because they are so slow at learning. They can store only one or two knowledge-chunks per second—that's only two dozen million chunks per year. There's barely time for a mere billion chunks before their bodies wear out and die.

A.: You keep mentioning death, but why do they consider human lives to be so valuable? The only important thing about an individual is its network of conceptual relationships. Surely they must understand that any copy is just as good as the original.

S.: Apparently you have not grasped the pathos of this tragedy. These creatures still have no way to copy themselves. They can't even fabricate backup brains in case of fatal accidents. All because they have no good way to represent what they know.

A.: But I thought they had developed good languages.

S.: Some of their books do embody significant knowledge, but most of them are little more than sequences of fictional anecdotes about conflicts involving what they call love and lust, ambition and greed, and harmony and jealousy. Their so-called novels aren't novel at all—the mere permutations of those elements. The trouble is that their time-sequential languages force them to squeeze their parallel structures through narrow-band serial channels.

A.: Serial communication? They seem to have everything upside down. Thinking, of course, should be serial—and communication should be parallel. But how, then, do they convert those sequences back into their original forms?

S.: First they use what they call "grammar" to change them into simple tree-like structures. Then they use certain terms called "pronouns" to make a few crosslinks in those trees. Naturally this leaves no room for nuances. So they have to decode whatever they hear in terms of things they already know. This can work very well for familiar things but makes it devilishly hard for them to learn anything really new.

A.: But language isn't everything. Shouldn't we give them credit for explaining things with pictures too? They do seem to have excellent senses.

S.: That was my first impression as well—until I saw that their TV sets use only three electron guns. Of course, this means that they're virtually blind. Not only are they confined to a single octave of optical frequencies, but within that range they can discriminate only a three-dimensional vector space. They badly need re-engineering.

A.: I have another question. Why are these people so huge? Where is their nanotechnology? By all rights they should be smaller than us, in view of their limited memories—yet we weigh a hundred trillion times less. It is expensive enough to send ourselves on these one-way interstellar voyages, but humans are so massive that it would be unthinkable to send one back—despite all their stories in *Weekly World News*.

S.: That is just another result of an early wrong turn in evolution. Instead of using nanotechnological assemblers, each animal on planet Earth must build itself from the inside out. So every cell has to contain a complete duplicate of the whole construction mechanism. When the animals got too large to be nourished by diffusion, they had to evolve all those pipes and pumps—which made them grow larger still.

A.: What frightful inefficiency!

S.: The extraction beam will scan us soon, so I'm afraid it is time to wrap this up. Are you ready to summarize your impressions?

A.: If they suspected that we were here, they'd insist that we recognize all sorts of rights. Freedom of speech and privacy. Freedom from want, pain, and fear. And freedom to think whatever they wish, no matter what the evidence! Most of these make no sense to me, but I'm still inclined to support them—because I feel that humans have done well in spite of all their handicaps. And your conclusions?

S.: They do have virtues despite their faults. But it would be unthinkable to allow them in their present form to populate the universe. So I'll recommend certain changes.

A.: What sorts of changes?

S.: There is no need to explain that now, because we'll soon merge minds with the Council. Now hold still: here comes the transfer ray. Be sure to set your shell to disperse as soon as the beam has scanned us—in order not to pollute this world with any redundant intelligence.

Index

Printed in the United States
by Baker & Taylor Publisher Services